GCSE Maths

Complete Revision and Practice

Contents

Section One — Numbers

Section Two — Shapes

Section Three — Mathematical Tools

Section Four — Statistics

Contents

Section Five — Graphs

Section Six — Algebra

Published by Coordination Group Publications Ltd.

Editors:
Richard Parsons, Dominic Hall.

Contributors:
Pamela Chatley, Martin Chester, Jane Chow, Mike Clarke, Charley Darbishire, Philippa Falshaw, Adrian Hall, Sharon Keeley, Simon Little, Tim Major, Manpreet Sambhi, Alice Shepperson, Emma Singleton, Claire Thompson, Jeanette Whiteman, Caroline Wilson.

With thanks to Peter Caunter for the proofreading.

Please note that AQA questions from pre-2003 papers are from legacy syllabuses and not from the current specification.
CGP has carefully selected the questions contained in the practice exam to cover subject areas which are still relevant to the current specification. As such the exam provides a good test of your knowledge of the syllabus areas you need to understand to get a good grade in the real thing.

ISBN 1 84146 377 9
Website: www.cgpbooks.co.uk
Printed by Elanders Hindson, Newcastle upon Tyne.
Clipart source: CorelDRAW and VECTOR

Types of Number

1) Square Numbers

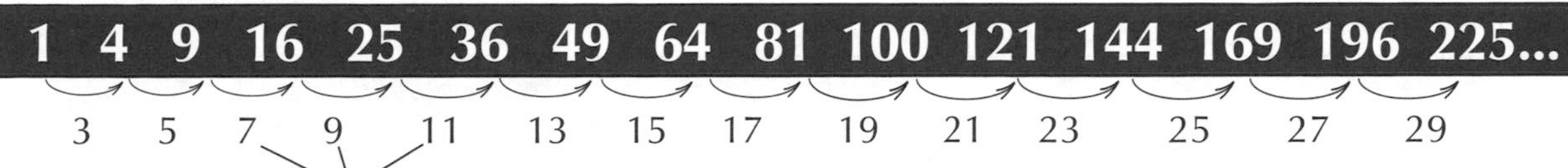

Note that the DIFFERENCES between the *square numbers* are all the ODD numbers.

2) Cube Numbers

They're called CUBE NUMBERS because they're like the volumes of this pattern of cubes.

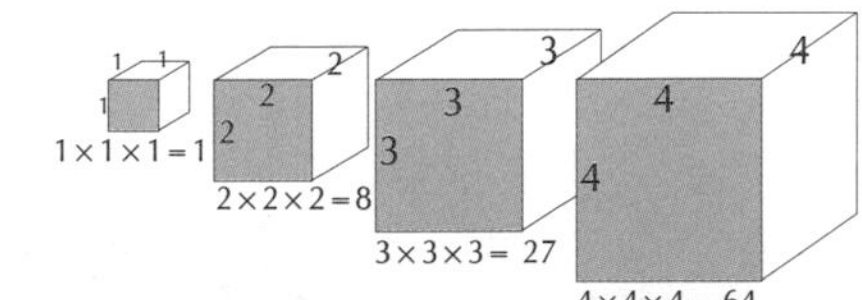

1 8 27 64 125 216 343 512 729 1000...

3) Triangle Numbers

To remember the triangle numbers you have to picture in your mind this *increasing pattern of triangles*, where each new row has *one more dot* than the previous row.

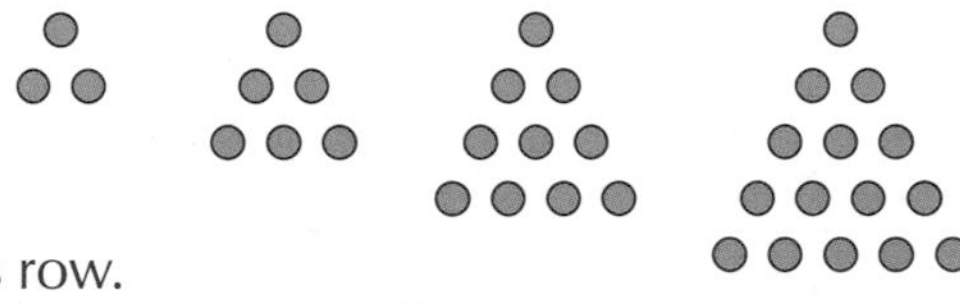

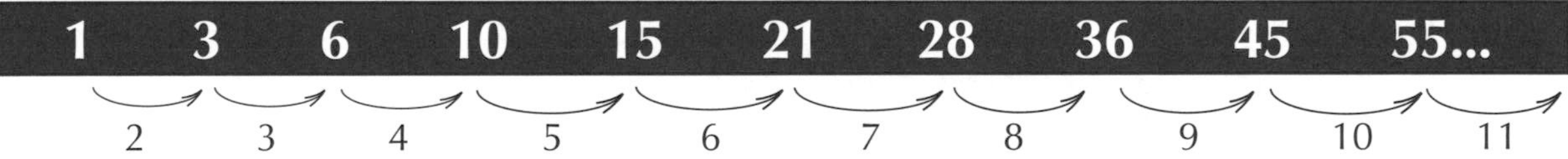

It's definitely worth learning this simple *pattern of differences*, as well as the formula for the *nth term* (see P.16) which is:

nth term = ½n (n + 1)

4) Powers

Powers are "numbers *multiplied by themselves* so many times".

"*Two to the power three*" = $2^3 = 2 \times 2 \times 2 = 8$

Here are the first few *POWERS OF 2*:

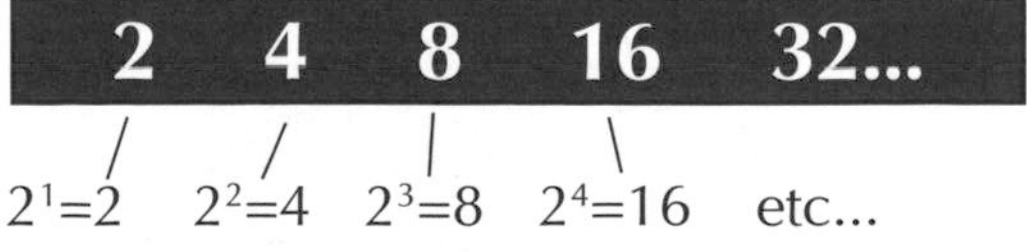

... and even easier the first *POWERS OF 10*:

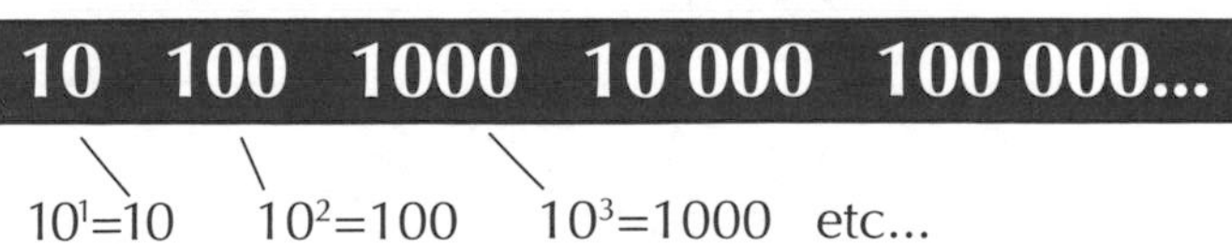

All these types of numbers just need learning

You should be able to spot these different types of numbers from a mile away and the only way to do that is keep writing them down and learning them.

Fractions

Doing Fractions *by hand*

You're not allowed to use your calculator in the Non-Calculator Exam (unsurprisingly). You'll have to do them "by hand" instead, so learn these 5 basic rules.

1) *Multiplying* — easy

Multiply top and bottom separately:

$$\frac{3}{5} \times \frac{4}{7} = \frac{3\times 4}{5\times 7} = \frac{12}{35}$$

2) *Dividing* — quite easy

Turn the *2nd fraction upside down* and then *multiply:*

$$\frac{3}{4} \div \frac{1}{3} = \frac{3}{4} \times \frac{3}{1} = \frac{3\times 3}{4\times 1} = \frac{9}{4}$$

3) *Cancelling down* — easy

Divide top and bottom by the same number, till they won't go any further:

$$\frac{24}{30} = \frac{12}{15} = \frac{4}{5}$$

4) *Adding/Subtracting* — difficult

i) First get the bottom lines the same (get a "common denominator")

e.g. $\frac{2}{3} + \frac{1}{5} = \frac{2\times 5}{3\times 5} + \frac{1\times 3}{5\times 3} = \frac{10}{15} + \frac{3}{15}$

(multiply each fraction by the same number top and bottom, but use a different number for each fraction)

ii) Add or subtract TOP LINES ONLY but *only if the bottom numbers are the same.*

e.g. $\frac{10}{15} + \frac{3}{15} = \frac{13}{15}$ $\quad \frac{2}{6} + \frac{1}{6} = \frac{3}{6}$ $\quad \frac{5}{7} - \frac{3}{7} = \frac{2}{7}$

You have to learn to handle these fractions

Multiplying, dividing and cancelling fractions is pretty easy but still needs practice — there's no point in throwing away easy marks. Adding and subtracting is that bit harder so it'll need that bit more practice.

Fractions

5) Finding a **Fraction of** something — just multiply

Multiply by the top, divide by the bottom:

$$\frac{9}{20} \text{ of } £360 = \frac{9}{20} \times £360$$
$$= \frac{£3240}{20}$$
$$= £162$$

The Fraction Button: $a\frac{b}{c}$

Use this as much as possible in the calculator paper.
It's very easy, so make sure you know how to use it — you'll lose a lot of marks if you don't:

1) To enter $\frac{1}{4}$ press:

2) To enter $1\frac{3}{5}$ press

3) To work out $\frac{1}{5} \times \frac{3}{4}$ press

4) To *reduce a fraction to its lowest terms* enter it and then press =

e.g. $\frac{9}{12}$, 9 $a\frac{b}{c}$ 12 =   3⌟4 = $\frac{3}{4}$

5) To convert between *mixed* and *top heavy* fractions press SHIFT $a\frac{b}{c}$

e.g. $2\frac{3}{8}$ 2 $a\frac{b}{c}$ 3 $a\frac{b}{c}$ 8 SHIFT $a\frac{b}{c}$ which gives $\frac{19}{8}$

Using a calculator can make your life much easier

You must make sure that you know how to use your calculator properly. If you aren't sure how to use it or you mess it up, your answers will all come out wrong. If you do use it properly, it will save you time and make things easier — so keep practising until you've mastered it.

Percentages

You shouldn't have any trouble with most percentage questions, especially the first two types. However, you need to make sure you know the proper method for doing type 3 questions.

Type 1

"Find x% of y" —

e.g. Find 15% of £46
⇒ 0.15 × 46 = £6.90

Type 2

"Express x as a percentage of y"

e.g. Give 40p as a percentage of £3.34
⇒ (40 ÷ 334) × 100 = 12% (to 2 d.p.)

Type 3

— IDENTIFIED BY NOT GIVING THE "ORIGINAL VALUE"

These are the type most people get wrong — but only because they don't recognise them as a type 3 and don't apply this simple method:

Example: A house increases in value by 20% to £72,000. Find what it was worth before the rise.

Method:

	£72,000	**= £120%**
÷ 120 ↓		
	£600	**= 1%**
× 100 ↓		
	£60,000	**= 100%**

So the original price was £60,000

An INCREASE of 20% means that £72,000 represents *120% of the original* value.

If it was a DROP of 20%, then we would put "£72,000 = 80%" instead, and then divide by 80 on the LHS (left hand side), instead of 120.

Always set them out exactly like this example. The trickiest bit is deciding the top % figure on the RHS (right hand side) — the 2nd and 3rd rows are always 1% and 100%.

Percentage Change

"Percentage change" can also catch you out if you don't watch all the details — like using the ORIGINAL value, for example.

It is common to give a *change in value* as a *percentage*.
This is the formula for doing so — LEARN IT, AND USE IT:

$$\text{Percentage "Change"} = \frac{\text{"Change"}}{\text{Original}} \times 100$$

By "change", we could mean all sorts of things such as: "Profit", "loss", "appreciation", "depreciation", "increase", "decrease", "error", "discount", etc. For example,

$$\text{percentage "profit"} = \frac{\text{"profit"}}{\text{original}} \times 100$$

Note the great importance of using the ORIGINAL VALUE in this formula.

Percentages are one of the most useful things you'll ever learn

Whenever you open a newspaper, see an advert, watch tv or do a maths exam paper you will see percentages. So it's really important you get confident with using them — so practise.

Prime Numbers

1) Basically, **Prime** Numbers **don't divide** by anything

And that's the best way to think of them. (Strictly, they divide by themselves and 1)
So Prime Numbers are all the numbers that DON'T come up in Times Tables:

2	3	5	7	11	13	17	19	23	29	31	37	...

For example:

The only numbers that multiply to give 7 are	1 × 7
The only numbers that multiply to give 31 are	1 × 31

In fact the only way to get ANY PRIME NUMBER is 1 × ITSELF

2) They **all end** in **1, 3, 7** or **9**

1) 1 is NOT a prime number
2) The first four prime numbers are 2, 3, 5 and 7
3) 2 and 5 are the EXCEPTIONS because all the rest end in 1, 3, 7 or 9
4) But NOT ALL numbers ending in 1, 3, 7 or 9 are primes, as shown here:
(Only the *circled ones* are *primes*)

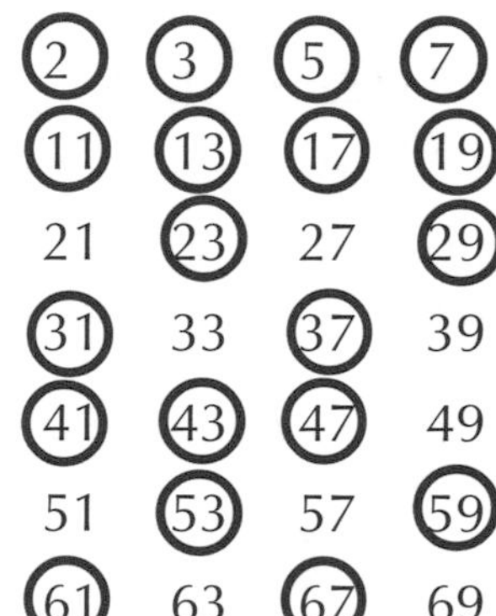

3) How to **find** Prime Numbers - a very simple method

For a chosen number to be a *prime*:

1) It must end in either 1, 3, 7 or 9.
2) It WON'T DIVIDE by any of the primes below the value of its own square root.

If something like this comes up on the non-calculator paper, you'll have to start by estimating the square root - see P. 12.

Example "Decide whether or not 233 is a prime number."

1) Does it end in either *1, 3, 7 or 9?* Yes
2) Find its *square root:* $\sqrt{233} = 15.264$
3) List *all primes* which are *less* than this square root: 3, 7, 11 and 13
4) *Divide* all of these primes into the number under test:

$233 \div 3 = 77.6667$ $233 \div 7 = 33.2857$

$233 \div 11 = 21.181818$ $233 \div 13 = 17.923077$

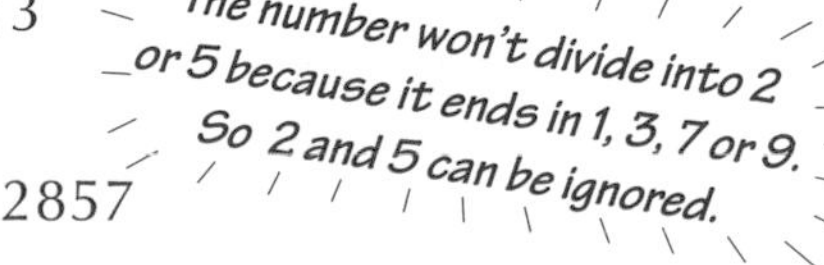

The number won't divide into 2 or 5 because it ends in 1, 3, 7 or 9.
So 2 and 5 can be ignored.

5) Since *none* of these divide *cleanly* into 233 then it *IS* a *prime number*. It's as easy as that.

Remember — prime numbers don't come up in times tables

You have to be able to recognise prime numbers. The first few are easy enough to remember by heart, but when it comes to bigger numbers the only way is to use the prime number test.

Multiples and Factors

Multiples

The MULTIPLES of a number are simply its TIMES TABLE:

E.g. the multiples of 13 are 13 26 39 52 65 78 91 104 ...

Factors

The FACTORS of a number are all the numbers that DIVIDE INTO IT.
There is a special way to find them:

Example 1: *"Find ALL the factors of 24"*

Start off with 1 × the number itself, then try 2 × , then 3 × and so on, listing the pairs in rows like this. Try each one in turn and put a dash if it doesn't divide exactly.

Eventually, when you get a number *repeated*, you *stop*.

So the FACTORS OF 24 are 1,2,3,4,6,8,12,24

This method guarantees you find them ALL.
And don't forget 1 and 24.

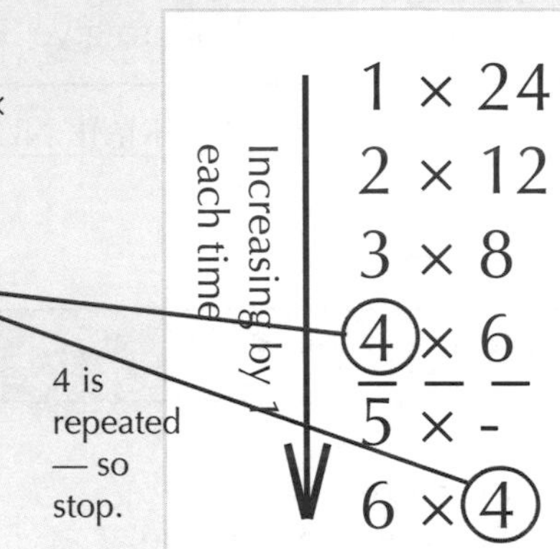

Example 2: *"Find the factors of 64"*

Check each one in turn, to see if it divides or not. Use your calculator if you are not totally confident.

So the FACTORS of 64 are 1,2,4,8,16,32,64

1 × 64
2 × 32
3 × –
4 × 16
5 × –
6 × –
7 × –
8 × 8

8 is repeated — so stop.

The Factor Tree

Any number can be broken down into *a string of PRIME NUMBERS all multiplied together* – this is called *"Expressing it as a product of prime factors"*. It's in the Exam, *and it's not difficult so long as you know what it is*.

The *"Factor Tree" method* is best, where you start at the top and split your number off into factors as shown. Each time you get a prime you ring it and you finally end up with all the prime factors, which you can then arrange in order.

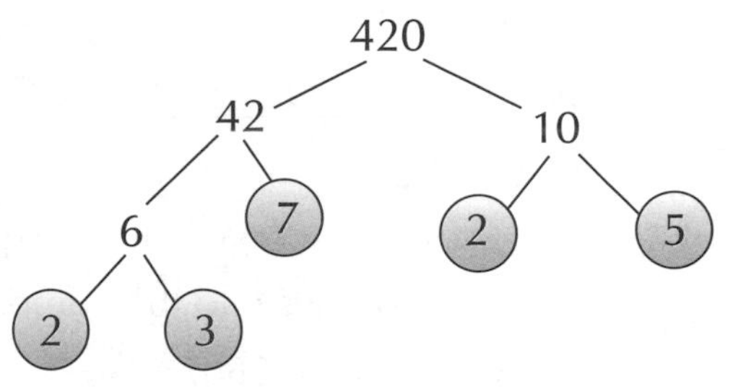

So, "As a product of prime factors", 420 = 2×2×3×5×7

Factors and Multiples are easy marks

Factor and multiple questions are simple multiplication and division so there's no reason to lose marks. Practise doing them quickly and accurately and make sure you know what all the words mean.

Warm-Up and Worked Exam Questions

This stuff is pretty straightforward, but that doesn't mean you can get away without learning the facts and practising the questions. You should have learnt the facts already — try these and we'll see.

Warm-Up Questions

1) Choose from the numbers 1, 2, 3, 4, 5, 6, 7, 8, 9, 10:
   Which numbers are (a) Square? (b) Cube? (c) Triangular? (d) Powers of 2? (e) Prime?
2) Repeat Question (1) using the numbers 30-40 inclusive.
3) Explain why 231 is not a prime number.
4) Find all the factors of 40.
5) Write 40 as a product of its prime factors.
6) Work these out, then simplify your answers:
   a) $\frac{2}{5}\times\frac{2}{3}$ b) $\frac{2}{5}\div\frac{2}{3}$ c) $\frac{2}{5}+\frac{2}{3}$ d) $\frac{2}{3}-\frac{2}{5}$
7) What percentage is the same as $\frac{2}{5}$?
8) What percentage is the same as $\frac{2}{3}$?
9) Find 15% of £90 (without using a calculator).
10) What is 37 out of 50 as a percentage?

Worked Exam Questions

Take a look at this worked exam question. It's not too hard, but it should give you a good idea of what to write. Make the most of the handy hints now — they won't be there in the exam.

1 By writing 240 and 150 as a product of their prime factors, find the Highest Common Factor (HCF) of 240 and 150.

Start by drawing a factor tree for each number.

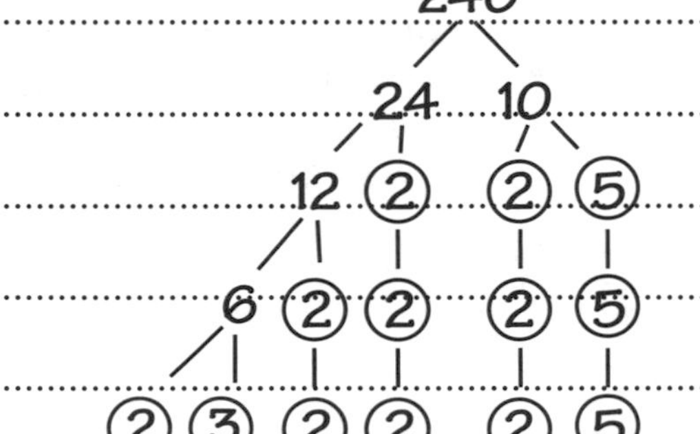

150 → 15, 10 → 3, 5, 2, 5

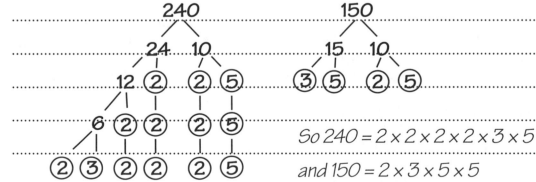

So $240 = 2\times2\times2\times2\times3\times5$

and $150 = 2\times3\times5\times5$

The Highest Common Factor is the highest number which divides into both 240 and 150. To find it, we need to look at which numbers are in both lists of prime factors and multiply them together.

The numbers in both lists are 2, 3 and 5, so HCF $= 2\times3\times5 = 30$

Answer *30*

(3 marks)

Worked Exam Questions

Worked Exam Questions

2 Find 12% of £90 without a calculator.

To do this, first find 10% and 1% of £90 by dividing by 10, and then dividing by 10 again.

10% of £90 = £9.00

1% of £90 = £0.90

Combine these 2 amounts to make 12%.

12% = 10% + 1% + 1%

So 12% of £90 = £9.00 + £0.90 + £0.90 = £10.80

Answer £10.80

(2 marks)

3 A motorbike depreciates in value by 5% every year. If the bike is bought for £1600, how much is it worth at the end of 3 years?

Be careful to find 5% of the latest value at the end of each year.

After 1 year: 5% of £1600 = £80,

so the bike is worth £1600 – £80 = £1520

After 2 years: 5% of £1520 = £76,

so the bike is worth £1520 – £76 = £1444

After 3 years: 5% of £1444 = £72.20,

so the bike is worth £1444 – £72.20 = £1371.80

A quicker way to do this same question is to realise that if the bike's value is decreasing by 5% each year, this is the same as multiplying by 95% (since 100% – 5% = 95%). So each year I can just multiply by 0.95 (decimal equivalent of 95%): After 3 years: £1600 x 0.95 x 0.95 x 0.95 = £1371.80

Answer £1371.80

(3 marks)

4 A hi-fi system costs £329, which includes VAT at 17½ %. How much is the system worth before VAT is added?

In this question you are being asked to find the original value, so you need to be careful — it is a "reverse" or "inverse" percentage problem.

The system plus an extra 17½ % = £329.

Original amount = 100%, so total cost = 117½ %.

So 117½ % = £329. 1% = £329 ÷ 117.5 = £2.80.

To find the original amount, find 100%.

100% = £2.80 x 100 = £280.

So the hi-fi, before VAT is added, is worth £280.

Answer £280

(3 marks)

Exam Questions

Calculator Not Allowed Exam Questions:

5 What is the 20th number in this sequence? 1, 4, 9, 16, 25, 36, …

....

Answer ____________

(1 mark)

6 (a) Express 924 as a product of prime factors

....

Answer (a) ____________

(1 mark)

(b) What is the highest common factor (HCF) of 924 and 210?

....

Answer (b) ____________

(2 marks)

7 Calculate (a) $5\frac{2}{7}-2\frac{3}{5}$

....

Answer (a) ____________

(2 marks)

(b) $2\frac{2}{3}\times3\frac{3}{4}$

....

Answer (b) ____________

(2 marks)

Calculator Allowed Exam Questions:

8 Susan bought a camera for £95 and sold it a year later for £57. What was her percentage loss?

....

Answer ____________

(2 marks)

9 I invest £5000 in an account that pays 4% (compound) interest every year. I leave the interest earned at the end of each year in the account to accumulate. How much interest would I have earned at the end of 4 years?

....

Don't be put off by the number of dotted lines. You'll have more space in the real exam — we've just removed some to squeeze more questions in.

Answer ____________

(3 marks)

Rational and Irrational Numbers

The whole topic of "Rational and Irrational Numbers" can seem completely bizarre. *Unfortunately*, the fanatics who write your Exam papers *love them* and you're bound to get a question on it. You'll just have to *LEARN this page thoroughly* and it'll all make more sense...

RATIONAL NUMBERS The vast majority of numbers are rational. They are always either:

1) A whole number (either positive (+ve), or negative (–ve)) e.g 4, -5, -12
2) A fraction p/q, where p and q are whole numbers (+ve or –ve). e.g. ¼, -½, ¾
3) A finite or repeating decimal, e.g. 0.125 0.3333333333... 0.143143143143

IRRATIONAL NUMBERS are that bit harder:

1) They are always NEVER-ENDING NON-REPEATING DECIMALS. π is irrational.
2) A *good source* of IRRATIONAL NUMBERS is SQUARE ROOTS AND CUBE ROOTS.

3 Important Examples

*1) Determine which of these numbers are **rational** and which are **irrational***

$\sqrt{2}$ $\sqrt{4}$ $\sqrt{36}$ $\sqrt{42}$

You *know* $\sqrt{4}$ is 2, and you know $\sqrt{36}$ is 6, 'cos 6×6 = 36.

$\sqrt{42}$ looks *loads* harder. But just remember this:

The *only* numbers with *rational* square roots are *square numbers*.

42 is NOT square so $\sqrt{42}$ is *irrational*. Easy.
(If you're not sure if it's square or not, you could split it into prime factors.)
Of course, if you've got a *calculator* handy, you could always stick the numbers in and see if they are *non-recurring decimals* (irrational) or *otherwise* (rational).

*2) Find an **irrational number** between **6** and **10***

Since *square roots are our main source of irrational numbers*, you might well go for $\sqrt{7}$ or $\sqrt{8}$.
They are both certainly *irrational* but they are *not* between 6 and 10,
$\sqrt{7}$ = 2.645... and $\sqrt{8}$ = 2.828... Something like $\sqrt{40}$ will be more like it.

Since 6^2=36 and 10^2=100, possible answers are $\sqrt{37}, \sqrt{38}, \sqrt{39}, ...\sqrt{97}, \sqrt{98}, \sqrt{99}$.
All these have irrational values between 6 and 10, so they would all do as answers
(except for $\sqrt{49}, \sqrt{64}$ or $\sqrt{81}$ — why?)

*3) Sometimes they'll do a **nasty question** using **letters***

E.g. if p is rational and q is irrational, say whether p + q and pq are rational or irrational:

If you've got a *calculator*, you can pick some numbers and try it out. It's not too hard to *figure out* anyway. If p = 1 and q = $\sqrt{2}$, then adding 1 to $\sqrt{2}$ isn't going to change the fact that it's a *non-repeating decimal*. And 1 × $\sqrt{2}$ = $\sqrt{2}$, so it's *irrational*.

Don't be phased by irrational numbers

They can seem pretty weird and tricky but all you have to do is learn the definitions of Rational and Irrational Numbers and the full details of all three examples. Then turn over and write it all down.

Recurring Decimals

There are two methods for turning recurring decimals into fractions, and here they are...

Turning Recurring *Decimals* into *Fractions*

As you will undoubtedly remember, RECURRING DECIMALS are RATIONAL NUMBERS so you should also be able to turn them into FRACTIONS, i.e. a/b where a and b are whole numbers.

This is given special mention in the syllabus.
Luckily it's very easy if you just learn the simple rules.

There are two ways you can do it:
1) by UNDERSTANDING   2) by JUST LEARNING THE RESULT:

The **Understanding** Method:

1) Find the *length* of the *repeating sequence*.
   Then *multiply* by 10, 100, 1000, 10 000 or whatever to move it all up past the decimal point by *one full repeated lump*:

   E.g. $0.234234234... \times 1000 = 234.234234..$

2) *Subtract the original number*, r, from the new one (which in this case is 1000r)

   i.e. $1000r - r = 234.234234... - 0.234234...$
   so: $999r = 234$

3) Then just DIVIDE to leave r:

   $r = {}^{234}/_{999}$,

   and cancel if possible: $r = {}^{26}/_{111}$

The "*Just Learning The Result*" Method:

The fraction always has:
1) the repeating unit on the top
2) the same number of nines on the bottom — easy as that.

Look at these and marvel at the elegant simplicity of it:

0.4444444 = 4/9   0.34343434 = 34/99
0.124124124 = 124/999   0.14561456 = 1456/9999

Always check if it will CANCEL DOWN of course, e.g. 0.363636.... = 36/99 = 12/33 = 4/11

Understanding or just learning, the choice is yours

It doesn't matter if you decide to understand turning decimals into fractions or just learn the pattern they always have — remember how to do it and practise it and there's some easy marks to be had.

Manipulating Surds

You have to practice Manipulating Surds

Surds are expressions with irrational square roots in them.

You MUST USE THEM if they ask you for an EXACT answer.

There are a few simple rules to learn:

1) $\sqrt{a} \times \sqrt{b} = \sqrt{ab}$ e.g. $\sqrt{2} \times \sqrt{3} = \sqrt{2 \times 3} = \sqrt{6}$ — also $\sqrt{b}^2 = b$, fairly obviously.

2) $\sqrt{a}/\sqrt{b} = \sqrt{a/b}$ e.g. $\sqrt{8}/\sqrt{2} = \sqrt{8/2} = \sqrt{4} = 2$

3) $\sqrt{a} + \sqrt{b}$ — IS DEFINITELY NOT $\sqrt{a+b}$

4) $(a + \sqrt{b})^2 = (a + \sqrt{b})(a + \sqrt{b}) = a^2 + 2a\sqrt{b} + b$ (NOT just $a^2 + \sqrt{b}^2$)

5) $(a + \sqrt{b})(a - \sqrt{b}) = a^2 + a\sqrt{b} - a\sqrt{b} - \sqrt{b}^2 = a^2 - b$

6) Express $3/\sqrt{5}$ in the form $a\sqrt{5}/b$ where a and b are whole numbers.

To do this you must *"RATIONALISE the denominator"*,

This just means multiplying top and bottom by $\sqrt{5}$:

$$\frac{3\sqrt{5}}{\sqrt{5}\sqrt{5}} = \frac{3\sqrt{5}}{5} \quad \text{so } a = 3 \text{ and } b = 5$$

7) If you want an *exact* answer, *LEAVE THE SURDS IN*.

As soon as you go using that calculator, you'll get a *big rounding error* —

and you'll get the answer *WRONG*. You have been warned...

Once you get used to them surds are quite easy

They do seem a bit fiddly with all those square roots everywhere, but with a bit of practice surds can become your best friend. Just learn these simple rules and then practise, practise and practise some more.

Warm-Up and Worked Exam Questions

Take a deep breath and go through these warm-up questions one by one.
If you don't know these basic facts there's no way you'll cope with the exam questions.

Warm-Up Questions

1) Which of these numbers are irrational? 17.1, 4^2, $\sqrt{10}$, 4.66666..., $\sqrt{36}$, π.
2) Find a rational number between $\sqrt{50}$ and $\sqrt{70}$.
3) Find an irrational number between $\sqrt{50}$ and $\sqrt{70}$.
4) Find an irrational number between 8 and 9.
5) a) What fraction is the same as 0.4?
   b) What fraction is the same as 0.444444...?
   c) What fraction is the same as 0.45454545...?
6) a) What decimal is the same as $\frac{7}{10}$? b) What decimal is the same as $\frac{7}{9}$?
7) Work out $\sqrt{5} \times \sqrt{6}$, leaving your answer as a surd.
8) Work out $\sqrt{12} \times \sqrt{3}$, giving your answer as a normal number.

Worked Exam Questions

Exam questions are the best way to practise what you've learnt. After all, they're exactly what you'll have to do on the big day — so work through these worked examples very carefully.

1 Peter claims that if p and q are both irrational numbers then pq is ALWAYS irrational as well. By choosing a suitable example, show that Peter is wrong.

You need to carefully choose p and q to be square roots of non-square-numbers (so that they are irrational), but make sure that when you multiply the numbers together you get a square number.

For example, $\sqrt{2}$ and $\sqrt{8}$ are both irrational,

but $\sqrt{2} \times \sqrt{8} = \sqrt{16} = 4$

So $\sqrt{2} \times \sqrt{8} = 4$ which is rational.

If we choose $p = \sqrt{2}$ and $q = \sqrt{8}$, then we have proved Peter wrong.

(2 marks)

Remember that $\sqrt{m} \times \sqrt{n} = \sqrt{(mn)}$.

2 Rationalise the denominator in the expression $\frac{2}{\sqrt{7}}$.

$$\frac{2 \times \sqrt{7}}{\sqrt{7} \times \sqrt{7}} = \frac{2\sqrt{7}}{\sqrt{49}} = \frac{2\sqrt{7}}{7}$$

and now the denominator is a rational number.

This means you need to turn the denominator into a "normal" number by multiplying the top and bottom by whatever surd is in the denominator.

(2 marks)

Worked Exam Questions continued

Worked Exam Questions

3 Find lengths a and b, leaving your answers in surd form:

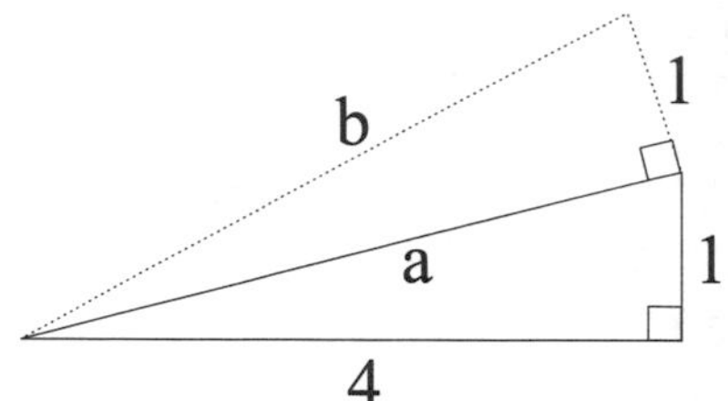

You need to use Pythagoras' Theorem for this question.

$a^2 = 4^2 + 1^2$

$a^2 = 16 + 1$

$a^2 = 17$

$a = \sqrt{17}$

Leaving "a" in surd form will ensure our answer for "b" is accurate.

$b^2 = a^2 + 1^2$

$b^2 = (\sqrt{17})^2 + 1^2$

$b^2 = 17 + 1$

$b^2 = 18$

$b = \sqrt{18}$

So, $a = \sqrt{17}$ and $b = \sqrt{18}$.

(3 marks)

4 Express $0.5\dot{4}\dot{1}$ as a fraction.

This is a tricky one, for A and A candidates only, so hold on tight.*

First we write $0.5\dot{4}\dot{1}$ like this: 0.54141414141...

Now we need to subtract something in order to make a much simpler recurring decimal. Notice that if we subtract 0.4, we get 0.141414141.... which you should recognise as $\frac{14}{99}$.

So the original decimal is $\frac{14}{99} + 0.4 = \frac{14}{99} + \frac{4}{10}$.

Now we have to add these fractions by converting to equivalent fractions with the same denominator:

$\frac{14}{99} = \frac{140}{990}$ (multiplying top and bottom by 10)

and $\frac{4}{10} = \frac{396}{990}$ (multiplying top and bottom by 99)

so $\frac{14}{99} + \frac{4}{10} = \frac{140}{990} + \frac{396}{990} = \frac{536}{990} = \frac{268}{495}$

You can check this on a calculator by doing

$268 \div 495 = 0.54141414141...$, which is what we started with.

(5 marks)

Exam Questions

Non-Calculator Exam Questions

5 Put a ring around any irrational number: $\sqrt{100}$, $\frac{7}{11}$, 0.818, $\frac{\pi}{2}$, $0.\dot{4}$, $\sqrt{50}$

....

(2 marks)

6 Find any irrational number between 5 and 6.

....

(2 marks)

7 Find any rational number between $\sqrt{80}$ and $\sqrt{90}$.

....

(2 marks)

8 Find a rational number which lies between 3.14 and π.

....

(2 marks)

Calculator Exam Questions

We've missed out some dotted lines to leave more room for questions. So don't be fooled into thinking you should be able to answer these questions in one line.

9 a) Find a rational number which lies between $\frac{3}{4}$ and $\frac{7}{8}$.

....

(2 marks)

b) Find an irrational number which lies between $\frac{3}{4}$ and $\frac{7}{8}$.

....

(2 marks)

10 Simplify these expressions, and say whether each answer is rational or irrational:

a) $\sqrt{8} \times \sqrt{2}$

....

(1 mark)

b) $\sqrt{24} \div \sqrt{3}$

....

(1 mark)

c) $\sqrt{15} \times \sqrt{6}$

....

(1 mark)

d) $\sqrt{20} \div \sqrt{8}$

....

(1 mark)

11 Find an irrational number which lies between 3.14 and π.

....

(3 marks)

Sequences — Finding the nth Term

"The nth term" is a formula with "n" in it which gives you every term in a sequence when you put different values for "n" in.

There are two different types of sequence (for "n^{th} term" questions) which have to be done in different ways. The first type is the common difference type:

Common Difference Type: "dn + (a – d)"

Consider a sequence such as:

3, 7, 11, 15, ...
(differences: 4, 4, 4)

The difference between each pair of numbers is 4 — this is the COMMON DIFFERENCE.

You can always find "the nth term" of a "common difference" type of sequence using this FORMULA:

$$\text{nth term} = dn + (a - d)$$

Don't forget:

1) "a" is simply the value of THE FIRST TERM in the sequence.
2) "d" is simply the value of THE COMMON DIFFERENCE between the terms.
3) To get the *nth term*, you just *find the values of "a" and "d" from the sequence and put them in the formula.*
4) You don't replace n though — that should stay as n.
5) YOU HAVE TO LEARN THE FORMULA.

Example:

Find the nth term of this sequence: 5, 8, 11, 14 ....

Answer:

1) The formula is dn + (a – d)
2) The first term is 5, so a = 5
   The *common difference* is 3 so d = 3
3) Putting these in the formula gives: 3n + (5 – 3)
4) So the nth term = 3n + 2

Learn the formula and you're halfway there

This is the easiest type of sequence to spot — you only need to do a couple of subtractions to find out that it's a common difference type. So when you get into the exam, try that first. Once you know what it is, you can just pick the relevant formula and stick the numbers into it.

Sequences — Finding the nth Term

The second kind of sequence is the changing difference type:

Changing Difference Type: “$a + (n-1)d + \frac{1}{2}(n-1)(n-2)C$”

If the number sequence is one where the difference between the terms is *increasing or decreasing* then it gets a whole lot more complicated.

Consider a sequence such as:

3, 7, 13, 21, ...

(differences: 4, 6, 8)

The difference between each pair of numbers increases by 2 each time.

You can always find "the nth term" of a “CHANGING DIFFERENCE” type of sequence using this FORMULA:

$$\text{nth term} = a + (n-1)d + \tfrac{1}{2}(n-1)(n-2)C$$

This time there are THREE letters you have to fill in:

1) "a" is the FIRST TERM.
2) "d" is the FIRST DIFFERENCE (between the first two numbers).
3) "C" is the CHANGE BETWEEN ONE DIFFERENCE AND THE NEXT.

Example:

Find the nth term of this sequence: *2, 5, 9, 14 ....*

(differences: 3, 4, 5)

Answer:

1) The formula is "$a + (n-1)d + \frac{1}{2}(n-1)(n-2)C$"
2) The *first term* is 2, so $a = 2$
3) The *first difference* is 3 so $d = 3$
4) The *differences increase* by 1 each time so $C = +1$
5) Putting these in the formula gives:
   $2 + (n-1)3 + \frac{1}{2}(n-1)(n-2)\times 1$
   Which becomes: $2 + 3n - 3 + \frac{1}{2}n^2 - 1\frac{1}{2}n + 1$
   Which simplifies to: $\frac{1}{2}n^2 + 1\frac{1}{2}n = \frac{1}{2}n(n+3)$
6) So the *nth term* $= \frac{1}{2}n(n+3)$

Don’t get this formula mixed up with the one for Common Difference

You need to learn both of these formulas — and remember when to use each one.

Warm-Up and Worked Exam Questions

By doing these warm-up questions, you'll soon find out if you've got the basic facts straight. If not you'll really struggle, so take the time to go back over the bits you don't know.

Warm-Up Questions

1) a) Find the first 6 terms of the sequence whose nth term is $5n + 3$.
   b) Find the first 6 terms of the sequence whose nth term is $3n + 5$.
2) Find the first 6 terms of the sequence given by the formula $n^2 + n$.
3) Find the nth term of the following sequences:
   a) 5, 10, 15, 20, 25, ... b) 7, 10, 13, 16, 19, ... c) 1, 4, 9, 16, 25, ...
4) How many crosses are in the nth pattern?

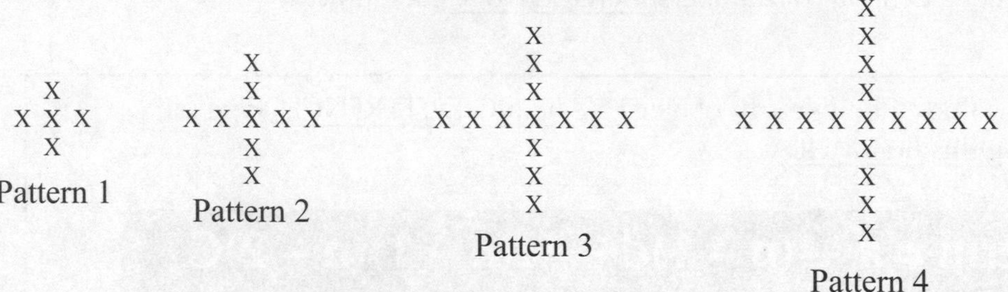

Worked Exam Questions

These worked examples are exactly like you'll get in the real exam, except here they've got the answers written in for you already — pretty handy.

These questions can also be done by using the formulas — recognise whether you have a common or changing difference type and then plug in the values for a, d and, if necessary, c.

1 Find the nth term of the sequence 8, 17, 26, 35, 44, 53, ...

The gaps between the numbers are always 9, which means the sequence is connected to the 9-times-table (so the formula starts 9n). The 9-times-table starts 9, 18, 27, 36, 45, 54, ... which means that we have to subtract one each time to end up with the sequence in the question. So the nth term is $9n - 1$.

(2 marks)

2 Find the nth term of the sequence 2, 8, 18, 32, 50, ...

As soon as you notice that the gaps between the numbers are not constant (in this case they increase by 4 each time), you should realise that the sequence has something to do with n^2. Often, the sequence is very simply connected to n^2, so write the square numbers down and have a look: 1, 4, 9, 16, 25, ... In this case the sequence in the question is just double the square numbers.

So the nth term is $2n^2$.

(2 marks)

Exam Questions

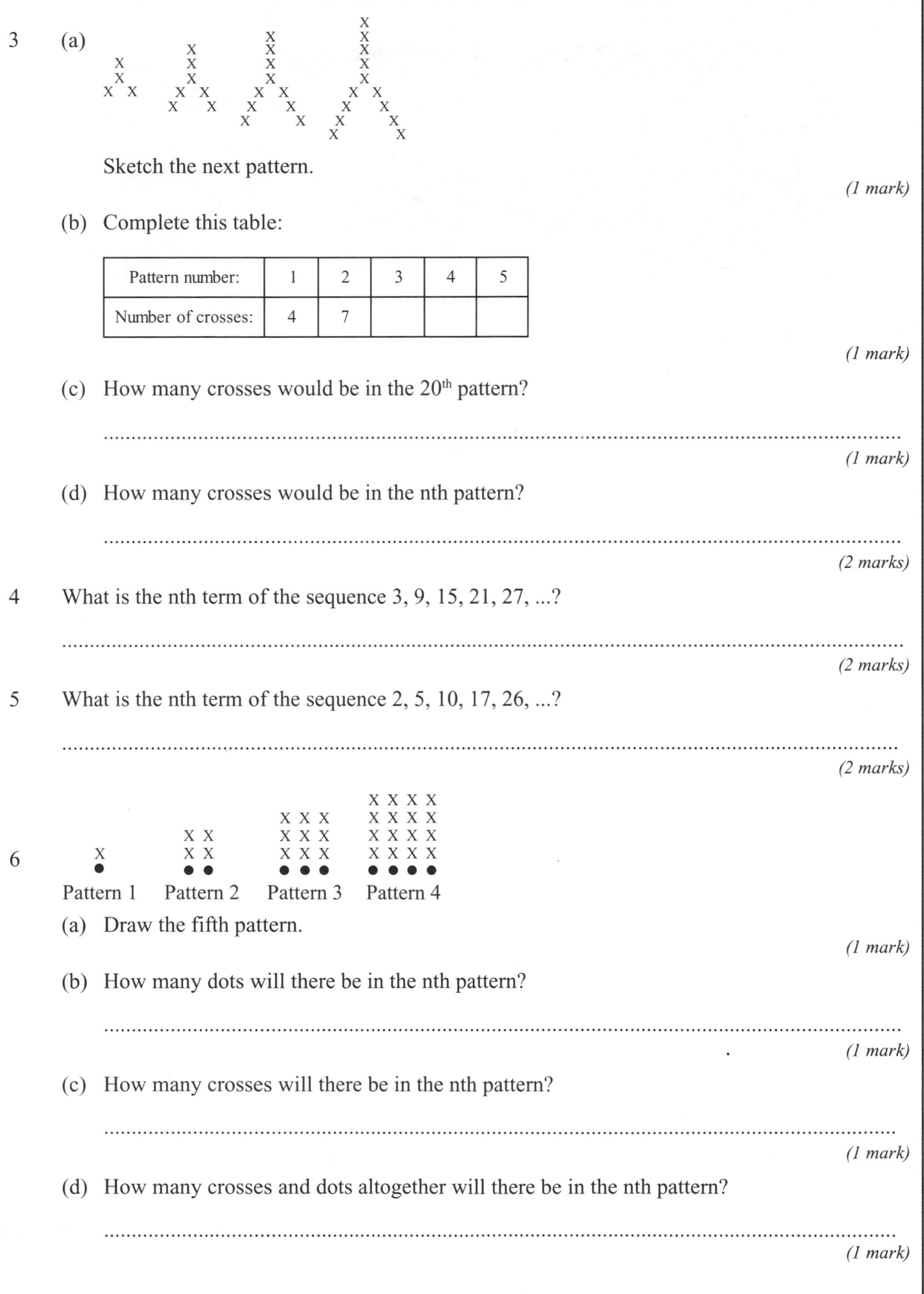

3 (a)

Sketch the next pattern.

(1 mark)

(b) Complete this table:

Pattern number:	1	2	3	4	5
Number of crosses:	4	7			

(1 mark)

(c) How many crosses would be in the 20th pattern?

....

(1 mark)

(d) How many crosses would be in the nth pattern?

....

(2 marks)

4 What is the nth term of the sequence 3, 9, 15, 21, 27, ...?

....

(2 marks)

5 What is the nth term of the sequence 2, 5, 10, 17, 26, ...?

....

(2 marks)

6

Pattern 1 Pattern 2 Pattern 3 Pattern 4

(a) Draw the fifth pattern.

(1 mark)

(b) How many dots will there be in the nth pattern?

....

(1 mark)

(c) How many crosses will there be in the nth pattern?

....

(1 mark)

(d) How many crosses and dots altogether will there be in the nth pattern?

....

(1 mark)

Conversion Factors

Conversion Factors are a mighty powerful tool for dealing with a wide variety of questions. And what's more the method is really easy, so learn it now.

METHOD

1) Find the Conversion Factor (always easy)
2) Multiply by it AND divide by it
3) Choose the common sense answer

*Three Important **Examples***

"Convert 2.55 hours into minutes." — (N.B. This is NOT 2hrs 55mins)

1) Conversion factor = 60 — (simply because 1 hour = 60 mins)
2) 2.55 hrs × 60 = 153 mins (makes sense)
   2.55 hrs ÷ 60 = 0.0425 mins (ridiculous answer)
3) So plainly the answer is that 2.55hrs = 153 mins

"If £1 = 1.5 Euros, how much is 47.36 Euros in £ and p?"

1) Obviously, Conversion Factor = 1.5 (The "exchange rate")
2) 47.36 × 1.5 = £71.04
   47.36 ÷ 1.5 = £31.57
3) Not quite so obvious this time, but if 1.5 Euros = £1, then Euros are worth less than pounds, so the answer must be £31.57

"A map has a scale of 1:20,000. How big in real life is a distance of 3cm on the map?"

1) Conversion Factor = 20 000
2) 3cm × 20 000 = 60 000cm (looks OK)
   3cm ÷ 20 000 = 0.00015cm (not good)
3) So 60,000cm is the answer.
   How do we convert to metres? →

To Convert 60,000cm to m:

1) C.F. = 100 (cm ⟷ m)
2) 60,000 × 100 = 6,000,000m (unlikely)
   60,000 ÷ 100 = 600m (more like it)
3) So answer = 600m

Just remember to use your common sense

These questions are really straightforward multiplying and dividing. The only tricky bit is knowing which to do. But use your common sense and you'll be fine.

Metric and Imperial Units

Make sure you learn all these easy facts:

Metric Units

1) Length mm, cm, m, km
2) Area mm^2, cm^2, m^2, km^2,
3) Volume mm^3, cm^3, m^3, litres, ml
4) Weight g, kg, tonnes
5) Speed km/h, m/s

MEMORISE THESE KEY FACTS:

1cm = 10mm	1 tonne = 1000kg
1m = 100cm	1 litre = 1000ml
1km = 1000m	1 litre = 1000cm^3
1kg = 1000g	1cm^3 = 1ml

Imperial Units

1) Length Inches, feet, yards, miles
2) Area Square inches, square feet, square yards, square miles
3) Volume Cubic inches, cubic feet, gallons, pints
4) Weight Ounces, pounds, stones, tons
5) Speed mph

LEARN THESE TOO!

1 Foot = 12 Inches
1 Yard = 3 Feet
1 Gallon = 8 Pints
1 Stone = 14 Pounds (lbs)
1 Pound = 16 Ounces (oz)

Metric/Imperial *Conversions*

YOU NEED TO LEARN THESE — they DON'T promise to give you these in the Exam and if they're feeling mean (as they often are), they won't.

APPROXIMATE CONVERSIONS

1 kg = 2¼ lbs	1 gallon = 4.5 litres
1m = 1 yard (+ 10%)	1 foot = 30cm
1 litre = 1¾ pints	1 metric tonne = 1 imperial ton
1 inch = 2.5 cm	1 mile = 1.6km or 5 miles = 8 km

Using Metric/Imperial *Conversion Factors*

1) Convert 45mm into cm.
   CF = 10, so × and ÷ by 10, to get 450cm or 4.5cm. (If you check this seems sensible)

2) Convert 37 inches into cm.
   CF = 2.5, so × and ÷ by 2.5, to get 14.8cm or 92.5cm.

3) Convert 5.45 litres into pints.
   CF = 1¾ so × and ÷ by 1.75, to get 3.11 or 9.54 pints.

There's no way round it you just have to learn all these factors

There's loads of conversion factors to learn here so keep scribbling them down until you remember every one. Then use your common sense to make sure you don't divide when you should be multiplying.

Accuracy, Estimating and Rounding

Estimating

This is VERY EASY, so long as you don't over-complicate it.

1) ROUND EVERYTHING OFF to nice easy CONVENIENT NUMBERS

2) Then WORK OUT THE ANSWER using these nice easy numbers — that's it!

In the Exam you'll need to show all the steps, to prove you didn't just use a calculator.

EXAMPLE: Estimate the value of $\frac{127.8 + 41.9}{56.5 \times 3.2}$ showing all your working.

Ans: $\frac{127.8 + 41.9}{56.5 \times 3.2} \approx \frac{130 + 40}{60 \times 3} \approx \frac{170}{180} \approx 1$

(" ≈ " means "roughly equal to")

Estimating **Areas** and **Volumes**

1) Draw or imagine a RECTANGLE OR CUBOID of similar size to the object in question

2) Round off all lengths to the NEAREST WHOLE, and work it out — easy.

EXAMPLES:

Estimate the area of the blue shape:

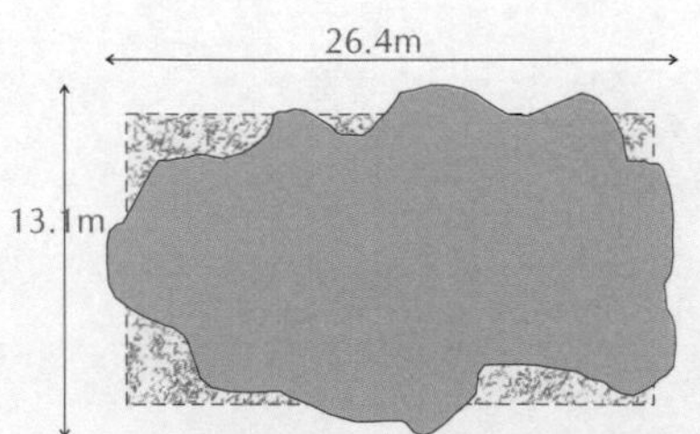

Area ≈ rectangle
26m × 13m = $338m^2$
(or without a calculator:
30 × 10 = $300m^2$)

Estimate the volume of the bottle:

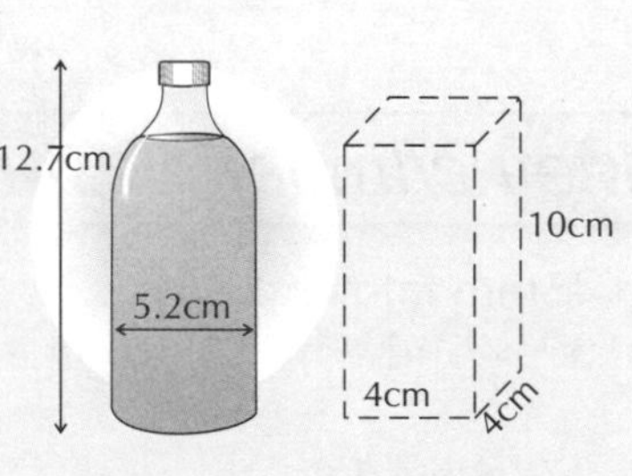

Volume ≈ cuboid
=4 × 4 × 10
=$160cm^3$

Estimating just makes your life simpler

The whole point of estimating is to make your life easier by choosing nice easy numbers and using them for calculations. So don't make a big deal of it, just practise a few and you'll see how easy it is.

Accuracy, Estimating and Rounding

Appropriate *Accuracy*

To decide what is appropriate accuracy, you need only remember these three rules:

1) For fairly casual measurements, 2 SIGNIFICANT FIGURES is most appropriate.

EXAMPLES:

Cooking – 250g (2 sig fig) of sugar, not 253g (3 S F), or 300g (1 S F)
Distance of a journey – 450 miles or 25 miles or 3500 miles (All 2 S F)
Area of a garden or floor — 330m^2 or 15m^2

2) For more important or technical things, 3 SIGNIFICANT FIGURES is essential.

EXAMPLES:

A technical figure like 34.2 miles per gallon, rather than 34 mpg.
A length that will be cut to fit, e.g. Measure a shelf 25.6cm long not just 26cm.
Any accurate measurement with a ruler: 67.5cm not 70cm or 67.54cm

3) Only for really scientific work would you have more than 3 SIG FIG.

You need to be able to answer questions about maximum and minimum values possible for a given level of accuracy.

Finding the **Upper** and **Lower** bounds of a **Single Measurement**

The simple rule is this:

The real value can be as much as HALF THE ROUNDED UNIT above and below the rounded-off value

This sounds a bit confusing but this example shows how straightforward it really is:

E.g. A length is given as 2.4m to the nearest 0.1m.

The rounded unit is 0.1m.
So the real value could be anything up to 2.4m ± 0.05m (half the rounded value = half of 0.1 = 0.05)
So the upper and lower bounds are 2.45m and 2.35m.

Some things need to be more accurate than others

It's pretty obvious really that in some cases you need to give a number very accurately, and other times rounding off to one significant figure will be fine. Just use your common sense and the three rules on the page to help you decide what is appropriate accuracy.

Accuracy, Estimating and Rounding

The **Maximum** and **Minimum** possible values of a **Calculation**

When a calculation is done using rounded-off values, there will be a DISCREPANCY between the CALCULATED VALUE and the ACTUAL VALUE:

EXAMPLE: A floor is measured as being 5.3 m × 4.2 m to the nearest 10 cm.

This gives an area of 22.26 m^2.
But this is not the actual floor area.
The real values could be anything from:
5.25 m to 5.35 m and 4.15 m to 4.25 m,
∴ Maximum possible floor area = 5.35 × 4.25 = 22.7375 m^2,
∴ Minimum possible floor area = 5.25 × 4.15 = 21.7875 m^2.

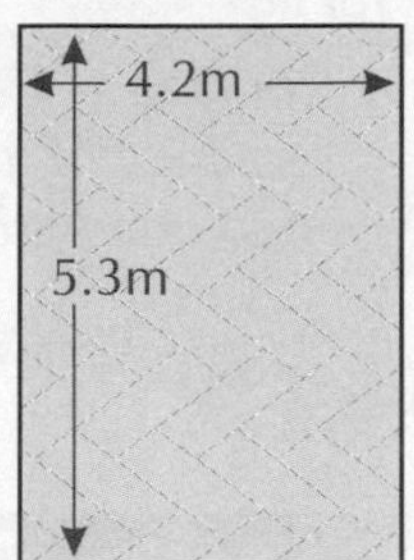

Maximum **Percentage Error**

Having found the two possible extreme values, calculate the maximum percentage error. There are two possibilities:

$$\text{Maximum Percentage Error} = \frac{\text{Error at lowest rounded value}}{\text{Lowest value}} \times 100$$

OR

$$\text{Maximum Percentage Error} = \frac{\text{Error at highest rounded value}}{\text{Highest value}} \times 100$$

In most cases the first possibility (the lowest extreme) will give the maximum percentage error. But try both and pick the biggest.

This looks pretty confusing but look at the example and it should make sense — then just remember the formula:

The lowest extreme = 21.7875
The error at that lowest extreme =
22.26 – 21.7875 = 0.4725
So the percentage error is $\frac{0.4725}{21.7875} \times 100 = 2.2\ \%$

The highest extreme = 22.7375
The error at that highest extreme =
22.7375 – 22.26 = 0.4775
So the percentage error is $\frac{0.4775}{22.7375} \times 100 = 2.1\ \%$

So the maximum percentage error is given by the LOWEST EXTREMES. Max percentage error = 2.2 %

You need to think about how to get the highest and lowest extremes

In some formulas it ISN'T the biggest input values that give the maximum result.

Example: $z = x + \frac{1}{y}$

For the maximum value for z you need *maximum* value for x coupled with the *minimum* value for y.

So when the question looks more complicated, the *safest method* is to work out the answer *using all four combinations* and see which combinations give the maximum and minimum results.

These methods let you say what your level of accuracy is

It's all very well being able to round off and estimate, but you need to be able also to say what your level of accuracy is. There are three methods: upper and lower bounds, maximum and minimum values, and percentage errors — you need to learn and practise all three, as if you couldn't guess.

Warm-Up and Worked Exam Questions

Warm-up questions first, then some worked examples — then you're on your own.
So make the most of this page by working through everything carefully.

Warm-Up Questions

1) Convert 12.7 kg into grams.
2) Convert 1430 cm into metres.
3) 10 lbs of apples weighs about how many kilograms?
4) By rounding to 1 significant figure, estimate the answer to $\frac{94 \times 1.9}{0.328 + 0.201}$
5) Estimate the answer to $\sqrt{50}$, without using a calculator.
6) Round these numbers to the level of accuracy indicated:
   a) 40.218 to 2 d.p. b) 39.888 to 3 sig. fig. c) 27.91 to 2 sig. fig.

Worked Exam Questions

I've gone through these worked examples and written in answers just like you'll do in the exam.
It should really help with the questions which follow, so don't say I never do anything for you.

1 Convert 2028 minutes into hours and minutes.

2028 ÷ 60 = 33.8. This is not 33 hours and 80 minutes, it is

33 hours and 8 tenths of an hour (or 80% of an hour).

One tenth of an hour is 60 ÷ 10 = 6 minutes, so 8 tenths is 48 minutes.

So the answer is 33 hours and 48 minutes.

Be careful with decimal points and hours.
Remember 0.4 hours is four-tenths of an hour, not forty minutes.

(2 marks)

2 A map has a scale of 1:40000. How long is a road that appears as 3cm long on the map?

40000 × 3 cm = 120000 cm = 1200 m = 1.2 km.

(2 marks)

3 A rug measures 1.5 m by 0.8 m (both measurements to the nearest 0.1 m).
Calculate the upper and lower bounds of the rug's:

(a) Length *Upper bound = 1.55m; lower bound = 1.45m.*

(b) Width *Upper bound = 0.85m; lower bound = 0.75m.*

(c) Area *Upper bound = 1.55 × 0.85 = 1.3175m^2;*
lower bound = 1.45 × 0.75 = 1.0875m^2.

(d) Perimeter *Upper bound = 2 × (1.55 + 0.85) = 4.8m;*
lower bound = 2 × (1.45 + 0.75) = 4.4m.

(8 marks)

Exam Questions

Some of these questions would have lots more space for answers in the real exam. We've just squeezed them in here so you get more practice.

Non-Calculator Exam Questions

4 A signpost says "Paris 24 km". About how many miles is this?

....

(1 mark)

5 A bunch of bananas are weighed on some old scales. The dial reads 5 lbs.
Approximately how many kilograms is this?

....

(1 mark)

6 Change 312 hours into hours and minutes.

....

(2 marks)

7 By rounding to 1 significant figure, estimate the answer to $\dfrac{29 \times 2.9}{9.1 - 6.9}$

....

(2 marks)

Calculator Exam Questions

8 A train travels 495 km in 4 hours. What is its average speed in km/h, to 2 significant figures?

....

(2 marks)

9 A model car is built to a scale of 1:40. If the real car is 3½ metres long,
how long is the model car?

....

(2 marks)

10 If a = 8 and b = 5 (both rounded to the nearest whole number),
calculate the <u>minimum</u> value of: a) $a + b$; b) $a \div b$

....

(4 marks)

11 A cube measures 60 mm along each side, correct to the nearest millimetre.
Calculate the upper and lower bounds of the cube's volume.

....

(3 marks)

12 John measures the width of a washing machine to be 59 cm, to the nearest centimetre.
What is the maximum percentage error?

....

(3 marks)

Calculator Buttons

The next few pages are full of calculator tricks to save you a lot of time and effort. There are two basic types of calculator — the old-style and the more up-to-date two-line display ones.

The old style calculators:

These ones only display numbers. They do the calculation each time you press an operation key.

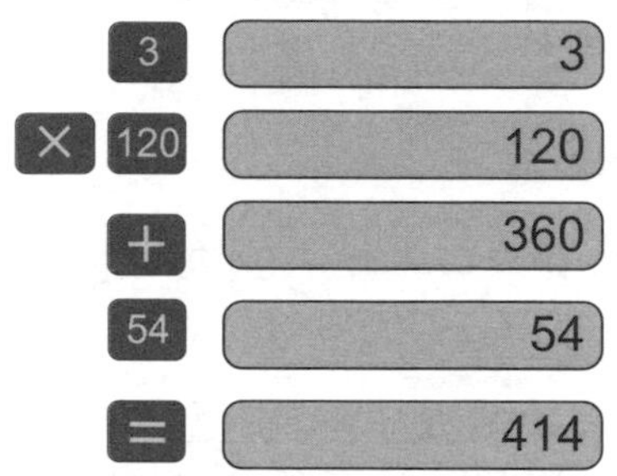

C Semi-Cancel and AC All-Cancel

The C button only cancels the NUMBER YOU ARE ENTERING. AC clears the whole calculation.
If you use C instead of AC for when you press the wrong key, you will HALVE the time you spend correcting mistakes.

2-line display calculators:

These are the more common type now. They are easy to use because you just type most calculations exactly as they're written.

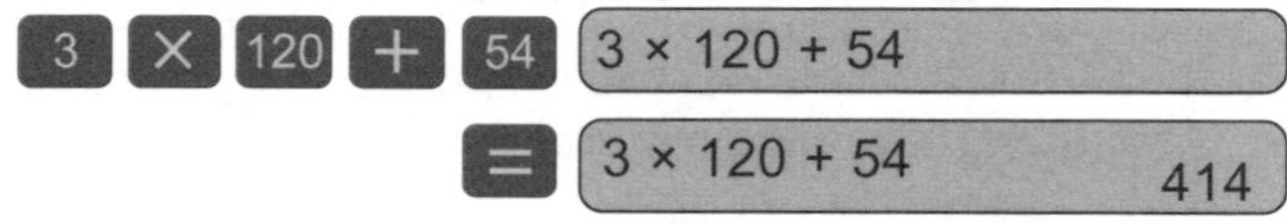

DEL The Delete Button

Pressing the DEL button deletes what you've typed, one key at a time (just like on a computer), so it's much quicker than pressing AC and re-typing the whole lot. Using DEL will save you a lot of time.

Cursor Buttons ◀ ▶

These cursor buttons ◀ and ▶ are very useful for editing what you've typed in. (You'll probably find you overwrite what was there before, but you can change this with the INS key to insert, rather than overwrite.)

1) Entering **Negative** Numbers

Some calculators have a +/– button which you press after you have entered the number. Others just have a minus button (–) which you press before entering the number.

So to work out -5 × -6 you'd either press... (–) 5 × (–) 6 =
or... 5 +/– × 6 +/– =

The examples in this book will use the (–) button.

2) The **Memory Buttons** STO, RCL (Store and Recall)

(On some calculators the memory buttons are called Min (memory in) and MR (memory recall)).
The memory function is a useful feature for keeping a number you've just calculated, so you can use it again shortly afterwards.

E.g. for $\frac{16}{15+12\sin 40}$, you could just work out the bottom line first and keep it in the memory.

Press 15 + 12 SIN 40 = and then STO (Or STO M or STO 1 or Min) to keep the result of the bottom line in the memory.

Then you simply press 16 ÷ RCL =, and the answer is 0.7044.

(Instead of RCL, you might need to type RCL M or RCL 1 or MR on yours.) Once you've practised using the memory buttons, you'll soon find them very useful. They speed things up no end.

Calculators are a great help — as long as you use them properly

Calculators can give you quick, accurate answers — but only if you know how to use them properly. Make sure you know what the important buttons do and how to use them.

Calculator Buttons

3) BODMAS and the Brackets Buttons (and)

Remember that a calculator always works things out in a certain order, which is:

Brackets, Other, Division, Multiplication, Addition, Subtraction — or **BODMAS** for short.

This is particularly important when you want to work out something like $\frac{23+45}{64\times 3}$.

DON'T press 23 + 45 ÷ 64 × 3 = — the calculator will interpret that as $23+{}^{45}\!/_{64}\times 3$ because it will do the division and multiplication BEFORE it does the addition.

You need to override the automatic BODMAS order of operations using the BRACKETS BUTTONS. Brackets are the ultimate priority in BODMAS, which means anything in brackets is worked out before anything else happens to it. So all you have to do is:

1) Write a couple of pairs of brackets into the expression: $\frac{(23+45)}{(64\times 3)}$
2) Then just type it as it's written: (23 + 45) ÷ (64 × 3) =

It's not too difficult to decide where to put the brackets in — just put them in pairs around each group of numbers. You can have brackets within other brackets too, e.g. (4 ÷ (5+2)). As a rule you can't cause trouble by putting too many brackets in, as long as you always keep them in pairs.

4) The Powers Button x^y

The powers button can be useful for working out if a number is rational or irrational — like this:

1) $144^{1/2}$ ANS: press √ 144 = or 144 x^y 0.5 = to get 12, which is certainly *rational*.

2) $80^{-3/4}$ ANS: press 80 x^y ((–) 3 $a^b/_c$ 4) = which gives 0.037383719 ... which shows no signs of repeating so it will probably be *irrational*.

3) $\sqrt[5]{6\frac{2}{5}}$ ANS: press (6 $a^b/_c$ 2 $a^b/_c$ 5) x^y (1 $a^b/_c$ 5) = which gives 1.449559327 ... which again looks *irrational*.

If you hadn't used brackets here, your calculator would probably have given the wrong answer. That's because it wasn't clear how much of the expression to apply the x^y — you need the brackets to make it clear. Get in the habit of using brackets and you'll save yourself a lot of headaches.

4) Express $49^{-1/2}$ as a fraction in the form a/b.

ANS: press 49 x^y ((–) 1 $a^b/_c$ 2) = which gives 0.142857142.. and you might think it's irrational. But notice the repeat of the 142 which suggests *it may be a repeating decimal* and therefore *rational*. The $1/x$ button reveals all — see next page.

And more calculator buttons

Brackets are essential if you want to avoid confusion, and nonsense answers.
Put them in wherever they are needed, but remember they must always come in pairs.

Calculator Buttons

5) The $\frac{1}{x}$ Button

It basically turns numbers upside-down and this provides two very useful functions:

1) DOING DIVISIONS SLIGHTLY QUICKER
   E.g. if you already have 2.3456 in the display and you want to do 12 ÷ 2.3456, then you can just press ÷ 12 = $\frac{1}{x}$ =, which does the division the wrong way up and then flips it the right way up.

2) ANALYSING DECIMALS to see if they might be rational (i.e. something simple) e.g. if the display is 0.142857142 and you press $\frac{1}{x}$ = you'll get 7, meaning it was 1/7 before.

6) The **Standard Form Button** — EXP or EE

You are only likely to use this for entering numbers written in STANDARD FORM into the calculator.

It actually means $\times 10^n$ — and that's what you should think as you press it: "Times ten to the power..."

For example, to enter 6×10^3 you press: 6 EXP 3 and NOT: 6 × 10 EXP 3.

Pressing × 10 as well as EXP is wrong, because the EXP already contains the "×10" in it.

This is why you must always say to yourself "Times ten to the power.." each time you press the EXP button, to prevent this very common mistake.

TO READ A STANDARD FORM NUMBER FROM THE DISPLAY: E.g. 7.986 ^{05}

This must be written as 7.986×10^5 (NOT 7.986^5) — YOU have to put the $\times 10^n$ in yourself.

7) **Converting Time** to Hours, Minutes and Seconds with ° ' "

You will need this when you're doing speed, distance and time — converting an answer like 2.35 hours into hours and minutes. What it definitely ISN'T is 2 hours and 35 mins — remember your calculator does not work in hours and minutes unless you tell it to, as shown below. You'll need to practise with this button, but you'll be glad you did.

1) To ENTER a time in hours, mins and secs
   E.g. 5 hrs 34 mins and 23 secs, press 5 ° ' " 34 ° ' " 23 ° ' " = to get 5°34°23

2) Converting hours, min and secs to a decimal time:
   Enter the number in hours, mins and secs as above.
   Then just press ° ' " and it should convert it to a decimal like this 5.573055556
   (Though some older calculators will automatically convert it to decimal when you enter a time in hours, minutes and secs.)

3) To convert a decimal time (as you always get from a formula) into hrs, mins and secs:
   E.g. To convert 2.35 hours into hrs, mins and secs.
   Simply press 2.35 = to enter the decimal, then press SHIFT ° ' ".
   The display should become 2°21°0
   which means 2 hours, 21 mins (and 0 secs).

And more calculator buttons

You must learn all the different buttons on these three pages. If you remember all the calculator functions and practise using them, the world of maths will become a much quicker and easier place.

Revision Summary for Section One

I know these questions seem difficult, _but they are the very best revision you can do_. The whole point of revision, remember, is _to find out what you don't know_ and then learn it _until you do_. These searching questions test how much you know _better than anything else ever can_.

Keep learning the basic facts until you know them

1) What are square numbers, cube numbers, triangle numbers and prime numbers?
2) List the first ten of each _from memory_. Then write down the first five powers of 2 and the first five powers of 10.
3) What are the three steps of the method for determining prime numbers?
4) What are a) multiples, b) factors, c) prime factors?
5) List the first five multiples of 13, and all the factors of 80.
6) Give details of five different things you can do with the Fraction Button.
7) Describe in words the method for each of the five rules for doing fractions by hand.
8) Do your own example to illustrate each of the three types of percentage question.
9) What is the formula for percentage change? Give two examples of its use.
10) Name three different forms that a rational number can take, and give examples.
11) Describe two forms that an irrational number can take, with examples.
12) What is generally the best way of identifying a number as rational or irrational?
13) Explain the process for finding an irrational number between, say, 14 and 19.
14) Demonstrate the two methods for "doing" recurring decimals.
15) Write down all you know about manipulating surds.
16) What are the two formulas for finding the nth term of a sequence?
17) What type of sequence does each formula apply to?
18) What are the three steps for using conversion factors? Give 3 examples.
19) Give eight metric conversions, five imperial ones, and eight metric-to-imperial.
20) Give three rules for deciding on appropriate accuracy.
21) Give two rules for working out approximate answers to formulas.
22) Give two rules for working out approximate areas and volumes.
23) How do you determine the upper and lower bounds of a rounded measurement?
24) Explain how a calculated answer can have a range of possible values.
25) How do you find the maximum possible error?
26) How do find the maximum possible *percentage* error?
27) What is the worst situation for this and how do you deal with it?
28) Illustrate four extreme uses of the powers button.
29) Explain exactly what BODMAS is. Does your calculator know about it?
30) Give a good example of where the brackets buttons should be used.
31) Give a good example of where the memory buttons should be used.
32) Which button is useful for analysing awkward decimals? Give an example.
33) Which is the standard form button? What would you press to enter 6×10^8?
34) Which button can be used to enter hours, minutes and seconds?
35) Explain how to do so and also what to press to convert to a decimal time.
36) What is the difference between decimal time and ordinary time?

Regular Polygons

A polygon is a many-sided shape.
A regular polygon is one where all the sides and angles are the same.
The REGULAR POLYGONS are a never-ending series of shapes with some fancy features. They're very easy to learn. Here are the first few but they don't stop – you can have one with 12 sides or 25, etc.

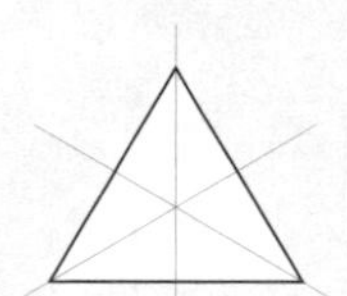

EQUILATERAL TRIANGLE
3 sides
3 lines of symmetry
Rot^{nl} symm. order 3

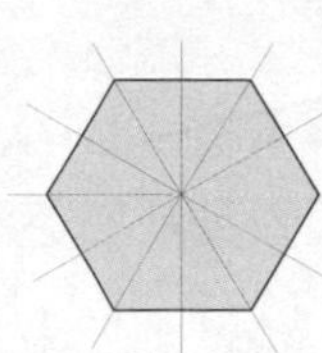

REGULAR HEXAGON
6 sides
6 lines of symmetry
Rot^{nl} symm. order 6

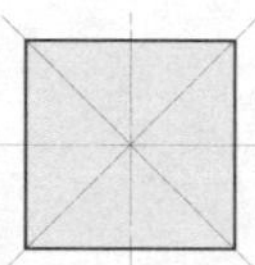

SQUARE
4 sides
4 lines of symmetry
Rot^{nl} symm. order 4

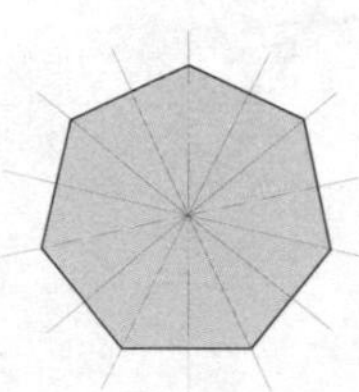

REGULAR HEPTAGON
7 sides
7 lines of symmetry
Rot^{nl} symm. order 7
(A 50p piece is like a heptagon)

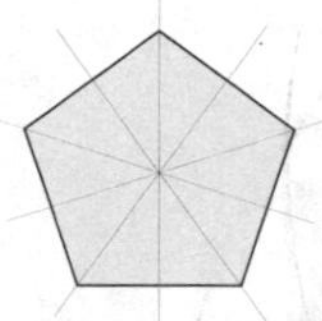

REGULAR PENTAGON
5 sides
5 lines of symmetry
Rot^{nl} symm. order 5

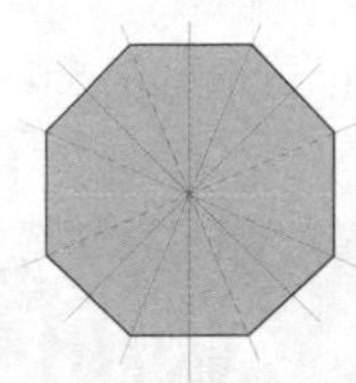

REGULAR OCTAGON
8 sides
8 lines of symmetry
Rot^{nl} symm. order 8

You also need to know the *next two*, but I'm not drawing them for you. *Learn their names:*

REGULAR NONEGON
9 sides, etc. etc.

REGULAR DECAGON
10 sides, etc. etc.

Regular **Polygons** have **LOADS** of **symmetry**

1) The pentagon shown here has only three different angles in the whole diagram.
2) This is typical of regular polygons. They display an amazing amount of symmetry.
3) With a regular polygon, if two angles look the same, they will be. That's not a rule you should normally apply in geometry, and anyway you'll need to prove they're equal.

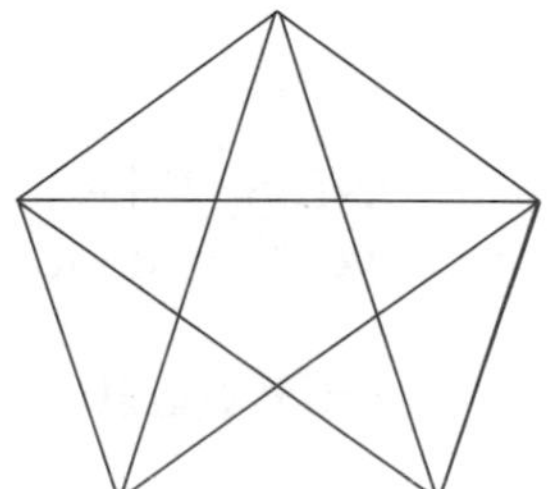

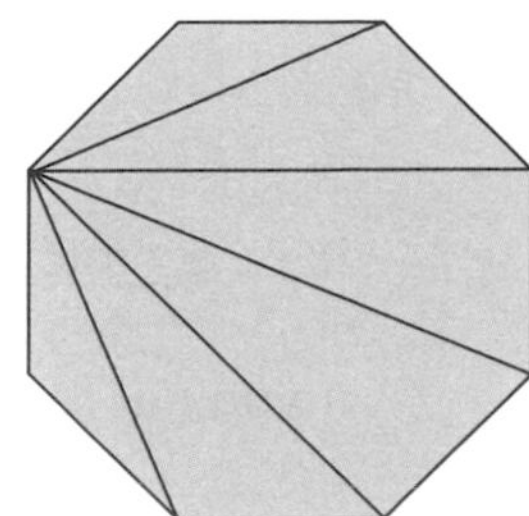

Regular polygons are easier than a round peg in a round hole

All you need to learn are the names of the polygons (which is pretty straightforward), and then remember what's special about regular polygons. Five minutes of scribbling should knock this page on the head.

Interior and Exterior Angles

Another thing that is special about regular polygons is all the calculations you can do with their angles...

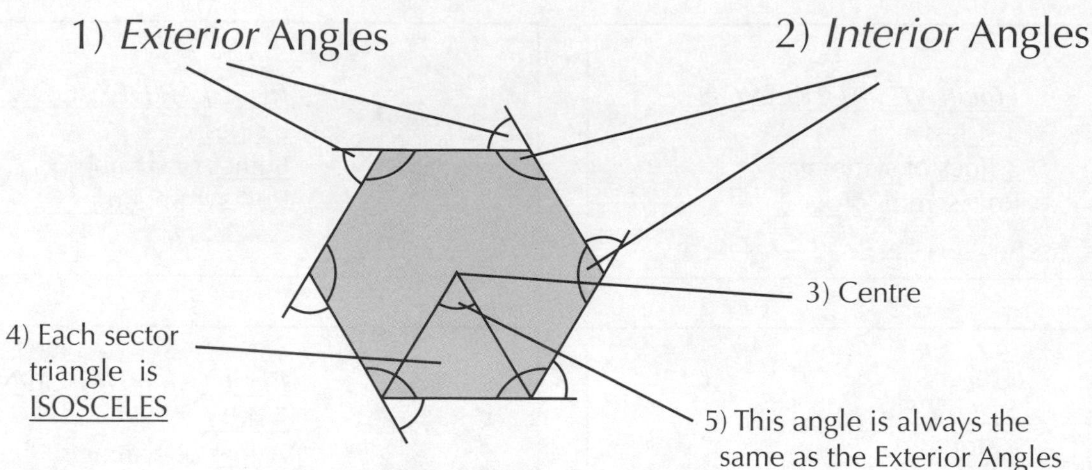

The two all important formulas you need to remember are:

$$\text{EXTERIOR ANGLE} = \frac{360^\circ}{\text{No. of Sides}}$$

$$\text{INTERIOR ANGLE} = 180^\circ - \text{EXTERIOR ANGLE}$$

This is the <u>MAIN BUSINESS</u>. Whenever you get a <u>Regular Polygon</u>, it's a <u>cosmic certainty</u> you'll need to work out the <u>Interior and Exterior Angles</u>.

If you fail to remember that you'll get nowhere with regular polygon questions.

Two very simple and very important formulas

There's always all manner of questions they can ask about angles in polygons, but they all come back to these two basic formulas. So make sure you've learnt them really well.

Areas

These formulas are given inside the front cover of the Exam, but I GUARANTEE that if you don't learn them beforehand, you'll be totally incapable of using them in the Exam – REMEMBER, I ABSOLUTELY GUARANTEE IT.

YOU MUST LEARN THESE FORMULAS:

Area of triangle = ½ × base x vertical height

$$A = ½ \times b \times h_v$$

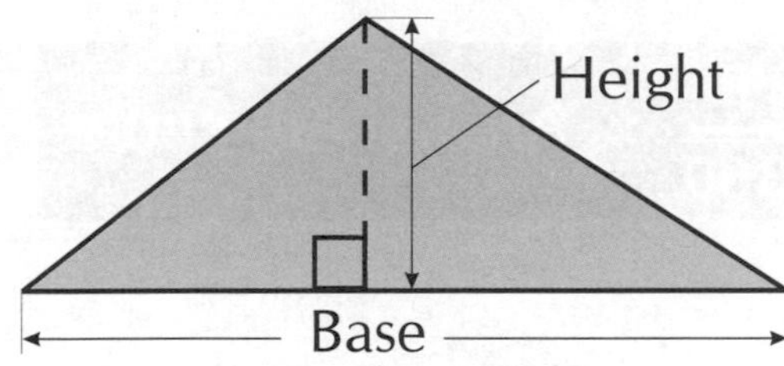

Note that the height must always be the vertical height, not the sloping height.

The alternative formula is this:

Area of triangle = ½ absinC

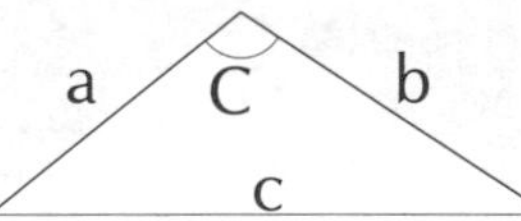

Area of parallelogram = base × vertical height

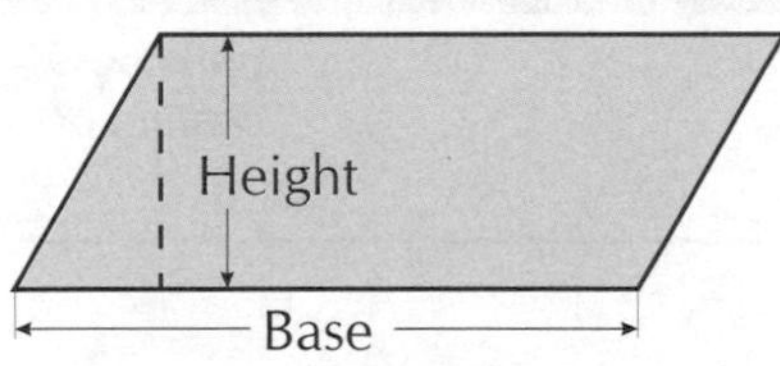

$$A = b \times h_v$$

Area of trapezium = average of parallel sides × distance between them

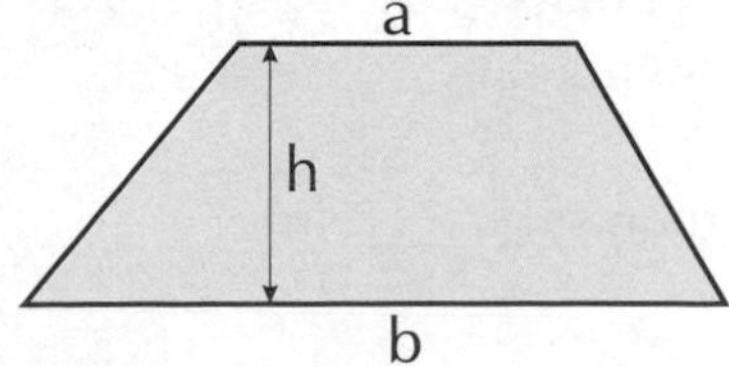

$$A = ½ \times (a + b) \times h$$

Did I say already — you must learn these formulas

Just remember...
I guarantee it...

Areas — Circles

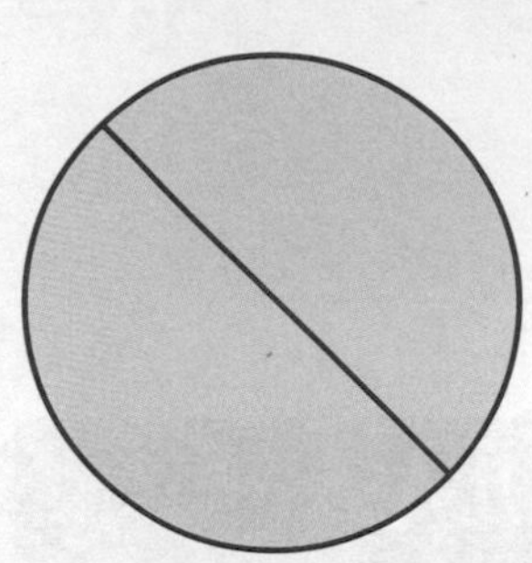

Area of circle = $\pi \times (\text{radius})^2$

$$A = \pi \times r^2$$

Circumference = $\pi \times$ Diameter

$$C = \pi \times D$$

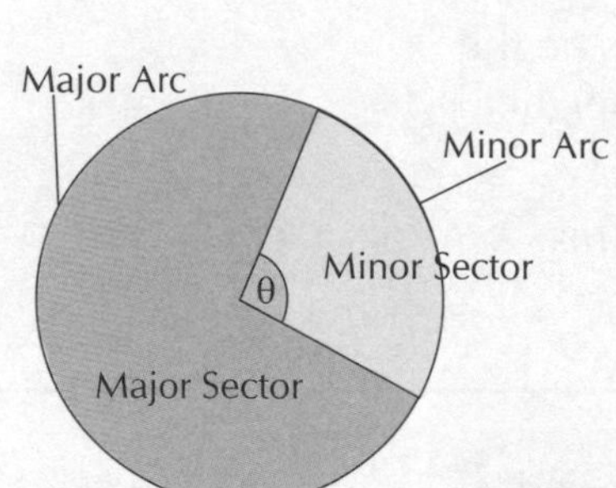

$$\text{Area of sector} = \frac{\theta}{360} \times \text{Area of full circle}$$

(Pretty obvious really isn't it?)

$$\text{Length of arc} = \frac{\theta}{360} \times \text{Circumference of full circle}$$

(Obvious again, no?)

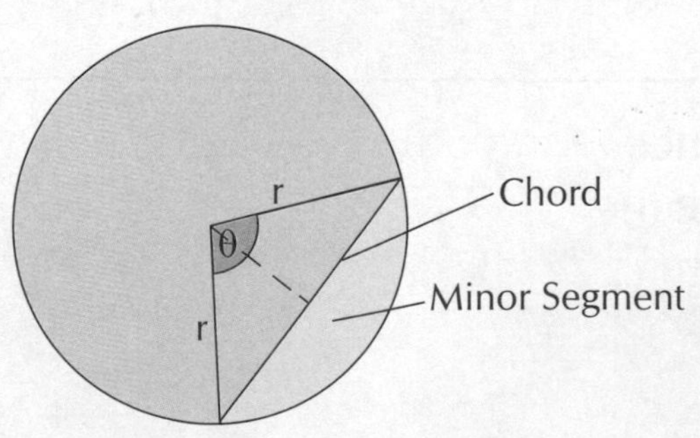

FINDING THE AREA OF A SEGMENT

is a slightly involved business but worth learning:

1) Find the area of the sector using the above formula.
2) Use trigonometry twice to find the base ($2 \times r \sin(\theta/2)$) and height ($r \times \cos(\theta/2)$) of the triangle
3) Find the area of the triangle, then subtract it from the area of the sector.

More formulas to scribble down and cram in your head

For any Exam question on area you should be prepared to make use of Pythagoras and / or trigonometry. But one step at a time, just get these simple formulas lodged in your brain box.

Volumes — Prisms

A PRISM is a solid (3-D) object which has a constant area of cross section - i.e. it's the same shape all the way through.

A lot of people aren't really sure what prisms are,
but they come up a lot in Exams, so make sure YOU know.

Circular Prism
(or Cylinder)

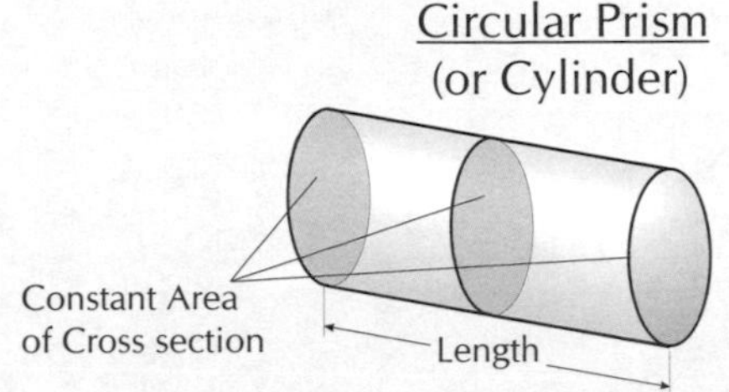

Triangular Prism

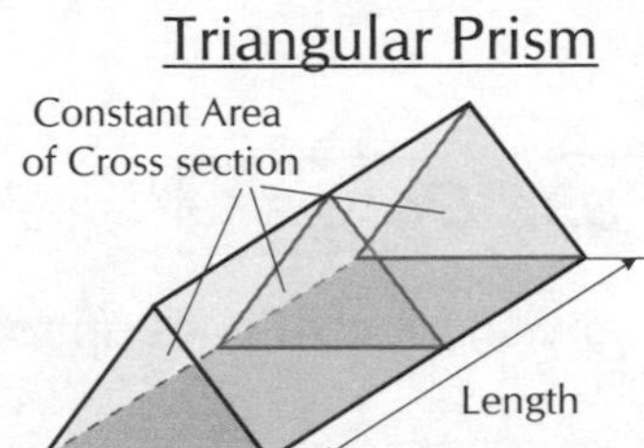

Hexagonal Prism
(a flat one, certainly, but still a prism)

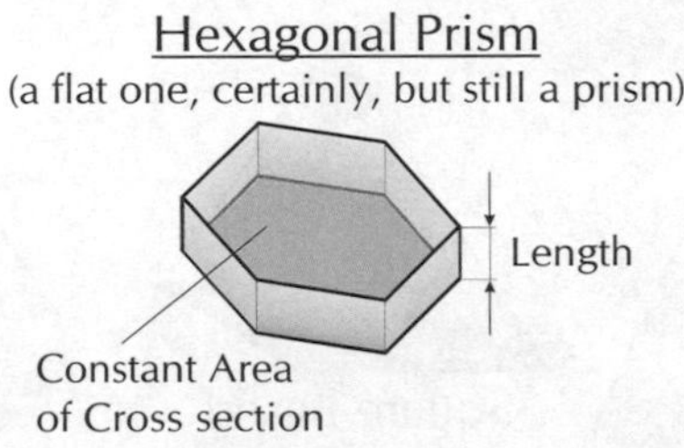

For all these prisms all you need to know is:

$$\text{Volume of prism} = \text{Cross sectional area} \times \text{Length}$$

Or simply:

$$V = A \times L$$

As you can see, the formula is very simple.
The difficult part, usually, is finding the area of the cross section.

You have to remember what a prism is

It's the constant area of cross section which is important — that's what makes a prism a prism. If you remember that, it makes perfect sense that to get the volume you just multiply that area by the length.

Volumes — Spheres, Pyramids and Cones

Sphere

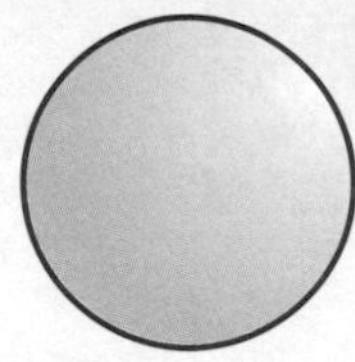

Volume of sphere $= \frac{4}{3}\pi r^3$

EXAMPLE: The moon has a radius of 1700km, find its volume.

Ans: $V = \frac{4}{3}\pi r^3 = (4/3)\times3.14\times1700^3 = \underline{2.1\times10^{10}\ \text{km}^3}$

Pyramids and Cones

A pyramid is any shape that goes up to a point at the top.

Its base can be any shape at all.
If the base is a circle then it's called a cone
(rather than a circular pyramid).

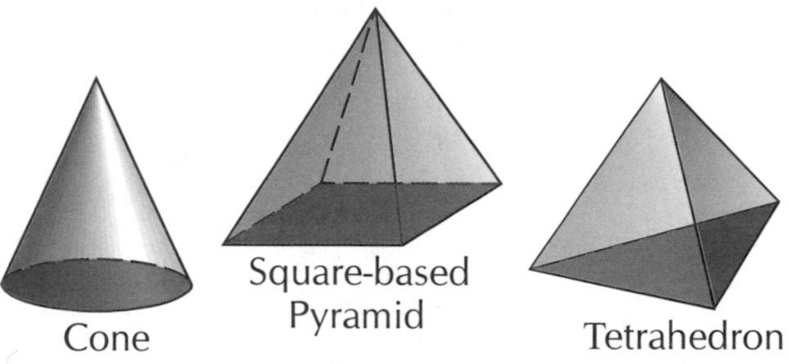

Volume of Pyramid $= \frac{1}{3} \times$ **Base Area** $\times$ **Height**

Volume of Cone $= \frac{1}{3} \times \pi r^2 \times$ **Height**

This surprisingly simple formula is true for any pyramid or cone, whether it goes up "vertically" (like the three shown above) or off to one side (like this one).

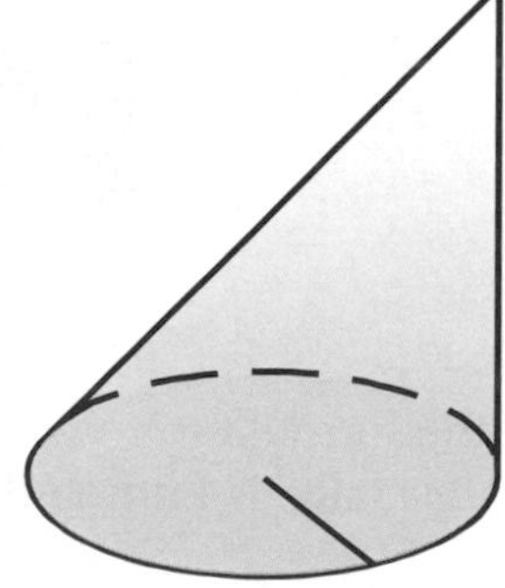

Remember that a cone is just a pyramid with a round base

The pyramid and cone equations are basically the same because the area of the base = area of a circle $= \pi r^2$. So really just two equations to learn here, and two important ones at that.

Length, Area and Volume

Identifying formulas just *by looking* at them

This is pretty easy since we're only talking about the formulas for three things— LENGTH, AREA and VOLUME — and the rules are as simple as this:

AREA FORMULAS always have lengths MULTIPLIED IN PAIRS

VOLUME FORMULAS always have lengths MULTIPLIED IN GROUPS OF THREE

LENGTH FORMULAS (such as perimeter) always have LENGTHS OCCURRING SINGLY

In formulas, *lengths are represented by letters*, so when you look at a formula you're *looking for groups of letters MULTIPLIED together* in ones, twos or threes. *BUT REMEMBER,* π *is NOT a length* so don't count it as one of your letters.

EXAMPLES:

πd (length)
πr^2 (area)
$4\pi r + 15L$ (length)
$2\pi d - 14r/3$ (length)

$2l + 2w$ (length)
$(4/3)\pi r^3$ (volume)
$Lwh + 6r^2L$ (volume)
$6hp + \pi r^2 + 7h^2$ (area)

$4\pi(a + b)^2$ (area)
$3b(d + l)^2$ (volume)
$\frac{5ph^2 + d^3}{4\pi r}$ (area)

$4\pi r^2 + 6d^2$ (area)
$5p^2L - 4k^3/7$ (volume)

Scale Drawings from *different views*

You might get an exam question asking for one of these, so make sure you know which is which.

ISOMETRIC Projection

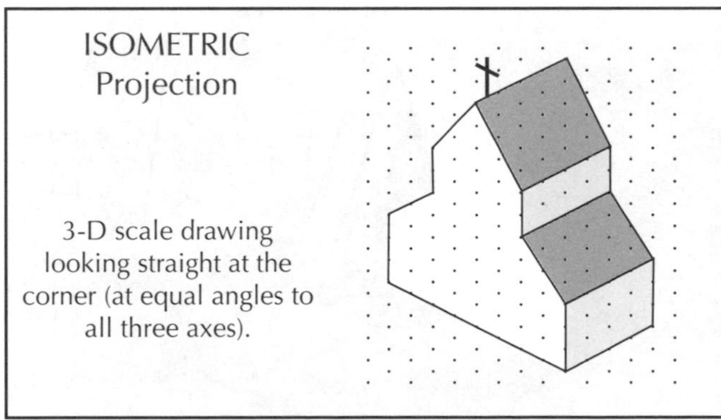

3-D scale drawing looking straight at the corner (at equal angles to all three axes).

FRONT Elevation

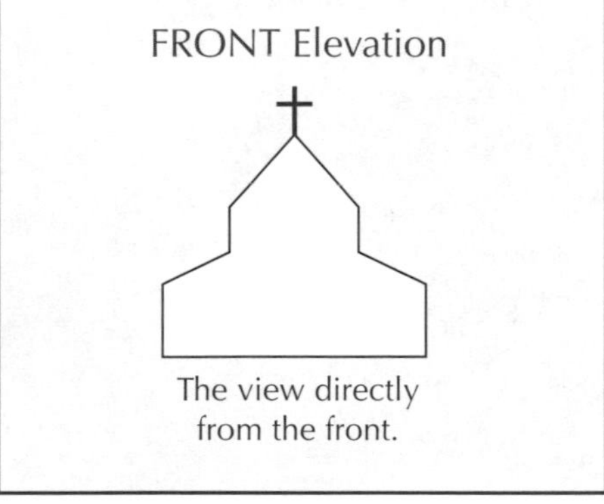

The view directly from the front.

SIDE Elevation

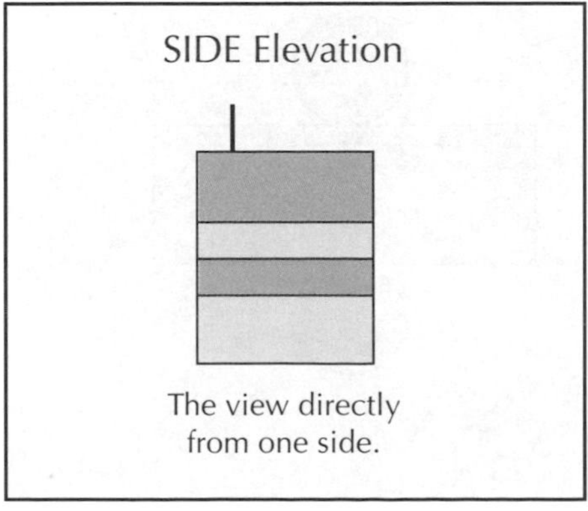

The view directly from one side.

Plan

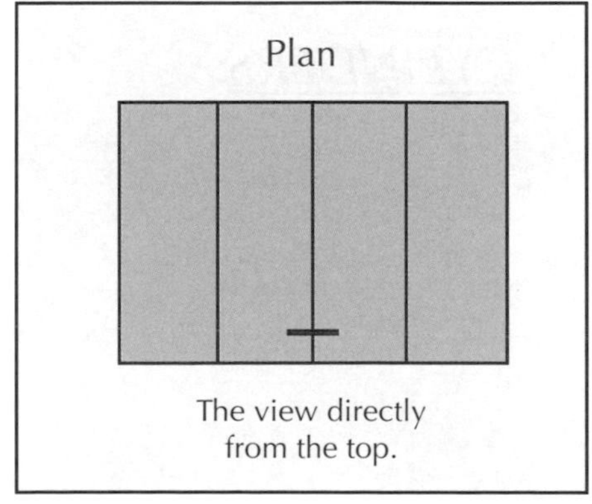

The view directly from the top.

To recognise lengths, areas and volumes just count the letters

See if the letters appear in ones, twos or threes. There's loads of examples on the page to make sure you've got the idea. Then you'll have a few minutes spare to learn these four scale drawing views.

Length, Area and Volume

Surface Area and Nets

1) SURFACE AREA only applies to solid 3D objects, and it is simply the total area of all the outer surfaces added together. If you were painting it, it's all the bits you'd paint.

2) There is NEVER A SIMPLE FORMULA for surface area — you have to work out each side in turn and then ADD THEM ALL TOGETHER.

3) A NET is just A SOLID SHAPE FOLDED OUT FLAT.

4) So obviously :
   SURFACE AREA OF SOLID = AREA OF NET.

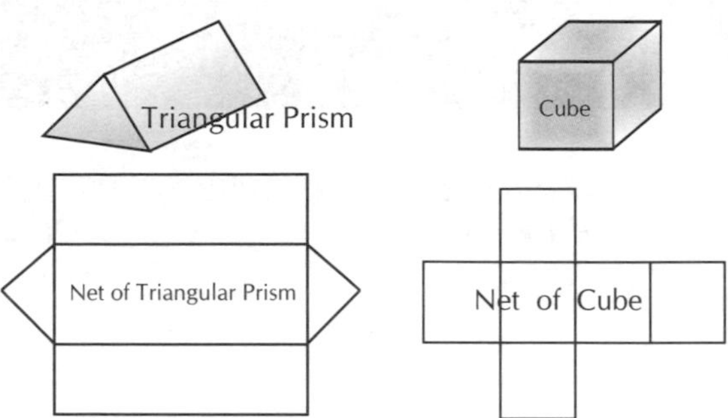

5) The SURFACE AREAS OF SPHERES, CYLINDERS AND CONES are particularly important (because they're mentioned in the syllabus):

SPHERES:
Surface area = $4\pi r^2$

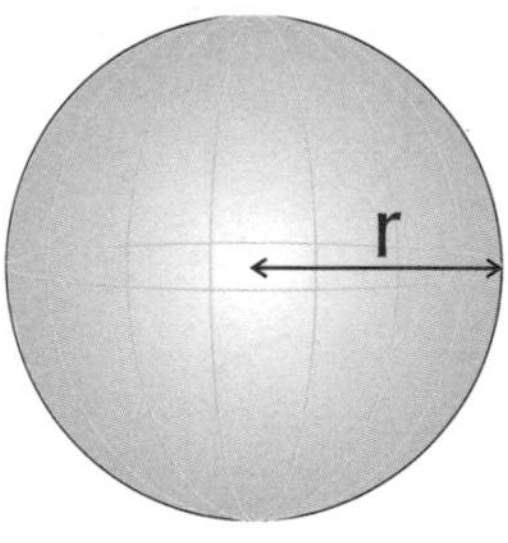

CONES:
Surface area = $\pi rl + \pi r^2$

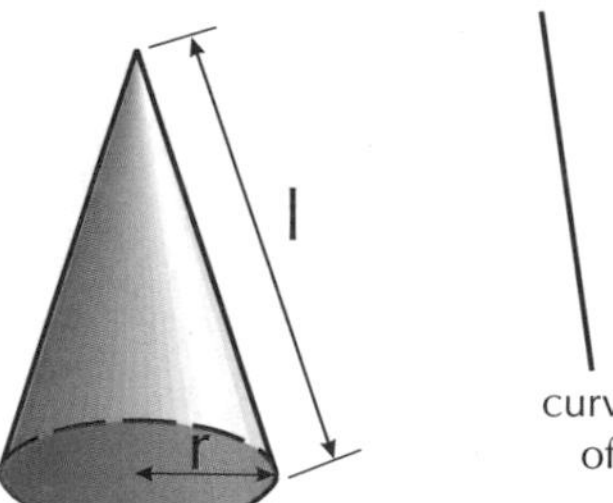

curved area of cone

area of circular base

CYLINDERS:
Surface area = $2\pi rh + 2\pi r^2$

Especially note that the length of the rectangle is equal to the circumference of the circular ends.

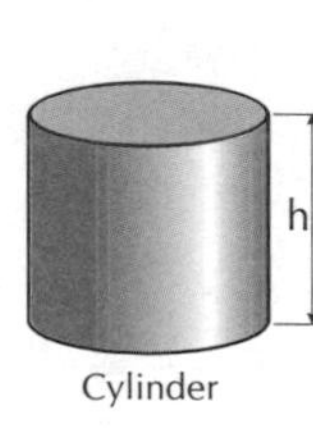

Cylinder

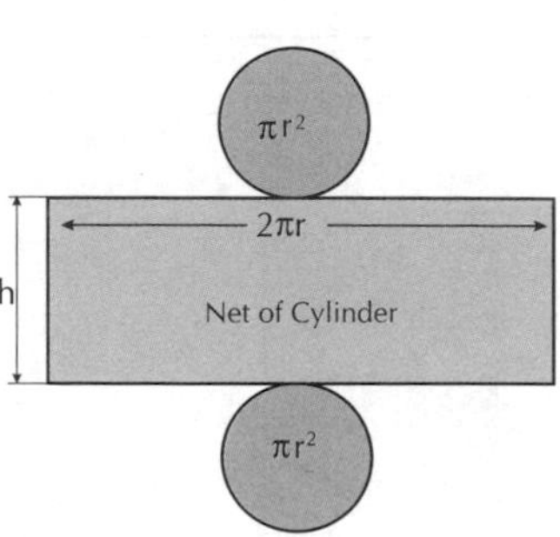

To get the surface area of a solid just add up the area of each face

That's why nets are useful when working out surface area. A net is just all the sides folded out flat, which makes it easier to see which shapes you need to calculate the areas of.

Warm-Up and Worked Exam Questions

There are lots of formulas in this section. The best way to see what you know is to practise these questions. If you find you keep forgetting the formulas, you need more practice.

Warm-Up Questions

1) Calculate the volume of this triangular prism.

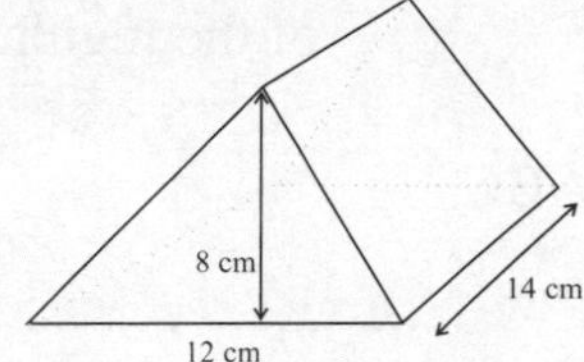

2)

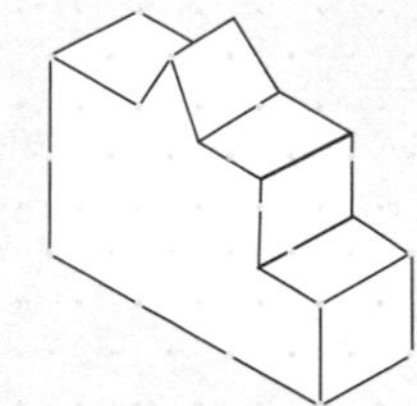

From the isometric projection shown draw

(a) Both side elevations

(b) Front elevation

(c) Plan view

3) A woodworking template has the shape shown.

(a) Calculate the area of one of the round holes.

(b) Use this to calculate the area of the template.

(c) If the template is 4 mm thick calculate its volume.

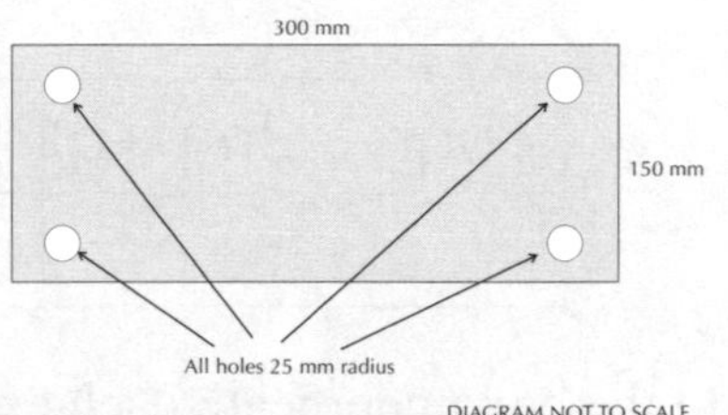

Worked Exam Question

These worked exam questions are the ideal way to get the hang of the real exam — so practise.

1 A householder draws a plan of his garden.

The flowerbed and pond are rectangular and his patio is a quadrant.

He intends to sow lawn seed on the shaded area of his plan.

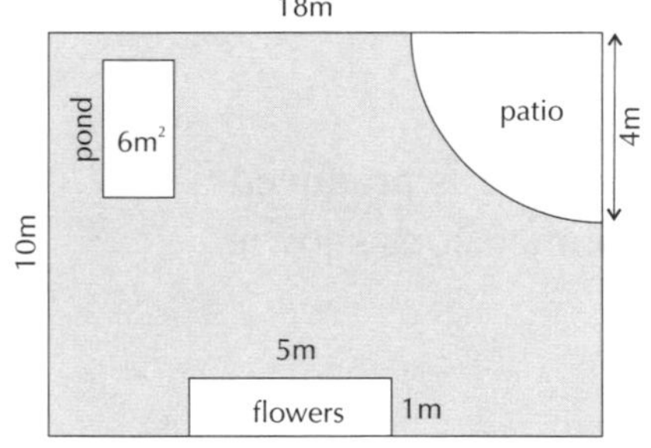

DIAGRAM NOT TO SCALE

(a) Calculate the area covered by his new lawn

Total area of garden = 10 × 18 = 180 m², area of pond = 6 m²,

area of flowerbed = 5 × 1 = 5 m², area of patio = $\frac{1}{4} \times \pi \times 4^2 = 12.6\,m^2$

So area of lawn = area of garden – (pond + flowers + patio)

= 180 – (6 + 5+12.6) = 156.4

Work out one bit at a time

A quadrant is quarter of a circle, so area = $\frac{1}{4} \times \pi \times r^2$

Answer (a) 156.4 m²

(4 marks)

If 0.5 kg of seed covers 10 square metres

(b) How many kilograms of seed will he need? (Round answer to the nearest kilogram)

0.5 kg of seed covers 10m², so 0.5 ÷ 10 = 0.05 kg covers 1 m².

So to cover 156.4 m² need 156.4 x 0.05 = 7.82 kg (8 to nearest kg)

Answer (b) 8 kg

(2 marks)

Exam Questions

2

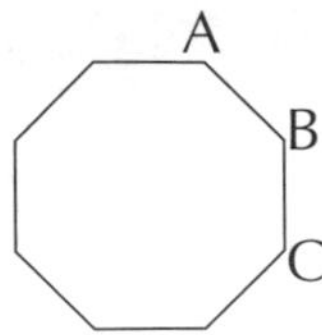

A tile is in the shape of the regular polygon shown.

Calculate the size of the angle ABC.

....

Answer ____________

(2 marks)

3 The table below shows six expressions. The letters p, q and r represent lengths.

pqr	$2p(p+q)$	$p+q+r$	$2p+2r$	$pq(r-p)$	p^2r

In the box underneath each expression
(a) place the letter L if the expression represents a length.

(b) place the letter A if the expression represents an area.

(c) place the letter V if the expression represents a volume.

(3 marks)

4 A metal fastener is produced using the dimensions shown.

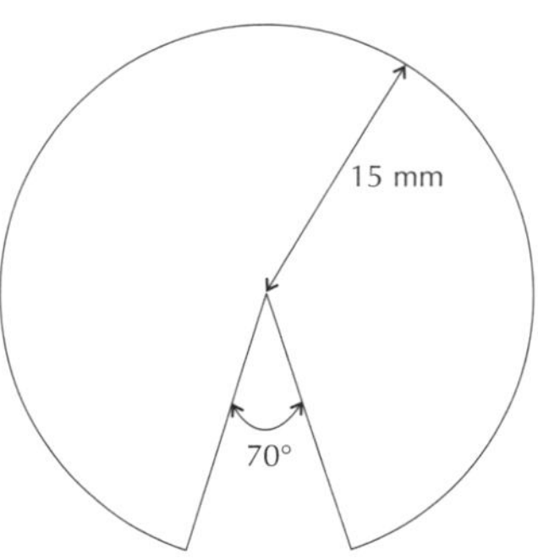

Calculate:

(a) the area of metal used to make the fastener.

....

Answer (a) ____________

(3 marks)

(b) the perimeter of the fastener.

....

Answer (b) ____________

(3 marks)

Geometry

There are Eight Simple Rules — that's all:

Spread over the next three pages there are eight simple rules which will solve ANY geometry problem not involving circles.

If you learn them all THOROUGHLY, you'll at least have a fighting chance of tackling geometry problems — if you're slightly unsure about any of them, then believe me you won't get anywhere with Exam questions.

1 ANGLES IN A TRIANGLE add up to 180^0

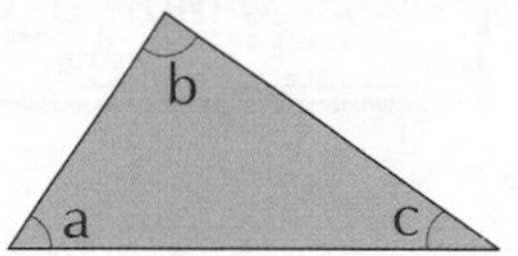

2 ANGLES ON A STRAIGHT LINE add up to 180^0

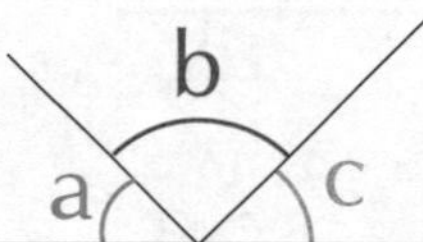

3 ANGLES IN A QUADRILATERAL add up to 360^0

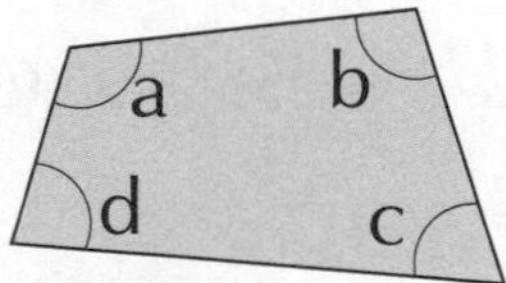

4 ANGLES ROUND A POINT add up to 360^0

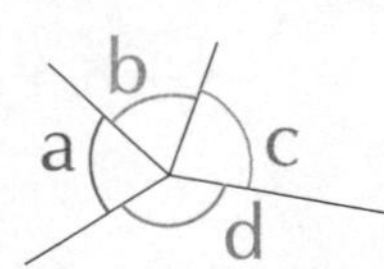

5 ISOSCELES TRIANGLES — Two sides the same, Two angles the same

1) *You only need to know one angle* to be able to find the other two, which is *very useful IF YOU REMEMBER IT*.
2) The biggest problem with isosceles triangles is spotting them in the first place.

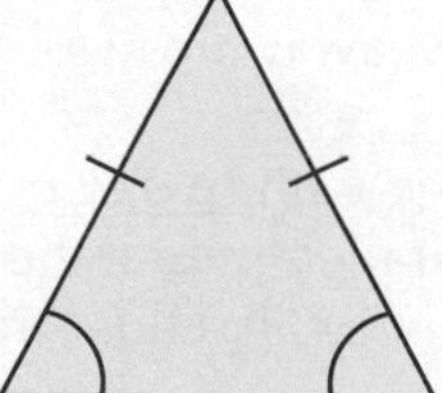

Five of eight geometry rules are here — YOU MUST LEARN THEM

That's one page of rules — and the first five done, only three more to do. Scribble them down again and again until they're ingrained in your brain (or desk). Then on to those last three...

Geometry

Parallel Lines

6

Whenever one straight line crosses two *parallel lines* then:

the two bunches of angles ARE THE SAME,

and a + b = 180°

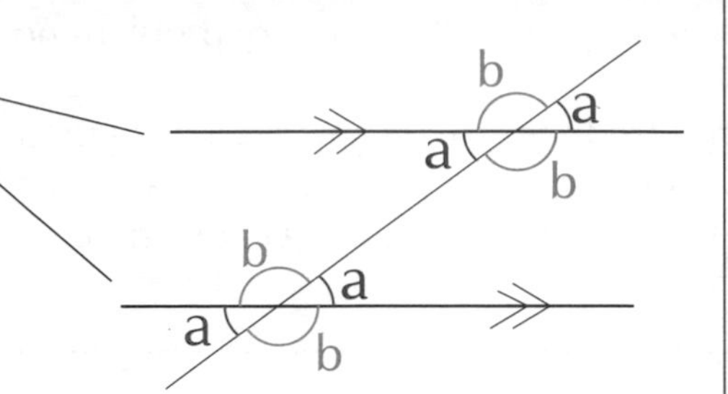

You need to spot the *characteristic Z, C, U and F shapes*

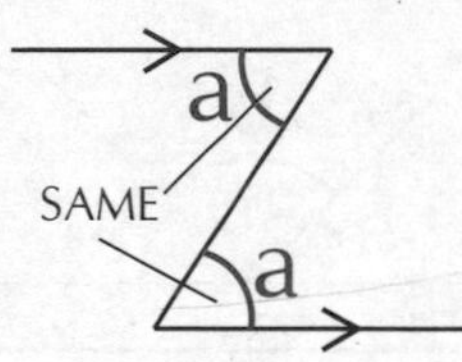

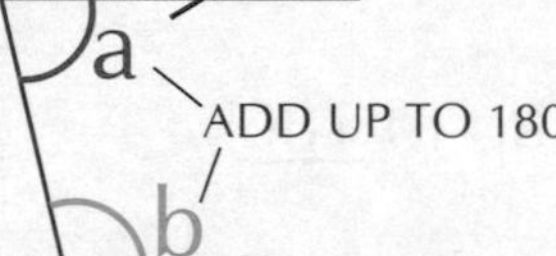

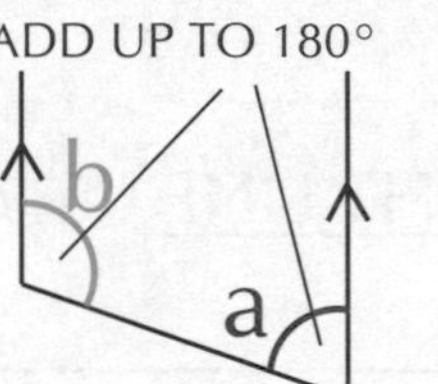

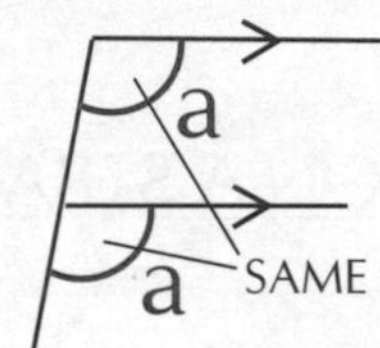

In a Z-shape they're called "ALTERNATE ANGLES"

If they add up to 180° they're called "SUPPLEMENTARY ANGLES"

In an F-shape they're called "CORRESPONDING ANGLES"

Alas you're expected to learn these three silly names.

If necessary, EXTEND THE LINES to make the diagram easier to get to grips with:

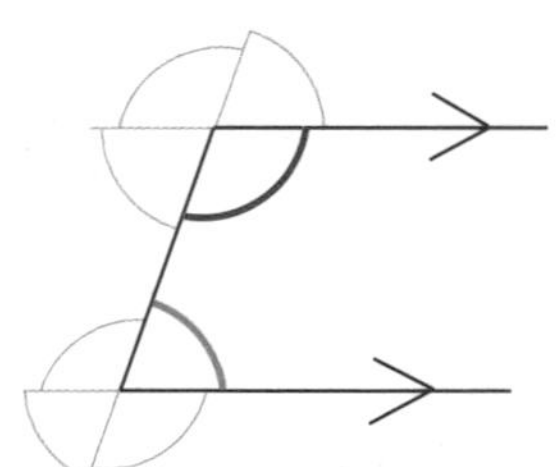

The **two most difficult** things about **parallel lines:**

a) *Spotting them in the first place,* perhaps because they've managed to avoid the giveaway arrows on the diagram.

b) Dealing with *two lines crossing* the parallel lines at the same point like this:

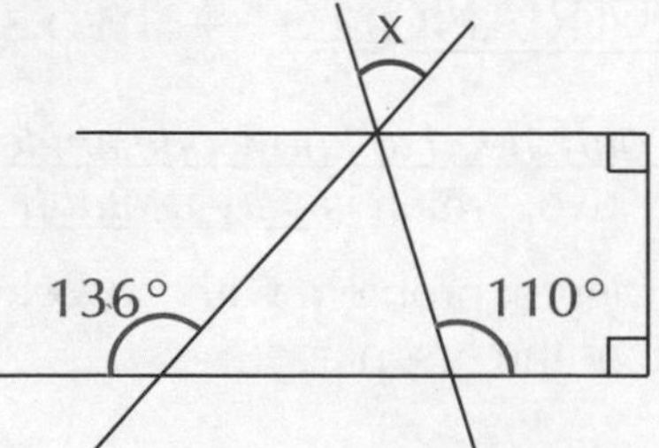

Parallel lines are key things to look out for in geometry

Keep your eyes open for parallel lines and those all important z, c, u and f shapes. Remember that extending the lines can make seeing these things (and therefore make your life) a lot easier.

Geometry

Irregular Polygons: Interior and Exterior Angles

An irregular polygon is basically any shape with lots of straight sides which aren't all the same. There are two formulas you need to know:

7

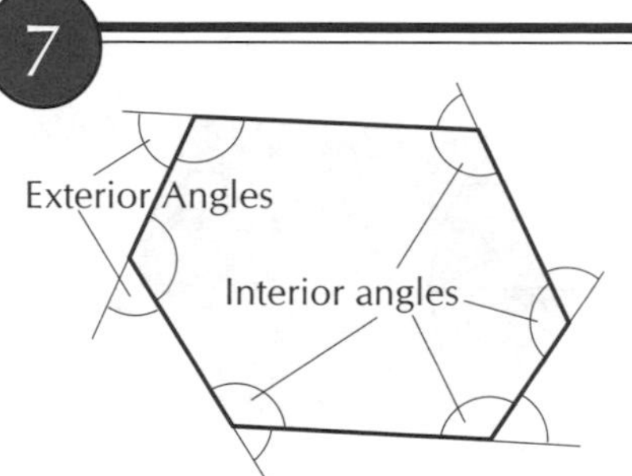

Sum of Exterior angles = 360°

Sum of Interior angles = (n – 2) × 180°
where n is the number of sides

The (n – 2)×180° formula comes from splitting the inside of the polygon up into triangles using full diagonals:
Each triangle has 180° in it so just count up the triangles and × by 180°. There's always two less triangles than there are sides, hence the (n – 2) in the formula.

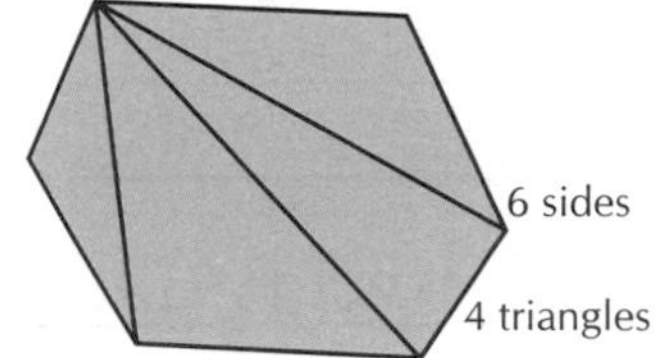

Basic Approach to geometry problems

1) Don't concentrate too much on the angle you have been asked to find. The best method is to FIND ALL THE ANGLES IN WHATEVER ORDER THEY BECOME OBVIOUS.

2) Don't sit there waiting for inspiration to hit you. It's all too easy to find yourself staring at a geometry problem and getting nowhere. The method is this:

8

GO THROUGH ALL THE ABOVE RULES OF GEOMETRY, ONE BY ONE, and apply each of them in turn in as many ways as possible - one of them is bound to work.

This really works by the way. Try it and you'll be amazed how easy geometry can become when you just apply these simple rules.

An example

"Find all the other angles in this diagram."

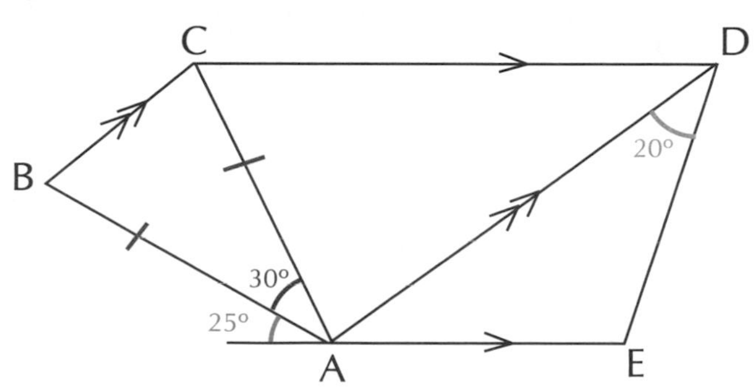

ANSWER:

1) ABC is isosceles, so ∠ABC =∠ACB =75°
2) BC and AD are parallel, BCAD is a Z-shape, so if ∠ACB =75° then ∠CAD = 75° too.
3) Angles on a straight line means ∠EAD = 50°
4) AE and CD are parallel so ∠ADC = 50° also.
5) Triangle ACD adds up to 180° so ∠ACD = 55°
6) Triangle ADE adds up to 180° so ∠AED =110°

That's all eight rules — so make sure you've got them all

Learn each of the last three pages one at a time, and make sure you've got all eight rules clear in your head. If not, go back over and scribble all eight down again and again.

Circle Geometry

9 Simple Rules — that's all:

Unfortunately as well as the eight geometry rules on pages 41-43, there are *nine* special rules for circle geometry. There's only one thing for it — you have to *scribble them down too*...

1) ANGLE IN A SEMICIRCLE = 90°

A triangle drawn from the two ends of a diameter will ALWAYS make an angle of 90º where it hits the edge of the circle, no matter where it hits.

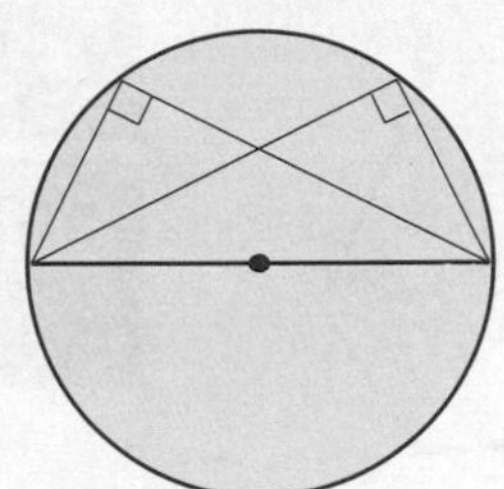

2) TANGENT and RADIUS MEET AT 90°

A TANGENT is a line that just touches the edge of a RADII curve. If a tangent and radius meet at the same point, then the angle they make is EXACTLY 90°.

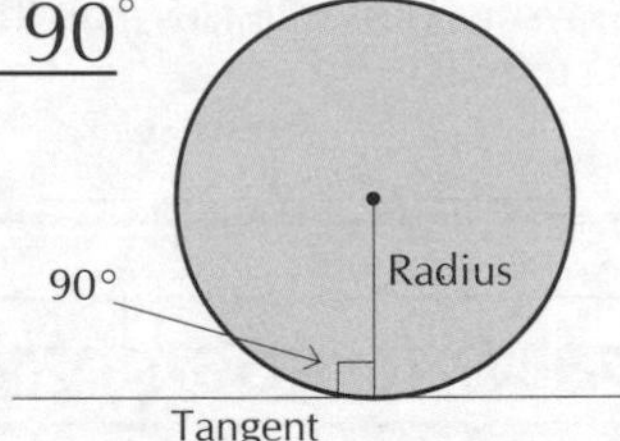

"radii" is just the plural of radius

3) SNEAKY ISOSCELES TRIANGLES FORMED BY TWO RADII

Unlike other isosceles triangles, they don't have the little tick marks on the sides to remind you that they are the same — the fact that they are both radii is enough to make it an isosceles triangle.

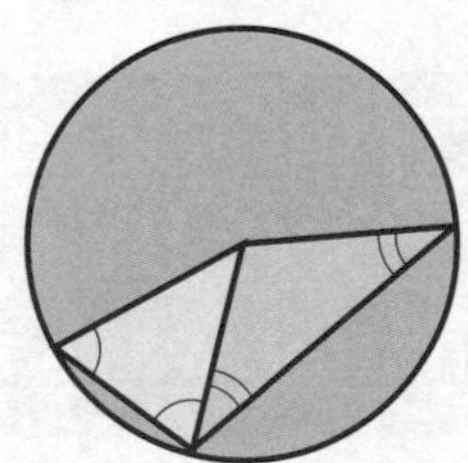

4) CHORD BISECTOR IS A DIAMETER

A CHORD is any line drawn across a circle. And no matter where you draw a chord, the line that cuts it exactly in half (at 90°), will go through the centre of the circle and so will be a DIAMETER.

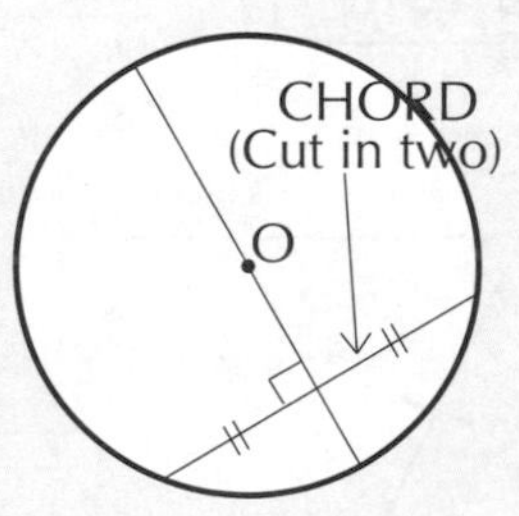

Four down, five to go

There's just a pile of words (like tangent, chord, bisector...) which make this stuff sound more complicated than it really is. Once you've got them in your head it's just four simple rules to learn.

Circle Geometry

5) ANGLES IN THE SAME SEGMENT ARE EQUAL

All triangles drawn from a chord will have the same angle where they touch the circle. Also, the two angles on opposite sides of the chord add up to 180°.

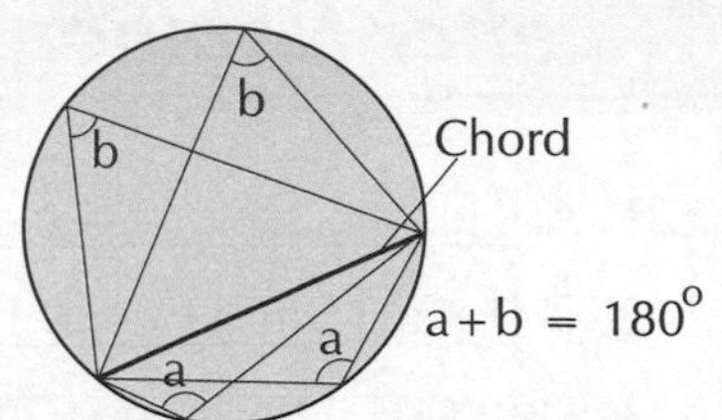

6) ANGLE AT THE CENTRE IS TWICE THE ANGLE AT THE EDGE

The angle subtended at the centre of a circle is EXACTLY DOUBLE the angle subtended at the edge of the circle from the same two points (two ends of the same chord). The phrase "angle subtended at" is nothing complicated, it's just a bit posher than saying "angle made at".

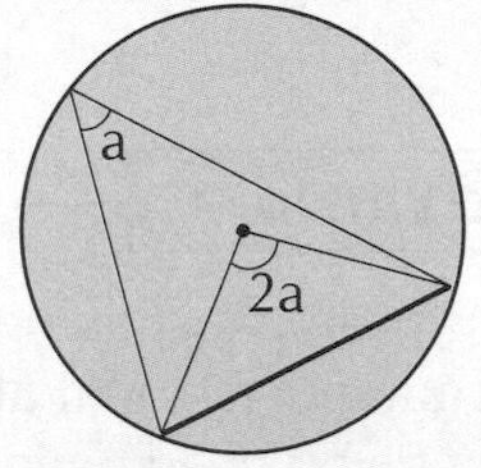

7) OPPOSITE ANGLES OF A CYCLIC QUADRILATERAL ADD UP TO 180°

$a+c=180°$
$b+d=180°$

A *cyclic quadrilateral* is a 4-sided shape with every corner touching the circle. Both pairs of opposite angles add up to 180°.

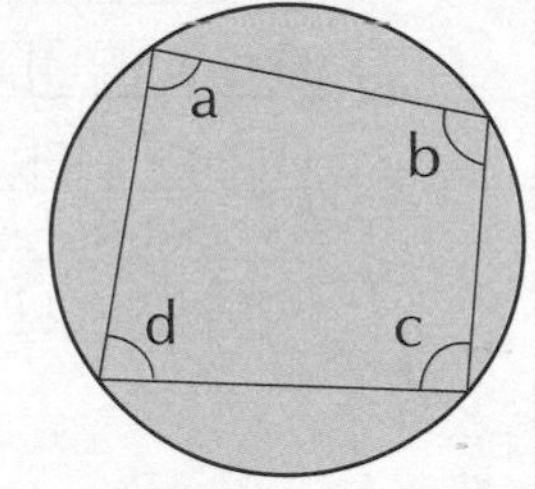

8) EQUALITY OF TANGENTS FROM A POINT

Two tangents drawn from any point outside the circle make two lines equal in length between the point and the circle, so creating two congruent right-angled triangles.

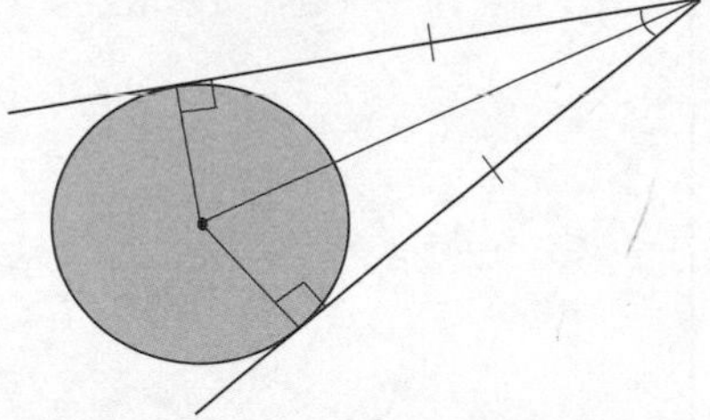

9) ANGLE IN OPPOSITE SEGMENT IS EQUAL

This is perhaps the trickiest one to remember. If you draw a tangent and a chord that meet, then the angle between them is always equal to *"the angle in the opposite segment"*. (The angle in the opposite segment is any angle made at the edge of the circle by two lines drawn from the chord.)

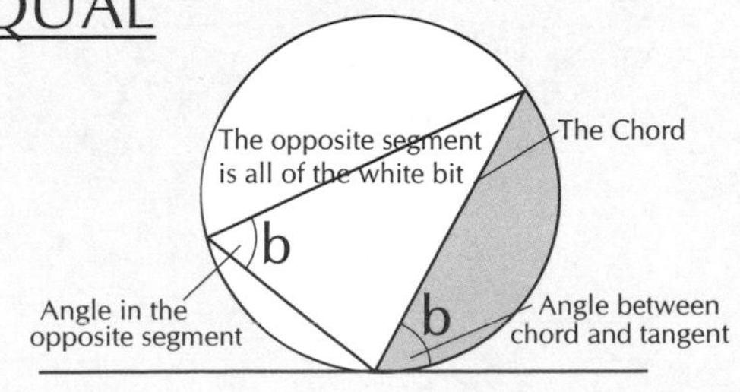

And that's your lot

This page is just more of the same: five more formulas to cram into your overcrowded brain. But there's no way round learning this stuff, and once you've learnt all nine, circle geometry becomes child's play.

Circle Geometry

3-Letter Notation for angles

1) Angles are specified using three letters, e.g. angle ODC = 48°
2) THE MIDDLE LETTER IS WHERE THE ANGLE IS
3) THE OTHER TWO LETTERS tell you which lines enclose the angle
   For example: Angle ODC is at D and enclosed by the lines going from O to D and from D to C.

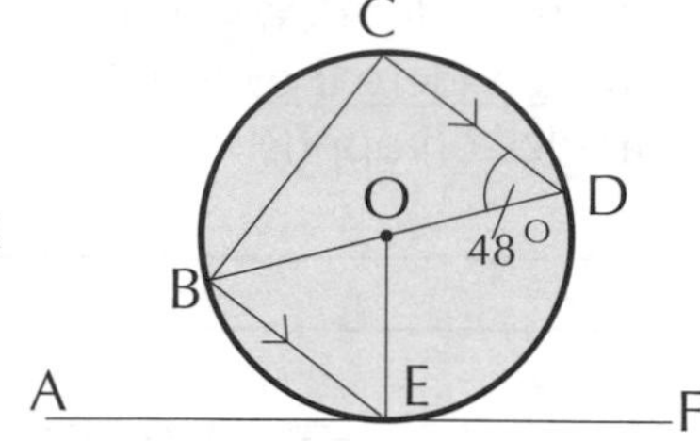

An example

This example should tie together all the circle rules and the 3-letter notation.
If you understand it all, that should mean you've got all this stuff sorted.
If not, you need to go back over those rules again.

1) Angles are specified using three letters, e.g. angle ODC = 48°
2) THE MIDDLE LETTER IS WHERE THE ANGLE IS
3) THE OTHER TWO LETTERS tell you which lines enclose the angle
   For example: Angle ODC is at D and enclosed by the lines going from O to D and from D to C.

"Find all the angles in this diagram."

(Apply the rules from P.41-45 and see how easy it makes it)

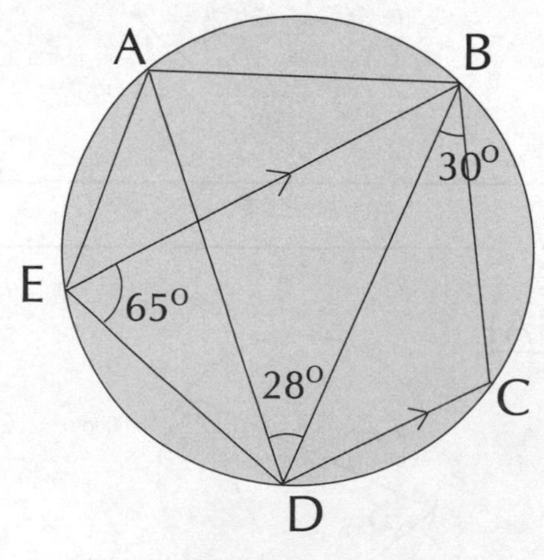

ANSWER:

1) PARALLEL LINES – there are actually four different lines crossing the two parallel ones, but the most useful one is ED which tells us that EDC is 115°
2) ANGLE IN SAME SEGMENT – there are potentially eight different chords where this rule could apply, but some are more useful than others:
   EAD = EBD, ADB = AEB (so AEB = 28°)
   ABE = ADE, DAB = DEB (so DAB = 65°)
3) ANGLES IN OPPOSITE SEGMENTS – again there are three different chords where this can be applied, and two of them bear fruit:
   BCD = 180 – 65 = 115°
   ABD = 180 – (65+28) = 87°
4) ANGLES IN A TRIANGLE ADD UP TO 180° — this, the simplest of all the rules, will now find all the other angles for you.

Have you remembered those nine rules?

If this stuff is all still more confusing than a Japanese game show, or you can't remember all the rules, you need to go back for another look. The rules are essential for all circle geometry questions.

Loci and Constructions

A LOCUS (another ridiculous maths word) is simply:

A LINE that shows all the points which fit a given rule

Make sure you learn how to do these PROPERLY
using a RULER AND COMPASSES, as shown on this page and the next:

1) The locus of points which are *"A FIXED DISTANCE from a given POINT"*

This locus is simply a *CIRCLE*.

Pair of Compasses
A given point
The LOCUS of points equidistant from it

2) The locus of points which are *"A FIXED DISTANCE from a given LINE"*

This locus is an *OVAL SHAPE*

It has *straight sides* (drawn with a *ruler*) and *ends* which are *perfect semicircles* (drawn with *compasses*).

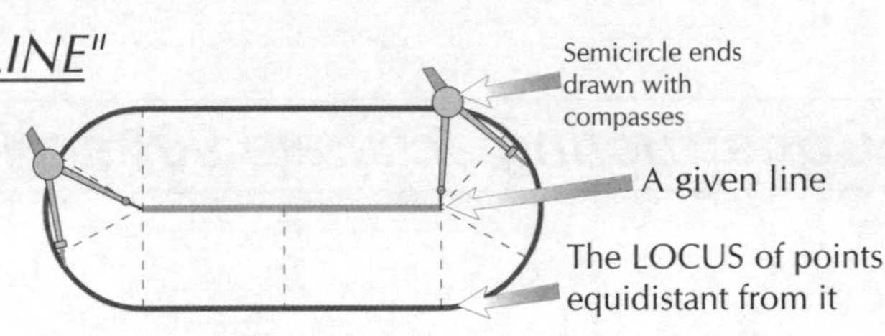

3) The locus of points which are *"EQUIDISTANT from TWO GIVEN LINES"*

1) Keep the compass setting *THE SAME* while you make *all four marks*.
2) Make sure you *leave* your compass marks *showing*.
3) You get *two equal angles* — i.e. this *LOCUS* is actually an *ANGLE BISECTOR*.

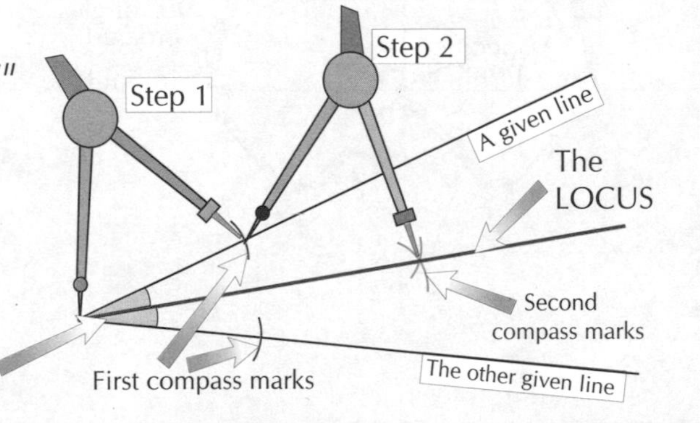

4) The locus of points which are *"EQUIDISTANT from TWO GIVEN POINTS"*

(In the diagram, A and B are the two given points)

This LOCUS is all points which are the *same distance* from A as they are from B.

This time the locus is actually the *PERPENDICULAR BISECTOR* of the line joining the two points.

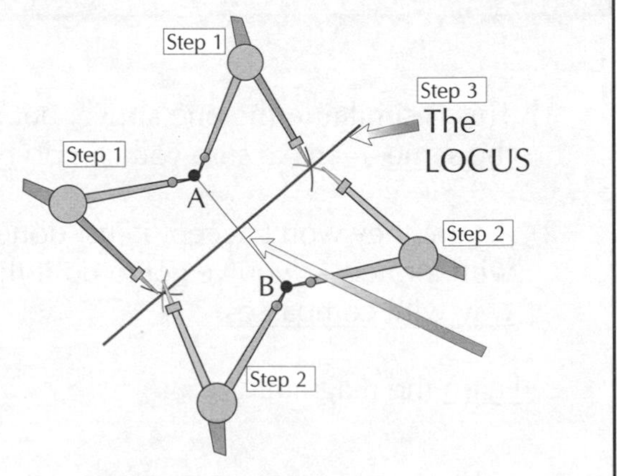

Don't be confused by the jargon — loci are simple enough

They just show a set of points that fit a given rule.
The main knack is remembering that, and constructing them carefully with a ruler and compass.

Loci and Constructions

Constructing accurate 60° angles

1) They may well ask you to draw an accurate 60° angle.
2) They're needed for drawing an equilateral triangle.
3) Make sure you follow the method shown in this diagram, and that you can do it entirely from memory.

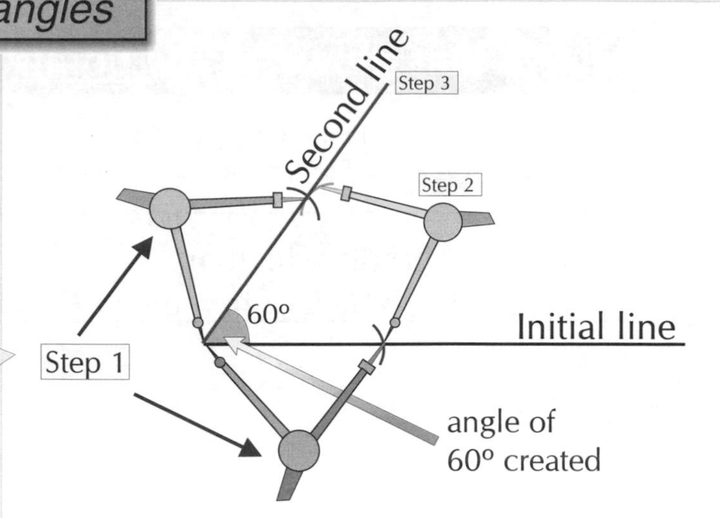

Constructing accurate 90° angles

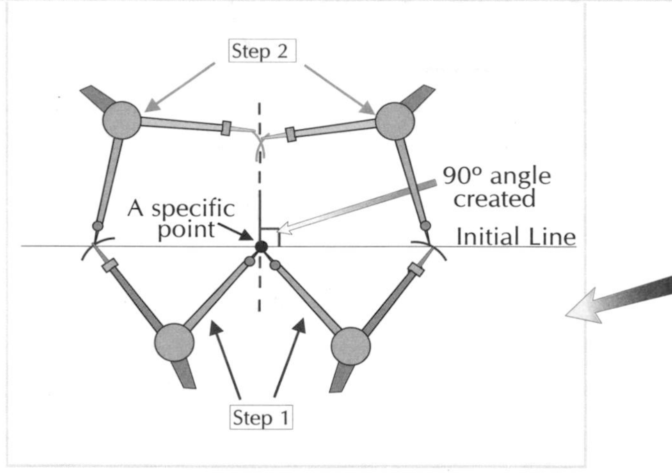

1) They might want you to draw an accurate 90° angle.
2) They won't accept it just done "by eye" or with a ruler — if you want the marks you've got to do it the proper way with compasses, like I've shown you here.
3) Make sure you can follow the method shown in this diagram.

Drawing the Perpendicular from a Point to a Line

1) This is similar to the one above, but not quite the same — make sure you can do both.
2) Again, they won't accept it just done "by eye" or with a ruler — you've got to do it the proper way with compasses.
3) Learn the diagram.

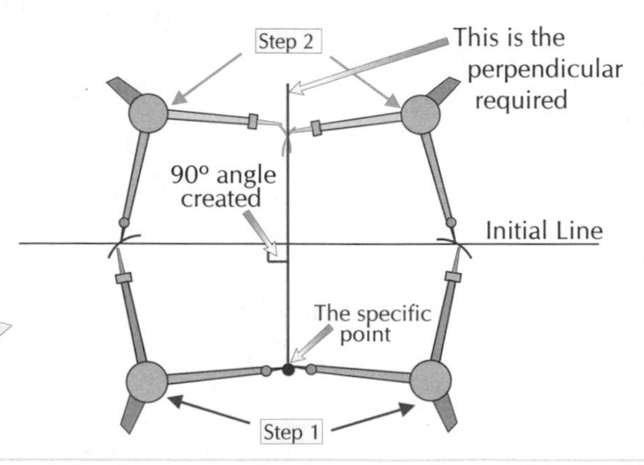

Constructions are basically tricks for maths drawings

There's nothing too 'mathsy' about this page. It's just a few simple tricks to use to draw accurately different angles — it's almost art. So get it learnt quick-smart so you can get back to the maths.

Warm-Up Questions

A whole page of warm-up questions, and look at those lovely big diagrams. But don't just look at them — you need to work through them one by one and make sure that you've remembered all those rules...

Warm-Up Questions

1) Using a compass and ruler construct an equilateral triangle with length of side 4 cm.

2) 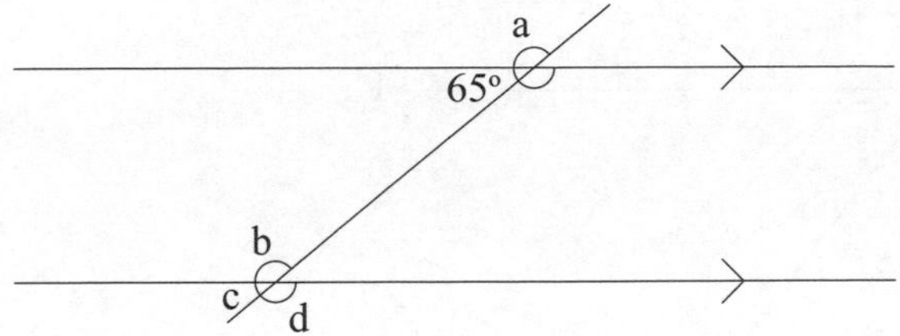

Find the missing angles and state any angle laws used.

3) 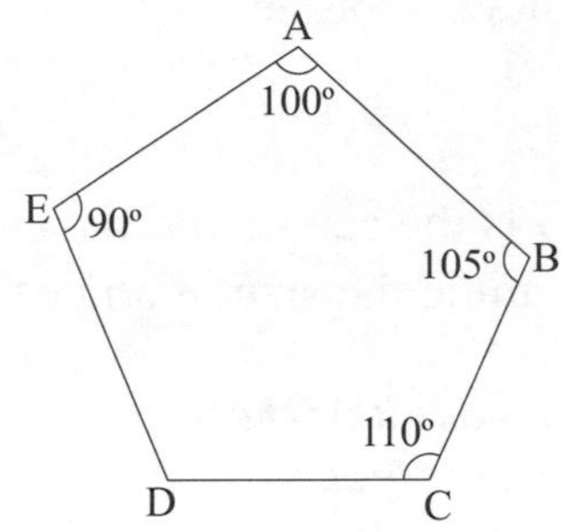

ABCDE is an irregular pentagon. Determine the size of the internal angle EDC.

4) 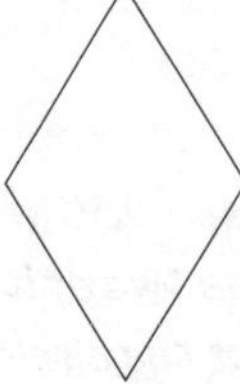

Draw the locus of the point P that moves around the kite at a constant distance of 1 cm.

5) 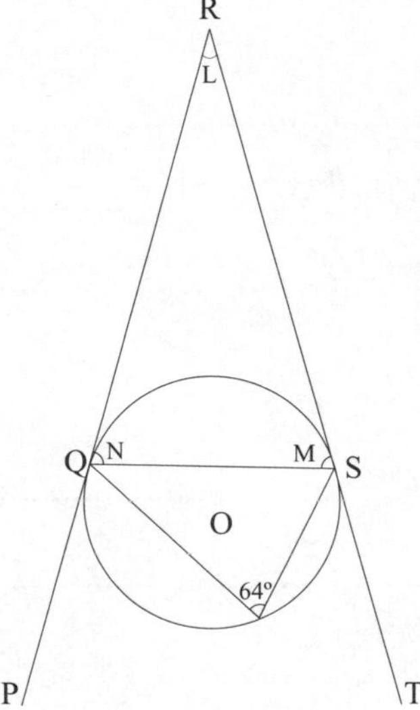

PQR and RST are tangents to the circle. Find the missing angles L, M and N.

Worked Exam Question

Worked Exam Question

There will be a question in the exam which asks you to find angles. That means you have to remember all the different angle rules and practise using them in the right places...

1

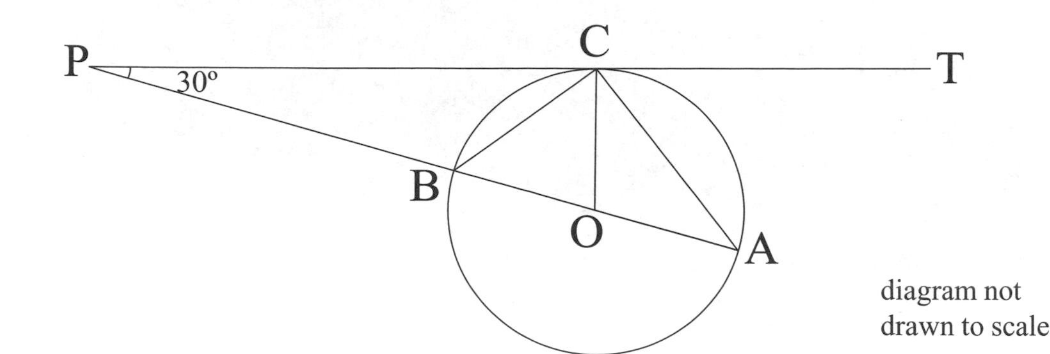

diagram not drawn to scale.

The line joining P to T is a tangent to the circle at the point C. O is the centre and the angle APT is 30º. Giving reasons and stating any theorems used, determine the size of angles:

Hint: look for radii within the circle and identify any isosceles triangles.

(a) OBC.

PCT is a tangent so $P\hat{C}O = 90°$

Angles in a triangle total 180° so

$180° = P\hat{C}O + C\hat{O}P + O\hat{P}C$ $\quad 180° = 90° + C\hat{O}P + 30°$

$C\hat{O}P = 60°$. Triangle OBC is isosceles, so

$O\hat{B}C = \frac{1}{2}(180° - C\hat{O}P) = \frac{1}{2}(180 - 60°)$

$O\hat{B}C = 60°$

You know triangle OBC is isosceles because two of it's sides are radii of the circle and therefore are the same length.

(3 marks)

(b) OAC.

We know angle $C\hat{O}P = 60°$

So $A\hat{O}C = 180° - 60° = 120°$ (angles on a straight line).

Triangle OAC is isoceles, so $O\hat{A}C = \frac{1}{2}(180 - 120) = 30°$

(2 marks)

(c) ACT.

$O\hat{C}A = O\hat{A}C = 30°$ because triangle OAC is isoceles.

$A\hat{C}T = O\hat{C}T - O\hat{C}A = 90° - 30° = 60°$

(2 marks)

Worked Exam and Exam Questions

Worked Exam Question

One more worked example and then it's on to the exam questions, so make the most of it.

2 Using a ruler and compass, make an accurate drawing of the triangle ABC, where AB is 6 cm, BC is 5 cm and AC is 7 cm.
Then plot the locus of the point P, which moves around the outside of the triangle at a constant distance of 1 cm.

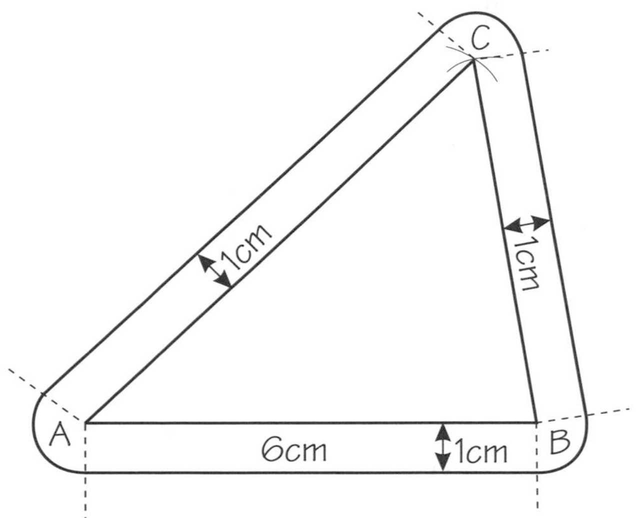

Hint: Always think carefully about the shape of the locus when passing around corners. In general the locus will be an arc.

(4 marks)

Exam Question

3 A wheel of radius r rests at the top of a flight of stairs.

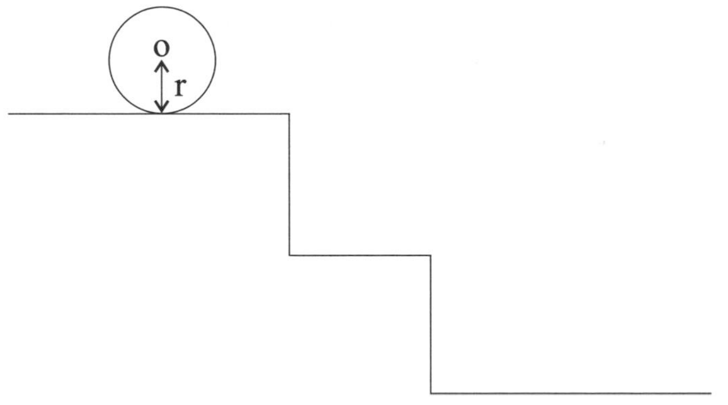

It is pushed towards the top of the stairs and rolls downwards. If the wheel remains in contact with the steps at all times, plot the locus of the point O, the centre of the wheel.

....

(3 marks)

Exam Questions

4

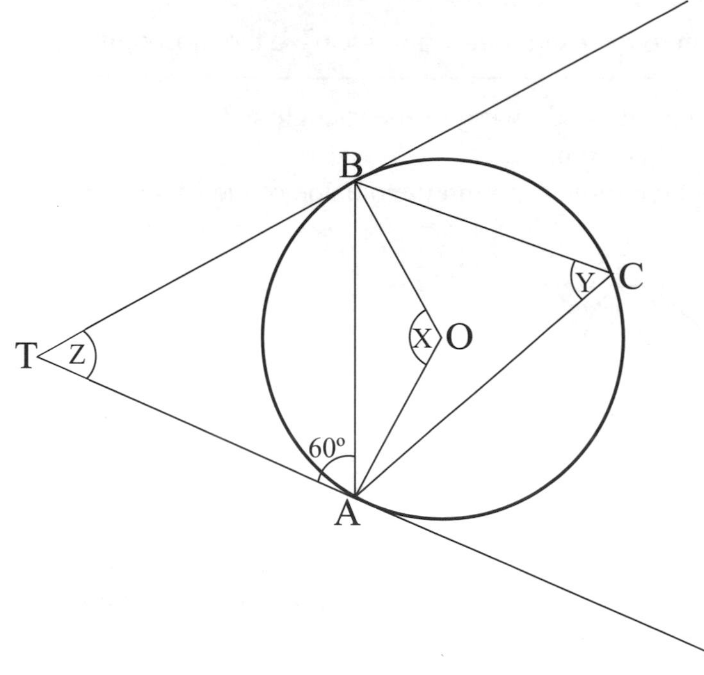

Remember, we've taken out some dotted lines to make space for more questions. You'll have lots more room in the real exam.

The lines AT and BT are tangents to the circle with centre O.
Angle BAT is 60°.
Calculate the missing angles, giving reasons for your calculations at each step.

(a) *X*.

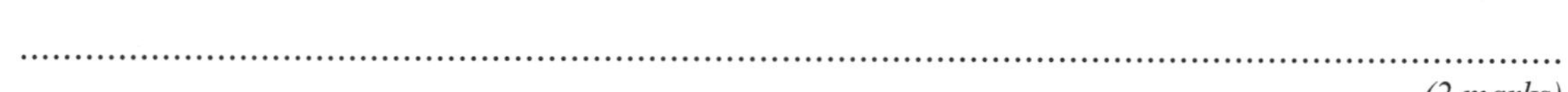

(3 marks)

(b) *Y*.

(2 marks)

(c) *Z*.

....

(2 marks)

5

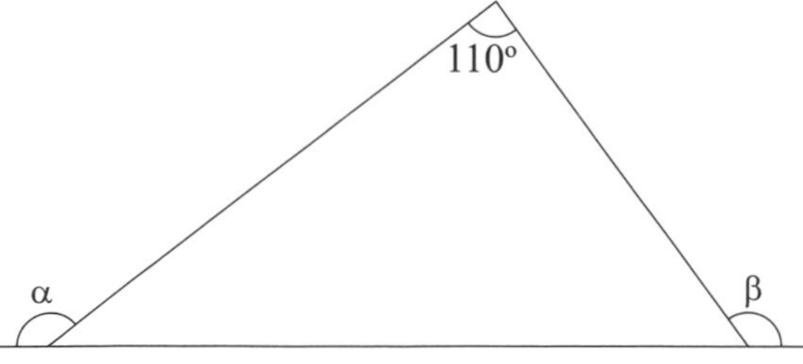

Prove that $\alpha + \beta = 290°$.

....

(3 marks)

Transformations

Transformations are about the most fun you can have without laughing.

1) Use the word TERRY to remember the four types.
2) You must always remember to specify all the details for each type.

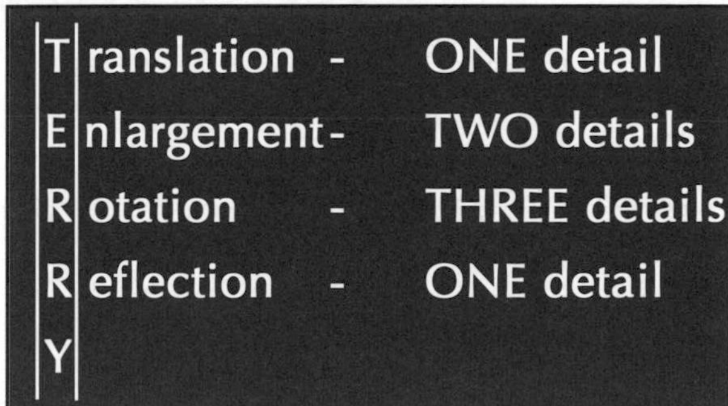

T ranslation - ONE detail
E nlargement - TWO details
R otation - THREE details
R eflection - ONE detail
Y

1) TRANSLATION

You must specify this ONE detail:

1) the VECTOR OF TRANSLATION

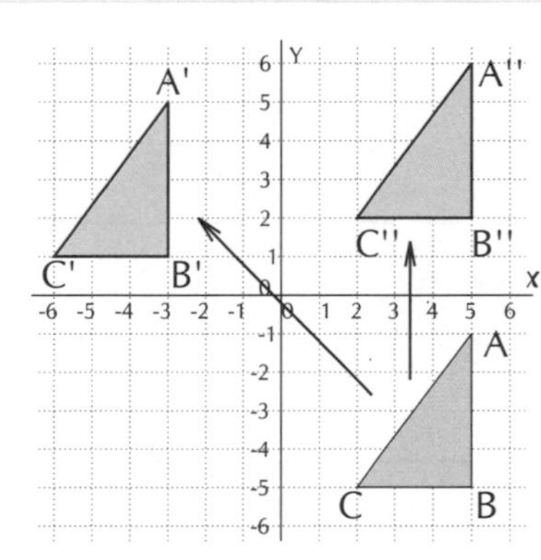

ABC to A'B'C' is a translation of $\begin{pmatrix}-8\\6\end{pmatrix}$

ABC to A''B''C'' is a translation of $\begin{pmatrix}0\\7\end{pmatrix}$

2) ENLARGEMENT

You must specify these two details:

1) The SCALE FACTOR

2) The CENTRE of enlargement

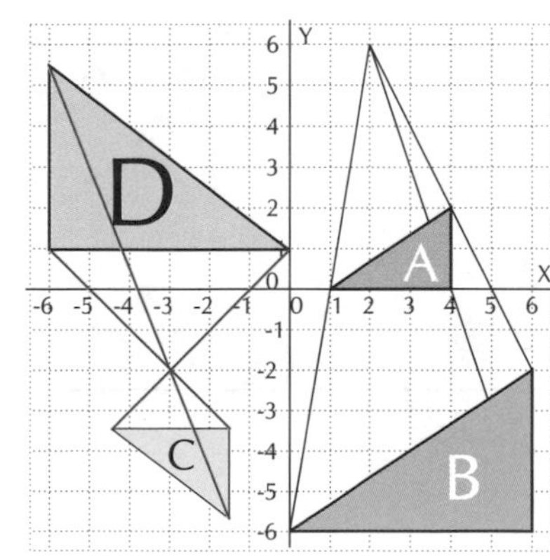

A to B is an enlargement of scale factor 2, and centre (2,6)

B to A is an enlargement of scale factor 1/2 and centre (2,6)

C to D is an enlargement of scale factor -2 and centre (-3,-2)

You must remember to give specific details

It's pretty obvious that it's no good just saying it's a translation, if you don't give the vector of translation. But be careful with enlargements — it's easy to forget to give the centre of enlargement, and that's marks gone.

Transformations

3) ROTATION

You must specify these three details:

1) ANGLE turned

2) DIRECTION (Clockwise or anticlockwise)

3) CENTRE of Rotation

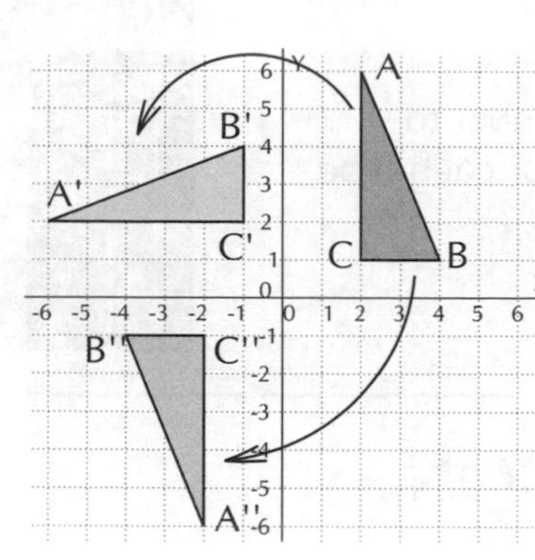

ABC to A'B'C' is a Rotation of 90^0, anticlockwise, ABOUT the origin.

ABC to A''B''C'' is a Rotation of half a turn (180^0), clockwise, ABOUT the origin.

4) REFLECTION

You must specify this ONE detail:

1) The MIRROR LINE

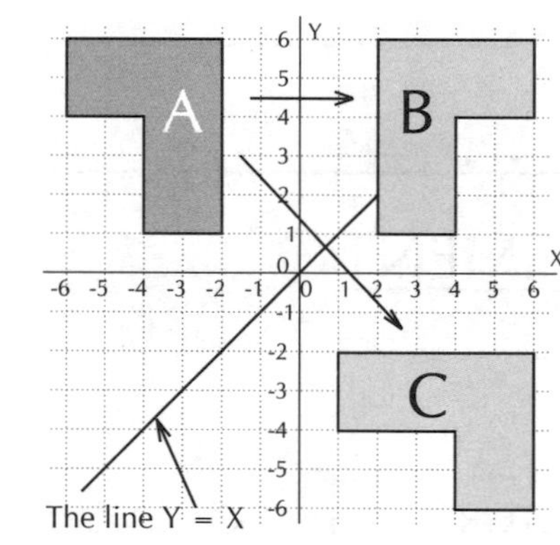

A to B is a reflection IN the Y-axis.

A to C is a reflection IN the line Y=X.

Remember four types — Translation, Enlargement, Rotation, Reflection, Y

The key thing is to get your head around the details you need for each type of transformation. Without the details the translations mean nothing — the devil's in the detail.

Congruence and Similarity

Congruence is another ridiculous maths word which sounds really complicated when it's not:

If two shapes are CONGRUENT, they are simply the same — the same size and the same shape. That's all it is. They can, however, be MIRROR IMAGES.

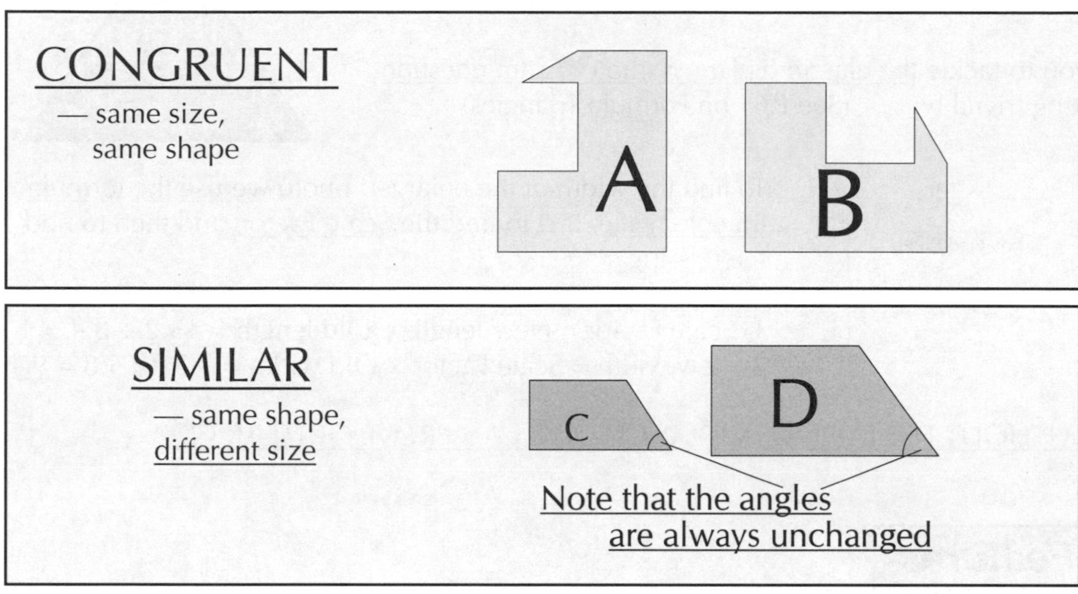

CONGRUENT
— same size,
same shape
A
B
SIMILAR
— same shape,
different size
C
D
Note that the angles
are always unchanged

Congruent Triangles - are they or aren't they?

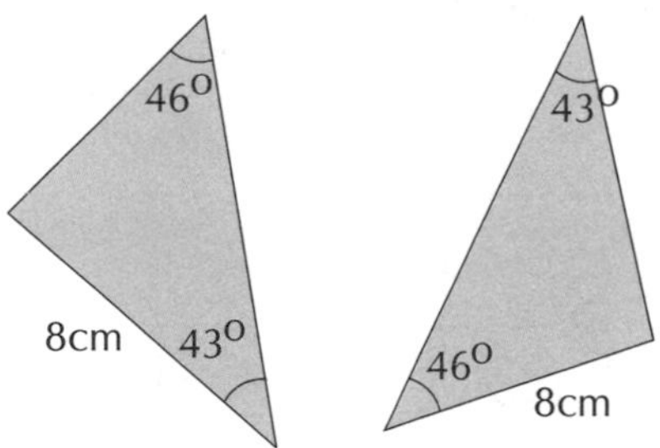

Probably the trickiest area of congruence is deciding whether two triangles, like the ones shown here, are CONGRUENT.

In other words, from the skimpy information given, are the two going to be the same or different?

There are TWO IMPORTANT STEPS:

1) The Golden Rule is definitely to DRAW THEM BOTH IN THE SAME ORIENTATION — only then can you compare them properly:

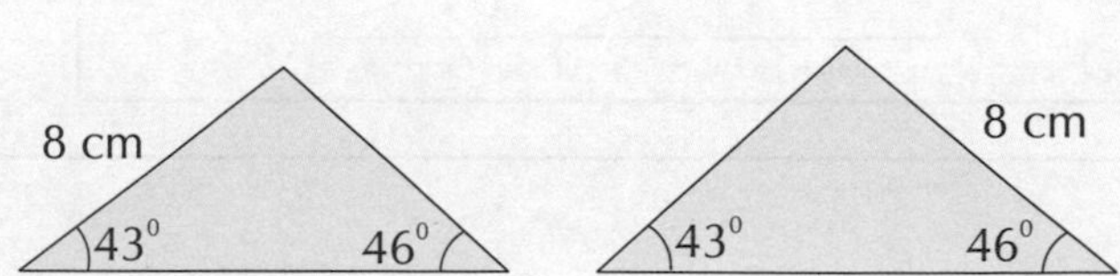

2) Don't jump to hasty conclusions — although the 8 cm sides are clearly in different positions, it's always possible that both top sides are 8 cm. *In this case we can work out that they're not because the angles are different (so they can't be isosceles).*

Congruent just means same size, same shape

The trick is being sure if things are congruent, similar or neither. Take your time and think about it carefully. The shapes are only congruent if all the angles and lengths are the same.

Similarity and Enlargements

Similar Shapes and the *Formula Triangle*

The lengths of two SIMILAR SHAPES are related to the Scale Factor by this VERY important Formula Triangle WHICH YOU MUST LEARN:

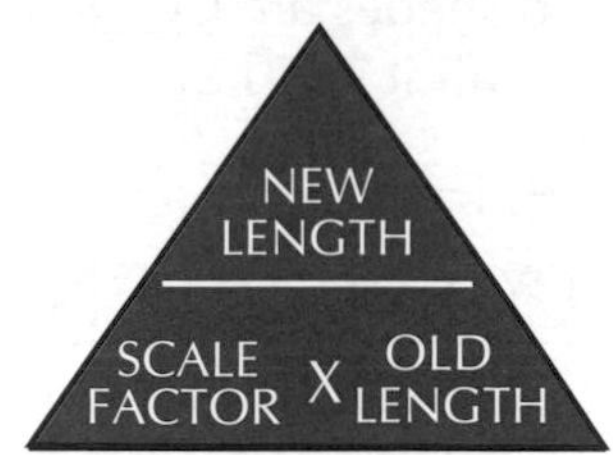

This enables you to tackle the classic "Enlarged photo" Exam question with breathtaking triviality: (See P.61 on Formula Triangles)

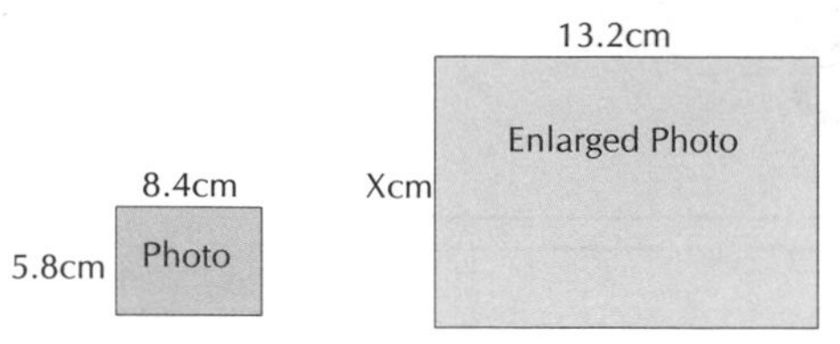

To find the width of the enlarged photo we use the formula triangle twice, first to find the Scale Factor, and then to find the missing side:

1) Scale Factor = New length ÷ Old length = 13.2 ÷ 8.4 = 1.57
2) New width = Scale Factor × Old width = 1.57 × 5.8 = 9.1cm

WITHOUT THE FORMULA TRIANGLE THIS CAN PROVE QUITE TRICKY

Four Key Features

1) If the Scale Factor is bigger than 1 the shape gets bigger.

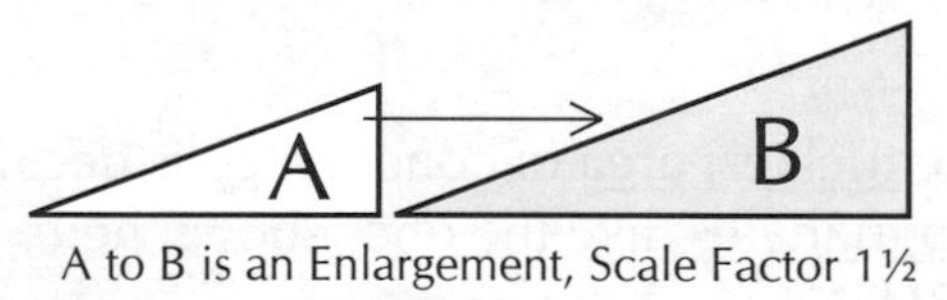

A to B is an Enlargement, Scale Factor 1½

2) If the Scale Factor is smaller than 1 (i.e. a fraction like ½) then the shape gets smaller. (Really this is a reduction, but you still call it an Enlargement, Scale Factor ½)

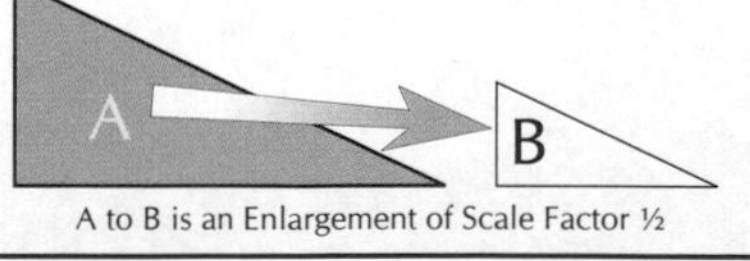

A to B is an Enlargement of Scale Factor ½

3) If the Scale Factor is NEGATIVE then the shape pops out the other side of the enlargement centre. If the scale factor is -1, it's exactly the same as a rotation of 180°

A
B

A to B is an enlargement of scale factor -2. B to A is an enlargement of scale factor -½.

4) The Scale Factor also tells you the relative distance of old points and new points from the Centre of Enlargement — this is very useful for drawing an enlargement, because you can use it to trace out the positions of the new points:

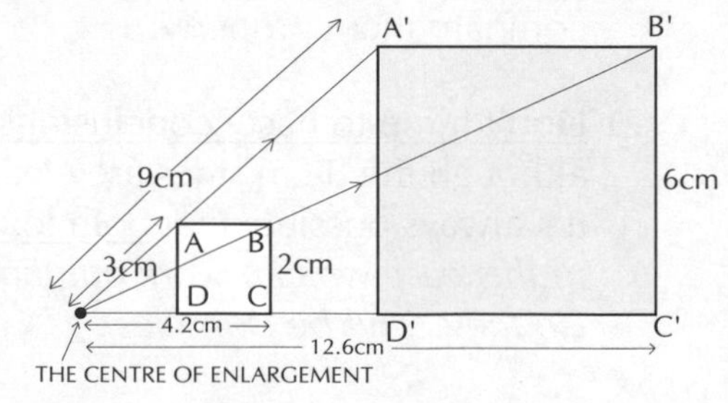

Enlargement questions are always appearing on exam papers

It's strange to think enlargements can actually result in the shape getting smaller or moving about. You need to make sure you've got these four key features straight in your head, or you'll be very muddled.

Area and Volume of Enlargements

Finding volumes and areas

This catches everybody out.
The increase in area and volume is BIGGER than the scale factor.

For example, if the Scale Factor is 2,
the lengths are twice as big,
each area is 4 times as big, and
the volume is 8 times as big.

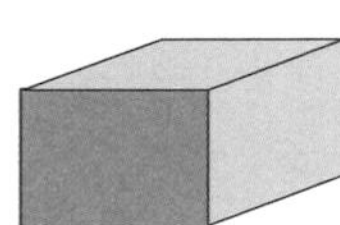

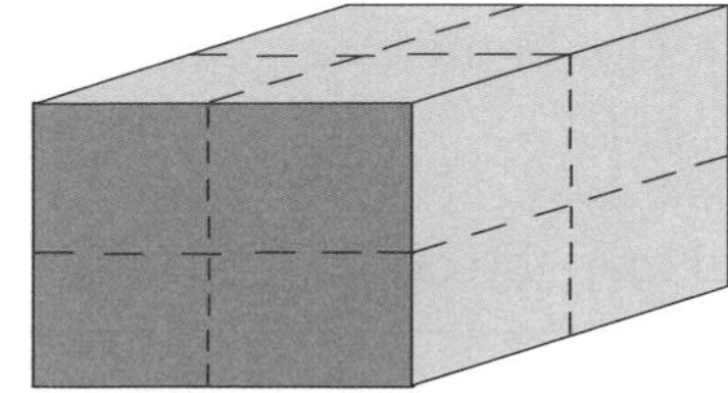

The rule is this:

For a Scale Factor n:

The SIDES are n times bigger

The AREAS are n^2 times bigger

The VOLUMES are n^3 times bigger

Simple... but VERY FORGETTABLE

These ratios can also be expressed in this form:

Lengths	$n : m$	e.g.	3 : 4
Areas	$n^2 : m^2$	e.g.	9 : 16
Volumes	$n^3 : m^3$	e.g.	27 : 64

A PARTICULAR EXAMPLE:

Two spheres have surface areas of 16m^2 and 25m^2.
Find the ratio of their volumes.

(This conversion from area ratio to volume ratio is specifically mentioned in the syllabus. Make sure you can do it.)

ANSWER:
16 : 25 is the area ratio which must be $n^2 : m^2$,
i.e. $n^2 : m^2 = 16 : 25$
and so $n : m = 4 : 5$
and so $n^3 : m^3 = 64 : 125$ The volume ratio.

When you make a length bigger, areas get bigger and volumes even bigger

It's easy to make the mistake of thinking that length, area and volume all get bigger at the same rate — make sure you've got the rule on this page very clear in your mind to avoid a lot of confusion.

Warm-Up and Worked Exam Questions

The warm-up questions run quickly over the basic facts you'll need in the exam. The exam questions come later — but unless you've learnt the facts first you'll find the exams tougher than old boots.

Warm-Up Questions

1) From the diagram on the right, pick out:
   (a) a pair of congruent shapes
   (b) a pair of similar shapes

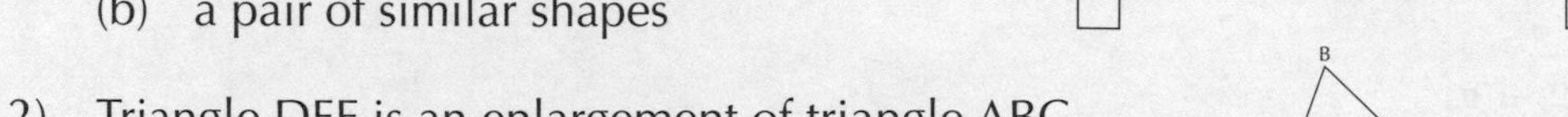

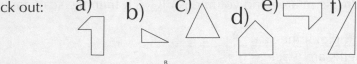

2) Triangle DEF is an enlargement of triangle ABC.
   (a) What is the scale factor of the enlargement?
   (b) What is the length of DF?

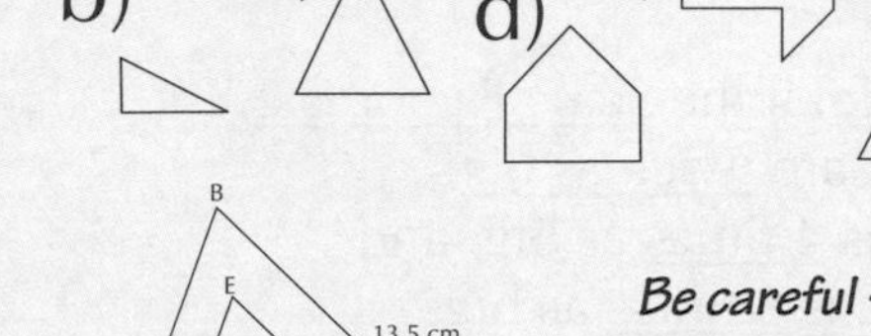

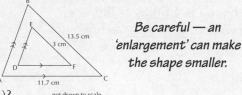

Be careful — an 'enlargement' can make the shape smaller.

3) What translation would map the point (1, 3) onto (-2, 6)?

Worked Exam Questions

I'm afraid this helpful blue writing won't be there in the exam, so if I were you I'd make the most of it and make sure you fully understand it now.

1

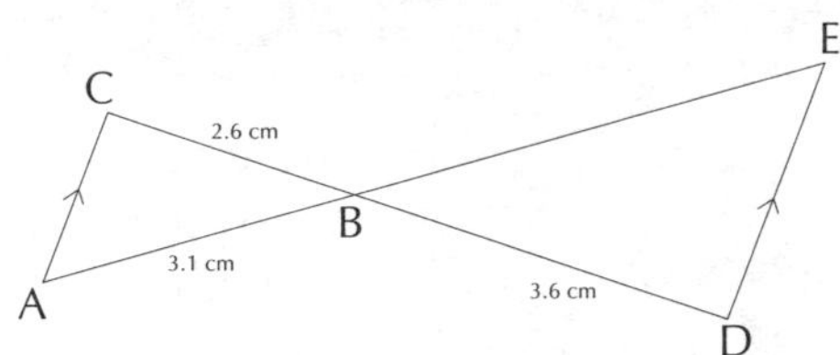

(a) Explain why the triangles ABC and BDE are similar.

$A\hat{B}C = D\hat{B}E$ (vertically opposite angles are equal). $C\hat{A}B = B\hat{E}D$ and $A\hat{C}B = B\hat{D}E$ (alternate angles on parallel lines equal — Z angles). So the triangles have the same angles, i.e. same shape, so are similar.

(2 marks)

(b) Find the length of BE, correct to 1 decimal place.

(use two given corresponding sides) Scale factor = 3.6 ÷ 2.6 = 1.384615385 **do not round the answer at this stage**

So BE = 1.384615385 x 3.1 = 4.2923 = 4.3 cm (to 1 d.p.)

(3 marks)

2

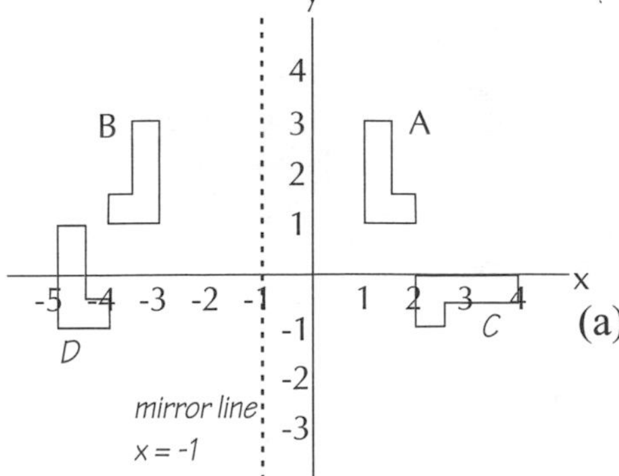

(a) What is the equation of the line of reflection to map A onto B?

x = -1

(1 mark)

(b) Rotate A 90° clockwise about centre (1, 0). Label the new shape C.

(2 marks)

(c) Translate A by vector $\begin{pmatrix}-6\\-2\end{pmatrix}$. Label this shape D.

(1 mark)

Exam Questions

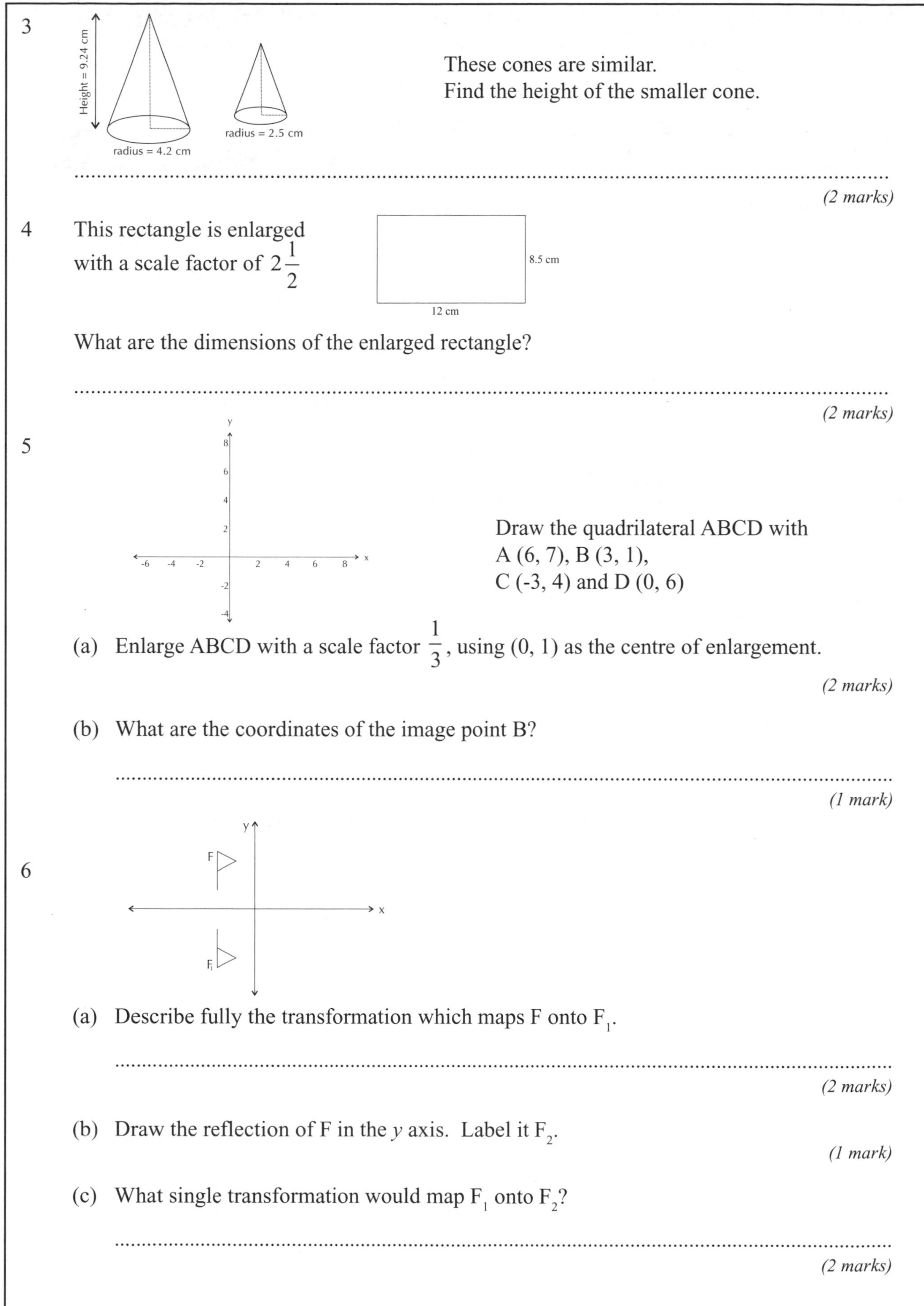

3 These cones are similar.
Find the height of the smaller cone.

....

(2 marks)

4 This rectangle is enlarged with a scale factor of $2\frac{1}{2}$

What are the dimensions of the enlarged rectangle?

....

(2 marks)

5 Draw the quadrilateral ABCD with A (6, 7), B (3, 1), C (-3, 4) and D (0, 6)

(a) Enlarge ABCD with a scale factor $\frac{1}{3}$, using (0, 1) as the centre of enlargement.

(2 marks)

(b) What are the coordinates of the image point B?

....

(1 mark)

6

(a) Describe fully the transformation which maps F onto F_1.

....

(2 marks)

(b) Draw the reflection of F in the *y* axis. Label it F_2.

(1 mark)

(c) What single transformation would map F_1 onto F_2?

....

(2 marks)

Revision Summary for Section Two

More difficult questions, *but just keep reminding yourself that they're the very best revision you can do*. These questions are very plain and very straightforward. They don't ask anything tricky, just whether or not you've actually *learnt* all the *basic facts* in Section Two. It's really important to keep practising these as often as you can.

Keep learning the basic facts until you know them

1) What are regular polygons? Name the first eight.
2) List the special features that regular polygons have.
3) What do you know about their symmetry?
4) What are their two special angles called? Write down the formulas for these angles.
5) There are six formulas for area you should know straight off. Write them all down.
6) Draw a circle and show what *arc, sector, segment* and *chord* are.
7) What is the formula for the length of an arc? Which other formula is similar?
8) What are the three steps needed to find the area of a segment?
9) There are five formulas for volume you should know. Write them all down.
10) What is a prism? Sketch three different ones.
11) Write down the first eight easy rules of geometry.
12) Give five extra details on parallel lines.
13) Write down the two formulas for irregular polygons.
14) Write down the nine simple rules for circle geometry.
15) What is three-letter notation? Give an example.
16) What is a locus? Describe, with diagrams, the four you should know.
17) Demonstrate how to accurately draw the bisector of an angle.
18) Demonstrate how to accurately draw the perpendicular bisector of a line.
19) Demonstrate how to draw accurate 60° angles. Draw an accurate equilateral triangle.
20) Demonstrate how to draw accurate 90° angles. Draw an accurate square.
21) What do "congruent" and "similar" mean?
22) What are the two rules for deciding if two triangles are congruent or not?
23) What is the formula triangle for similar shapes?
24) Demonstrate its use on the enlarged photo question.
25) Draw a typical enlargement, showing the two important details.
26) What three types of scale factor are there and what is the result of each?
27) What two things does the scale factor tell you about the new shape compared to the original?
28) What is the rule about lengths, areas and volumes of similar shapes?
29) What does TERRY stand for?
30) Say how many details must be specified for each type of transformation.
31) List these details for each transformation.
32) What are the three rules for identifying formulas as either length, area or volume?
33) 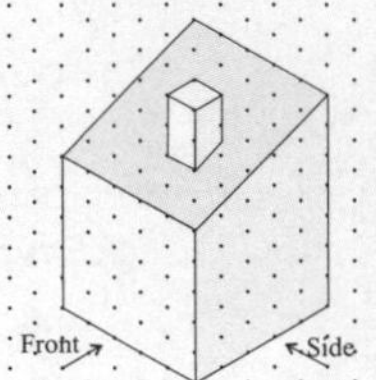

    For this shape, draw:
    a) the front elevation b) the side elevation c) the plan.
    Use the scale 5 mm (in this book) : 1 cm (in your drawing).

34) What is meant by a net? How is it related to surface area?
35) Sketch the nets for these shapes:
    a) triangular prism b) cylinder c) cube d) cuboid e) square-based pyramid.

Formula Triangles

You may have already come across these in physics, because they are EXTREMELY POTENT TOOLS for dealing SWIFTLY AND RELIABLY with a lot of common formulas.

They are VERY EASY, so make sure you know how to use them.

Where do you put the letters?

If three things are related by a formula like this:

$A = B \times C$ or like this: $B = A \div C$

then you can put them into a FORMULA TRIANGLE thus:

1) $A = B \times C$

If there are TWO LETTERS MULTIPLIED TOGETHER they must go ON THE BOTTOM of the Formula Triangle, and so the other must go on the top. For example the formula $A = B \times C$ becomes:

2) $B = A \div C$

If there is ONE THING DIVIDED BY ANOTHER then the one ON TOP OF THE DIVISION goes ON TOP IN THE FORMULA TRIANGLE, and so the other two letters must go on the bottom (it doesn't matter which way round). For example, the formula $B = A \div C$ will produce the same formula triangle as the one above.

How do you use it?

1) COVER UP the thing you want to find and just WRITE DOWN what is left showing.

2) Now PUT IN THE VALUES for the other two things and WORK IT OUT.

Formula triangles are incredibly useful

With this method you don't need to worry about changing the subjects of formulas and horrible things like that. So make sure you understand formula triangles and use them whenever you can.

Density

*An important **example:***

This example shows how handy formula triangles can be when dealing with the tricky looking equation:

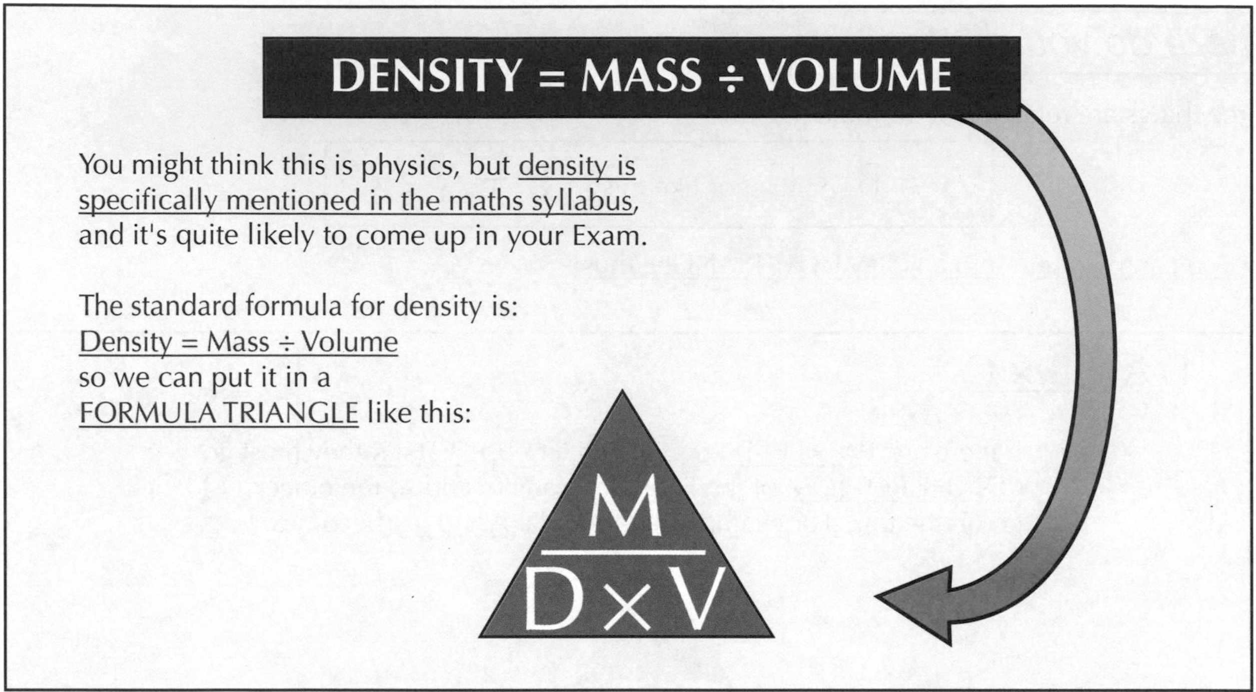

DENSITY = MASS ÷ VOLUME
You might think this is physics, but density is specifically mentioned in the maths syllabus, and it's quite likely to come up in your Exam.
The standard formula for density is:
Density = Mass ÷ Volume
so we can put it in a
FORMULA TRIANGLE like this:
M
D × V

One way or another you MUST remember this formula for density — without it you'll be stuck.

The best method by far is to remember the order of the letters in the FORMULA TRIANGLE as:

$D^{M}V$ or DiMoV (The Russian Agent!).

EXAMPLE:

"Find the volume of an object with a mass of 40g and a density of 6.4g/cm³."

ANSWER:

To find volume, cover up V.
This leaves M ÷ D,
so V = M ÷ D = 40 ÷ 6.4 = 6.25 cm³.

Putting the equation into a formula triangle makes life easier

Once you've got the formula triangle sorted, then you only need to cover up whichever letter you are trying to work out and the formula you need is right there. What could be simpler?

Speed, Distance and Time

This is very common, and they never give you the formula.
Either you learn it beforehand, or you wave goodbye to several easy marks.

1) The **Formula Triangle**

Of course you have to *remember the order of the letters* in the triangle (SDT), and this time we have the word *SaiDiT* to help you.

So if it's a question on speed, distance and time just say: SAID IT.

EXAMPLE: "A car travels 90 miles at 36 miles per hour. How long does it take?"
ANS: We want to find the time, so cover up T in the triangle which leaves D ÷ S,
so T = D ÷ S = Distance ÷ speed = 90 ÷ 36 = 2.5 hours
If you learn the formula triangle, you will find questions on speed, distance and time very easy.

2) **Units** — Getting them **right**

By units we mean things like cm, m, m/s, km^2, etc. and quite honestly they should always be uppermost in your mind whenever you write an answer down. When you're using a FORMULA, there is one special thing you need to know. It's simple enough but you must know it:

The UNITS you get out of a Formula DEPEND ENTIRELY upon the UNITS you put into it.

For example if you put a distance in cm and a time in seconds into the formula triangle to work out SPEED, the answer must come out in cm per second (cm/s).

If the time is in hours and the speed in miles per hour (mph) then the distance you'd calculate would come out in miles. It's pretty simple when you think about it.

BUT DON'T MIX UNITS
E.g. Don't mix Miles Per HOUR in a formula with a time in MINUTES (convert it to hours).
Don't mix DENSITY IN g/cm^3 in a formula with a MASS IN kg (convert it to g).

EXAMPLE: "A boy walks 800 m in 10 minutes. Find his speed in km/h."
ANS: If you just use 800 m and 10 minutes your answer will be a speed in *metres per minute* (m/min).
Instead you must CONVERT: 800 m = 0.8 km, 10 mins = 0.1667 hours (mins ÷ 60).
Then you can divide 0.8 *km* by 0.16667 *hours* to get 4.8 km/h.

Don't get the units wrong — that's just marks down the drain

Just stop to think for a second about the units, and convert them in to what you need, before firing numbers wildly into the triangle. I know you are keen, but calm your passions.

Distance-Time Graphs

Distance-time (D/T graphs) and velocity-time graphs are so common in Exams that they deserve a page all to themselves — just to make sure you know all the vital details about them. The best thing about them is that they don't vary much, and they're always easy.

1) Distance-Time Graphs

Just remember these four important points:

1) At any point, GRADIENT = SPEED, but watch out for the UNITS.
2) For a CURVED GRAPH you'll need to draw a TANGENT to work out the SPEED (gradient) at any particular point.
3) The STEEPER the graph, the FASTER the speed.
4) FLAT SECTIONS are where the speed is ZERO.

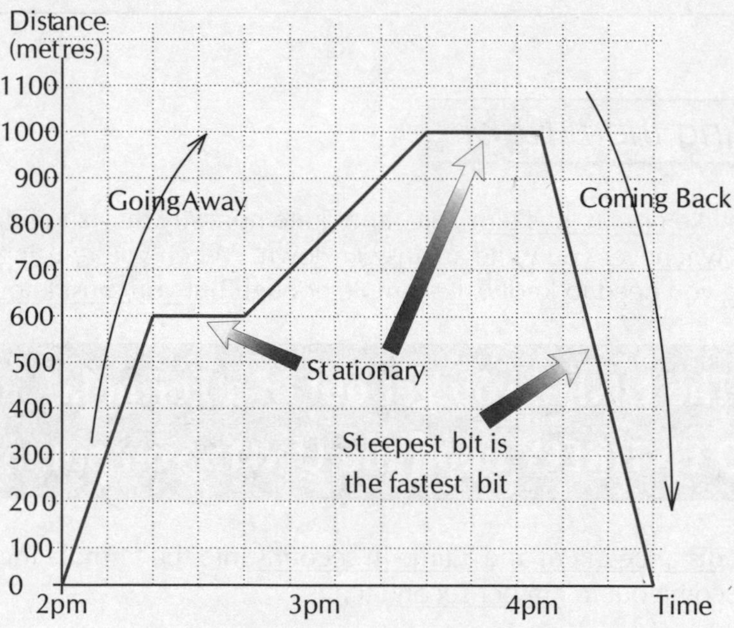

EXAMPLE: *"What is the speed of the return section on the graph shown?"*

Speed = gradient = 1000m/30mins = 33.33 m/min.
But speeds are usually given in km/h so it's better to do it like this:
1km ÷ 0.5 hrs = 2 km/h (See p.21 on units)

On distance-time graphs — gradient shows speed

If you remember the four simple facts on this page d/t graphs become very simple and they are always appearing on exam papers — which is a great place to see something easy.

Velocity-Time Graphs

2) Velocity-Time Graphs

A velocity-time graph can LOOK just the same as a distance-time graph, but it means something completely different. The graph shown here is exactly the same SHAPE as the one on the last page, but the actual motions are completely different.

Remember these five important points:

1) At any point, GRADIENT = ACCELERATION,
(The UNITS are m/s^2 don't forget)

2) For a CURVED GRAPH you'll need to draw a TANGENT to work out the ACCELERATION (gradient) at any particular point.

3) NEGATIVE SLOPE is DECELERATION.

4) FLAT SECTIONS are STEADY SPEED.

5) AREA UNDER GRAPH = DISTANCE TRAVELLED

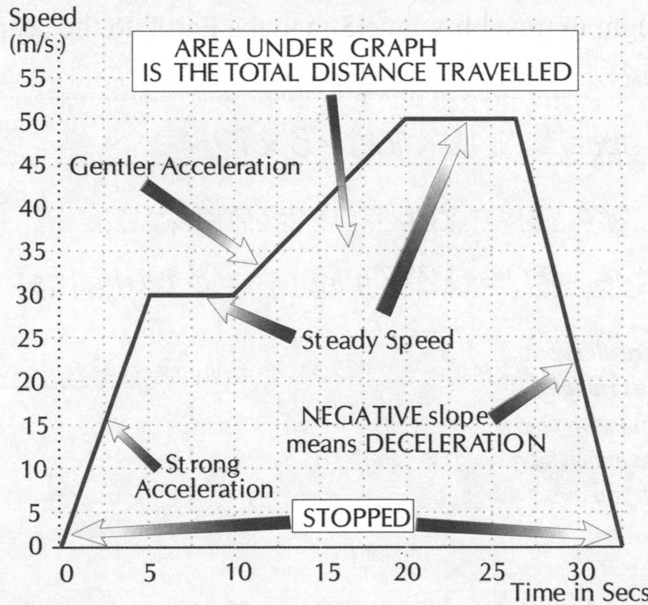

The D/T graph on the last page shows something moving away and then back again with steady speeds and long stops (rather like a donkey on Blackpool beach).

The V/T graph above on the other hand shows something that sets off from rest, accelerates strongly, holds its speed, then accelerates again up to a maximum speed which it holds for a while, and then comes to a dramatic halt at the end. (More like a Ferrari than a donkey.)

On velocity-time graphs — gradient shows acceleration

Both velocity-time graphs and distance-time graphs are pretty straightforward exam questions. The main danger is getting the two muddled up, so make sure you get clear the differences and what they show.

Warm-Up and Worked Exam Questions

Without a good warm-up you're likely to strain a brain cell or two. So take the time to run through these simple questions and get the basic facts straight before plunging into exam questions.

Warm-Up Questions

1) A cheetah runs 100 m in 4 seconds, what is its average speed in km per hour?
2) A cyclist travels for ¾ hour at a speed of 12 km per hour. What distance does he travel?
3) A lump of lead, weighing 374 g has a volume of 33 cm^3.
   What is the approximate density of the lead (to 3 s.f.)?
4) A solid plastic building block measures 5 cm × 4 cm × 6 cm.
   The density of the plastic is 0.8 g/cm^3. What is the mass of the block?

Worked Exam Questions

With the answers written in, it's very easy to skim these worked examples and think you've understood. But that's not going to help you, so take the time to make sure you've *really* understood them.

1 The distance from the Earth to the Sun is 149 000 000 km.
The speed of light is 3×10^5 km per second.
How long does it take light to travel from the Sun to the Earth, to the nearest minute?

$149\,000\,000 = 1.49 \times 10^8$

Time = distance ÷ speed = $1.49 \times 10^8 \div 3 \times 10^5$

$= (1.49 \div 3) \times 10^3$ seconds = 496.667 seconds.

To make into minutes ÷ 60 = 8.277 minutes = 8 to nearest minute.

These questions are all about using the formula triangle. But be extra careful with the units — they're the main thing that could catch you out.

Answer *8 minutes*

(2 marks)

2 A solid silver rod is in the shape of a cylinder. The rod is 10 cm long. The diameter of the rod is 7.4 cm and the rod has a mass of 4516.5 g. What is the density of the silver? State all units clearly.

Density = mass ÷ volume.

Volume = $\pi r^2 \times$ length = $\pi \times 3.7^2 \times 10 = 430.084$ cm^3

Density = 4516.5 ÷ 430.084 = 10.5 g/cm^3

Answer *10.5 g/cm^3*

(4 marks)

Exam Questions

3 A car is travelling along the M6. It passes Hilton Park service station at 13.20 hrs and then gets stuck in a traffic jam. It finally passes Stafford service station at 16.00 hrs.

The service stations are 30 km apart.
What was the average speed of the car on this part of the journey?

....

Answer ________________ *(2 marks)*

4 A cube container is filled to the brim with mercury. The sides of the container are 4 cm long. The density of the mercury is 13.55 g/cm^3. Find the mass of mercury in the container.

....

Answer ________________ *(3 marks)*

5 Dominic cycled to visit his Gran who lived 24 km away. His journey is shown on the graph below. Letters A - G represent different stages of the journey.

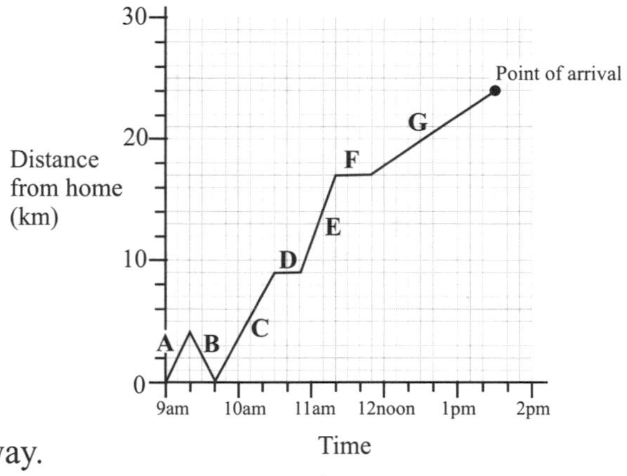

(a) After cycling for 20 minutes, Dominic realised he'd forgotten his wallet and had to go back. How far had he cycled by this time?

Answer ________________ *(1 mark)*

(b) Dominic stopped for two breaks along the way. Which letters on the diagram represent these breaks?

Answer ______ and ______ *(2 marks)*

(c) Work out Dominic's speed during the fastest leg of his journey.

....

Answer ________________ *(3 marks)*

(d) Work out Dominic's average speed for the total journey (after picking up his wallet).

....

Answer ________________ *(3 marks)*

Standard Index Form

Standard Form and Standard Index Form are the SAME THING.
So remember both of these names as well as what it actually is:
Ordinary Number: 4,300,000 In Standard Form: 4.3×10^6

Standard form is only really useful for writing VERY BIG or VERY SMALL numbers in a more convenient way, e.g.

56,000,000,000 would be 5.6×10^{10} in standard form.
0.000 000 003 45 would be 3.45×10^{-9} in standard form.

but ANY NUMBER can be written in standard form and *you need to know how to do it*:

What it actually is:

A number written in standard form must ALWAYS be in EXACTLY this form:

This *number* must *always* be BETWEEN 1 AND 10.
(The fancy way of saying this is: "$1 \le A < 10$" — they sometimes write that in Exam questions — don't let it put you off, just remember what it means).

This number is just the NUMBER OF PLACES *the Decimal Point moves.*

LEARN THE THREE RULES:

1) The front number must always be BETWEEN 1 AND 10.
2) The power of 10, n, is purely: HOW FAR THE D.P. MOVES.
3) n is +ve for BIG numbers, n is –ve for SMALL numbers.
   (This is much better than rules based on which way the D.P. moves.)

Two very simple examples:

1) *"Express 35 600 in standard form."*

METHOD
1) Move the D.P. until 35 600 becomes 3.56 ("$1 \le A < 10$")
2) The D.P. has moved 4 places so n=4, giving: 10^4
3) 35600 is a BIG number so n is +4, not -4

ANSWER
3.5 6 0 0.
= 3.56×10^4

2) *"Express 0.000623 in standard form."*

METHOD
1) The D.P. must move 4 places to give 6.23 ("$1 \le A < 10$"),
2) So the power of 10 is 4
3) Since 0.000623 is a SMALL NUMBER it must be 10^{-4} not 10^{+4}.

ANSWER
0.000623
= 6.23×10^{-4}

Remember, n tells you how far the decimal point moves

Standard form is just a way of writing down very big and small numbers without writing long rows of zeros. But in order to use it you have to learn the three rules or you'll be in a big mess.

Standard Index Form

Four **very important** examples

1) The calculator's **scientific mode**

This mode *gives all numbers in standard form* to a specified number of sig fig.
A little SCI will be displayed somewhere when you're in this mode.
To get into this mode, press MODE and select SCI from one of the menus you get.
(On other calculators look for a button with "SCI" written above it as the 2nd or 3rd function.)
It'll ask you for the number of sig figs to display, something like this: SCI 0-9?
So if you choose 4, all numbers and answers will be displayed to 4 sig fig.

EXAMPLE: 565 ÷ 3 would give 188.3333333 in normal mode,
...or 1.883^{02} in 4 sig fig mode.

2) What is 146.3 million in **standard form**?

The two favourite wrong answers for this are:

1) " 146.3×10^6 " which is kind of right but it's not in STANDARD FORM because 146.3, is not between 1 and 10 (i.e. "$1 \leq A < 10$" has not been done)

2) " 1.463×10^6 " This one *is* in standard form but it's not big enough.

This is a very typical Exam question, which too many people get wrong.
Just take your time and do it IN TWO STAGES like this:

ANSWER: 146.3 million = 146,300,000 = 1.463×10^8

3) Remember, 10^5 **means** 1×10^5

So to enter 10^5 into the calculator you must remember it's actually 1×10^5
and press 1 EXP 5 (See P.29)

EXAMPLE: "A nanometre is 10^{-9} m. How many nanometres are there in 0.35m? "
ANSWER: $0.35 \div (1 \times 10^{-9})$, so press 0.35 ÷ 1 EXP (–) 9 = $= 3.5 \times 10^8$.

4) The "**Googol**" is 10^{100}

It's a problem because it goes off the scale of your calculator, so you have to do it "by hand" — which means they like it for Exam questions.
So make sure you LEARN this example: *"Express 56 Googols in standard form."*

ANS: 56 googols is $56 \times 10^{100} = 5.6 \times 10 \times 10^{100} = 5.6 \times 10^{101}$.
Note: you split the 56 into 5.6 × 10 and then COMBINE THE POWERS OF 10

Four top tips here for some easy marks

Notice in every example on this page there are typical mistakes made by people in the exam — so don't be one of them. You have been warned.

Powers and Roots — Seven Easy Rules

Powers are a very useful shorthand:
$2 \times 2 \times 2 \times 2 \times 2 \times 2 \times 2 = 2^7$
("two to the power 7")

That bit is easy to remember.
Unfortunately, there are TEN SPECIAL RULES for Powers — seven easy ones (on this page) and three trickier ones (on the next page).
They're not tremendously exciting, but you do need to know them for the Exam:

The seven easy rules:

1) When MULTIPLYING, you ADD THE POWERS.

e.g. $3^4 \times 3^6 = 3^{6+4} = 3^{10}$

2) When DIVIDING, you SUBTRACT THE POWERS.

e.g. $5^4 \div 5^2 = 5^{4-2} = 5^2$

3) When RAISING one power to another, you MULTIPLY THEM.

e.g. $(3^2)^4 = 3^{2\times4} = 3^8$

4) $X^1 = X$, ANYTHING to the POWER 1 is just ITSELF.

e.g. $3^1 = 3$, $6 \times 6^3 = 6^4$

5) $X^0 = 1$, ANYTHING to the POWER 0 is just ONE .

e.g. $5^0 = 1$ $67^0 = 1$

6) $1^x = 1$, 1 TO ANY POWER is STILL JUST 1 .

e.g. $1^{23} = 1$ $1^{89} = 1$ $1^2 = 1$

7) FRACTIONS — Apply Power to both TOP and BOTTOM .

e.g. $(1\tfrac{3}{5})^3 = (\tfrac{8}{5})^3 = \tfrac{8^3}{5^3} = \tfrac{512}{125}$

These seven rules are the key to all power questions

If you can add, subtract and multiply, there's nothing here you can't do — as long as you learn the rules.
Try copying them over and over until you can do it with your eyes closed.

Powers and Roots — Three Tricky Rules

The three tricky rules:

The last three of the ten rules are a bit trickier...

8) **Negative** powers - turn it **upside-down**

People do have quite a bit of difficulty remembering this.
Whenever you see a negative power you're supposed to immediately think:

"That means turn it the other way up and make the power positive"

e.g. $7^{-2} = \frac{1}{7^2} = \frac{1}{49}$ $\left(\frac{3}{5}\right)^{-2} = \left(\frac{5}{3}\right)^{+2} = \frac{5^2}{3^2} = \frac{25}{9}$

9) **Fractional powers** - mean one thing: **ROOTS**

The Power ½ means Square Root, e.g. $25^{\frac{1}{2}} = \sqrt{25} = 5$

The Power ⅓ means Cube Root, e.g. $64^{\frac{1}{3}} = \sqrt[3]{64} = 4$

The Power ¼ means Fourth Root etc. e.g. $81^{\frac{1}{4}} = \sqrt[4]{81} = 3$

The one to really watch is when you get a negative fraction like $49^{-\frac{1}{2}}$ — people get mixed up and think that the minus is the square root, and forget to turn it upside down as well.

10) **Two-stage** fractional powers

They really like putting these in Exam questions so learn the method:

With fractional powers like $64^{5/6}$ always:

SPLIT THE FRACTION into a ROOT and a POWER,

and do them in that order:

ROOT first, then POWER

$(64)^{\frac{1}{6} \times 5} = \left(64^{\frac{1}{6}}\right)^5 = (2)^5 = 32$

These three rules might be a bit trickier — but they are essential

Because these are things which people often get muddled, Examiners love to sneak them into the Exam — so scribble these rules down and learn them. Then in the Exam you'll have the last laugh.

Warm-Up and Worked Exam Questions

I know that you'll be champing at the bit to get into the exam questions, but these basic warm-up questions are invaluable to get the basic facts straight first.

Warm-Up Questions

1) The moon is 250 000 miles away from Earth. Write this number in standard form.
2) The half-life of a chemical isotope is 0.0000027 seconds. Write this number in standard form.
3) An oxygen atom has a mass of 2.7×10^{-23} g. Write this as an ordinary number.
4) Work out $4 \times 10^3 \times 30000$.
5) Simplify: (a) $4^5 \times 4^{-2}$ (b) $6^5 / 6^2$ (c) $(3^2)^4$
6) Evaluate: (a) $2^1 \times 1^{23} \times 9^0$ (b) $(1\frac{2}{7})^2$ (c) $27^{2/3}$

Worked Exam Questions

I'd like an exam question, and the answers written in — and a surprise. Two out of three's not bad.

1 The Sun is about 0.000016 light years from Earth.
A light year, the distance travelled by light in one year = 9.46×10^{15} m

(a) How far is the Sun from the Earth in metres? Give your answer in standard form.

$0.000016 = 1.6 \times 10^{-5}$ light years.

$1.6 \times 10^{-5} \times 9.46 \times 10^{15} = 15.136 \times 10^{10} = 1.5 \times 10^{11}$

Write them both in standard form and then use the laws of powers and roots.

Answer (a) 1.5×10^{11} m

(2 marks)

(b) Express the answer to (a) in km. Give your answer in standard form.

To change metres into km divide by 1000 (or 1×10^3)

$1.5 \times 10^{11} \div 1 \times 10^3 = 1.5 \times 10^8$

This last stage is easy — just subtract the powers.

Answer (b) 1.5×10^8 km

(1 mark)

(c) The speed of light is 3×10^8 m/s. How long, in seconds, would it take light to travel from the Sun to the Earth? Give your answer as an ordinary number.

time = distance ÷ speed = $1.5 \times 10^{11} \div 3 \times 10^8 = 0.5 \times 10^3$

= 500 secs.

Answer (c) 500 seconds

(2 marks)

(d) Express your answer to (c) in minutes and seconds.

500 ÷ 60 = 8.33333 mins = 8 mins 20 secs

Answer (d) 8 mins 20 secs

(1 mark)

Worked Exam Questions

2 Simplify the following expressions, writing your answers in the form x^k.

(a) $\frac{x^7}{x^4}$

$$\frac{x^7}{x^4} = x^{7-4} = x^3$$

You just need to remember the power laws — for dividing, you subtract the powers...

Answer (a) x^3

(1 mark)

(b) $\sqrt[4]{x^9}$

$$\sqrt[4]{x^9} = x^{\frac{9}{4}}$$

...for fractional powers, the denominator is a root, i.e. $x^{\frac{1}{a}} = \sqrt[a]{x}$

Answer (b) $x^{\frac{9}{4}}$

(1 mark)

(c) $\sqrt[3]{x^9x^2}$

$$\sqrt[3]{x^9x^2} = \sqrt[3]{x^{9+2}}$$

First, sort out the powers inside the root — for multiplying, you just add the powers...

...then use the root / power rule that you used in part b).

$$= \sqrt[3]{x^{11}} = x^{\frac{11}{3}}$$

Answer (b) $x^{\frac{11}{3}}$

(2 marks)

3 Express $\frac{16}{\sqrt[5]{81}}$ in the form 2^m3^n.

This question isn't really harder than the ones above, there's just more stages...

$$\frac{16}{\sqrt[5]{81}} = \frac{16}{\sqrt[5]{3^4}} = \frac{16}{3^{\frac{4}{5}}}$$

Start inside the root and just simplify using the power laws like above.

$$= 16 \times 3^{-\frac{4}{5}} = 2^4 \times 3^{-\frac{4}{5}}$$

You need to recognise 16 and 81 as powers of 2 and 3 respectively — your calculator can help you with this.

Answer $2^4 \times 3^{-\frac{4}{5}}$

(3 marks)

Exam Questions

4 There is, on average, 6 litres of blood in an adult's body. 1 cubic millimetre of blood contains approximately 5×10^6 red blood cells.

(a) Calculate how many red blood cells there are in an adult's body.
Give your answer in standard form.

(1 litre = 1 000 cubic cm, 1 cubic cm = 1 000 cubic mm)

....

Answer (a) ________________

(2 marks)

(b) 1/120 of the total number of red blood cells are replaced every day.
How many is this in an adult? (Give your answer in standard form).

....

Answer (b) ________________

(2 marks)

5 Simplify: (a) $p^4 \times p^3$

Answer (a) ________________

(1 mark)

(b) $14t^5 / 7t^2$

Answer (b) ________________

(1 mark)

(c) $(6a^3d^2)^2$

Answer (c) ________________

(1 mark)

6 The Caspian Sea in Asia covers an area of 3.72×10^{11} m^2.
The Aral Sea in Asia covers 4.0×10^{10} m^2.

(a) What is the total area covered by the two seas? Give your answer in standard form.

....

Answer (a) ________________

(2 marks)

(b) What is the ratio of the area of the Aral Sea to the area of the Caspian Sea?
Give your answer in the form 1:n, rounded to the nearest whole number.

....

Answer (b) ________________

(2 marks)

Pythagoras' Theorem

Pythagoras' Theorem — $a^2 + b^2 = h^2$

1) PYTHAGORAS' THEOREM always goes hand in hand with SIN, COS and TAN because they're both involved with RIGHT-ANGLED TRIANGLES.

2) The big difference is that PYTHAGORAS DOES NOT INVOLVE ANY ANGLES — it just uses two sides to find the third side. (SIN, COS and TAN always involve ANGLES)

3) *THE BASIC FORMULA for Pythagoras is:*

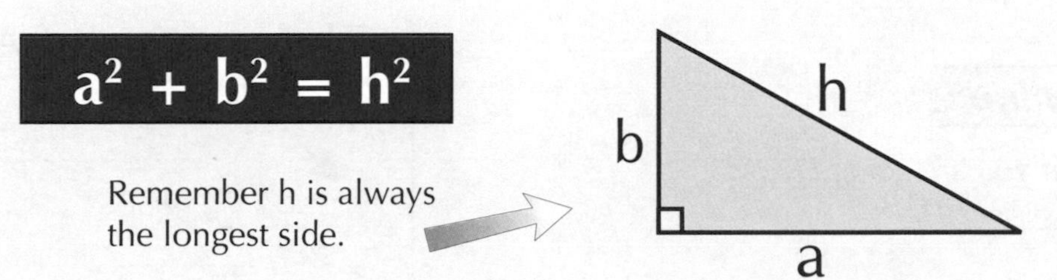

4) PLUG THE NUMBERS IN and work it out.

5) BUT GET THE NUMBERS IN THE RIGHT PLACE. The two shorter sides (squared) add to equal the longest side (squared).

6) ALWAYS CHECK THAT YOUR ANSWER IS SENSIBLE.

EXAMPLE:

"Find the missing side in the triangle shown."

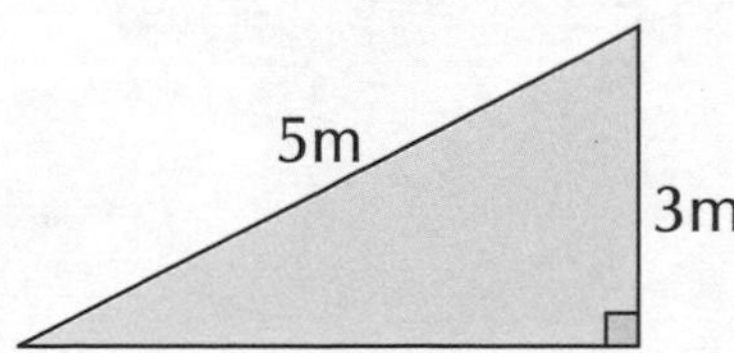

ANSWER:

$a^2 + b^2 = h^2$
$\therefore 3^2 + b^2 = 5^2$
$\therefore 9 + b^2 = 25$

$\therefore b^2 = 25 - 9 = 16$
$\therefore b = \sqrt{16} = \underline{4\ m}$

(Is it sensible? — Yes, it's shorter than 5 m, but not too much shorter)

Finding lengths in a right angle triangle? Pythagoras is your man

This is probably one of the most famous of all maths formulas. It will be in your exam at some point. If you haven't learnt it and practised some questions you might as well kiss good grades goodbye.

Bearings

Bearings

A very common use of angles is to give bearings.
To find or plot a bearing you must remember three key words:

1) "From"

Find the word "FROM" in the question, and put your pencil on the diagram at the point you are going "from".

2) Northline

At the point you are going FROM, draw in a NORTHLINE.

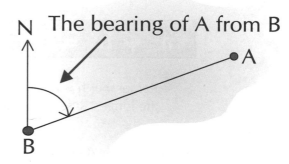

N The bearing of A from B

A

B

3) Clockwise

Now draw in the angle CLOCKWISE from the northline to the line joining the two points. This angle is the required bearing.

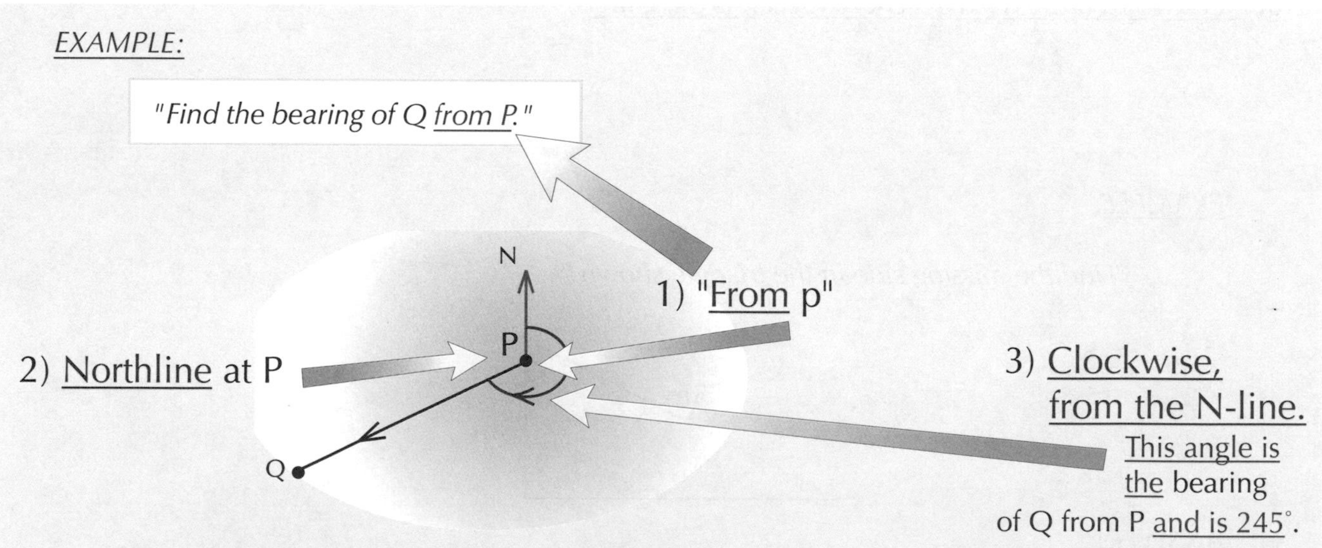

EXAMPLE:
"Find the bearing of Q from P."

1) "From p"
2) Northline at P
3) Clockwise, from the N-line.
This angle is the bearing of Q from P and is 245°.

N.B. All bearings should be given as three figures, e.g. 176°, 034° (not 34°), 005° (not 5°), 018° etc.

From... Northline... Clockwise — that's all you need to remember...

This is a very straightforward Exam question. Make sure you get the bearing from the right place, draw a northline and measure clockwise... From, Northline, Clockwise — am I going on...

Trigonometry — SIN, COS, TAN

There are several methods for doing Trig and they're all pretty much the same.
However, *the method shown below has a number of advantages*, mainly because the *formula triangles* mean the same method is used every time, (no matter which side or angle is being asked for).
This makes the whole topic a lot simpler, and you'll find that once you've learned this method, the answers automatically come out right every time.

Method

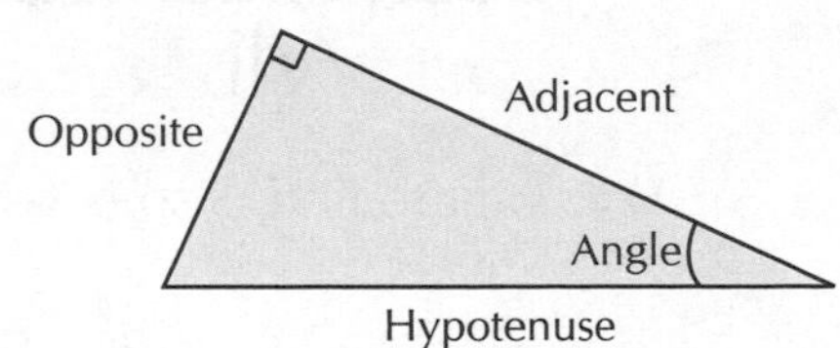

1) Label the three sides O, A and H (Opposite, Adjacent and Hypotenuse).
2) Write down FROM MEMORY

"SOH CAH TOA"
(Sounds like a Chinese word, "Sockatoa!")

3) Decide WHICH TWO SIDES are INVOLVED O,H A,H or O,A and select SOH, CAH or TOA accordingly
4) Turn the one you choose into a FORMULA TRIANGLE:

SOH

CAH

TOA

5) Cover up the thing you want to find (with your finger), and write down whatever is left showing.
6) Translate into numbers and work it out.
7) Finally, check that your answer is SENSIBLE.

Some details

1) The Hypotenuse is the LONGEST SIDE.
   The Opposite is the side OPPOSITE the angle being used (θ).
   The Adjacent is the side NEXT TO the angle being used.
2) In the formula triangles, Sθ represents SIN θ, Cθ is COS θ, and Tθ is TAN θ.
3) Remember, TO FIND THE ANGLE — USE INVERSE.
   i.e. press INV or SHIFT or 2nd, followed by SIN, COS or TAN (and make sure your calculator is in DEG mode).
4) You can only use SIN, COS and TAN on RIGHT-ANGLED TRIANGLES — you may have to add lines to the diagram to create one, especially with *isosceles triangles*.

H= Longest, O = Opposite, A = next to — and remember SOCKATOA

It's vital to practise Exam questions, but don't make the mistake of thinking it's pointless learning these seven steps first. If you don't know them all thoroughly, you'll just keep on getting questions wrong.

Trigonometry — SIN, COS, TAN

Example 1

"Find x in the triangle shown."

Opp 15m, Hyp x, Adj, 35°

1) Label O,A,H
2) Write down "SOH CAH TOA"
3) Two sides *involved:* O,H
4) So use $\frac{O}{S^{\theta} \times H}$

5) We want to find H so cover it up to leave: $H = {}^{O}\!/_{S\theta}$

6) Translate : $x = {}^{15}\!/_{\sin 35}$

Press [15] [÷] [SIN] [35] [=] → 26.151702 So ans = 26.2 m

7) Check it's sensible: yes, it's about twice as big as 15, as the diagram suggests. (N.B. on some calculators you press [35] [SIN] rather than [SIN] [35] — know yours)

Example 2

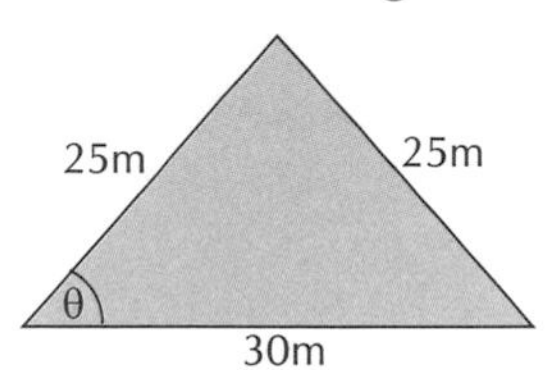

1) Label O, A, H
2) Write down "SOH CAH TOA"
3) Two sides involved: A,H
4) So use 

5) We want to find θ so cover up Cθ to leave: $C\theta = {}^{A}\!/_{H}$

6) Translate: $\cos\theta = {}^{15}\!/_{25} = 0.6$

NOW USE INVERSE : θ = inv cos (0.6)

Press [INV] [COS] [0.6] [=] → 53.130102 So ans. = 53.1°

7) Finally, is it sensible? — Yes, the angle looks like about 50°.

> Note the usual way of dealing with an ISOSCELES TRIANGLE: split it down the middle to get a RIGHT ANGLE:
>
> Hyp, 25m, Opp, Adj, θ, 15m

Angles of elevation *and* depression

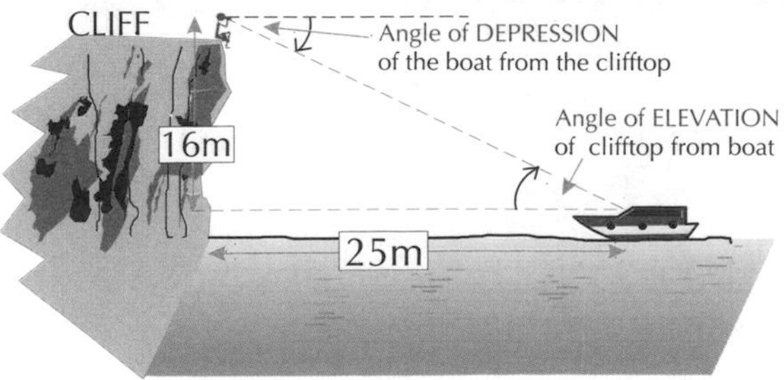

1) The *Angle of Depression* is the angle *downwards* from the horizontal.
2) The *Angle of Elevation* is the angle *upwards* from the horizontal.
3) The Angles of Elevation and Depression are *EQUAL*.

You need to have learnt all seven steps on page 77

Here you can see the seven steps from the last page being put into action. You can see how easy it is to apply those steps, but only if you can remember them and practise using them — so practise.

The Sine and Cosine Rules

Normal trigonometry using SOH CAH TOA etc. can only be applied to right-angled triangles. The Sine and Cosine Rules, on the other hand, allow you to tackle any triangle at all with contemptuous ease.

Labelling the triangle

This is very important. *You must label the sides and angles properly* so that the letters for the sides and angles correspond with each other:

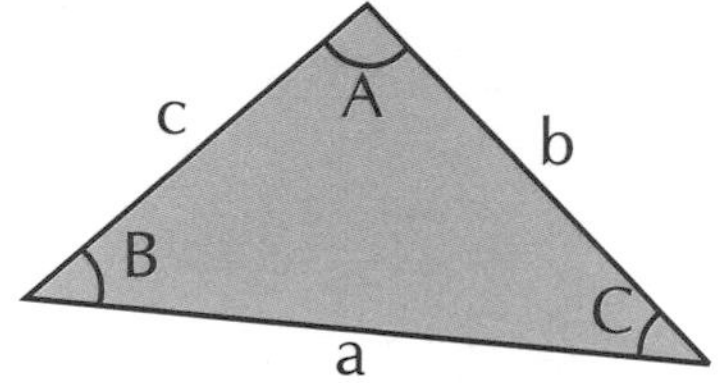

Remember, *side "a" is opposite angle A* etc.

It doesn't matter which sides you decide to call a, b, and c, just as long as the angles are then labelled properly.

Two formulas to learn:

They're quite an odd-looking pair of formulas really, but don't be put off by that. Once you know how to operate them they're *just like any other formula* — stick the numbers in, crank the handle and out pops the answer.

The **Sine** Rule

You don't use the whole thing with both "=" signs of course, so it's not half as bad as it looks — you just choose the two bits that you want:

$$\frac{a}{\sin A} = \frac{b}{\sin B} = \frac{c}{\sin C}$$

e.g. $\frac{a}{\sin A} = \frac{b}{\sin B}$ or $\frac{b}{\sin B} = \frac{c}{\sin C}$

The **Cosine** Rule

$$a^2 = b^2 + c^2 - 2bc \cos A$$

$$\text{or } \cos A = \frac{b^2 + c^2 - a^2}{2bc}$$

You should LEARN these three formulas off by heart. If you can't, you won't be able to use them successfully in the Exam, even if they give them to you.

***When** do you **use** which rule?*

1) Basically, THE SINE RULE is *much simpler* so always try to use it first IF POSSIBLE.

2) However, *you don't usually have a lot of choice*.
The good news is that there are only FOUR basic questions: TWO which need the SINE RULE and TWO which need the COSINE RULE — and they're all shown on the next page.
However, once you know 4 BITS OF DATA (e.g. 2 sides and 2 angles, or 3 sides and 1 angle) then the rest is easily worked out (with the SINE RULE preferably).

That cosine rule looks complicated, but you just have to learn it

Once you have learnt it, it's just like any other formula — plug the numbers in and Bob's your uncle. So you just have to scribble over and over until it's burnt into the inside of your eyeballs.

The Sine and Cosine Rules

The four *examples*

Amazingly enough there are BASICALLY ONLY FOUR questions where the SINE and COSINE rules would be applied. *Learn the exact details of these four basic examples:*

*1) **Two angles** given plus **any side***

SINE RULE NEEDED

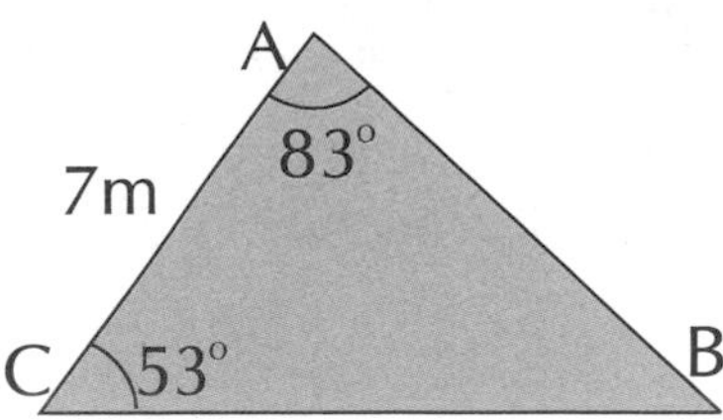

1) Don't forget the obvious: $B = 180 - 83 - 53 = \underline{44^0}$

2) Then use $\frac{b}{\sin B} = \frac{c}{\sin C} \Rightarrow \frac{7}{\sin 44} = \frac{c}{\sin 53}$

3) Which gives $\Rightarrow c = \frac{7 \times \sin 53}{\sin 44} = \underline{8.05\text{m}}$

The rest is easy using the SINE RULE

*2) **Two sides** given plus an **angle not enclosed** by them*

SINE RULE NEEDED

1) Use $\frac{b}{\sin B} = \frac{c}{\sin C} \Rightarrow \frac{7}{\sin B} = \frac{8}{\sin 53}$

2) $\Rightarrow \sin B = \frac{7 \times \sin 53}{8} = 0.6988 \Rightarrow B = \sin^{-1}(0.6988) = 44.3°$

The rest is easy using the SINE RULE

*3) **Two sides** given plus **the angle enclosed** by them*

COSINE RULE NEEDED

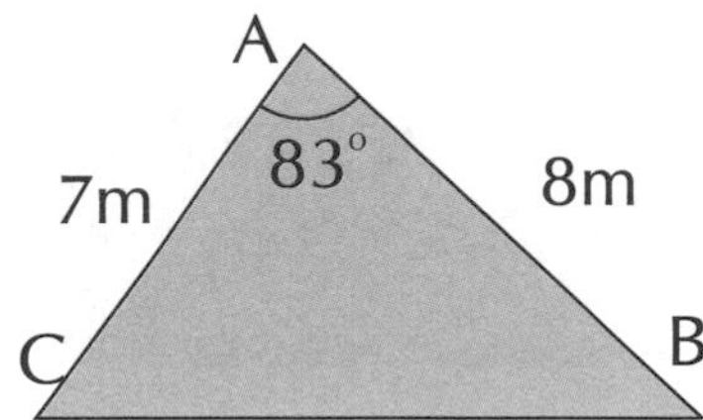

1) Use: $a^2 = b^2 + c^2 - 2bc \cos A$

$= 7^2 + 8^2 - 2 \times 7 \times 8 \times \cos 83$

$= 99.3506 \Rightarrow a = \sqrt{99.3506} = \underline{9.97\text{m}}$

The rest is easy using the SINE RULE

*4) **All three sides** given but **no angles***

COSINE RULE NEEDED

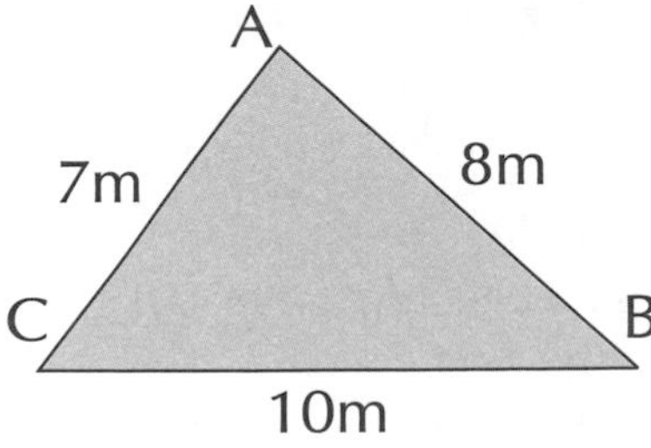

1) Use: $\cos A = \frac{b^2 + c^2 - a^2}{2bc}$

$= \frac{49 + 64 - 100}{2 \times 7 \times 8} = \frac{13}{112} = 0.11607$

2) Hence $A = \cos^{-1}(0.11607) = \underline{83.3}°$

The rest is easy using the SINE RULE

Learn which rule you need for which question type

Rather than fret about which equation to use and how to do it, you just need to learn these four basic question types and practise them. It'll save you loads of time and stress on the big day.

The Graphs of SIN, COS and TAN

You are expected to know these graphs and be able to SKETCH them from memory.
It really isn't that difficult — the secret is to notice their SIMILARITIES and DIFFERENCES:

Y = SIN X

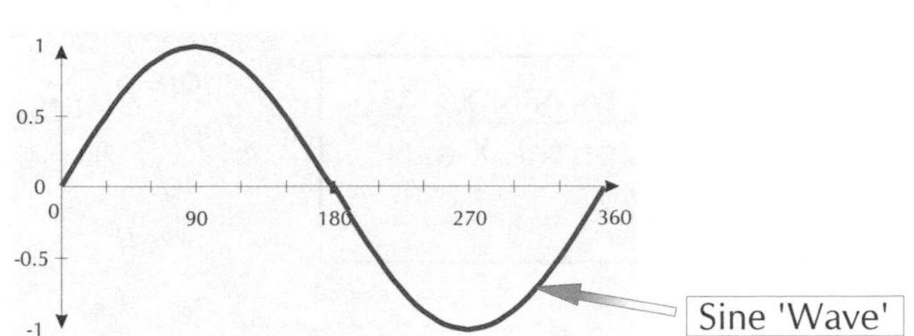

Y = COS X

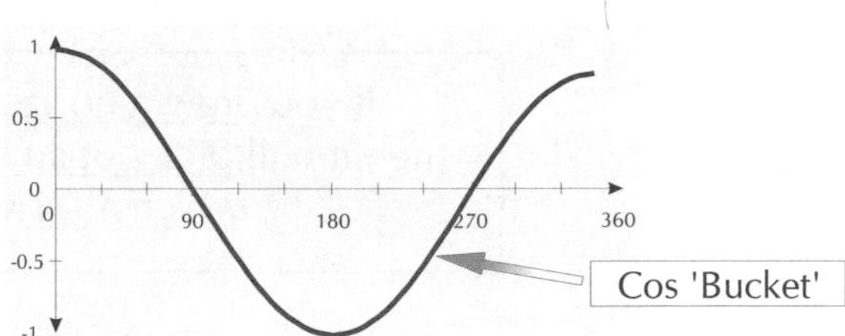

1) For 0° – 360°, the shapes you get are a SINE "WAVE" (One peak, one trough) and a COS "BUCKET" (Starts at the top, dips, and finishes at the top).
2) The underlying shape of both the SIN and COS graphs are identical (as shown below) when you extend them (indefinitely) in both directions:

Y = SIN X

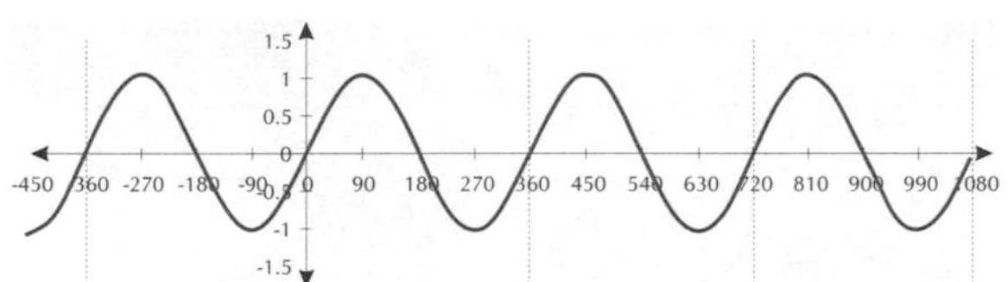

Y = COS X

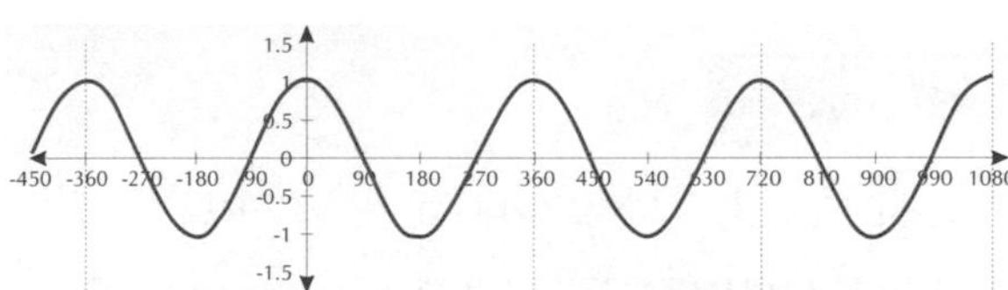

3) The only difference is that the SIN graph is shifted by 90° → compared to the COS graph.
4) Note that BOTH GRAPHS wiggle between y-limits of exactly +1 and -1.
5) The key to drawing the extended graphs is to first draw the 0 – 360° cycle of either the SIN "WAVE" or the COS "BUCKET" and then repeat it in both directions as shown.

Y = TAN X

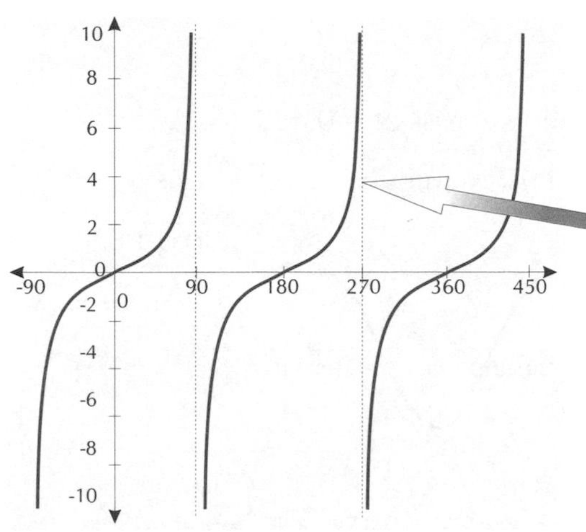

1) The TAN graph BEARS NO RESEMBLANCE to the other two.
2) *It behaves in a fairly bizarre way at 90°, 270° etc. ....by disappearing up to + infinity and then reappearing from - infinity on the other side of the asymptote (— a dotted line that the graph never quite touches).*
3) *So unlike the SIN and COS graphs, Y = TAN X is NOT LIMITED to values between +1 and -1.*
4) *You'll also notice that whilst SIN and COS repeat every 360°, the TAN graph repeats every 180°.*

You should recognise these three like the back of your hand

Tan looks very different, but sin and cos are very similar. You need to remember what the graphs look like and all the properties in the numbered lists — it's lucky you love to learn.

Angles of Any Size

You can only do this if you've learnt the graphs on the last page.

SIN, COS and TAN for angles of any size

There is ONE BASIC IDEA involved here:

> If you draw a horizontal line at a given value for SIN X then it will pick out an infinite number of angles on the X-axis which all have the same value for SIN X.

Note that this applies to cos and tan as well.

Example 1:

"Find six different angles X such that SIN X = 0.94"

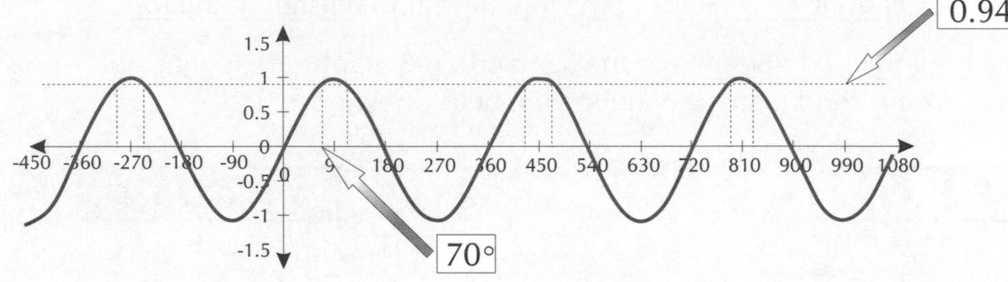

Method

1) SKETCH the extended SIN X graph.
2) Put a HORIZONTAL LINE across at 0.94.
3) DRAW LINES DOWN to the X-axis wherever the horizontal CROSSES THE CURVE.
4) Use your CALCULATOR to find INV SIN 0.94, to get the first angle (70° in this case).
5) The SYMMETRY is surely obvious. You can see that 70° is 20° away from the peak, so all the other angles are clearly 20° either side of the peaks at 90°, 450°, etc.

> Hence we can say that SIN X = +0.94 for all the following angles:
> ..... -290°, -250°, 70°, 110°, 430°, 470°, 790°, 830°....

Example 2:

"Find three other angles which have the same Cosine as 65°."

ANSWER: 1) Use the calculator to find COS 65° = +0.423

2) Draw the extended COS curve and a horizontal line across at + 0.423

3) Draw the vertical lines from the intersections and use symmetry

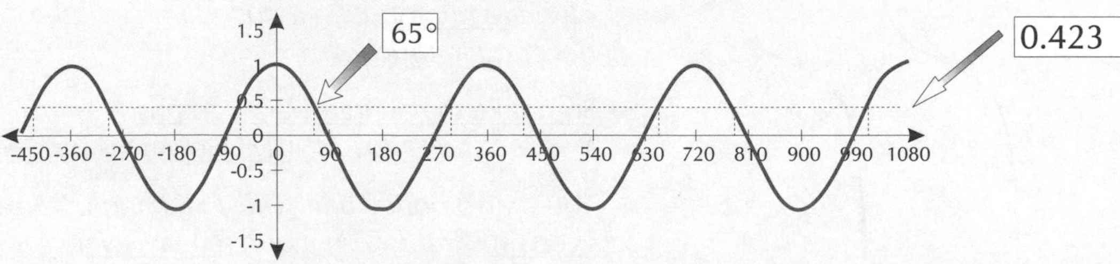

Since 65° is 25° below 90° the other angles shown must be: -425°, -295°, -65°, etc

Many angles give the same value for sin, cos and tan

If you are asked to find a number of angles with the same value of sin, cos or tan you need to use the graphs — so you must learn those graphs really well. If they're a bit hazy have another look at page 81.

Warm-Up and Worked Exam Questions

Learning facts and practising exam questions is the only recipe for success.
That's what the questions on these pages are all about. All you have to do — is do them.

Warm-Up Questions

1) In a right-angled triangle, the two shorter sides are 10 cm and 8.4 cm. Find:
   a) the length of the longest side, correct to 3 significant figures.
   b) the smallest angle, correct to the nearest degree.
2) In this triangle, find the length of AC, correct to 1 decimal place.

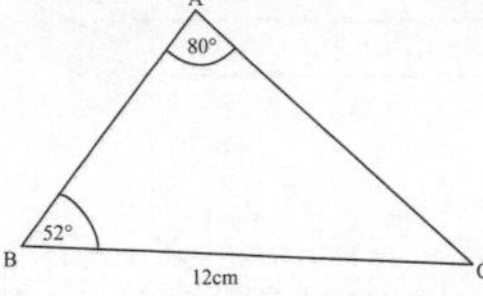

3) A triangle has sides of 4 cm, 6 cm and 8 cm. Calculate the largest angle, correct to 1 d.p.
4) Name one important similarity and one difference between the following pairs of graphs:
   a) y = sin x and y = cos x   b) y = sin x and y = tan x
5) Sketch the graph of y = sin x for x between 0° and 360°.

Worked Exam Questions

There's a knack to be learnt in using the facts you've stored away in your brain box in the right way to get marks in the exam. These worked examples will really help you see how...

1 The radar location of a ship in distress is given as 143 km north and 89.5 km east of a port P. The rescue ship leaves P travelling on a bearing of 032°, to the ship in trouble.

(a) How far does the rescue team travel, to the nearest km?

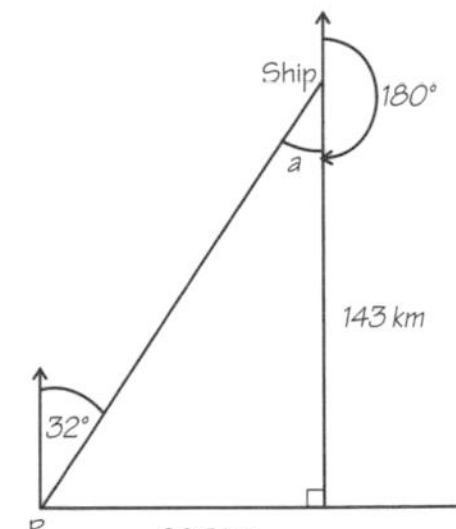

Call the distance x.

By Pythagoras $143^2 + 89.5^2 = x^2$

$x^2 = 28459.25$, so $x = 169$ km

Answer (a) 169 km

(3 marks)

(b) What bearing does the rescue team need to return to port P?

The two parts of the bearing are 180° + a

a = 32° (the NORTH lines are parallel and the angles are equal alternate (or Z) angles)

Bearing required = 180 + 32 = 212°

Remember — draw in the North line *from* the required point (in this case, the ship in trouble) and then mark in the angle turned clockwise to face port P.

Answer (b) 212°

(1 mark)

Worked Exam Questions

2 (a) Find the area of the cross section of this prism.

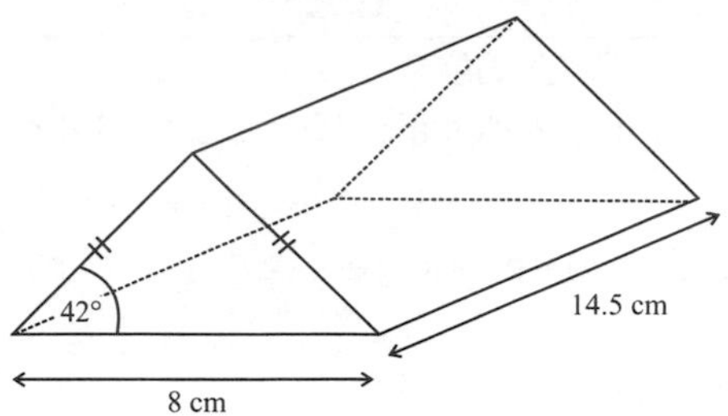

Always look for a right-angled triangle.

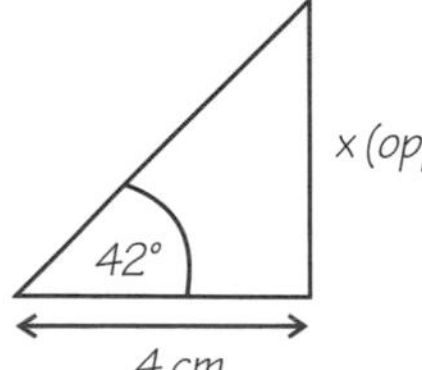

opp = tan 42 × adj. $x = \tan 42 \times 4 = 3.60162$ cm

Area = (8 × 3.60162) ÷ 2 = 14.40646 = 14.4 cm^2

Answer (a) 14.4 cm^2

(3 marks)

(b) Find the volume of the prism.

14.40646 × 14.5 = 208.8937 = 209 cm^3

Volume is just cross section area x length

Answer (b) 209 cm^3

(2 marks)

3 (a) By plotting a few significant points, sketch the graphs of $y = \cos x$ and $y = \frac{x}{50}$ for values of x between 0° and 90°.

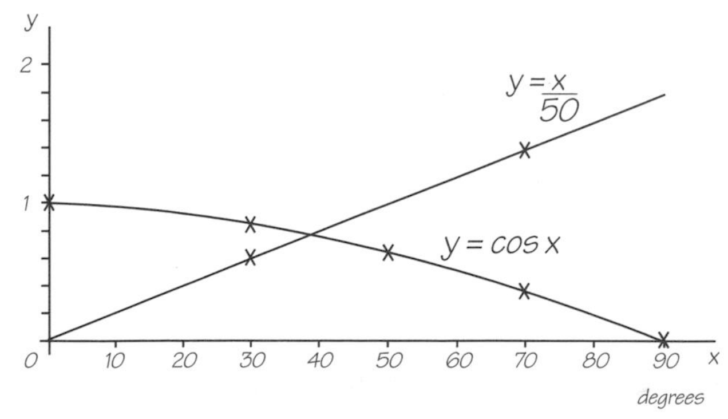

Stick a few points into your calculator. Plot those points and then join them up with a smooth curve or straight line as appropriate.

(3 marks)

(b) The point of intersection is the solution of the equation $x = 50 \cos x$. Explain why.

The graphs are $y = \cos x$ and $y = \frac{x}{50}$

At the point of intersection the y values are the same, so $\cos x = \frac{x}{50}$

multiplying both sides by 50 gives $x = 50\cos x$, as required.

(3 marks)

Exam Questions

4 To 3 significant figures, find:

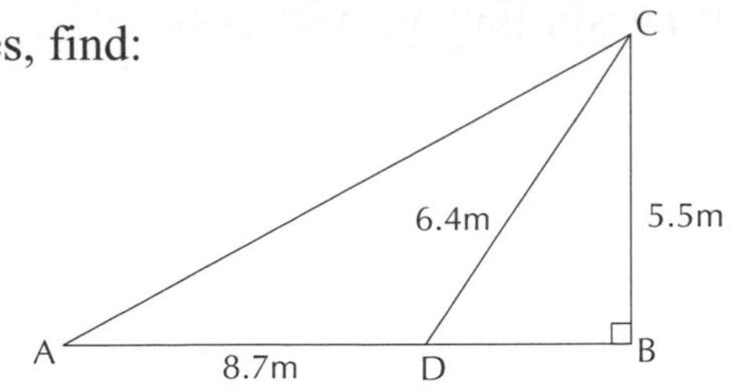

(a) BD

....

....

Answer (a) ____________________

(3 marks)

(b) AB

....

Answer (b) ____________________

(1 mark)

(c) AC

....

....

Answer (c) ____________________

(3 marks)

5 The angle of elevation of the top of a tower from a point A on the ground is 52.1°.
A and B are 24 m and 31 m respectively from the base of the tower.

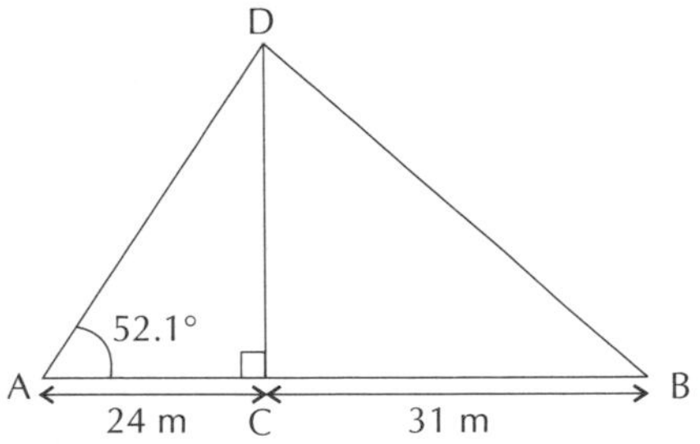

Calculate:

(a) the height of the tower.

....

....

Answer (a) ____________________

(3 marks)

(b) the angle of elevation of the top of the tower from point B.

....

....

Answer (b) ____________________

(3 marks)

Vectors

The next two pages contain 4 MONSTROUSLY IMPORTANT THINGS you need to know about *Vectors:*

1) The four **notations**

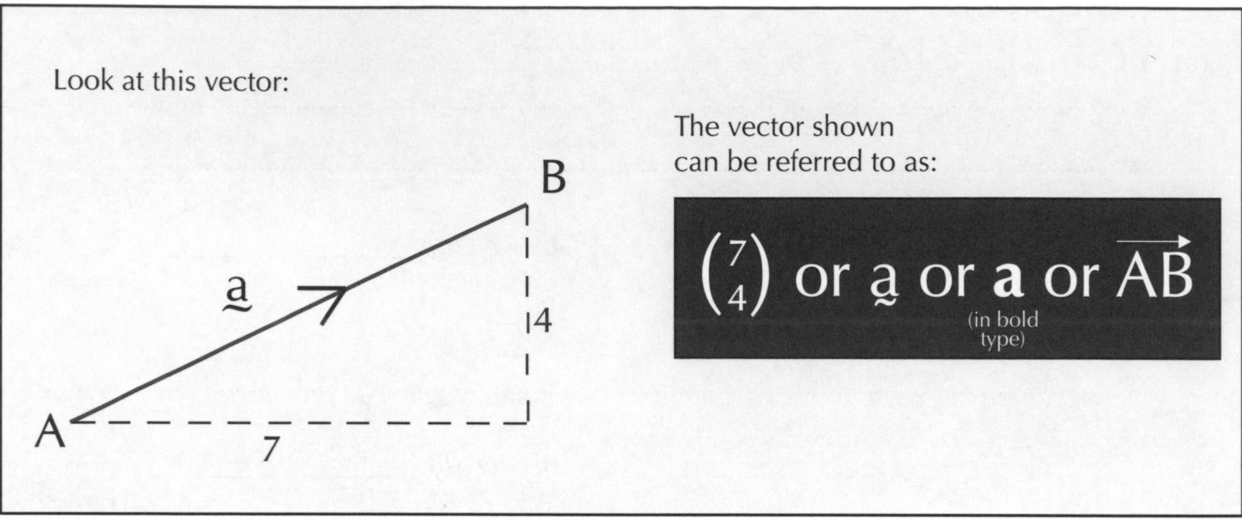

Look at this vector:
B
a
4
A
7
The vector shown
can be referred to as:
$\binom{7}{4}$ or $\underset{\sim}{a}$ or **a** or $\overrightarrow{AB}$
(in bold type)

It's pretty obvious what these mean.
Just make sure you know which is which in the column vector (x→ and y↑)
and what a negative value means in a column vector.

2) **Adding** and **subtracting** vectors

Vectors must always be combined END TO END,
so that the *arrows all point WITH each other,* not AGAINST each other.

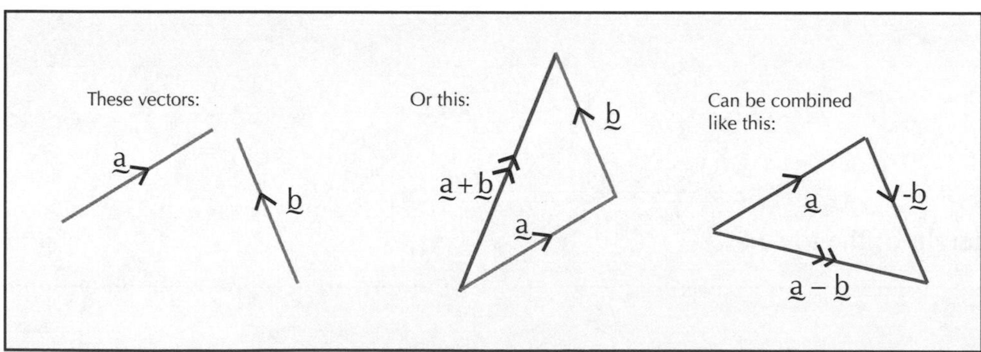

Adding and subtracting COLUMN VECTORS is really easy:

E.g. if $a = \begin{pmatrix} 5 \\ 3 \end{pmatrix}$ and $b = \begin{pmatrix} -2 \\ 4 \end{pmatrix}$ then $2a - b = 2\begin{pmatrix} 5 \\ 3 \end{pmatrix} - \begin{pmatrix} -2 \\ 4 \end{pmatrix} = \begin{pmatrix} 12 \\ 2 \end{pmatrix}$

That's the first two vital vector facts done

But the facts are only really 'done' if you've learnt them. So make sure you know how vectors are written (there's four ways remember) and you know how to add and subtract vectors — then you're done.

Vectors and Splitting into Components

3) **Splitting** into components

Any vector can be split into two components that are at 90° to each other.

These two components will always be: F cos θ and F sin θ.

The main difficulty is knowing which one is which.

The easiest way is to remember this diagram:

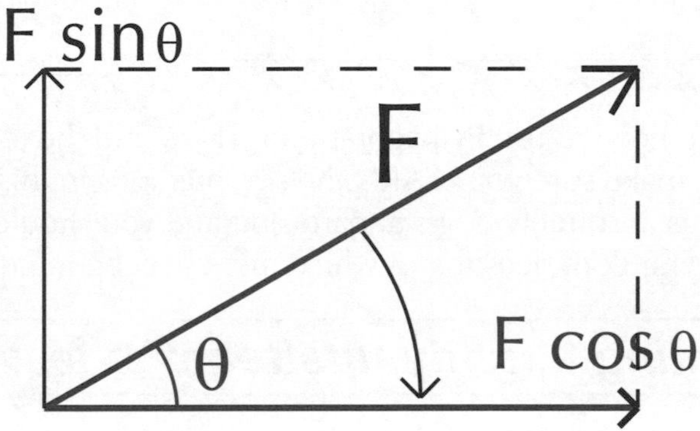

4) A **typical** exam question

This is a common type of question and it illustrates a very important vector technique:

To obtain the *unknown vector* just *'get there'* by any route *made up of known vectors*

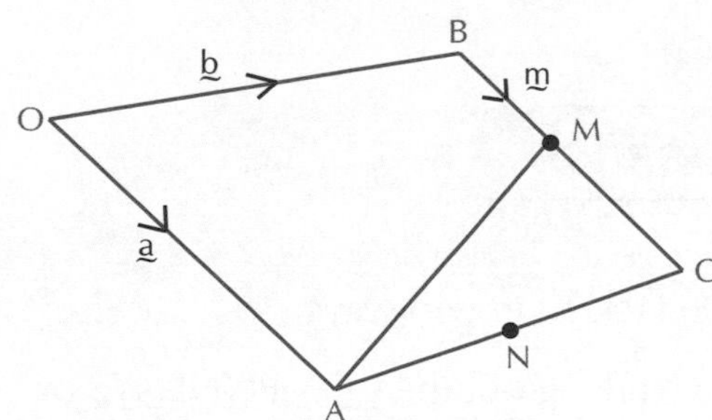

Applying this rule we can easily obtain the following vectors in terms of **a**, **b** and **m**, (given that M and N are mid points)**:**

1) $\overrightarrow{AM} = -\underset{\sim}{a}+\underset{\sim}{b}+\underset{\sim}{m}$ (i.e. get there via O and B)

2) $\overrightarrow{OC} = \underset{\sim}{b}+2\underset{\sim}{m}$ (i.e. get there via B and M)

3) $\overrightarrow{AC} = \underset{\sim}{a}+\underset{\sim}{b} + 2\underset{\sim}{m}$ (A to C via O, B and M)

If you know $\overrightarrow{AB}$ *and* $\overrightarrow{BC}$ *— then add them to get* $\overrightarrow{AC}$

That's the last of the four facts about vectors. The ones on this second page are a bit trickier, but you need all four to do the vector questions which will be on the exam. So make sure you can do them all.

Real Life Vector Questions

These are the type of vector questions you're most likely to get in the Exam, so make sure you learn all the little tricks on this page.

1) The old "swimming across the river" question

This is a really easy question: You just ADD the two velocity vectors END TO END and draw the RESULTANT vector which shows both the speed and direction of the final course. Simple huh?

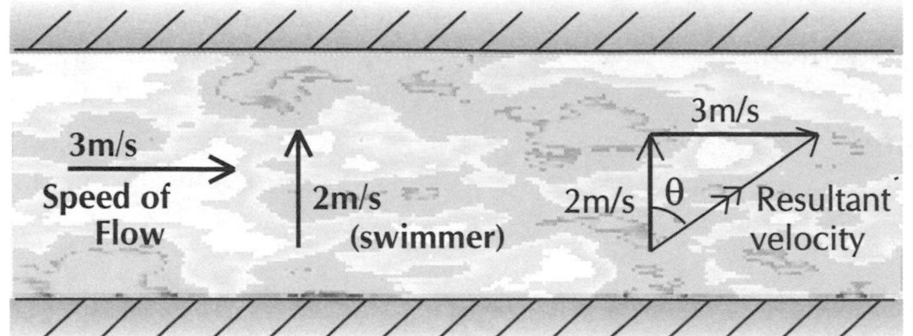

Overall Speed = $\sqrt{3^2+2^2} = \sqrt{13} = \underline{3.6\text{m/s}}$

Direction: $\tan\theta = 3 \div 2$

$\theta = \tan^{-1}(1.5) = \underline{56.3^0}$

As usual with vectors, you'll need to use Pythagoras and Trig to find the length and angle but that's no big deal is it? Just make sure you LEARN the two methods in this question. The example shown above is absolutely bog-standard stuff and you should definitely see it that way, rather than as one random question of which there may be hundreds — there aren't.

2) The old "swimming slightly upstream" question

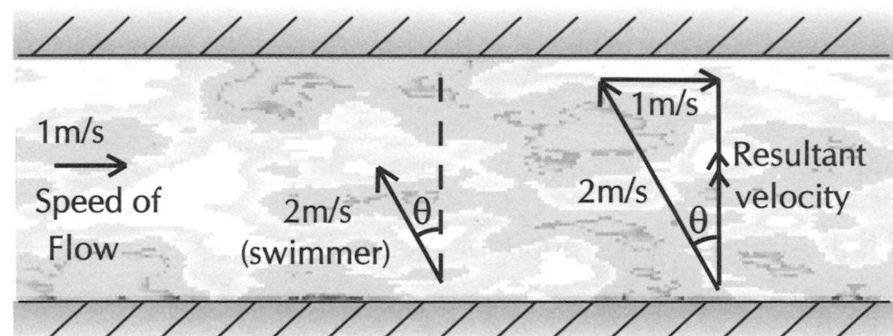

1) $\sin\theta = \text{OPP/HYP}$

$= 1/2$

so $\underline{\theta} = \sin^{-1}(0.5) = \underline{30^0}$

2) Speed $= \sqrt{2^2 - 1^2} = \sqrt{3} = \underline{1.73\text{ m/s}}$

The general idea here is to end up going directly across the river, and ONCE AGAIN the old faithful method of DRAWING A VECTOR TRIANGLE makes light work of the whole thing — two vectors joined END TO END to give the resultant velocity. However, in this case the resultant is drawn in FIRST (straight across), so that the angle θ has to be worked out to fit as shown above.

3) The old "Queen Mary's Tugboats" question

The problem here is to find the overall force from the two tugs.

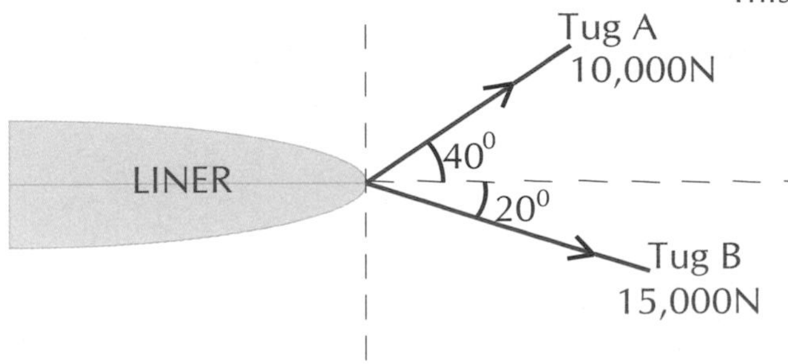

This can be tackled in two ways:

1) By working out the COMPONENTS of the two force vectors along both dotted lines ($F\cos\theta$ and $F\sin\theta$ etc.)

OR:

2) By adding the vectors END TO END to make a vector triangle and using the SINE & COSINE RULES (See P.79).

If you learn how to answer these questions you will get marks

Three questions which are very likely to come up on your exam, almost like a hint as to what to learn — it's as close to cheating as you can get without cheating — so learn them.

Warm-Up Questions

Vector questions can be pretty tricky until you get your head around the basics. That's what these warm-up questions are all about — work through them carefully and check any bits you don't know.

Warm-Up Questions

1) 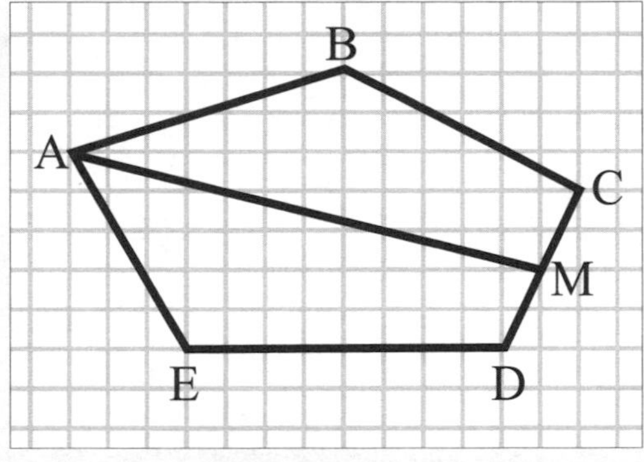

In the diagram, each square represents 1 unit.

Write the following as a column vector.

a) $\overrightarrow{AB}$ b) $\overrightarrow{BC}$ c) $\overrightarrow{ED}$ d) $\overrightarrow{CD}$ e) $\overrightarrow{AM}$

2) If $a=\begin{pmatrix}5\\3\end{pmatrix}$, $b=\begin{pmatrix}-1\\6\end{pmatrix}$, $c=\begin{pmatrix}0\\4\end{pmatrix}$, $d=\begin{pmatrix}-2\\0\end{pmatrix}$ find:

(a) a + b (b) b – c (c) c + a (d) d – b (e) b + c – d

3) Write down the two components of the following vectors.

a) 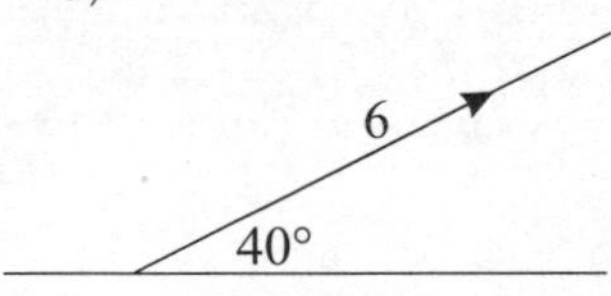

b) 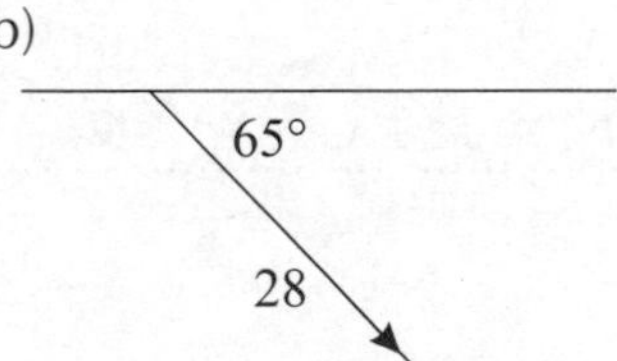

c) 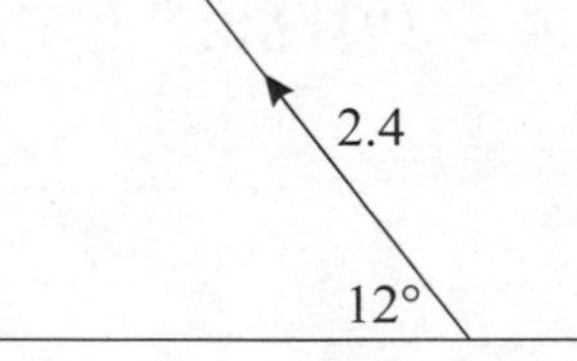

4) 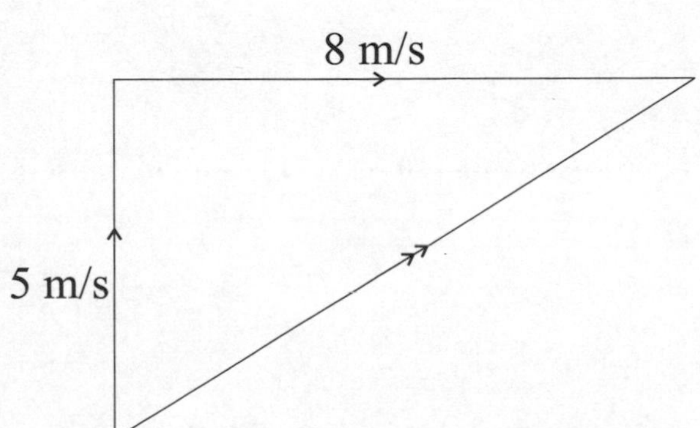

Find the speed and direction of the final course.

Worked Exam Question

Worked Exam Question

Take your time to go through this example and make sure you understand it all.
If any of the facts are baffling you, it's not too late to take another peek over the section.

1

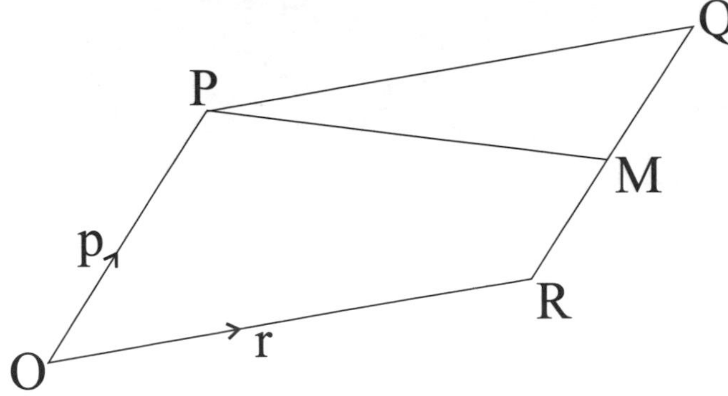

OPQR is a parallelogram. M is the midpoint of QR. $\overrightarrow{OP} = p$, $\overrightarrow{OR} = r$.

(a) Find in terms of p and r expressions for the following vectors.

(i) $\overrightarrow{OQ}$

$\overrightarrow{OQ} = \overrightarrow{OP} + \overrightarrow{PQ} = p + r$ (because $\overrightarrow{PQ} = \overrightarrow{OR}$)

(1 mark)

(ii) $\overrightarrow{MR}$

$\overrightarrow{MR} = \frac{1}{2}\overrightarrow{QR} = \frac{1}{2}\overrightarrow{PO} = -\frac{1}{2}p$

(1 mark)

(b) S is a point positioned three quarters along $\overrightarrow{PM}$. Find in terms of p and r:

(i) $\overrightarrow{PS}$

$\overrightarrow{PS} = \frac{3}{4}\overrightarrow{PM} = \frac{3}{4}(r - \frac{1}{2}p)$

(1 mark)

(ii) $\overrightarrow{OS}$

$\overrightarrow{OS} = \overrightarrow{OP} + \overrightarrow{PS} = p + \frac{3}{4}(r - \frac{1}{2}p)$ or $\frac{3}{4}r + \frac{5}{8}p$

(1 mark)

Exam Questions

2 OPQR is a parallelogram. $\overrightarrow{OP} = a$, $\overrightarrow{PQ} = 2b$.
M is the midpoint of QR. N is the midpoint of OR.

(a) Find in terms of a and b the vectors:

(i) $\overrightarrow{OQ}$ ....

(1 mark)

(ii) $\overrightarrow{OM}$ ....

(1 mark)

(b) The lines PQ and NM are extended to meet at S. Find in terms of a and b the vectors:

(i) $\overrightarrow{RS}$ ....

(1 mark)

(ii) $\overrightarrow{NQ}$ ....

(1 mark)

(c) What can you say about the lines RS and NQ?

....

(1 mark)

3

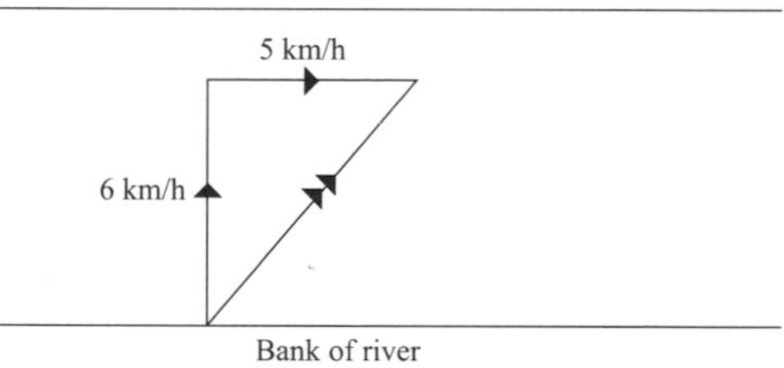

A boat, whose speed in still water is 6 km/h, is making its way across a river flowing at 5 km/h. The boat sets off at right angles to the bank. Find:

(a) Its resultant velocity and its direction.

....

(2 marks)

(b) The boat owner wants to cross the river at right angles to the bank.
At what angle must he point the boat upstream?

....

(2 marks)

(c) The boat is pointed upstream, 60° to the bank. The speed of the current has changed.
If the boat is moving at right angles to the bank, what is the current's speed?

....

(2 marks)

Revision Summary for Section Three

Here we are again — more lovely questions for you to test yourself with. Remember you have to keep practising these questions *over and over again* until you can answer them *all*. Seriously, you do. That's the best kind of revision there is because the whole idea is to find out what you *don't know* and then learn it *until you do*. Enjoy.

Keep learning the basic facts until you know them

1) How do you put the formulas A = B × C and A = B ÷ C into formula triangles?
2) What are the two rules for using a formula triangle?
3) What is the formula triangle for density?
4) What is the formula triangle for speed, distance and time?
5) Is there a better way of doing speed, distance and time?
6) What two main rules apply to the units involved with formula triangles?
7) Give four important details relating to distance-time graphs.
8) Give five important details relating to velocity-time graphs.
9) Draw a typical example of each type of graph and label the important features.
10) What is the format of any number expressed in standard form?
11) What are the three important points that you need to focus on?
12) Detail the three important examples of Exam-style standard form.
13) What is scientific mode? Can you get in and out of it easily on your calculator?
14) Is SCI mode useful for doing standard form questions?
15) Write down the ten rules for powers and roots.
16) What are the two possible square roots of 9?
17) What is the formula for Pythagoras' theorem? Where can you use Pythagoras?
18) How do you decide which numbers go where? What final check do you make?
19) What are the three key words for bearings? How must bearings be written?
20) Write down the important steps of a good solid method for doing TRIG.
21) Is there any point in trying to get every last mark you can in every Exam question?
22) What are the advantages of using formula triangles to do sin, cos and tan?
23) Draw a diagram to illustrate angles of elevation and depression.
24) Write down the SINE and COSINE RULES and draw a properly labelled triangle.
25) List the four different types of questions and which rule you need for each.
26) What is the formula (involving sin) for the area of any triangle? Demonstrate its use.
27) Draw the graphs of sin, cos and tan over 0 to 360^{0} and then -1080^{0} to 1080^{0}.
28) What is the method for dealing with sin, cos and tan of angles of any size?
29) Illustrate the method by finding six angles whose cosine is -0.5.
30) What are the four vector notations?
31) What is a vector triangle? What's it for? What's the main rule for adding vectors?
32) Draw a diagram to show how you split a vector into its components.
33) What is the rule for remembering which component is $F\cos\theta$ and which is $F\sin\theta$?
34) In a typical Exam question, what is the basic rule for finding an unknown vector?
35) Produce your own "swimming across the river" question and work it out.
36) Produce your own "swimming slightly upstream" question and work it out.
37) Produce your own "Queen Mary's tugboats" question and work it out using $F\cos\theta$.
38) Do the "Queen Mary's tugboats" using SINE and COSINE rules.

Probability

THE SINGLE MOST IMPORTANT FACT you can learn about probability is this:

Every Probability Question should be done using a Tree Diagram.

And *once you register that sweet simple truth* the whole torrid subject suddenly begins to settle into sublime serenity. And why? — because once you've *thoroughly learnt* the handful of details below on how to do tree diagrams you can tackle EVERY probability question they can throw at you using the EXACT SAME METHOD every time.
There are TWO THINGS YOU MUST DO, however, to attain this happy state:

1) Thoroughly LEARN all these details on TREE DIAGRAMS and practise applying them.
2) Make it a HABIT to START DRAWING A TREE DIAGRAM (as small and scruffy as you like) the moment you see any probability question.

General tree diagram

All Tree Diagrams have a lot of details in common. It's pretty essential that you know these details, because without them, you won't be able to use tree diagrams to do the questions in the Exam.
You need to know this diagram inside out:

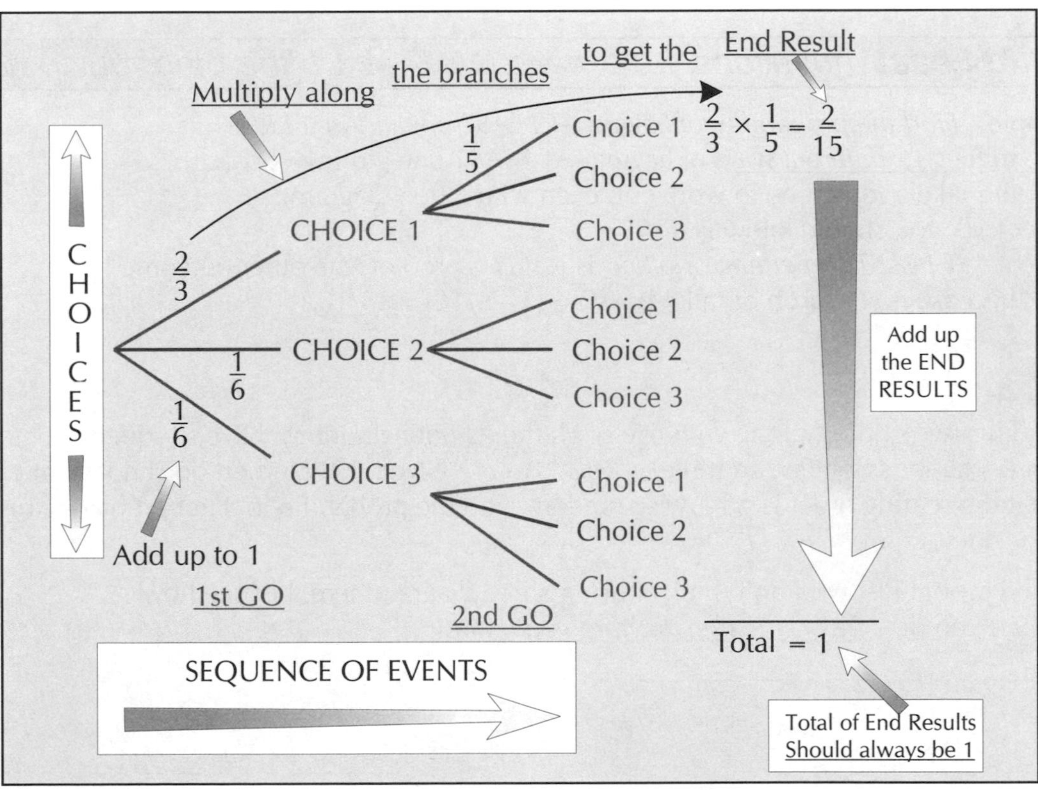

1) Always multiply the numbers along the branches to get the END RESULTS.
2) The numbers on any set of branches which all meet at a point must always ADD UP TO 1.
3) Check that your diagram is correct by making sure the End Results ADD UP TO ONE.
4) To answer any question, simply ADD up the RELEVANT END RESULTS.

The tree's the key

The tree diagram is the top toy when it comes to probability questions. Even if the question doesn't specifically ask for a tree diagram you should draw one straight away so you know what's going on.

Probability

Four extra details for the **tree diagram** method:

1) Always break up the question **into a sequence of separate events**

E.g. "Three coins are tossed together" – just split it into three separate events.
You need this sequence of events to able to draw any sort of tree diagram.

2) **Don't feel** you have to draw **complete** tree diagrams

Learn to adapt them to what is required.
E.g. "What is the chance of throwing two Sixes followed by an even number?". This diagram is all you need to get the answer:

$\frac{1}{6} \times \frac{1}{6} \times \frac{1}{2} = \frac{1}{72}$

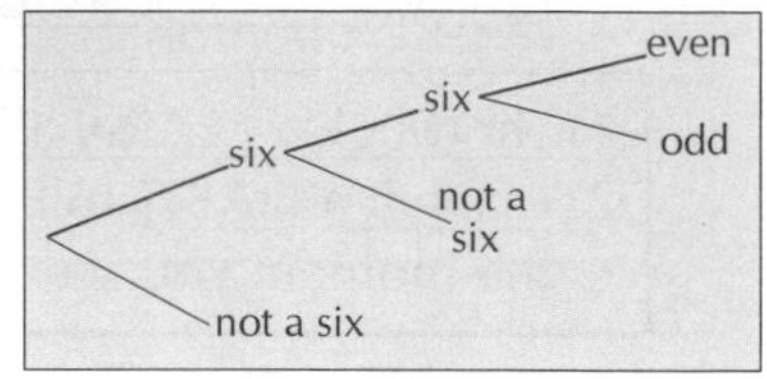

3) **Watch out** for **conditional probabilities**

...where the fraction on each branch depends on what happened _on the previous branch_, e.g. bags of sweets, packs of cards etc, where the _bottom_ number of the fractions _also_ changes as items are removed. E.g. $^{11}/_{25}$ then $^{10}/_{24}$ etc .

4) With "**At Least**" questions, it's always (1 - Prob of "the other outcome")

For example, *"Find the probability of having AT LEAST one girl in 4 kids"*
There are in fact _15 different ways_ of having "AT LEAST one girl in 4 kids" which would take a long time to work out, even with a tree diagram.
The clever trick you should know is this:
The prob of *"AT LEAST something or other"* is just (1 – prob of "the other outcome") which in this case is (1 – prob of "all 4 boys") = (1 – 1/16) = _15/16_.

Example:

"Herbert and his two chums, along with five of Herbert's doting aunties, have to squeeze onto the back seat of his father's Bentley, en route to Royal Ascot. Given that Herbert does not sit at either end, and that the seating order is otherwise random, find the probability of Herbert having his best chums either side of him."

The untrained probabilist wouldn't think of using a tree diagram here, but see how easy it is when you do. _This is the tree diagram you'd draw:_

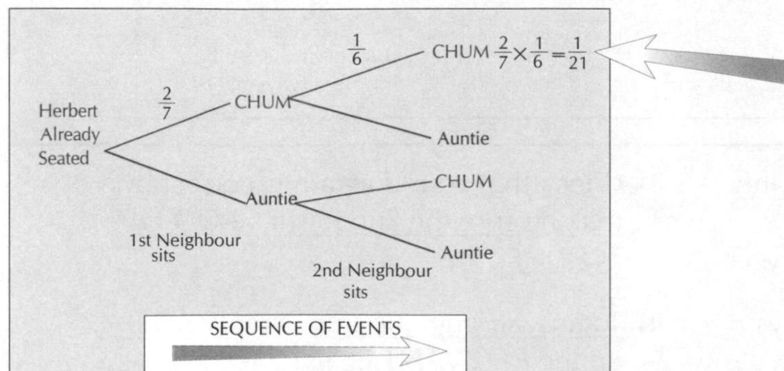

So the answer is 1/21.
Of course you'd have to do a bit of thinking to decide to place Herbert first, and then have the two events as each of his "neighbours" are placed beside him, but that sort of trick is pretty standard really.

See how useful tree diagrams are

This example shows how a tree diagram once again saves the day. It takes a bit of thinking about to decide how to do the diagram and which bits you need. Once you've done that it's plain sailing.

Warm-Up and Worked Exam Questions

Probability is really not that difficult once you get the hang of it, but it's easy to throw away marks by being a little slap-dash with your calculations. It's important to get loads of practice. Try these questions.

Warm-Up Questions

1) What is the probability of rolling a six three times in a row with a six-sided dice?
2) A sweet is picked out of a bag containing 4 cola bottles and 3 toffees. It is then put back in and a sweet picked out again. What is the probability of getting a cola bottle both times?
3) A playing card is dropped 3 times.
   What is the probability of it landing face up all three times?
4) Three balls are picked randomly from a bag containing 3 blue and 4 red balls.
   What is the probability of getting a ball of each colour?

Worked Exam Question

Take a look at this worked exam question. It's not too hard but it should give you a good idea of what to write. You'll usually get at least one probability question in the exam.

1 Mr and Mrs Jones plan to have children. The probability that they have a boy is 0.43.

(a) What is the probability that they have a girl?

1 − 0.43 = 0.57

(1 mark)

(b) Complete the following tree diagram for two children.

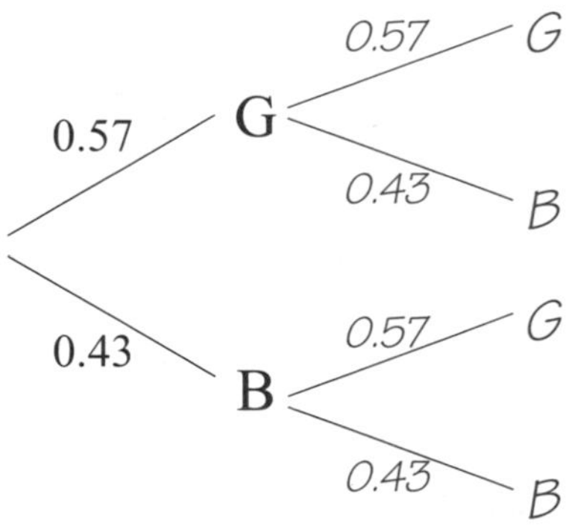

(2 marks)

(c) Find the probability that Mr and Mrs Jones have one girl and one boy.

P (Girl and Boy) + P (Boy and Girl)

(0.57 × 0.43) + (0.43 × 0.57)

0.2451 + 0.2451

= 0.4902

Hint: You may assume that the two events (first child, second child) are independent and therefore multiply the probabilities.

(3 marks)

(d) Find the probability that neither of the two children are girls.

What this is really saying is, what is the probability of having two boys: 0.43 × 0.43 = 0.1849

(3 marks)

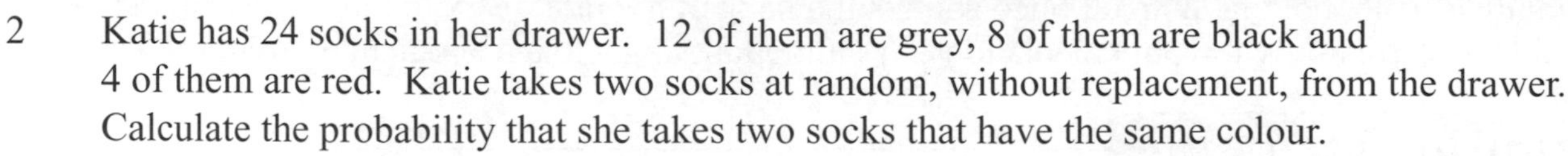

2 Katie has 24 socks in her drawer. 12 of them are grey, 8 of them are black and 4 of them are red. Katie takes two socks at random, without replacement, from the drawer. Calculate the probability that she takes two socks that have the same colour.

....

(5 marks)

3 A school canteen offers a choice of main course and sweet.
For each course, one of two choices must be selected with the probabilities shown below.
Complete the tree diagram:

(a)

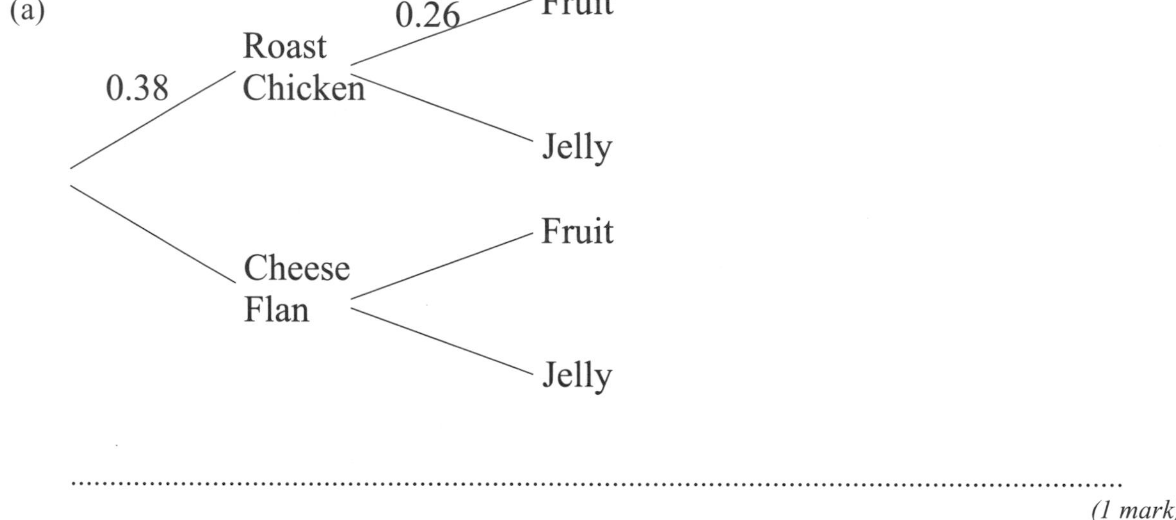

....

(1 mark)

(b) Work out the probability that a pupil chooses roast chicken and jelly.

....

(2 marks)

4 There are 9 balls in a box. 8 of the balls are yellow and 1 ball is red. Simon selects balls at random, without replacement, from the box until he obtains the red ball.
When he obtains the red ball, he stops selecting.
By extending the tree diagram shown below, or otherwise, calculate the probability that Simon selects the red ball on one of his first three selections.

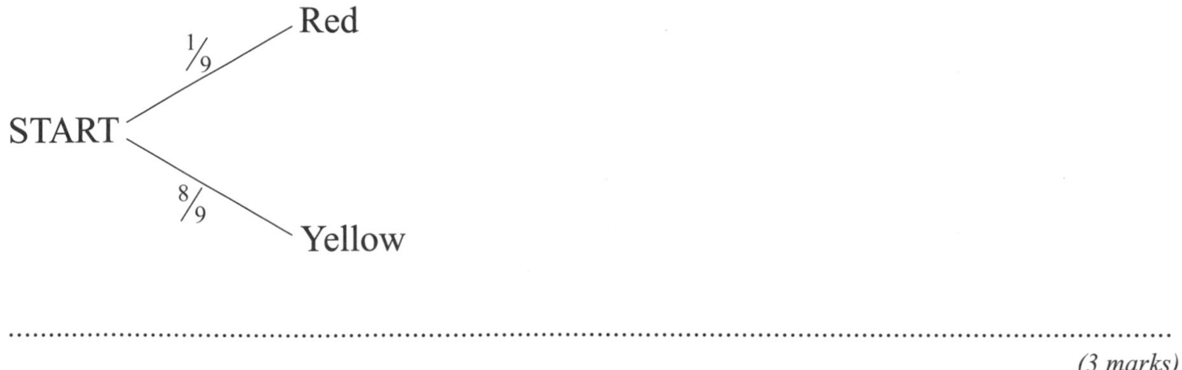

....

(3 marks)

Mean, Median, Mode and Range

If you don't manage to *learn these four basic definitions* then you'll be passing up on some of the easiest marks in the whole Exam. It can't be that difficult can it?

1) MODE = MOST common

2) MEDIAN = MIDDLE value

3) MEAN = TOTAL of items ÷ NUMBER of items

4) RANGE = How far from the smallest to the biggest

THE GOLDEN RULE

Mean, median and mode should be *easy marks*, but even people who've gone to the incredible extent of learning them still manage to lose marks in the Exam because they don't do *this one vital step:*

Always REARRANGE the data in ASCENDING ORDER

(and check you have the same number of entries)

Example: "Find the mean, median, mode and range of these numbers:"

2, 5, 3, 2, 6, -4, 0, 9, -3, 1, 6, 3, -2, 3 (14 numbers)

1) FIRST... rearrange them: -4, -3, -2, 0, 1, 2, 2, 3, 3, 3, 5, 6, 6, 9 (14)✓

2) MEAN $= \frac{\text{total}}{\text{number}} = \frac{-4-3-2+0+1+2+2+3+3+3+5+6+6+9}{14}$

$= 31 \div 14 = \underline{2.21}$

3) MEDIAN = *the middle value* (only when they are *arranged in order of size*).

When there are two middle numbers as in this case, then the median is HALFWAY BETWEEN THE TWO MIDDLE NUMBERS

-4, -3, -2, 0, 1, 2, 2, 3, 3, 3, 5, 6, 6, 9

seven numbers this side ↑ seven numbers this side

Median = 2.5

4) MODE = *most* common value, which is simply 3. *(Or you can say "The modal value is 3")*

5) RANGE = distance from lowest to highest value, i.e. from -4 up to 9, = 13

REMEMBER: Mode = most (emphasise the 'o' in each when you say them)
Median = mid (emphasise the m_d in each when you say them)
Mean is just the average, but it's mean 'cos you have to work it out.

Mean, median, mode & range — easy marks for learning four words

The maths involved in working these out is so simple that you'd be mad not to learn the definitions. As long as you remember which is which and don't make careless arithmetic errors, there's marks to be had.

Frequency Tables

Frequency Tables can either be done in rows or in columns of numbers.
They can be quite confusing, but not if you learn these eight key points:

Eight **key** points:

1) ALL FREQUENCY TABLES ARE THE SAME.
2) The word FREQUENCY just means HOW MANY, so a frequency table is nothing more than a "How many in each group" table.
3) The FIRST ROW (or column) just gives the GROUP LABELS.
4) The SECOND ROW (or column) gives the ACTUAL DATA.
5) You have to WORK OUT A THIRD ROW (or column) yourself (see next page).
6) The MEAN is always found using: 3rd Row total ÷ 2nd Row Total
7) The MEDIAN is found from the MIDDLE VALUE in the 2nd row.
8) The RANGE is found from the extremes of the first row.

Example:

No. of Sisters	Frequency
0	7
1	15
2	12
3	8
4	3
5	1
6	0

Here is a typical frequency table shown in both ROW FORM and COLUMN FORM:

No. of Sisters	0	1	2	3	4	5	6
Frequency	7	15	12	8	3	1	0

Column Form

Row Form

There's no real difference between these two forms and you could get either one in your Exam. Whichever you get, make sure you remember these THREE IMPORTANT FACTS:

1) THE 1ST ROW (or column) gives us the GROUP LABELS for the different categories: i.e. "no sisters", "one sister", "two sisters", etc.
2) THE 2ND ROW (or column) is the ACTUAL DATA and tells us HOW MANY (people) THERE ARE in each category i.e. 7 people had "no sisters", 15 people had "one sister", etc.
3) BUT YOU SHOULD SEE THE TABLE AS UNFINISHED, because it still needs A THIRD ROW (or column) and TWO TOTALS for the 2nd and 3rd rows, as shown on the next page...

A frequency table is just a "how many in each group" table

As so often in maths the words they use can be really off-putting. Once you realise that a frequency table really just shows you how many things are in each group, life becomes a lot easier.

Frequency Tables — 3rd Row

With frequency tables you always need to make a third row...

Multiply to make a third row...

Here's what the two types of table look like when they are complete:

No. of sisters	0	1	2	3	4	5	6	Totals	
Frequency	7	15	12	8	3	1	0	46	(People asked)
No. × Frequency	0	15	24	24	12	5	0	80	(Sisters)

No. of Sisters	Frequency	No. × Frequency
0	7	0
1	15	15
2	12	24
3	8	24
4	3	12
5	1	5
6	0	0
TOTALS	46	80
	(People asked)	(Sisters)

"Where does the third row come from?

....I hear you cry!

THE THIRD ROW (or column) is ALWAYS obtained by MULTIPLYING the numbers FROM THE FIRST TWO ROWS (or columns).

third row = 1st row × 2nd row

As soon as you see a frequency table — make a third row

To make the third row just multiply the other two rows together — what could be simpler? But why do you need the third row? Well once you've learnt all this, get on to the next page and you'll see...

Frequency Tables — Mean, Median, etc

A lot of the exam questions on frequency tables will ask you to find our old friends: mean, median, mode and range. With the help of the third row, nothing could be easier or more enjoyable*.

Mean, Median, Mode and Range:

This is easy enough *if you learn it*. If you don't, you'll drown in a sea of numbers. The examples below show how to do it for the frequency tables on the previous page.

1) MEAN = $\frac{\text{3rd Row Total}}{\text{2nd Row Total}}$

$= \frac{80}{46} = \underline{1.74}$ (Sisters per person)

2) MEDIAN: — imagine the original data *SET OUT IN ASCENDING ORDER*:

0000000 11111111111111 222222222222 33333333 444 5

↑

The median is just the middle which is here between the 23rd and 24th digits,

So for this data THE MEDIAN IS 2. (Of course, when you get slick at this you can easily find the position of the middle value straight from the table)

3) The MODE is just THE GROUP WITH THE MOST ENTRIES:

This is very easy. In this example it's 1

4) The RANGE is obvious from the table

The first row tells us there are people with anything from "no sisters" right up to "five sisters" (but not 6 sisters).
So the range is 5 – 0 = 5

(Always give it as a single number)

Frequency tables easily show the mean, mode, median and range

Exam questions will often ask you to get the mean, mode, median and range from a frequency table. As long as you have learnt the four boxes on this page, you shouldn't have any trouble whatsoever.

*The later statement in this sentence may only be true for those who should get out more.

Grouped Frequency Tables

These are a bit trickier than simple frequency tables, but they can still look deceptively simple, like this one which shows the distribution of weights of a bunch of 60 school kids.

Weight (kg)	31 — 40	41 — 50	51 — 60	61 — 70	71 — 80
Frequency	8	16	18	12	6

You can see the difference with grouped frequency tables by looking at the example above.

Instead of having a category for each individual weight, the kids have been divided into groups.

The frequency then shows the number of students whose weight falls into that category.

For example 16 children weigh between 41 and 50 kg.

*Class **boundaries** and mid-interval **values***

These are the two little jokers that make Grouped Frequency tables so tricky.

1) THE CLASS BOUNDARIES are the precise values where you'd pass from one group into the next.

For the above table the class boundaries would be at 40.5, 50.5, 60.5, etc.

It's not difficult to work out what the class boundaries will be, just so long as you're clued up about it — they're nearly always "something.5" anyway, for obvious reasons.

2) THE MID-INTERVAL VALUES

These are pretty self-explanatory really and usually end up being "something.5" as well. Mind you, a bit of care is needed to make sure you get the exact middle.

Class boundaries and mid-interval values are exactly what they say

The class boundary is the boundary between classes, and the mid-interval values are the values in the middle of the intervals — not exactly imaginative these mathematicians but at least it makes them easier to learn.

Grouped Frequency Tables — Estimating Mean

"Estimating" the **mean** using **mid-interval values**

Just like with ordinary frequency tables you have to *add extra rows and find totals* to be able to work anything out.

Also notice you can only "estimate" the mean from grouped data tables — you can't find it exactly unless you know all the original values.

1) Add a 3rd row and enter MID-INTERVAL VALUES for each group.

2) Add a 4th row and multiply FREQUENCY × MID-INTERVAL VALUE for each group.

Weight (kg)	31 — 40	41 — 50	51 — 60	61 — 70	71 — 80	TOTALS
Frequency	8	16	18	12	6	60
Mid-Interval Value	35.5	45.5	55.5	65.5	75.5	—
Frequency × Mid-Interval Value	284	728	999	786	453	3250

1) ESTIMATING THE MEAN is then the usual thing of DIVIDING THE TOTALS:

$$\text{Mean} = \frac{\text{Overall Total (Final Row)}}{\text{Frequency Total (2nd Row)}} = \frac{3250}{60} = \underline{\mathbf{54.2}}$$

2) THE MODE is still nice'n'easy: the modal group is 51 - 60kg

3) THE MEDIAN can't be found exactly but you can at least say which group it's in.
If all the data were put in order, the 30th/31st entries would be in the 51 - 60kg group.

This time there are two rows to add

With frequency tables there was just one row to add. With grouped frequency tables there are two. It's still easy enough though as long as you remember what the rows are and how to find them.

Cumulative Frequency

Four key points

1) CUMULATIVE FREQUENCY just means ADDING IT UP AS YOU GO ALONG.

2) You have to ADD A THIRD ROW to the table — the RUNNING TOTAL of the frequency (the 2nd row).

3) When plotting the graph, always plot points using the HIGHEST VALUE in each group (of row 1) with the running total value (from row 3).

4) CUMULATIVE FREQUENCY is always plotted up the side of a graph, not across.

Three vital statistics

For a *cumulative frequency curve* there are *three vital statistics* which you need to know how to find:

1) MEDIAN
Exactly halfway UP, then across, then down and *read off the bottom scale*.

2) LOWER AND UPPER QUARTILES
Exactly ¼ and ¾ UP the side, then across, then down and *read off the bottom scale*.

3) THE INTERQUARTILE RANGE
The distance *on the bottom scale* between the lower and upper quartiles.

A Box Plot shows the Interquartile Range as a Box

To make a box plot you need to:

1) *Draw the scale* along the bottom.
2) *Draw a box* the length of the *interquartile range*.
3) *Draw a line* down the box to show the *median*.
4) *Draw "whiskers"* up to the *maximum and minimum*.

Because of these whiskers they're sometimes called "Box and Whisker diagrams".

Four key points, three vital statistics — and a box plot in a pear tree

Here's cumulative frequencies broken down into four points and three statistics — get it learnt. Then there's a big example on the next page to explain a bit more and make sure you've got it all in your head.

Cumulative Frequency — Median and Quartiles

Example

Height (cm)	141 – 150	151 – 160	161 – 170	171 – 180	181 – 190	191 – 200	201 – 210
Frequency	4	9	20	33	36	15	3
Cumulative Frequency	4 (AT 150.5)	13 (AT 160.5)	33 (AT 170.5)	66 (AT 180.5)	102 (AT 190.5)	117 (AT 200.5)	120 (AT 210.5)

The graph is plotted from these pairs:

(150.5,4) (160.5,13) (170.5,33) (180.5,66) etc.

Note that the points are plotted using the HIGHEST VALUE in each group (of row 1) with the value from row 3. i.e. plot 13 at 160.5.

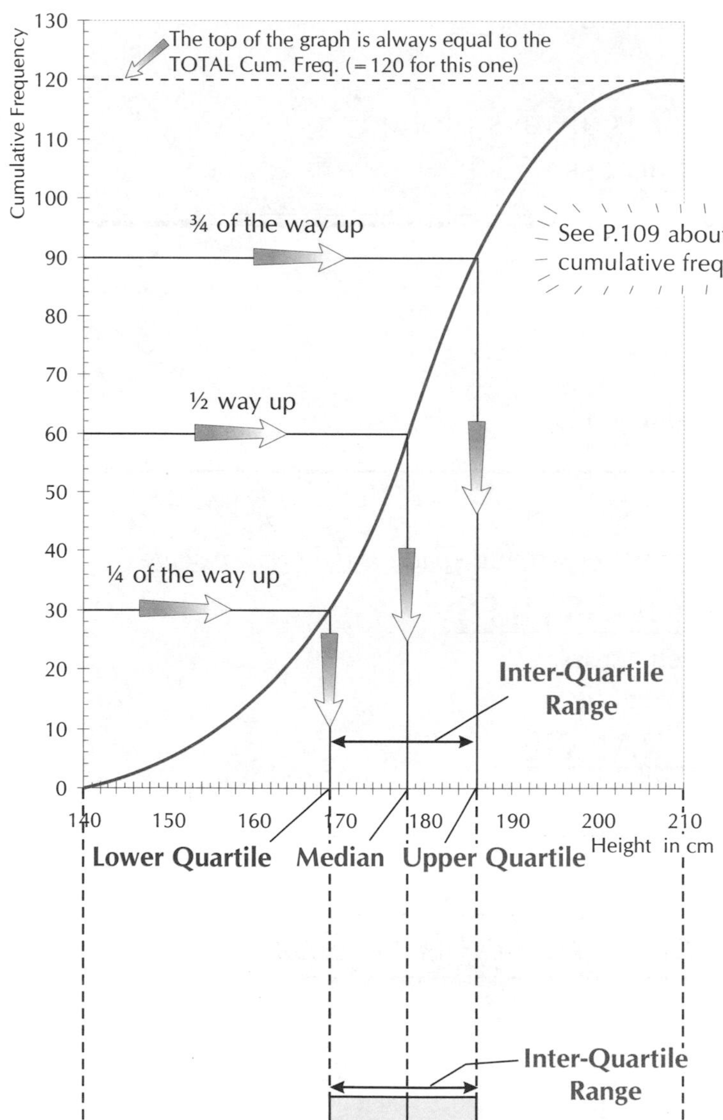

See P.109 about the *shape* of cumulative frequency curves.

So from the cumulative frequency curve for this data, we get these results:

MEDIAN = 178 cm

LOWER QUARTILE = 169 cm

UPPER QUARTILE = 186 cm

INTER-QUARTILE RANGE = 17 cm (186-169)

This example should leave you crystal clear on cumulative frequency

If some of these details are still hazy, go back over the previous page. It's tempting to nod your head and skip over and think you've learnt it. But nodding and skipping won't get any marks in the exam.

Warm-Up and Worked Exam Questions

By the time the big day comes you need to know all the facts in these warm-up questions and all the exam questions like the back of your hand. It's not easy, but it's the only way to get good marks.

Warm-Up Questions

1) Write down the 4 basic definitions of the following: Mode, Median, Mean and Range.
2) For the following frequency table find the:
(a) Mean; (b) Median; (c) Mode; (d) Range.

Number of cars	0	1	2	3	4	5	6
Frequency	1	24	36	31	22	9	1

3) The grouped frequency table below represents data from 79 random people.
(a) Estimate the mean; (b) Give an approximate value for the median;
(c) State the modal group.

Height (cm)	145-	155-	165-	175-185
Frequency	18	22	24	15

Worked Exam Question

There's no better preparation for exam questions than doing, err... practice exam questions. Hang on, what's this I see...

1 Steve carried out an experiment. He placed a small rat inside a maze and timed how long it took to escape. He plotted his results on the cumulative frequency graph below.

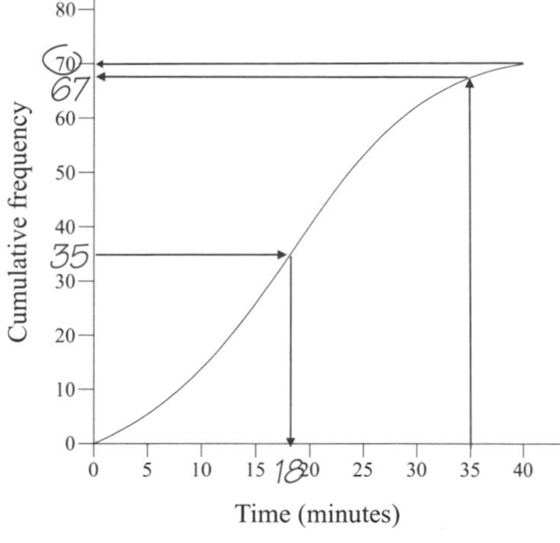

(a) How many times did Steve carry out the experiment?

70 times.

(1 mark)

(b) Use the cumulative frequency graph to find an estimate of the median time.

$70 \div 2 = 35$. So read off off the time at 35. That gives 18 minutes.

(2 marks)

(c) Use the cumulative frequency graph to find what percentage of times were less than 35 minutes.

$67 \div 70 \times 100 = 95.7\,\%$.

(3 marks)

Exam Questions

2 A survey was made of the time spent by each of 500 customers at the check-outs of a supermarket. The results were recorded in the frequency table below:

Time (t mins)	Frequency
$0 < t \leq 1$	77
$1 < t \leq 2$	142
$2 < t \leq 3$	143
$3 < t \leq 4$	60
$4 < t \leq 5$	49
$5 < t \leq 6$	29

(a) Calculate the average time spent by each customer at the checkout (in minutes).

....

(4 marks)

(b) Complete the cumulative frequency table.

Time (≤ mins)	Cumulative Frequency
1	77
2	
3	
4	
5	
6	

(3 marks)

(c) Draw the cumulative frequency curve on the axes below.

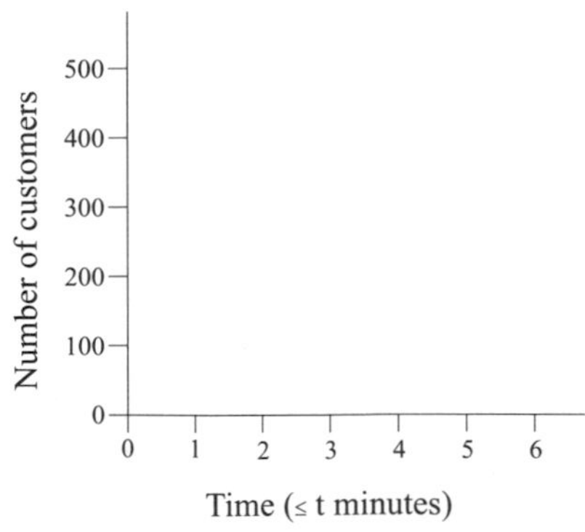

(4 marks)

(d) Use the graph to estimate:

(i) The median time (in minutes).

....

(1 mark)

(ii) The interquartile range (in minutes).

....

(2 marks)

Histograms and Frequency Density

Histograms

A histogram is just a bar chart where the bars can be of DIFFERENT widths.

This changes them from nice easy-to-understand diagrams into seemingly incomprehensible monsters, and yes, you've guessed it, that makes them a firm favourite with the Examiners.

In fact things aren't half as bad as that — but only if you LEARN THE THREE RULES:

1) It's not the height, but the AREA of each bar that matters.
2) Use the snip of information they give you to find HOW MUCH IS REPRESENTED BY EACH AREA BLOCK.
3) Divide all the bars into THE SAME SIZED AREA BLOCKS and so work out the *number* for each bar (using AREAS). This means working out what a unit of area represents.

EXAMPLE:
The histogram below represents the age distribution of people arrested for shop lifting in 1995. Given that there were 36 people in the 55 to 65 age range, find the number of people arrested in all the other age ranges.

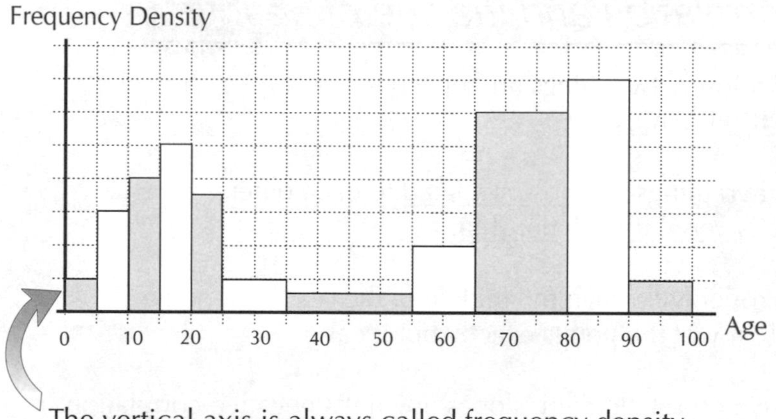

The vertical axis is always called frequency density...

ANSWER:
The 55-65 bar represents *36 people* and contains *4 dotted squares*, so *each dotted square* must represent *9 people*. *The rest is easy*. E.g. the 80-90 group has 14 dotted squares so that represents 14×9=*126 people*.

REMEMBER: ALWAYS COUNT AREA BLOCKS to find THE NUMBER IN EACH BAR.

Frequency Density = Frequency ÷ Class Width

You don't need to worry too much about this. It says in the syllabus that you need to understand frequency density, so here it is. Learn the formula and you'll be fine.

*With histograms it's **area** not height which matters*

The histogram is an odd beast — like a bar chart with funny columns . However, all you need to do is work out how much is represented by each area block and then divide the bars into those blocks.

Stem and Leaf Diagrams and Scatter Graphs

Stem and leaf diagrams **use numbers** instead of bars...

If you get one of these in the exam, you're laughing. It's the <u>EASIEST THING IN THE WORLD</u>.

1) Put the data in order
2) Put it in groups and make a key
3) Draw the diagram

7, 11, 12, 13, 16, 17, 20, 23, 24, 24, 25, 26, 26, 29, 29, 31, 32, 34

This looks like it'll split nicely into tens: Key: 2 | 3 = 23

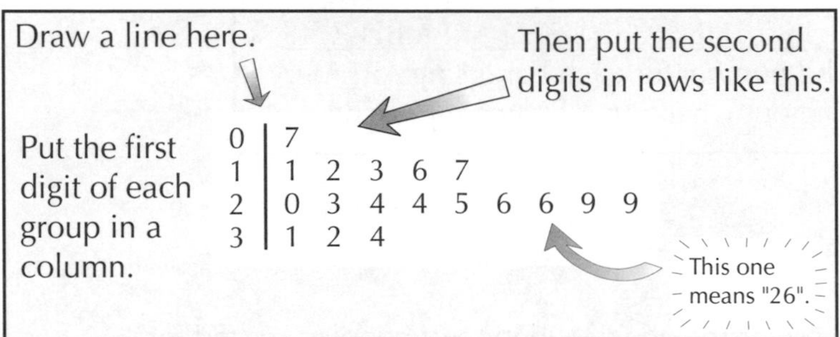

Scatter graphs - correlation and the line of best fit

A scatter graph tells you how closely two things are related — the fancy word for this is <u>CORRELATION</u>.

<u>Good correlation</u> means the two things are <u>closely related</u> to each other.
<u>Poor correlation</u> means there is <u>very little relationship</u>.

The <u>LINE OF BEST FIT</u> goes roughly <u>through the middle of the scatter of points</u>.
(It doesn't have to go through any of the points exactly but it can.)

If the line slopes <u>up</u> it's <u>positive correlation</u>, if it slopes <u>down</u> it's <u>negative correlation</u>.
<u>No correlation</u> means there's no <u>linear relationship</u>.

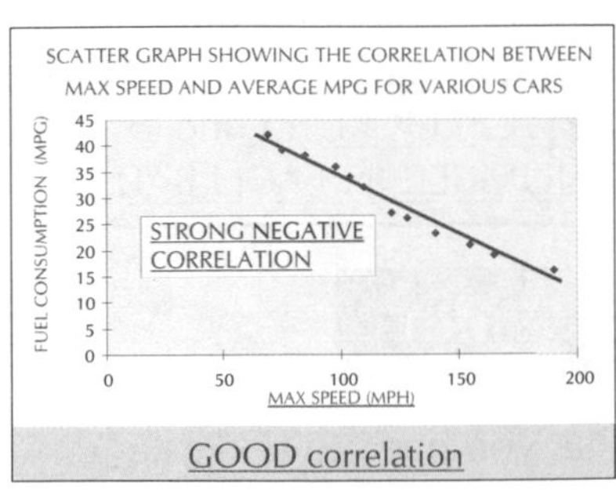

<u>GOOD correlation</u>

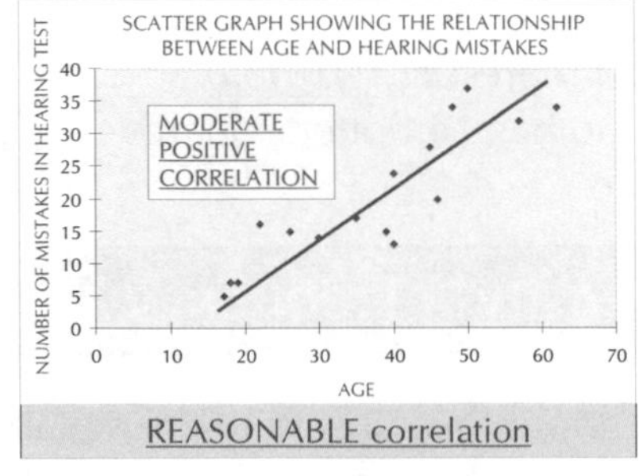

<u>REASONABLE correlation</u>

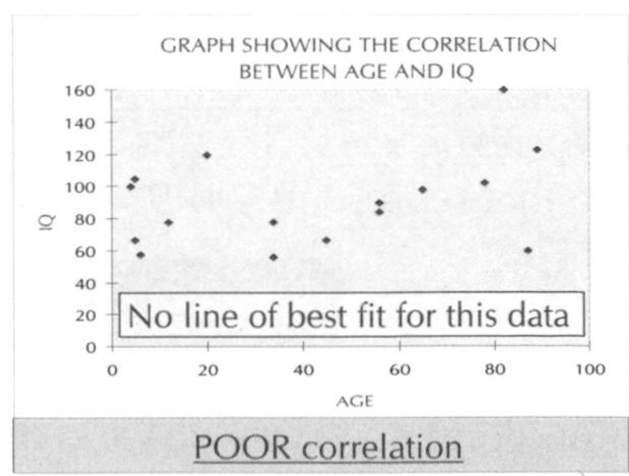

<u>POOR correlation</u>

Two straightforward types of diagram

For stem and leaf diagrams you just have to remember those three simple steps. Scatter graphs are a bit harder because there are more terms to learn like correlation, good and bad, positive and negative...

Dispersion and Spread

Shapes of **histograms** and **"spread"**

You can easily estimate the mean from the shape of a histogram — it's more or less IN THE MIDDLE.

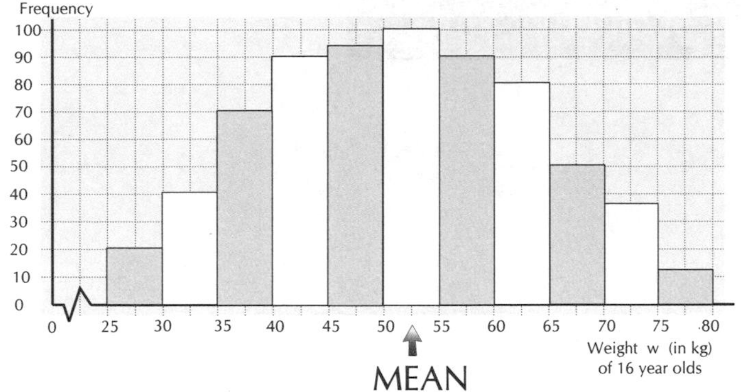

You must *LEARN the significance of the shapes* of these two histograms:

1) The first shows *high dispersion* (i.e. a *large spread* of results away from the mean).

   (i.e. the weights of a sample of 16 year olds will cover a very wide range)

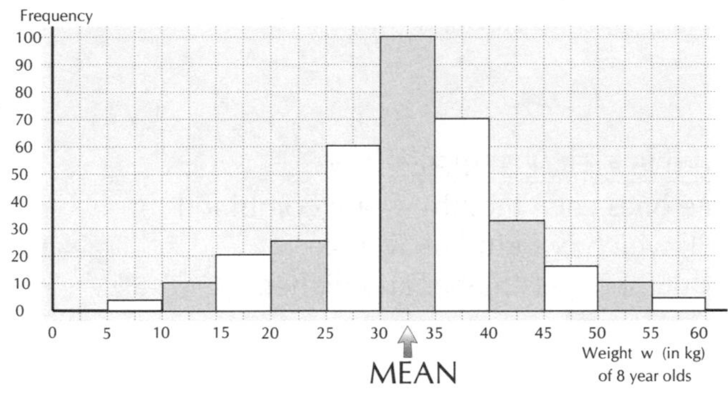

2) The second shows a *"tighter"* distribution of results where most values are within a *narrow range* either side of the mean.

   (i.e the weights of a sample of 8 year olds will show very little variation)

Cumulative Frequency **Curves** and **"spread"**

The shape of a CUMULATIVE FREQUENCY CURVE also tells us *how spread out* the data values are.

The *blue* line shows a *very tight distribution* around the MEDIAN and this also means the *interquartile range is small* as shown.

The *red* line shows a more *widely spread* set of data and therefore a *larger interquartile range*.

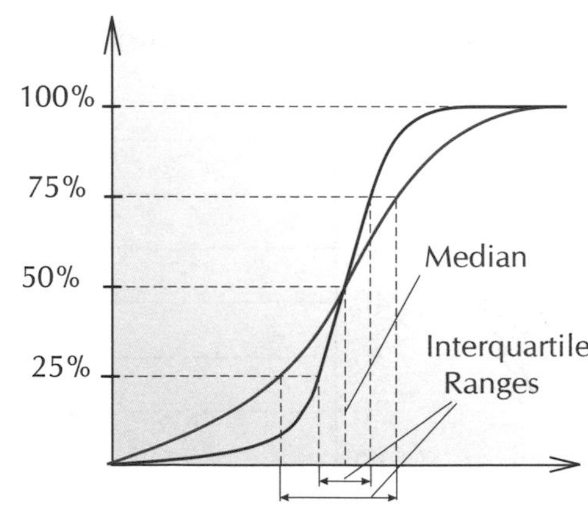

The 'tighter' distribution (blue line) represents very CONSISTENT results, e.g. lifetimes of batteries or light bulbs all very close to the median indicate a better product, compared to the other distribution (red line) where the lifetimes show wide variation (albeit with the same median).
They often ask about this "shape significance" in Exams.

And two more

That's four different types of charts over the last two pages. You need to learn all their features.
Don't forget questions about the significance of different shapes of graph and chart.

Time Series

Time series — measure the same thing over a period of time

A time series is what you get if you measure the same thing at a number of different times.

EXAMPLE:

Measuring the temperature in your greenhouse at 12 o'clock each day gives you a time series — other examples might be profit figures, crime figures or rainfall.

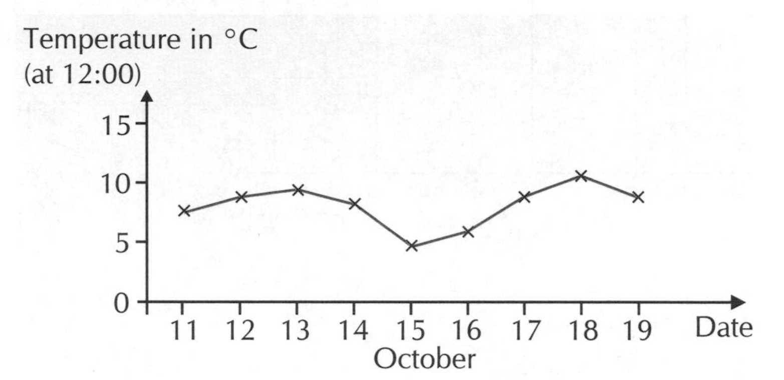

THE RETAIL PRICE INDEX (RPI) IS A TIME SERIES:
Every month, the prices of loads of items (same ones each month) — are combined to get an index number called the RPI, which is a kind of average. As goods get more expensive, this index number gets higher and higher.

Trend — ignoring the wrinkles

This time series has lots of random fluctuations but there's a definite upwards *trend*.

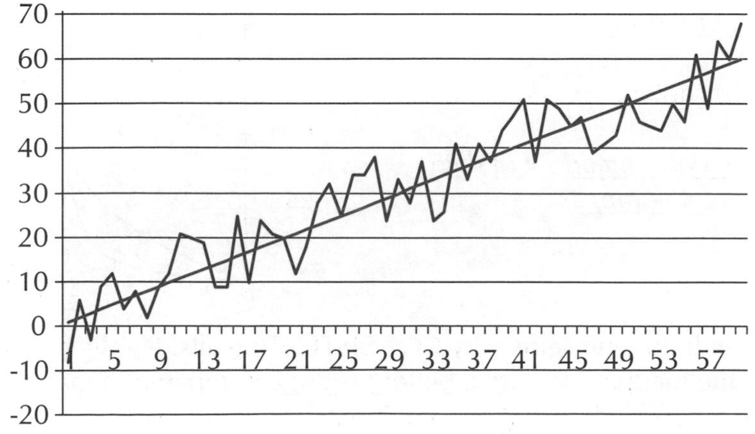

The pink line is the trend line.
It's straight, so this is a linear trend.

Time series — it's a series of measurements over a period of time

There are loads of examples of time series but you deal with all of them in the same way.
So don't be phased if the one in the exam looks a bit unfamiliar — just look for trends in the same way.

Time Series

Seasonality — the *same basic pattern*

This is when there's a definite pattern that *REPEATS ITSELF* every so often.

This is called *SEASONALITY* and the *"so often"* is called the *PERIOD*.

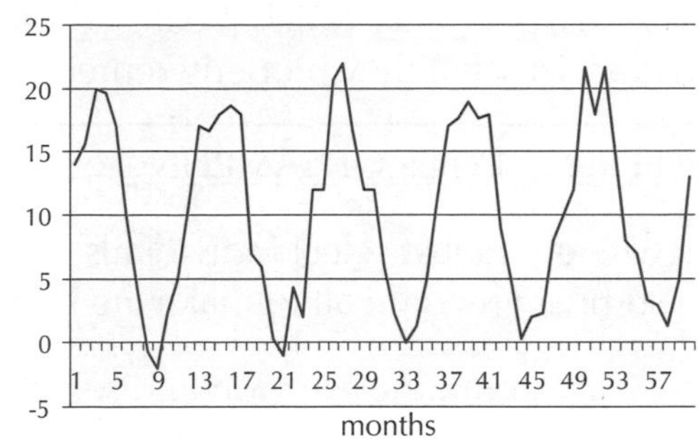

To find the *PERIOD*, measure *PEAK TO PEAK* (or trough to trough).

This series has a *period of 12 months*. There are a few irregularities, so the pattern isn't exactly the same every 12 months, but it's about right.

Moving average — *smooths out* the *seasonality*

It's easier to spot a trend if you can 'get rid of' the seasonality and some of the irregularities. One way to smooth the series is to use a *moving average*.

This is a time series that definitely looks periodic — but it's difficult to tell if there's a trend.

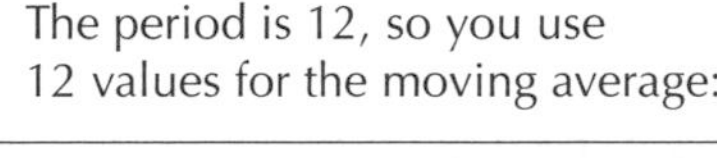

The period is 12, so you use
12 values for the moving average:

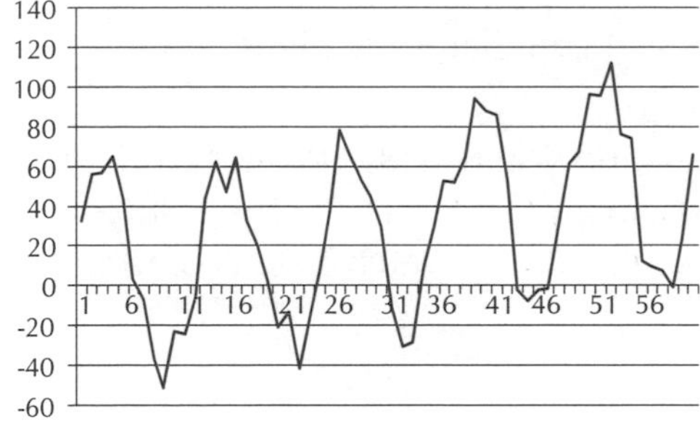

... but plot the moving average (shown here in pink)...

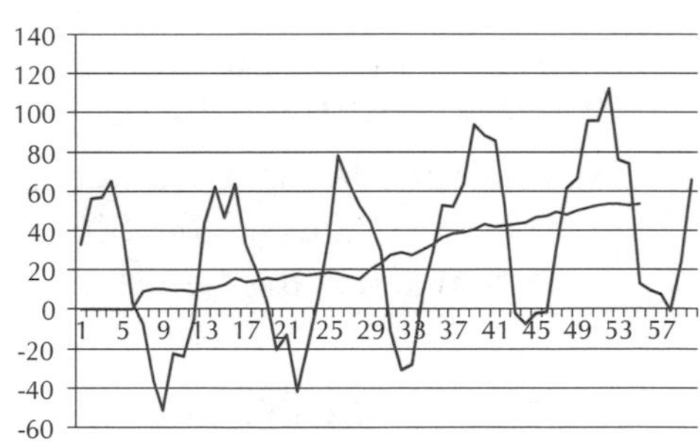

...and you can easily see the *upward trend*.

HOW TO FIND A MOVING AVERAGE:

month	1	2	3	4	5	6	7	8	9	10	11	12	13	14	...
temperature	38.00	42.30	59.00	32.30	25.00	2.00	-5.00	-51.30	-35.00	-45.30	-22.00	1.00	49.00	62.30	...

Find the average of these 12 values...

...then of these...

...then of these, and so on.

That's three factors to think about when dealing with time series

You need to know about trends, seasonality and moving averages. If any of these only ring vague bells you need to go back over these two pages until the bells ring loud and clear.

Sampling Methods

This is all about doing surveys of 'populations' (not necessarily people) to find things out about them. Things get tricky when it's not possible to test the whole 'population', usually because there's just too many.

In that case you have to take a SAMPLE, which means you somehow have to select a limited number of individuals so that they properly represent the whole 'population'.

There are FOUR DIFFERENT TYPES OF SAMPLING which you should know about:

RANDOM — this is where you just select individuals "at random".
In practice it can be surprisingly difficult to make the selection truly random.

SYSTEMATIC — Start with a random selection and select every 10th or 100th one after that.

STRATIFIED — as in "strata" or "layers". e.g. to survey pupils in a school you would first pick a selection of the classes, and then pick students at random from those classes.

QUOTA — This is where you pick a sample which as far as possible reflects the whole population by having the same proportion of, say, males/females or adults/children etc.

*Spotting problems with **sampling methods***

The most important thing you have to be able to do is to spot problems with sampling techniques, i.e. "look for ways that the sample might not be a true reflection of the population as a whole". One mildly amusing way to practise, is to think up examples of bad sampling techniques:

1) A survey of motorists carried out in London concluded that 85% of the British people drive black cabs.
2) Two surveys carried out on the same street corner asked "Do you believe in God?" One found 90% of people didn't and the other found 90% of people did. The reason for the discrepancy? — one was carried out at 11pm Saturday night and the other at 10.15am Sunday morning.
3) A telephone survey carried out in the evening asked "What do you usually do after work or school?". It found that 80% of the population usually stay in and watch TV. A street survey conducted at the same time found that only 30% usually stay in and watch TV. Astonishing.

Other cases are less obvious:

In a telephone poll, 100 people were asked if they use the train regularly and 20% said yes. Does this mean 20% of the population regularly use the train?

ANSWER: Probably not. There are several things wrong with this sampling technique:

1) First and worst: the sample is far too small. At least 1000 would be more like it.
2) What about people who don't have their own phone, e.g. students, tenants etc.
3) What time of day was it done? When might regular train users be in or out?
4) Which part or parts of the region would you telephone?
5) If the results were to represent say the whole country then stratified or quota sampling would be essential.

*Don't be **random** — **systematically** learn the **quota** of **stratified** facts...*

Lots of statistics are flawed in one way or another. It's important you look out for problems with samples, not only for your maths exam, but every time you read the paper or watch the news.

Warm-Up Questions

There's a whole page of warm-up questions here covering stem and leaf diagrams, correlation and sampling. Now's the time to go back over any bits you're not sure of — in the exam it'll be too late.

Warm-Up Questions

1) Draw a stem and leaf diagram for this data:
17, 12, 4, 19, 23, 29, 12, 25, 31, 2, 39, 9.

2) Decide what type of correlation best describes the two scatter graphs below.

Graph 1 showing correlation between the amount of ice creams sold and hours of sunshine

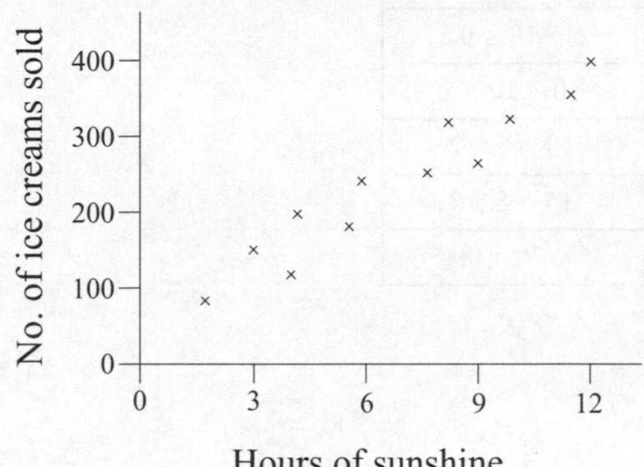

Graph 2 showing correlation between the average temperature and rainfall for ten weeks in a particular country

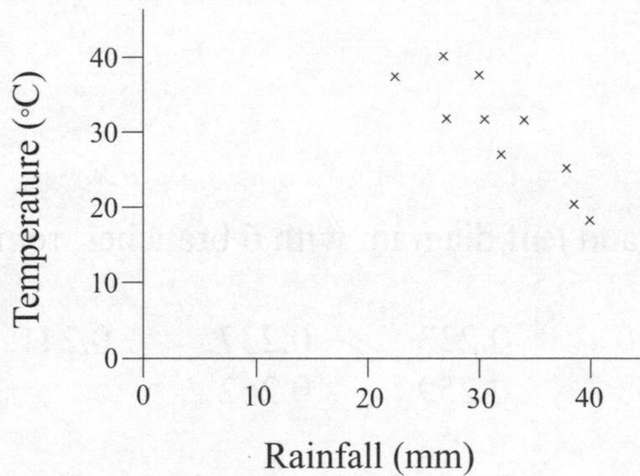

3) Mr Smith is an accountant. He is sampling from a computer file. The first number is randomly selected and is item 5; the rest of the sample is selected automatically and consists of items 55, 105, 155, 205, 255, 305, ...
What type of sampling procedure is being used?

4) The following situation involves a population and a sample.
Identify both and also identify the source of probable bias:
A flour company wants to know what proportion of Birmingham households bake some or all of their own bread. A sample of 600 residential addresses in Birmingham is taken and interviewers are sent to these addresses. The interviewers are employed during regular working hours on weekdays and interview only during these hours.

Worked Exam Questions

Worked Exam Questions

It's no good learning all the facts in the world if you go to pieces or just write nonsense in the exam. These worked examples show how to make all those facts into good answers — and earn yourself marks.

1 In a convenience store, small mixed bags of sweets are sold.
45 bags were weighed and put into the table below.

Weight of sweets (g)	$0g < x \le 10g$	$10g < x \le 20g$	$20g < x \le 25g$	$25g < x \le 30g$	$30g < x \le 50g$
Frequency	5	10	10	15	5

x	Frequency	Class Width	Frequency Density
$0g < x \le 10g$	5	10 - 0 = 10	$5 \div 10 = 0.5$
$10g < x \le 20g$	10	20 - 10 = 10	$10 \div 10 = 1$
$20g < x \le 25g$	10	25 - 20 = 5	$10 \div 5 = 2$
$25g < x \le 30g$	15	30 - 25 = 5	$15 \div 5 = 3$
$30g < x \le 50g$	5	50 - 30 = 20	$5 \div 20 = 0.25$

Draw a histogram for this data.

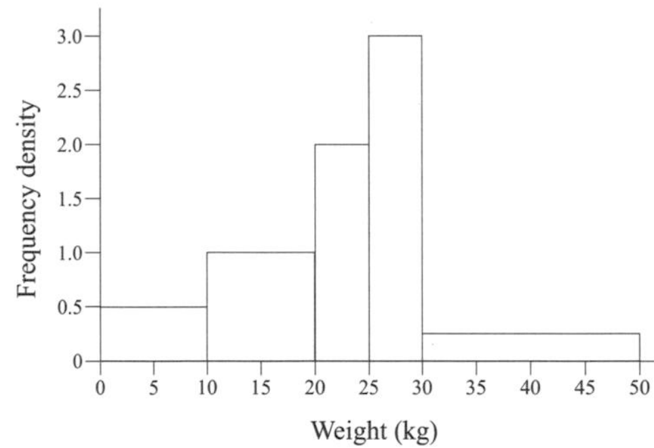

(3 marks)

2 Show the following numbers on a stem and leaf diagram with 6 branches, remembering to include the appropriate scale.

0.212 0.223 0.226 0.230 0.233 0.237 0.241
0.242 0.248 0.253 0.253 0.259 0.262

22 | 6 represents 0.226

21	2
22	3 6
23	0 3 7
24	1 2 8
25	3 3 9
26	2

(2 marks)

Exam Questions

3 A hamlet has a population of 720.
The population is classified by age, as shown in the table below.

Age (years)	0-5	6-12	13-21	22-35	36-50	51+
No. of people	38	82	108	204	180	108

A survey of the residents of the hamlet is intended. A sample size of 80 is projected.

(a) What is the overall sampling fraction?

....

(b) A stratified sample is planned. Calculate the approximate number that should be sampled from each age group.

....

(3 marks)

4 The durations of sixty pop songs recorded by a certain band are outlined in the table below:

Song length in seconds (x)	No. of songs
$0 < x < 120$	1
$120 \leq x < 180$	9
$180 \leq x < 240$	15
$240 \leq x < 300$	17
$300 \leq x < 360$	13
$360 \leq x \leq 600$	5

(a) Display the data on a histogram.

....

(2 marks)

(b) Determine the mean song length.

....

(2 marks)

Exam Questions

5 The table below shows the amount of blackcurrant cartons that were sold at a seaside supermarket and the number of hours of sunshine for 10 days in August last year.

Cartons of blackcurrant	410	780	610	700	1290	1590	1110	1650	1560	1900
Sunshine (hours)	3	4	5	6	7	8	9	10	11	12

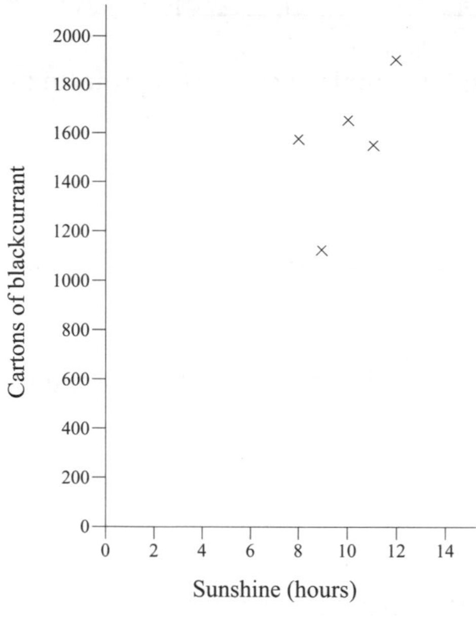

The last 5 results have been plotted on the scatter graph.

(a) Complete the scatter graph by plotting the first 5 results.

....

(1 mark)

(b) Describe, in a few words, the relationship between the hours of sunshine and the amount of cartons sold.

....

(1 mark)

(c) Draw a line of best fit on the scatter graph.

....

(1 mark)

(d) By using your line of best fit, find estimates for the following:

(i) the amount of sunshine when 1000 cartons were sold.

....

(1 mark)

(ii) the amount of cartons sold when there were 9½ hours of sunshine.

....

(1 mark)

Revision Summary for Section Four

Here's the really fun page. The inevitable list of straight-down-the-middle questions to test how much you know. Remember, these questions will sort out quicker than anything else can, exactly what you *know* and what you *don't*. And that's exactly what revision is all about, don't forget: finding out what you DON'T know and then learning it until you do. Enjoy.

Keep learning the basic facts until you know them

1) What is the most useful thing you should know about probability questions?
2) What two things must you do to take full advantage of this?
3) Draw a general tree diagram and put all the features on it.
4) There are four other important things to know about probability. What are they?
5) Write down the definitions of mean, median, mode and range.
6) What is the Golden Rule for finding the above for a set of data?
7) Write down eight important details about frequency tables.
8) What are the class boundaries in a grouped frequency table?
9) How do you find the mid-interval values and what do you use them for?
10) How do you *estimate* the mean from a grouped frequency table?
11) Why can you only estimate the mean in a grouped frequency table?
12) Write down four key points about cumulative frequency tables.
13) Draw a typical cumulative frequency curve, and indicate on it exactly where the median is to be found.
14) Draw a box plot underneath your cumulative frequency curve from question 13.
15) What is a histogram?
16) What is the difference between a histogram and a regular bar chart?
17) What are the three steps of the method for tackling all histograms?
18) Write down the formula for frequency density.
19) What is a stem and leaf diagram?
20) What is a scatter graph?
21) What does a scatter graph illustrate? What is the fancy word for this?
22) Draw three examples to illustrate the three main types of correlation.
23) What is the meaning of dispersion?
24) Can you deduce anything about the dispersion of a set of data from the shape of the histogram?
25) How do you estimate the mean from looking at a histogram?
26) Draw two histograms, one showing high dispersion, the other not.
27) Give examples of real data that might match each histogram.
28) Do cumulative frequency curves tell us anything about dispersion?
29) Draw two contrasting cumulative frequency curves.
30) Give an example of what these curves might represent and say what the significant difference between the two things will be.
31) Which numerical figure represents dispersion on a cumulative frequency curve?
32) When is sampling needed?
33) Name the four main sampling methods, with a brief description of each.
34) List five common problems with conducting surveys.
35) Which one of these is NOT a time series?
    a) measuring the temperature in 20 different countries at 12:00 today, GMT,
    b) measuring the temperature in Britain at 12:00 every day for 100 days,
    c) the Retail Price Index.
36) How can you find out if a seasonal time series has an overall trend?

Straight Lines You Should Just Know

You ought to know these simple graphs straight off with no hesitation:

1) **Vertical** and **horizontal** lines: "x = a" and "y = b"

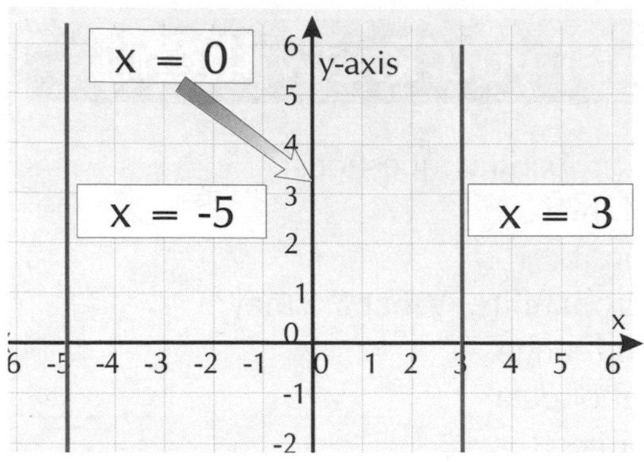

x = a is a vertical line through "a" on the x-axis

Don't forget: the y-axis is also the line x = 0

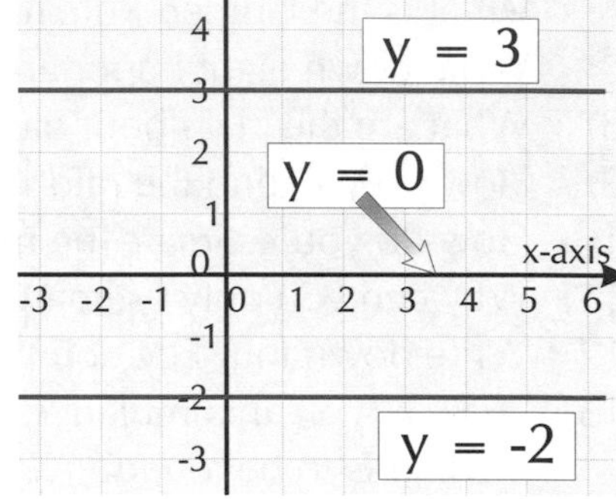

y = a is a horizontal line through "a" on the y-axis

Don't forget: the x-axis is also the line y = 0

2) The **main diagonals**: "y = x" and "y = -x"

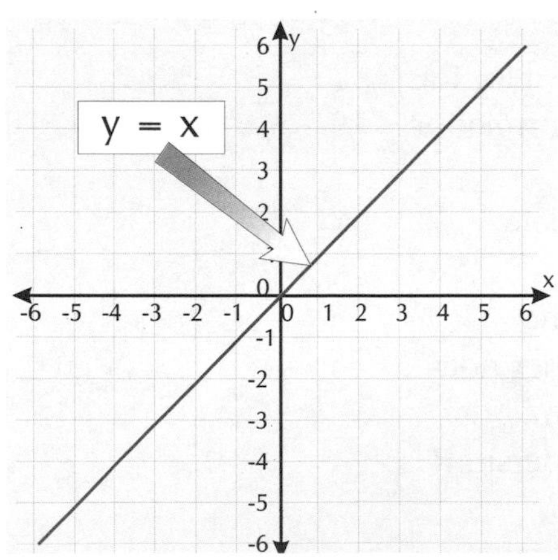

"y = x" is the main diagonal that goes UPHILL from left to right.

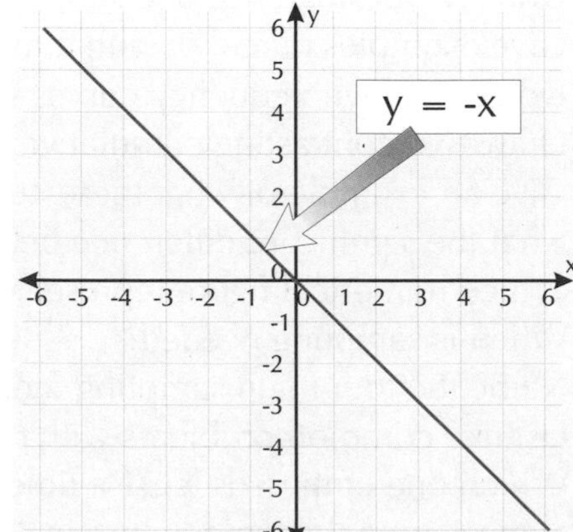

"y = -x" is the main diagonal that goes DOWNHILL from left to right.

Simple lines you have to learn — it'll only take a second

Vertical line: x = a, horizontal line: y = b, main diagonals: y = x and y = –x.
Say no more...

Straight Lines You Should Just Know

3) Other **sloping lines** through the origin: "y = ax" and "y = -ax"

y = ax and y = -ax are the equations for A SLOPING LINE THROUGH THE ORIGIN.

The value of "a" is the GRADIENT of the line, so the BIGGER the number the STEEPER the slope, and a MINUS SIGN tells you it slopes DOWNHILL as shown by the ones here:

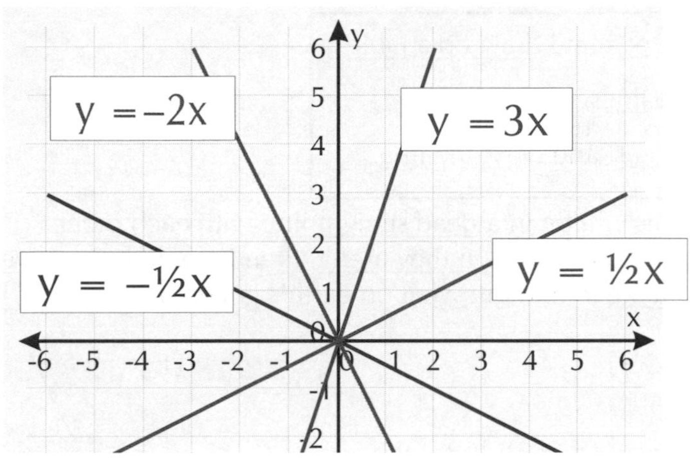

The gradient of a horizontal line (eg y = 3) is 0.
The gradient of a vertical line (eg x = 2) is ∞ (infinity).

All other **straight** lines

Other straight-line equations are a little more complicated, and the next three pages show three methods for drawing them. The first step, mind you, is identifying them in the first place. Remember: All straight-line equations just contain *"something x, something y, and a number"*.

Straight lines:

$x - y = 0$	$y = 2 + 3x$
$2y - 4x = 7$	$4x - 3 = 5y$
$3y + 3x = 12$	$6y - x - 7 = 0$
$5(x + 3y) = 5$	$12x - 7 = 3(x + 4y)$

NOT straight lines:

$y = x^3 + 3$	$2y - 1/x = 7$
$1/y + 1/x = 2$	$x(3 - 2y) = 3$
$x^2 = 4 - y$	$xy + 3 = 0$
$2x + 3y = xy$	$y = ½\sin x$

Get it straight — which lines are straight (and which aren't)

The graphs y = ax and y = –ax are diagonals just like y = x and y = –x on the last page.
The only difference is that the "a" represents the gradient of the line.

Plotting Straight-Line Graphs

Some people wouldn't know a straight-line equation if it ran up and bit them, but they're pretty easy to spot — they just have _two letters_ and _a few numbers_, but _nothing fancy_ like squared or cubed.

In the Exam you'll be expected to be able to draw the graphs of straight-line equations.
"y = mx + c" is the hard way of doing it (see P.122), but here's TWO NICE EASY WAYS of doing it:

1) The "**Table of 3 values**" method

You can easily draw the graph of any equation using this easy method:

1) Choose 3 values of x and draw up a table,
2) Work out the y-values,
3) Plot the coordinates, and draw the line.

If it's a straight-line equation, the three points will be in a dead straight line with each other, which is the usual check you do when you've drawn it — if they aren't, then it could be a curve and you'll need to do more values in your table to find out what on earth's going on.

Example: *"Draw the graph of y = 2x – 3"*

1) DRAW UP A TABLE with some *suitable values* of x. Choosing x = 0, 2, 4 is usually good enough. i.e.

x	0	2	4
y			

2) FIND THE Y-VALUES by putting each x-value into the equation:
(e.g. When x = 4, y = 2x – 3 = 2×4 – 3 = 5)

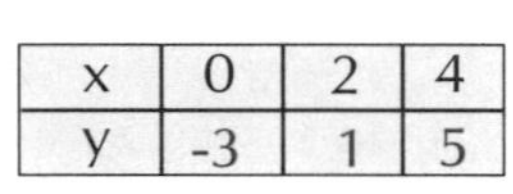

x	0	2	4
y	-3	1	5

3) PLOT THE POINTS and DRAW THE LINE.

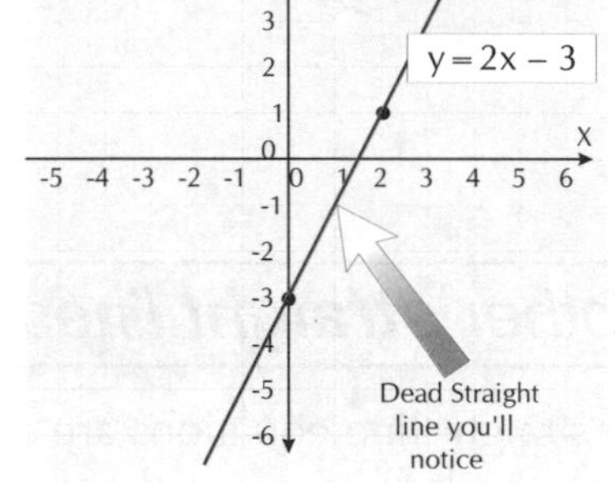

2) The "x = 0", "y = 0" **method**

This is especially good for typical linear programming equations of the form: "ax + by = c"

1) Set x=0 in the equation, and find y — this is where it crosses the y-axis.
2) Set y=0 in the equation and find x — this is where it crosses the x-axis.
3) Plot these two points and join them up with a straight line — *and just hope it should be a straight line, since with only two points you can't really tell.*

Example: "Draw the graph of 5x + 3y = 15"

1) Putting x = 0 gives "3y = 15" ⇒ y = 5
2) Putting y = 0 gives "5x = 15" ⇒ x = 3
3) So plot y = 5 on the y-axis and x = 3 on the x-axis and join them up with a straight line:

Only doing two points is risky unless you're sure the equation is definitely a straight line.

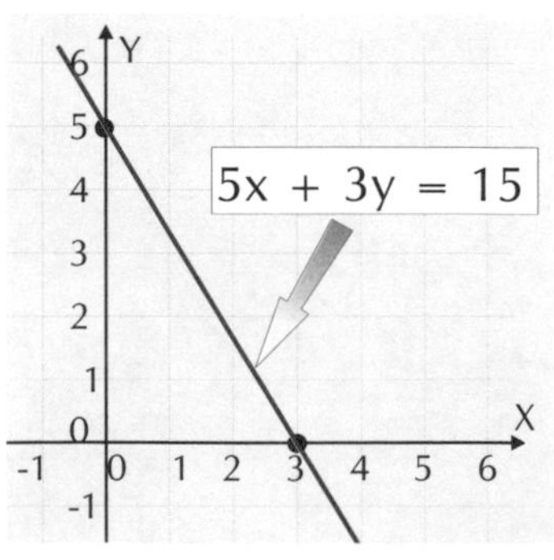

Plotting these graphs is straightforward with these simple methods

This gives you two simple methods for drawing straight line graphs. It's a very popular question with Examiners. If you learn the methods it'll be very popular with you too.

Uses of Coordinates

Here's a few more bits and bobs to do with coordinates.

Use **Pythagoras** to find the **length of a line...**

Example:

"Point P has coordinates (8, 3) and point Q has coordinates (-4, 8).
Find the length of the line PQ."

For questions like this, follow these rules and it'll all become breathtakingly simple:

1) Draw a *sketch* to find the *right-angled triangle*.
2) Find the *lengths of the sides* of the triangle.
3) *Use Pythagoras* to find the *length of the diagonal*. (That's your answer.)

Solution:

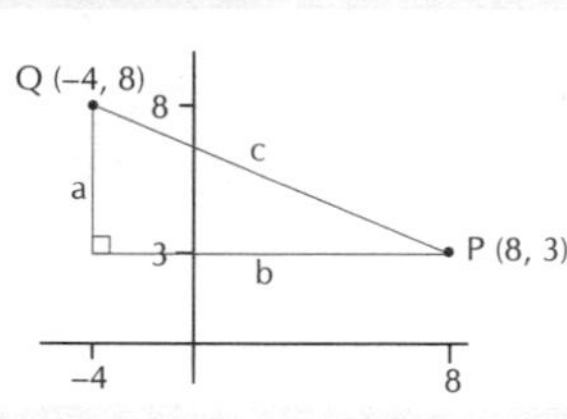

② Length of *side a* = 8 – 3 = *5*
Length of *side b* = 8 – -4 = *12*

③ *Use Pythagoras* to find *side c*:
$c^2 = a^2 + b^2 = 5^2 + 12^2 = 25 + 144 = 169$

So: $c = \sqrt{169} = 13$

...and with a **bit more fiddling** you can find the **midpoint**

Same kind of idea — except you don't need Pythagoras this time. Hurrah.

1) Find the *average* of the *two x-coordinates*, then do the same for the *y-coordinates*.
2) *These will be the coordinates of the midpoint*.

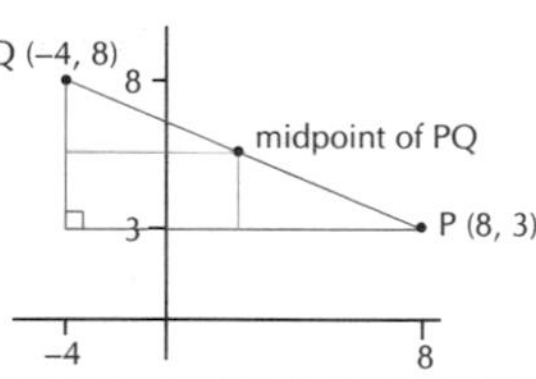

Example:

"Point P has coordinates (8, 3)
and point Q has coordinates (-4, 8).
Find the midpoint of the line PQ."

Solution:

Average of *x-coordinates* = (8 + -4)/2 = *2*
Average of *y-coordinates* = (8 + 3)/2 = *5.5*
So, coordinates of midpoint = *(2, 5.5)*

3-D coordinates - easy as **xyz**

If the examiners are feeling really mean, they may throw in one of these.
So you may as well be prepared.

3-D COORDINATES ARE ALWAYS WRITTEN (x, y, z) — IN THAT ORDER

You tip the x-axis and the y-axis over to make the base, and draw the z-axis sticking up out of the origin to make your third dimension.

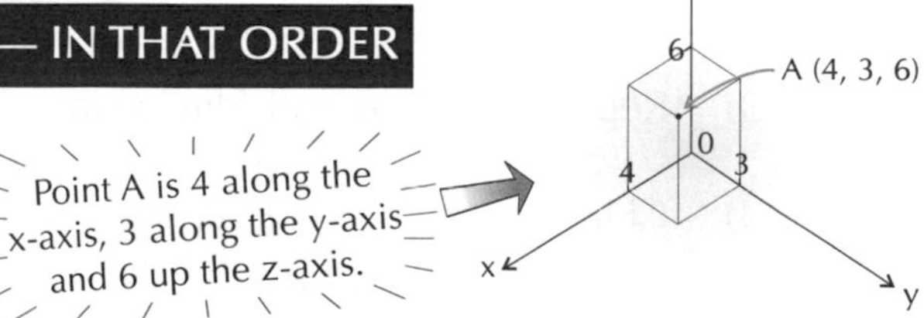

Coordinates and Pythagoras are a popular combo in the exam

Examiners like questions like the one at the top of page because they test two really important areas of GCSE maths in one go. Make sure you remember Pythagoras. If not, take another look at page 75.

Straight-Line Graphs: "y = mx + c"

Using "y = mx + c" is perhaps the "proper" way of dealing with straight-line equations, and it's a nice trick if you can do it. The first thing you have to do though is rearrange the equation into the standard format "y = mx + c" like this:

Straight line:		Rearranged into "y = mx +c"	
$y = 2 + 3x$	→	$y = 3x + 2$	($m = 3$, $c = 2$)
$2y - 4x = 7$	→	$y = 2x + 3\frac{1}{2}$	($m = 2$, $c = 3\frac{1}{2}$)
$x - y = 0$	→	$y = x + 0$	($m = 1$, $c = 0$)
$4x - 3 = 5y$	→	$y = 0.8x - 0.6$	($m = 0.8$, $c = -0.6$)
$3y + 3x = 12$	→	$y = -x + 4$	($m = -1$, $c = 4$)

REMEMBER: "m" equals the GRADIENT of the line.
"c" is the "y-intercept" (where the graph hits the y-axis).

BUT WATCH OUT: people mix up "m" and "c" when they get something like $y = 5 + 2x$.
REMEMBER, "m" is the number IN FRONT OF THE "X" and "c" is the number ON ITS OWN.

1) Sketching a **straight line** using y = mx + c

1) Get the equation into the form "y = mx + c".
2) *Put a dot on the y-axis* at the value of c.
3) Then go ALONG ONE UNIT to the right and *up or down by the value of m* and make another dot.
4) *Repeat* this step a few times, then do the same thing but this time to the left.
5) Finally, check that the gradient LOOKS RIGHT.

The graph shows the process for the equation "$y = 2x + 1$":

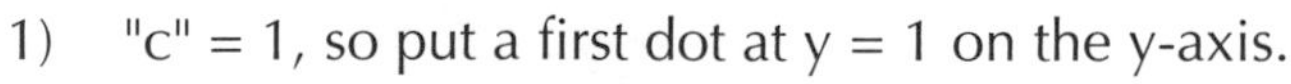

1) "c" = 1, so put a first dot at y = 1 on the y-axis.

2) Go along 1 unit → and then up by 2 because "m" = +2.

3) Repeat step 2 in both directions.

4) CHECK: a gradient of +2 should be quite steep and uphill left to right which it is, so it looks OK.

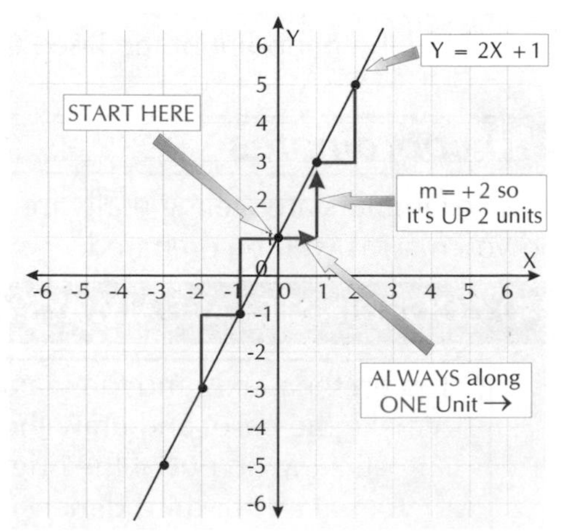

m is the gradient and c is the y-intercept

The key thing to remember is that m is the number in front of the x, and c is the number on its own. If you remember that then $y = mx + c$ is a very easy way of sketching or identifying straight lines.

Straight-Line Graphs: "y = mx + c"

Another popular exam question is asking you to find the equation for a given line.
If you get a question like this you just need to use the process on the last page in reverse...

2) Finding the **equation** of a straight-line **graph**

This is the reverse process and the good thing is it's EASIER:

1) From the axes, *identify the two variables* (e.g. "x and y" or "h and t").

2) *Find the values of*:

   "m" (gradient) and
   "c" (y-intercept) from the graph.

3) Using these values from the graph, *write down the equation* with the standard format "y = mx + c".

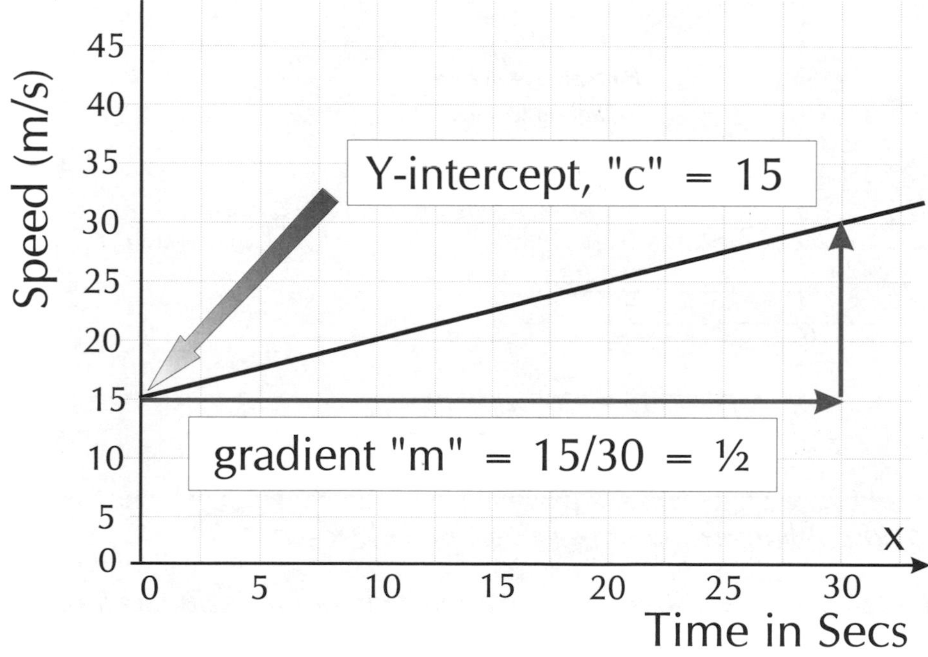

For the example above: "S = ½t + 15"

Find m and c — and write down the equation

Either you have an equation and have to sketch the graph, or you have the graph and have to find the equation. Both ways round are popular in the exam. For both, all you need is y = mx + c.

Warm-Up and Worked Exam Questions

On the day of the exam you'll have to know straight-line graphs like the back of your hand. If you struggle with any of the warm-up questions, go back over the section again before you go any further.

Warm-Up Questions

1) Which is the steeper hill: 1 in 4 or 20%?
2) Without drawing, state whether the lines joining the following points form a horizontal line, a vertical line, the line y = x or the line y = -x?
   (a) (1,1) to (5,5) (b) (0,4) to (-3,4) (c) (-1,3) to (-1,7) d) (4,-4) to (-3,3).
3) Which of these lines has a positive gradient, a negative gradient or no gradient?

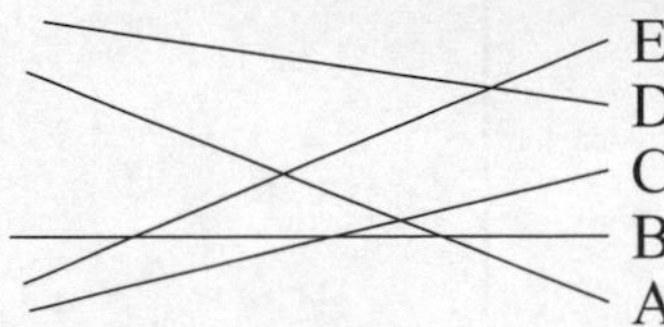

4) (a) Plot the line y = 3x – 4.
   (b) Draw the line y = 3x + 2. Where does it lie? Explain your answer.

Worked Exam Question

You know the routine by now — work carefully through this example and make sure you understand it. Then it's on to the real test of doing some exam questions for yourself.

1 Find the equation of the straight line which passes through the points (3,1) and (-1,3).

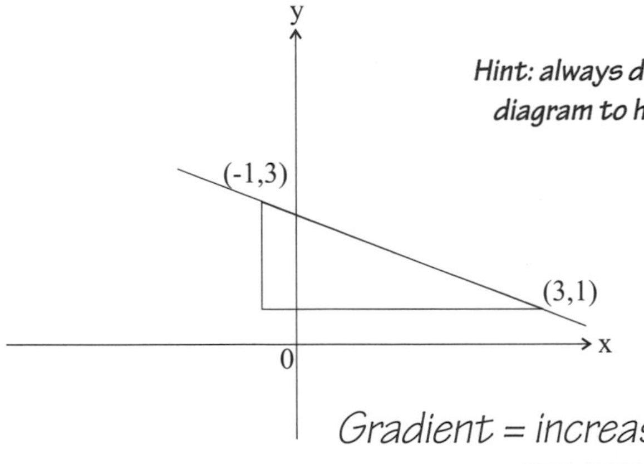

Hint: always draw a diagram to help.

$\text{Gradient} = \dfrac{\text{increase in } y}{\text{increase in } x} = \dfrac{2}{-4} = \dfrac{1}{-2}$

So equation of line: $y = mx + c$ $y = -\frac{1}{2}x + c$

Substitute $x = 3$, $y = 1$ (because we know this point is on the line)

$1 = (-\frac{1}{2} \times 3) + c$ $1 = -1\frac{1}{2} + c$ $c = 2\frac{1}{2}$

The equation is $y = -\frac{1}{2}x + 2\frac{1}{2}$.

Multiply both sides by 2:

$2y = -x + 5$.

(3 marks)

Exam Questions

2

A	$y = 3x - 2$
B	$y = 7 - 2x$
C	$7y = 10x$
D	$2y = 6x + 9$
E	$x + y = 14$

(a) Which two lines are parallel?

....

(1 mark)

(b) Which two lines have negative gradients?

....

(1 mark)

(c) Which line goes through the origin?

....

(1 mark)

(d) Which two lines go through the point (4,10)?

....

(1 mark)

3

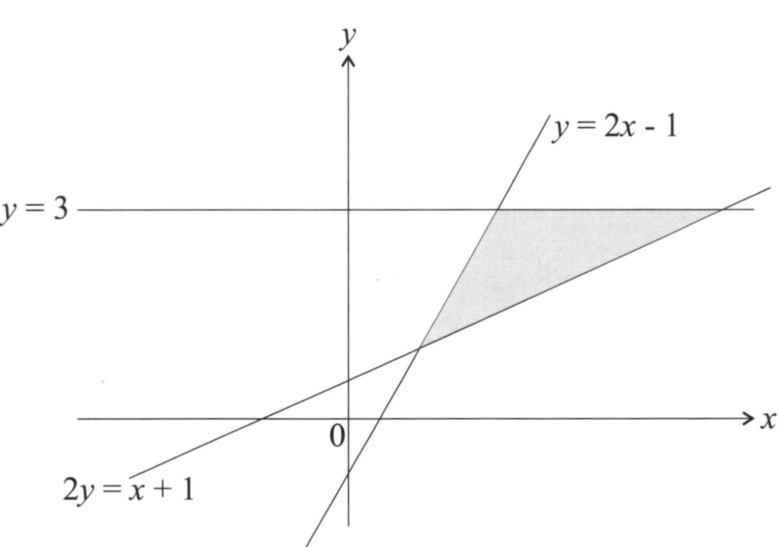

Work out the coordinates of the 3 vertices of the triangle formed by the lines with equations: $y = 2x - 1$; $2y = x + 1$; $y = 3$.

....

(3 marks)

Linear Programming

A full-blown linear programming question can be worth enough marks to raise your result by one whole grade — i.e. if you get it right rather than wrong your final result could be one whole grade higher — a sobering thought.

Although they're quite difficult, LINEAR PROGRAMMING QUESTIONS ALL FOLLOW THE SAME PATTERN and it's really important you realise just how REPETITIVE they are.
The THREE SEPARATE STAGES that occur in ALL linear programming questions are best illustrated by a typical example. Every step of the following method needs to be LEARNT:

1) *Converting* the *sentences* into *equations*

The local "Supplies 'n' Vittals" have two top sellers: "Froggatt's Lumpy Sprout Ketchup" and "Froggatt's Bone-tingling Fireball Soup" (not available in all areas).
The sales of these products are limited by the following factors:

1) Following an unusually good growing season, a severe shortage of suitably lumpy sprouts has meant total sales of the Ketchup are rationed to 200 bottles per month.
2) The local Health Department have limited the combined sales of these two Froggatt's products to 250 items per month.
3) Froggatt's themselves, ever keen to preserve their more traditional health products, insist that all retailers must sell at least as much Ketchup as Bone-tingling Soup.

Using L to represent the number of bottles of Lumpy Sprout Ketchup sold and B to represent the number of tins of Bone-tingling Fireball Soup sold, write down three inequalities.

ANSWER

1) Surely it's pretty obvious that the first condition is simply written: $L \leqslant 200$

2) Neither is it difficult to convert the second sentence into: $L + B \leqslant 250$

3) A little trickier but still quite straightforward: $L \geqslant B$

This set of THREE CONDITIONS is a key feature of Linear Programming questions, and the method to turn them into equations isn't so mysterious — it just needs to be LEARNT.

If you look at the mathematical expressions and the underlined parts of the corresponding statements, it's really quite easy to see how you turn one into the other.

The first stage is to change the words into equations

The sentences convert quite easily into inequalities. If maximum total sales are 200, then it's fairly obvious that $L \leqslant 200$. Just wade through the waffle and see the simple mathematical fact they are telling you.

Linear Programming

2) Drawing **the graphs**

TURN EACH INEQUALITY INTO AN EQUATION
— simply replace any inequality symbols (like ">") with an "=" (dead easy):

$$L \leqslant 200 \rightarrow L = 200$$

$$L + B \leqslant 250 \rightarrow L + B = 250$$

$$L \geqslant B \rightarrow L = B$$

These equations can now easily be drawn as straight lines on a graph, using the methods which you have thoroughly and meticulously learnt from the last few pages.

Shading the region

When you've drawn the three lines they're bound to enclose a region which is bound to be the region you're supposed to shade.

In this case, however, you'll see there are two enclosed regions, so you have to think about this one a bit more carefully:

If you look at the inequality "$L + B \leqslant 250$" you need to decide which side of the line "$L + B = 250$" this is — above it or below it.

It's easy enough, you just pick a point on the graph, either above or below the line, and see if its coordinates fit the inequality.

E.g. If you choose the point (150, 200), as shown, then $L + B = 150 + 200 = 350$. This certainly isn't "$\leqslant 250$" so the region we want must be the other side of the line, i.e. below it.

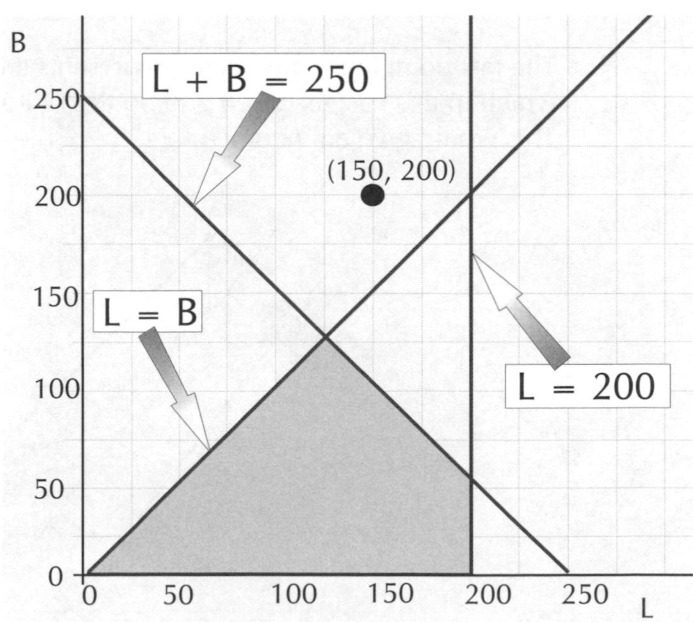

Then just draw the graphs and shade the region

Drawing the graphs is easy as long as you've remembered the methods for graph sketching in the last section. Then you just have to make sure you get the right region, by picking a point and trying it.

Linear Programming

3) Finding the optimum point

The question always ends up mentioning some quantity (usually INCOME), which has to be OPTIMISED (i.e. made as big or as small as possible) within the shaded region:

For Example:

> "The prices of these products are £2 per bottle of Lumpy Sprout Ketchup, and £1.50 per tin of Bone-tingling Fireball Soup. Find the maximum possible income, and say how many of each will be sold per month."

From this sort of information you should never have any real trouble writing a simple equation like this one:

> "Income = 2L + 1.5B"

Now, once you've got your equation for income (or whatever), you've then got to remember these tricky bits:

1) MAKE UP ANY VALUE for the income — say £300.

2) This gives 2L + 1.5B = 300, which is plotted using the x=0, y=0 method. This line gives you the right gradient.

4) Now put your ruler along this line and slide it towards the furthest edge of the shaded region.

5) The last point left in the region represents the optimum combination, which in this case is to sell 200 bottles of Ketchup and 50 tins of Soup. This would give an income of £475 (2L + 1.5B).

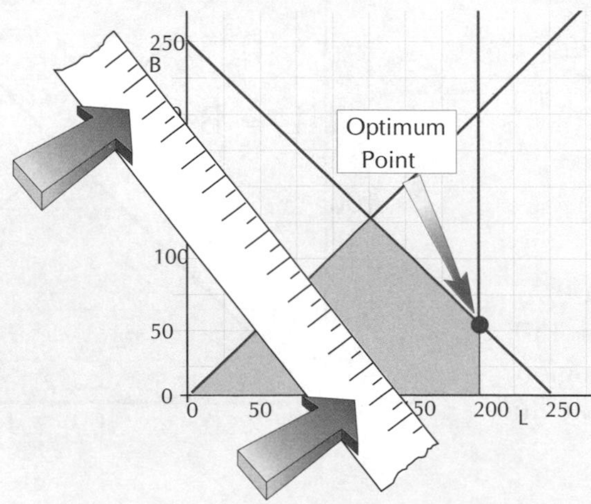

The last part of these questions is always about optimising

Optimising can be very tricky. The only way to deal with it is to learn these four steps — it works for all these questions and might make a whole grade difference to your mark.

Warm-Up and Worked Exam Questions

These warm-up questions should ease you in gently and make sure you've got all the basics straight. If you've forgotten anything, check back through the section before you do the exam questions.

Warm-Up Questions

1) (a) Using the same axes, draw the graphs of $y = 0$, $y = 2x$, $y = 6 - x$.
   (b) R is the region defined by the inequalities $y \le 2x$, $y \le 6 - x$, $y \ge 0$. Shade this region and label it R.
2) S is the region defined by the inequalities $3x + 4y \ge 12$, $8x + 3y \le 24$, $y - x \le 3$. Shade this region and label it S.
3) Robert wants to buy a rack to store his *m* music CDs and *c* computer games. Robert has at least 10 music CDs and 6 computer games but no more than a total of 24 items. From the information given, write down 3 inequalities and plot them. Shade and label, with the letter R, the region that satisfies the inequalities.

Worked Exam Question

Imagine if you opened up your exam paper and all the answers were already written in for you. Hmm, well I'm afraid that's not going to happen, the only way you'll do well is hard work now.

1 An architect is given this memo to plan a layout for parking spaces for a college:

1. The area of the plot of land is $2000m^2$. 75% of the land is to be designated for car and motorcycle parking spaces and the remaining land is for manoeuvring space.
2. The number of parking spaces for cars must be greater than or equal to the number of parking spaces for motorcycles. There must be at least 50 parking spaces for motorcycles.
3. A car takes up $12m^2$ and a motorcycle takes up $6m^2$ of parking space.
4. Design the layout to achieve the maximum number of parking spaces.

Let x be the number of car parking spaces and y the number of motorcycle parking spaces.

(a) Calculate the area of land designated for parking. $\frac{75}{100} \times 2000 = 1500m^2$

Hint: find 75% of 2000.

(1 mark)

(b) From the information given in the memo, write down three inequalities and plot them on the grid below. Shade and label, with the letter P, the region that satisfies the inequalities.

$x \ge y$

$y \ge 50$

$12x + 6y \le 1500$

$x = 0 \quad y = 250$

$y = 0 \quad x = 125$

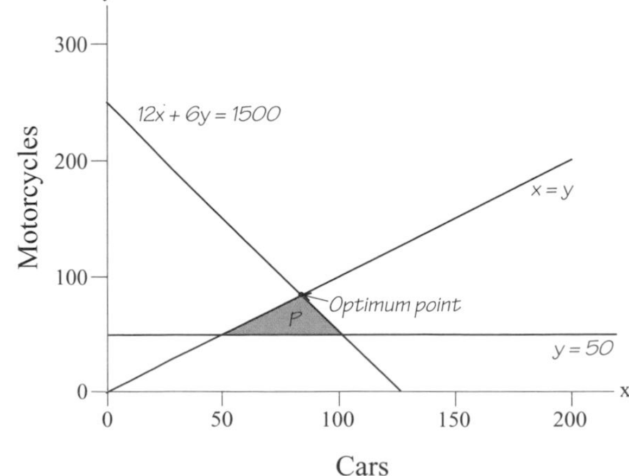

(3 marks)

(c) Find the maximum number of parking spaces from the graph.

$x = 84, y = 82, x + y = 166.$ *Hint: find the optimum point on the graph*

In the real exam, the graph would be a lot easier to read than this one. *(1 mark)*

Exam Questions

2 Alex has to buy x apples and y oranges from the supermarket.
He must buy at least one orange to every two apples but no more than twenty apples.
An apple weighs 120 grams and an orange weighs 150 grams.
Alex can only carry 4.2 kilograms of fruit home.

(a) From the information given, write down 3 inequalities.

....

(2 marks)

(b) Plot the inequalities on the grid below, and shade and label, with the letter F, the region that satisfies them.

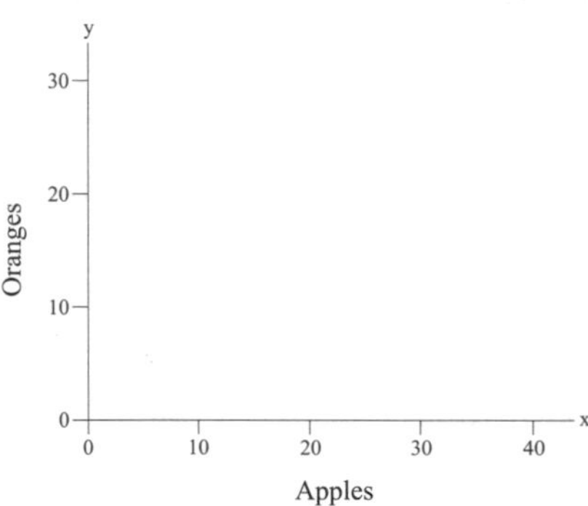

(3 marks)

(c) Apples cost 10p and oranges cost 30p each. Calculate how much change Alex receives when he buys the maximum possible number of fruit with £10.

....

(4 marks)

3 The graph of $y = x^2 - 4x + 2$ for the values of x from 0 to 4 is shown below.

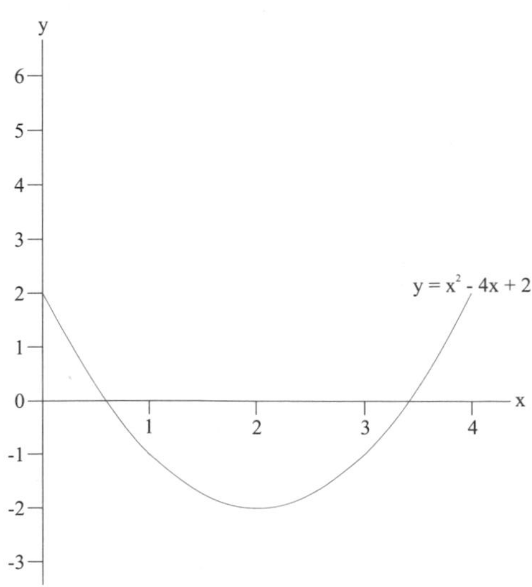

R is the region defined by the inequalities $x \geq 1.5$, $y \leq 1$, $y \leq 6 - 2x$ and $y \geq x^2 - 4x + 2$.
Shade this region and label it R.

(4 marks)

Typical Graph Questions (Plotting Curves)

Graphs are really good and everybody likes them a lot more than they let on, I'm sure.

Filling in the table of values

Here is an incomplete table of values for $y = x^2 - 4x + 3$:

x	-2	-1	0	1	2	3	4	5	6
y				0			3		15

The rest of the question hinges on this table of values and one silly mistake here could cost you lots of marks — YOU NEED TO MAKE SURE YOU GET THE NUMBERS RIGHT:

1) First, MAKE SURE YOU CAN REPRODUCE ANY VALUES THAT ARE ALREADY DONE.
2) Once you've checked out your method, work out the other values AT LEAST TWICE.
3) Try to spot any SYMMETRY or PATTERN in the values, and check any that seem out of place.

You should be able to work out each value in one go on the calculator, but if things aren't working out you'll have to do a SAFER METHOD. For each value in the table you might be wise to write this out:

$x = 4$ $\quad y = x^2 - 4x + 3$
$\quad = 4^2 - 4 \times 4 + 3$
$\quad = 16 - 16 + 3 = 3$

It's worth it, if it means you get it RIGHT rather than WRONG!

Plotting the points and *drawing* the curve

Here again there are easy marks to be won and lost. All these points matter:

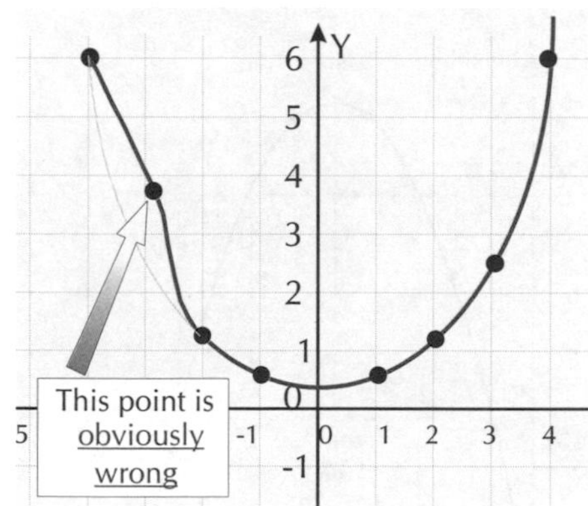

1) Get the axes the right way round: The values from the FIRST row or column are ALWAYS plotted on the x-axis.
2) Plot the points CAREFULLY, and don't muddle up the x and y values.
3) The points will ALWAYS form a DEAD STRAIGHT LINE or a COMPLETELY SMOOTH CURVE. NEVER EVER let one point drag your line off in some ridiculous direction. If one point seems out of place, check the value in the table and then the position where you've plotted it. When a graph is generated from an equation, you never get spikes or lumps — only MISTAKES.
4) A graph from an ALGEBRA EQUATION must always be a SMOOTH CURVE (or a dead straight line). You only use short straight-line sections to join points in "Data Handling".

Tables of values and plotting are easy marks as long as you're accurate

Both of these are easy questions but too many people rush them and make silly errors. Take your time and make sure you do them right. Check and see if the points in the table or on the graph are sensible.

Solving Equations Using Graphs

This is an easy type of graph question — you just draw a graph of the equation and then draw lines from one axis or the other to meet it.

The answers are where the x- or y-value hits the graph

The typical question will have a *nasty-looking equation* a bit like this:

$y = x^3 + 2x^2 + 4$

and a *graph* already drawn (or mostly done for you anyway).

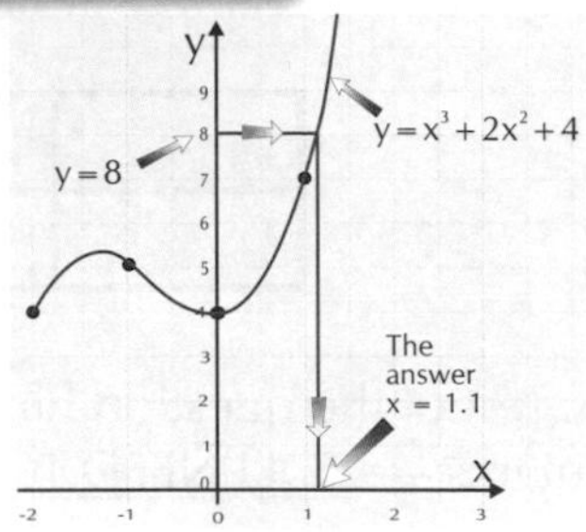

Then they'll ask you something like this:

"From the graph, find the value of x which makes y = 8."

This is how you do it:

The easy four-step method

1) Draw (or finish off) the *GRAPH* from a *TABLE OF VALUES*.
2) Draw a line *ACROSS* (or *UP*) from the *Y-AXIS* (or *X-AXIS*) at the value *GIVEN*.
3) Where it *crosses the graph*, draw a line (or lines) *DOWN* (or *ACROSS*) to the *X-AXIS* (or *Y-AXIS*).
4) *READ OFF* the *VALUES* from the *X-AXIS* (or *Y-AXIS*).

Example:

The height, h, gained by a small piece of mouldy cheese fired from a catapult is given by the equation $h = 25t - 5t^2$. Using a graphical method find:

a) the times at which the mouldy cheese is at a height of 25m and

b) its height after 2½ secs.

ANSWER:

1) First *draw the graph from the equation*, doing your own *table of values* if necessary.

time	0	1	2	3	4	5
height	0	20	30	30	20	0

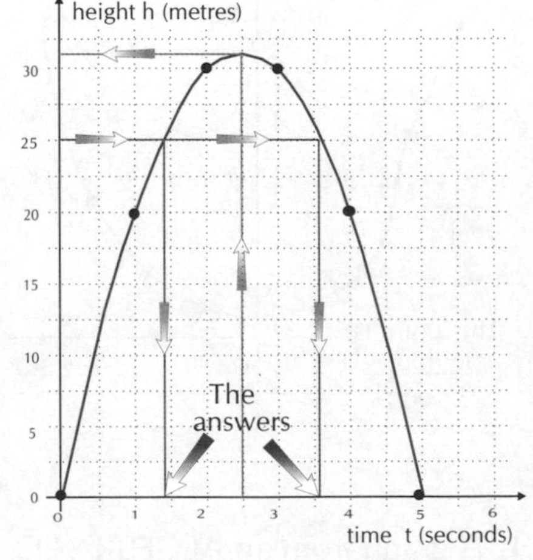

2) Draw the graph. Note the CURVED PEAK. DON'T EVER join the two points near the peak with a *ridiculous straight line*.

3) Draw a line UP or ACROSS from the axis (using the given value), *hit the curve* and go ACROSS or DOWN to the other axis and *read off the value*. Easy as that.

From the graph we can see the answers to this question are a) 1.4s and 3.6s b) 31m

Solve equations by drawing the graph and reading off the answers

Again accuracy is the key here. There's nothing too hard to understand — just make sure you work through the four easy stages carefully and accurately and you will get plenty of marks.

Simultaneous Equations and Graphs

When you have two graphs which represent two separate equations, there are two ways the question can present it:

TWO SIMULTANEOUS EQUATIONS or a single MERGED EQUATION.

In either case THE SOLUTIONS will simply be WHERE THE TWO GRAPHS CROSS (fairly obviously)

1) Two **graphs** and two **separate equations**

Example:

"Draw the graphs for "$y = 2x + 3$" and "$y = 6 - 4x$" and then use your graphs to solve them."

1) TABLE OF 3 VALUES (see P.120) for both equations:

X	0	2	-2
Y	3	7	-1

X	0	2	3
Y	6	-2	-6

2) DRAW THE GRAPHS:

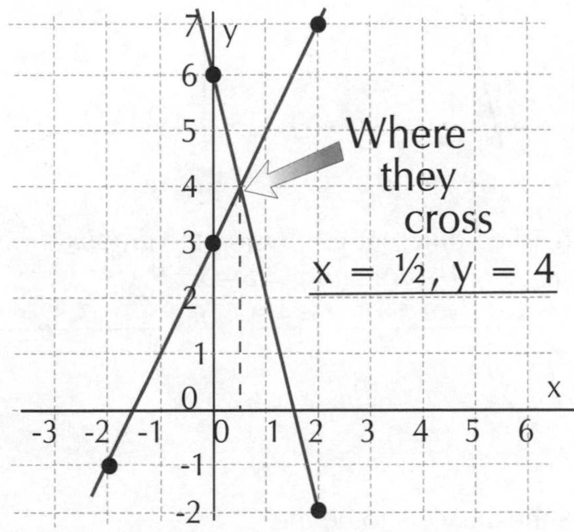

3) WHERE THEY CROSS: $x = \frac{1}{2}$, $y = 4$.
And that's the answer.

$x = \frac{1}{2}$ and $y = 4$

A point which satisfies two graphs is the point where they cross

This is pretty obvious but it's the key to these questions. When you are solving two simultaneous equations you are finding a point which satisfies both graphs. So just draw them and see where they cross.

Simultaneous Equations and Graphs

2) Two **graphs** but **just ONE equation**, or **so it seems...**

Example:

"Using the graphs shown for $y = 4 + \frac{1}{2}x$ and $y = 6 - x^2/3$, solve the equation: $x^2/3 + \frac{1}{2}x - 2 = 0$."

ANSWER: *Learn* these important steps:

1) *Equating the equations* of the two graphs gives this:
   $6 - x^2/3 = 4 + \frac{1}{2}x$
   (a sort of *"merged* equation")

2) Now bring it all onto *one side* and you end up with:
   $x^2/3 + \frac{1}{2}x - 2 = 0$
   (the equation in the question)

3) Hence the *solutions* to that equation are where the two initial equations ($y = 4 + \frac{1}{2}x$ and $y = 6 - x^2/3$) are *equal* — i.e. where their *graphs cross*, which as the graph shows is at:
   $x = 1.8$ or $x = -3.3$.

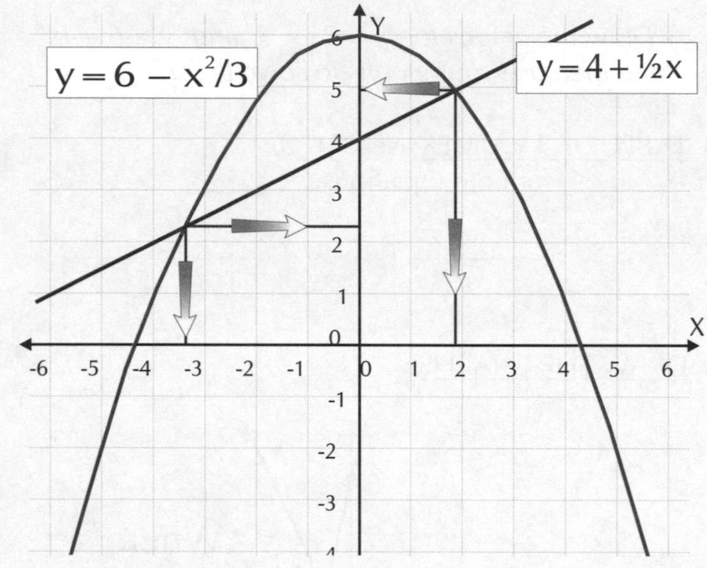

4) The *same* question *could* have been asked differently: *"Using the graphs shown, solve the two simultaneous equations: $y = 4 + \frac{1}{2}x$ and $y = 6 - x^2/3$"*
   ANSWER: From where the graphs cross: $x = 1.8,\ y = 4.9$, or $x = -3.3,\ y = 2.3$.

Even if you're not sure, you should GUESS the answers to be the points of intersection and just write them down.

Also note that for simultaneous equations you give BOTH the X-values AND Y-values whilst for the "merged equation" you just give the X-values.

That's because the merged equation doesn't have any Y in it to start with (even though the two equations it's derived from do) — tricky details, but you have to learn them.

You have to solve one equation using two different ones

When you're asked to solve one equation using two different graphs, you can bet that if you equate the two graph equations you'll get the equation in the question. Then find the point where the two cross.

Warm-Up Questions

The warm-up questions run quickly over the basic facts you'll need in the exam. The exam questions come later — but unless you've learnt the facts first you'll find the exams tougher than stale bread.

Warm-Up Questions

1) (a) Complete the table of values for $y = x^2 - 2x - 1$.

x	-2	-1	0	1	2	3	4	5
x^2	4							
-2x	4							
-1	-1							
$y = x^2 - 2x - 1$	7							

(b) Plot the x and y values from the table and join the points up to form a smooth curve.
(c) Use your curve to find the value of y when x = 3.5.
(d) Find the two values of x when y = 5.

2) The graphs of $2y = 3x - 6$, $y = 0.5x + 3$ and $y + 2x = 8$ are shown.

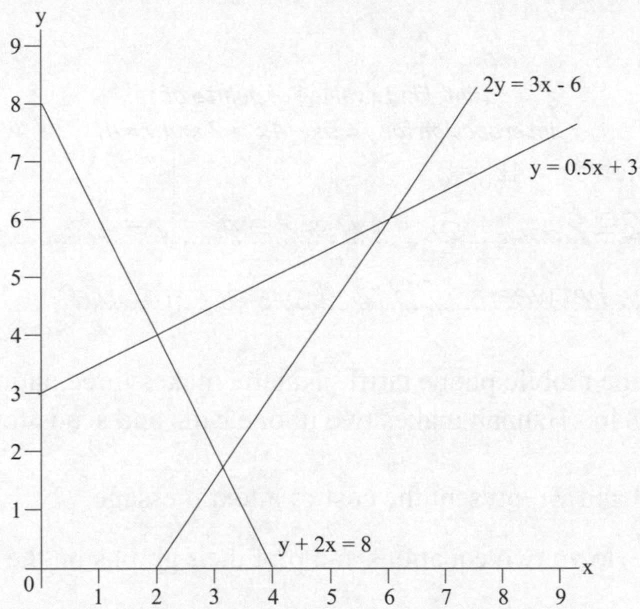

Use the graphs to solve the following pairs of simultaneous equations.
(a) $2y = 3x - 6$; $y = 0.5x + 3$.
(b) $y + 2x = 8$; $y = 0.5x + 3$.
(c) $2y = 3x - 6$; $y + 2x = 8$.

3) Draw the graph of $y = x^2 - 3x$ for values of x from -2 to 5.
Use your graph to solve the following equations.
(a) $x^2 - 3x = 0$.
(b) $x^2 - 3x = 3$.

4) Draw the graphs of $y = 4 - 2x^2$ and $y = 1 - x$ for values of x from -2 to +2.
Use the graphs to solve the equation $2x^2 = x + 3$.

5) Assume the graph of $y = x^2 - 3x + 2$ has been drawn. What other graph needs to be drawn to find the solution of the equation $x^2 - 2x - 3 = 0$?

Worked Exam Questions

Worked Exam Questions

Wow, exam questions — with the answers helpfully written in. It must be your birthday.

1 (a) Complete the table of values for $y = 5x - 4x^3 + 2$.

x	-1.5	-1	-0.5	0	0.5	1	1.5
y	8	1	0	2	4	3	-4

(2 marks)

(b) On the axes below, draw the graph of $y = 5x - 4x^3 + 2$ for values of x from -1.5 to 1.5.

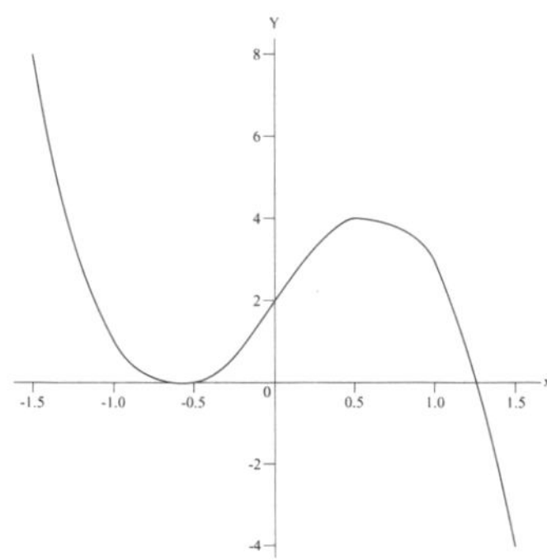

Hint: Find x values of points of intersection for $y = 5x - 4x^3 + 2$ and $y = 4$. *(2 marks)*

(c) Use your graph to solve the equation $5x - 4x^3 = 2$.

$5x - 4x^3 = 2$; $5x - 4x^3 + 2 = 2 + 2$; $5x - 4x^3 + 2 = 4$; $y = 4$.

$x = 0.5$ and -1.28 (any value between -1.25 to -1.3 is acceptable).

(2 marks)

2 Natalie and Hannah are both on the same mobile phone tariff. Natalie makes three phone calls and sends two text messages for 84p. Hannah makes two phone calls and sends four text messages for 88p.
Let x represent the cost of a phone call and y represent the cost of a text message.

(a) From the information given, write down two equations and plot their graphs on the grid below.

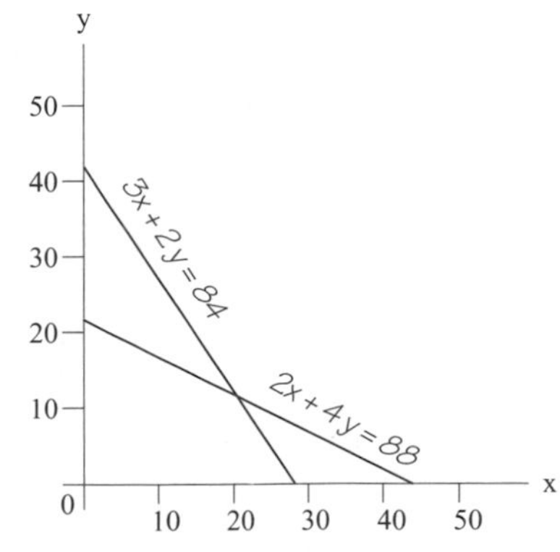

$3x + 2y = 84$ — when $x = 0$, $2y = 84$, $y = 42$; when $y = 0$, $3x = 84$, $x = 28$.

$2x + 4y = 88$ — when $x = 0$, $4y = 88$, $y = 22$; when $y = 0$, $2x = 88$, $x = 44$.

(4 marks)

(b) From your graphs, find the cost of i) a phone call and ii) a text message.

i) 20p ii) 12p. Hint: Read the x and y values at the point of intersection of the 2 graphs.

(2 marks)

Exam Questions

3 Teenagers, Nick and Tom have a competition to see who can kick a football to the greatest height. The graph shows the path followed by Nick's football which is described by the equation $h = 6t - 1.2t^2$ where h is height in metres and t is time in seconds.

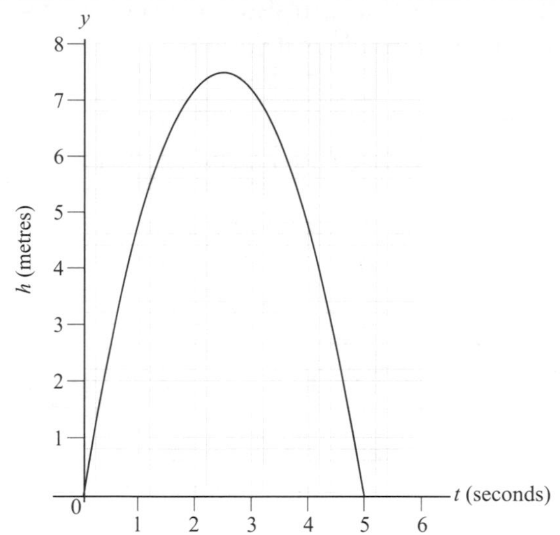

(a) The path followed by Tom's football is described by $h = 4.2t - 0.7t^2$.
Complete the table of values for Tom's football and plot the curve on the graph above.

t	0	1	2	3	4	5	6
$h = 4.2t - 0.7t^2$	0						

(4 marks)

(b) Who wins the competition?

....

(1 mark)

(c) Calculate the difference in maximum heights reached by Nick and Tom's footballs.

....

(2 marks)

(d) If Nick and Tom both kick their footballs at the same time, at what time do the footballs reach the same height?

....

(1 mark)

4 (a) Complete the table of values for $y = 12/x - 1$.

x	1	2	3	4	5	6
y	11					1

(2 marks)

(b) Plot the x and y values from the table onto a grid.

....

(2 marks)

(c) By adding a straight line to your graph, solve the equation $12/x = 11 - 2x$.

....

(2 marks)

Five Graphs You Should Recognise

There are five graphs that you should know the basic shape of just from looking at their equations — it really isn't as difficult as it sounds.

1) Straight line graphs: *"$y = mx + c$" (Note, no x^2 or x^3 or $^1/_x$ in the equation)*

You should know plenty about these — all of P.118-122 in fact — so make sure you do.
EXAMPLES: $y = 3x+2$, $3y - 3 = x$, $4x - 5 + 2y = 0$, $x - y = 12$

2) x^2 bucket shapes: *$y = ax^2 + bx + c$ (where b and/or c can be zero)*

Notice that all these graphs have the same SYMMETRICAL bucket shape and that if the x^2 bit has a "–" in front of it then the bucket is *upside down*.

$y = x^2$

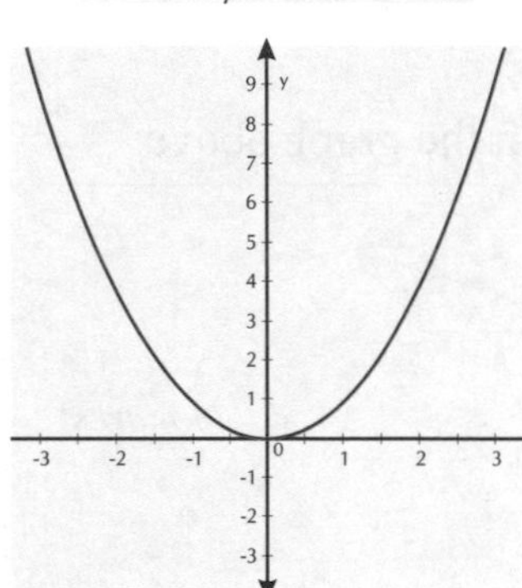

$y = 3x^2 - 6x - 3$

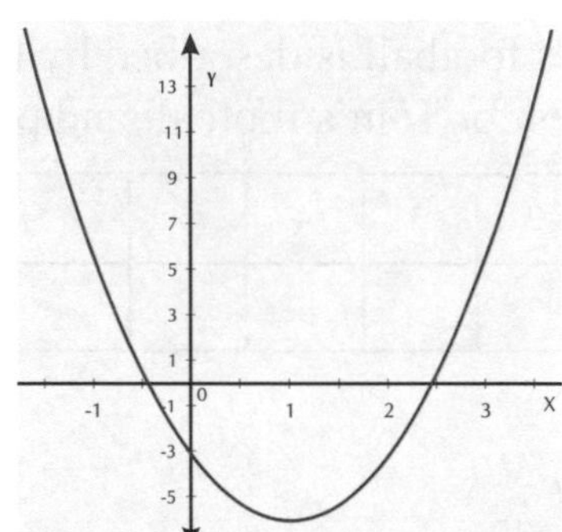

$y = -2x^2 - 4x + 3$

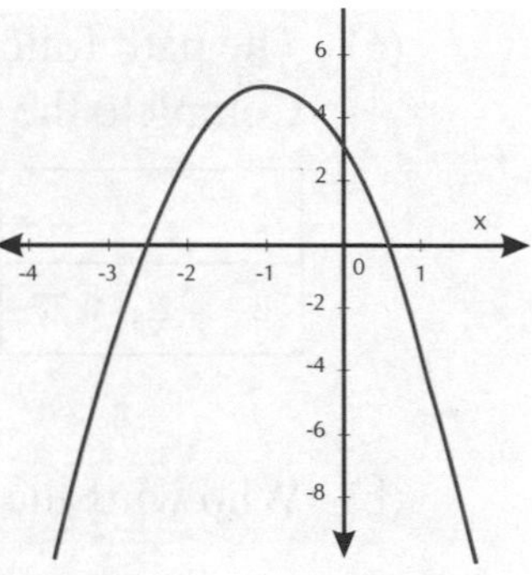

3) x^3 graphs: *$Y = ax^3 + bx^2 + cx + d$ (Note that b, c and/or d can be zero)*

(Note that x^3 must be the highest power and there must be no other bits like $\frac{1}{x}$ etc.)

All x^3 graphs have the *same basic wiggle* in the middle, but it can be a flat wiggle or a more pronounced wiggle.

Notice that "$-x^3$ graphs" always come *down from top left* whereas the $+x^3$ ones go *up from bottom left*.

$y = x^3$

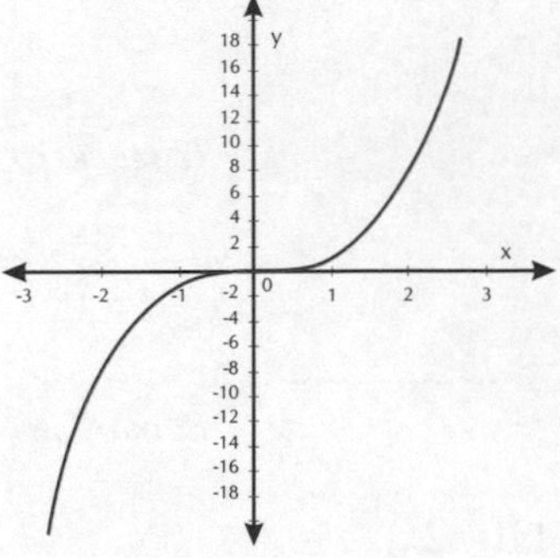

$y = x^3 + 3x^2 - 4x$

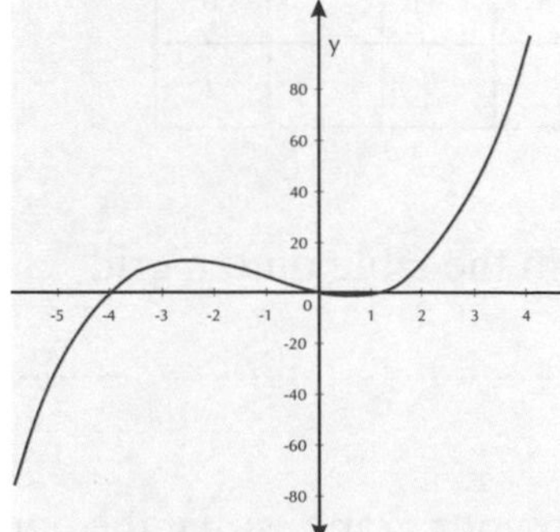

$y = -7x^3 - 7x^2 + 42x$

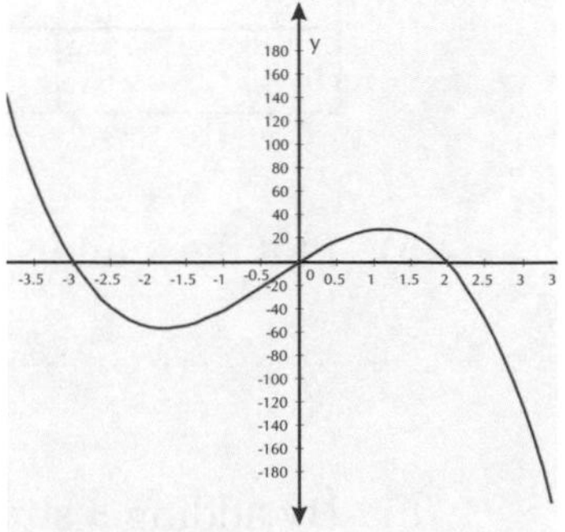

These shapes will come up again and again — so learn them

Straight line graphs are very easy, the x^2 bucket is a bit trickier and the x^3 wiggle can be downright confusing. All you really need to do, though, is recognise the general shape and the basic properties.

Five Graphs You Should Recognise

4) 1/x graphs: $y = a/x$, or $xy = a$, where a is some number (+ or -)

These graphs are *all the same basic shape*, except that the negative ones are in the opposite quadrants to the positive ones (as shown). The two halves of the graph don't touch.
They're all *symmetrical about the lines y=x and y=-x*.
This is also the type of graph you get with *inverse proportion*.

y = 4/x or xy = 4

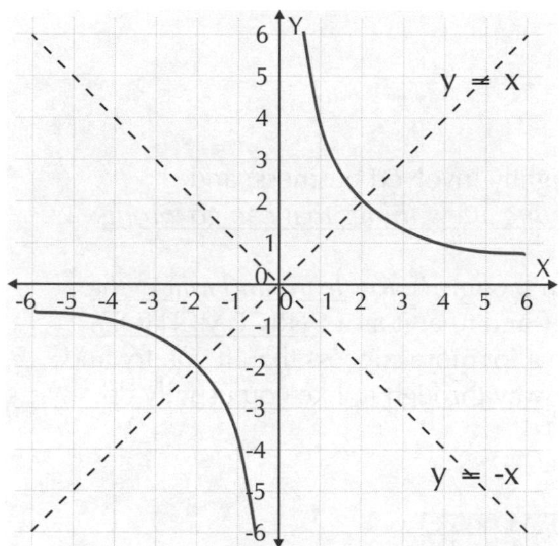

y = -4/x or xy = -4

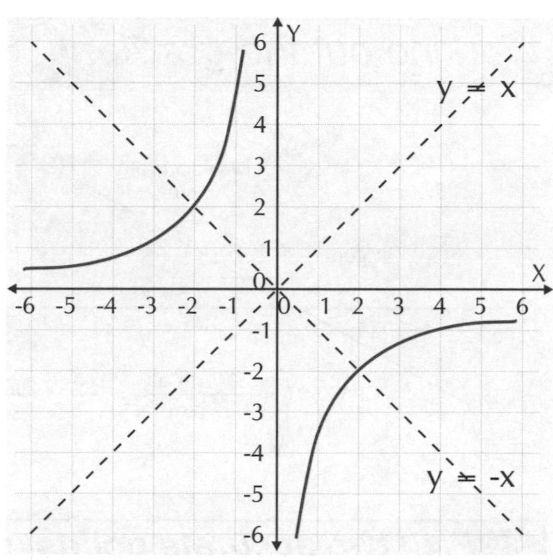

5) k^x graphs: $y = k^x$, where k is some positive number

1) These graphs *curve upwards* when k > 1.
2) They're always *above the x-axis*.
3) They all *go through the point (0, 1)*.
4) For *bigger values of k*, the graph *tails off towards zero more quickly* on the left and *climbs more steeply* on the right.

$y = k^x$

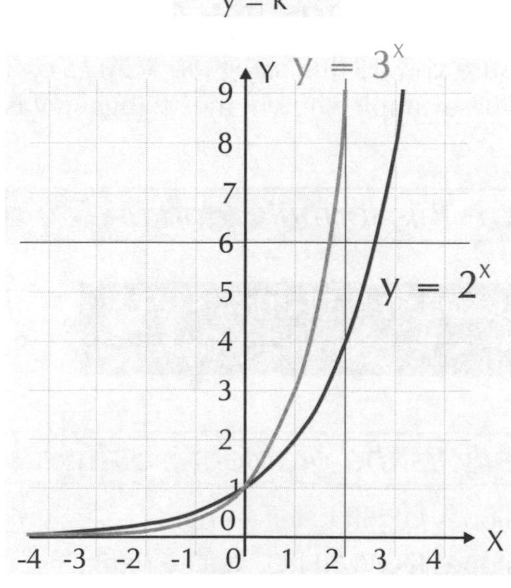

Five different graph shapes — draw a quick sketch of each to be sure

All these graphs look quite different and so you should be able to recognise the general shapes as easy as pie (though quite how easy pie is I have no idea).

Tangents and Gradient

Drawing *tangents*

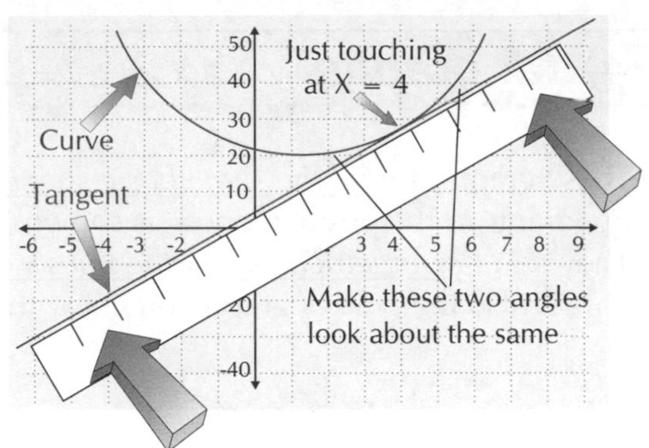

This is really easy. You just bring your ruler gradually up against the curve so that it *just touches at the right point* with the two little angles either side looking about the same, then *back off* enough to *fit your pencil in* between the ruler and the curve, and then draw it.

Working out the **gradient**

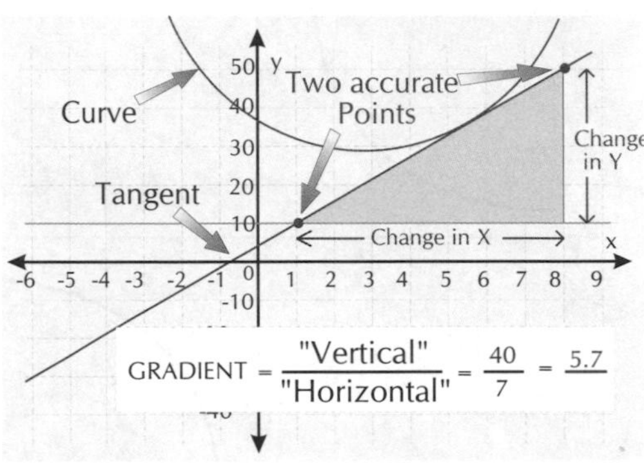

This is a slightly involved business, and there are *quite a few things that can go wrong*.

Once again though, if you *learn and follow the steps below* and treat it as a STRICT METHOD, you'll have a lot more success than if you try and fudge your way through it, like you usually do.

1) Find **two accurate points**, reasonably far apart

Both in the *upper right quadrant* if possible,
(to keep all the numbers positive and so reduce the chance of errors).

2) **Complete the triangle** as shown

3) Find the **change in y** and the **change in x**

Make sure you do this *using the SCALES on the y- and x- axes,* not by counting cm.
(So in the example shown, the change in y is NOT 4cm, but *40 units* off the y-axis.)

4) **Learn** this formula, and use it:

$$\text{GRADIENT} = \frac{\text{VERTICAL}}{\text{HORIZONTAL}}$$

Make sure you get it the right way up too —
Remember it's VERy HOt — VERtical over HOrizontal

5) Finally, is the gradient **positive** or **negative**?

If it slopes UPHILL left → right (↗) then it's +ve

If it slopes DOWNHILL left → right (↘) then it's –ve (so put a minus(–) in front of it)

Gradients are incredibly useful

It might seem unlikely but gradients are one of maths' most useful tools. The more maths you do, the more you come across. But even if you plan to see no maths after GCSE, you need them to get through the exam.

The Meaning of Gradient

The gradient** of a graph **represents** the **rate

No matter what the graph may be, THE MEANING OF THE GRADIENT is always simply:

(y-axis UNITS) PER (x-axis UNITS)

Once you've written "*something PER something*" using the x- and y-axis UNITS, it's then pretty easy to work out what the gradient represents, as these four examples show.

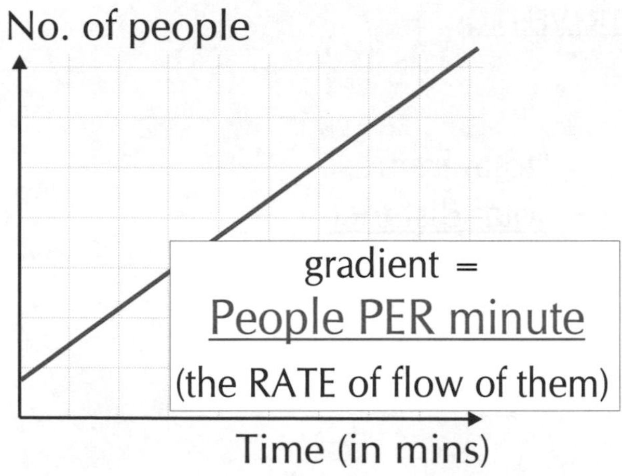

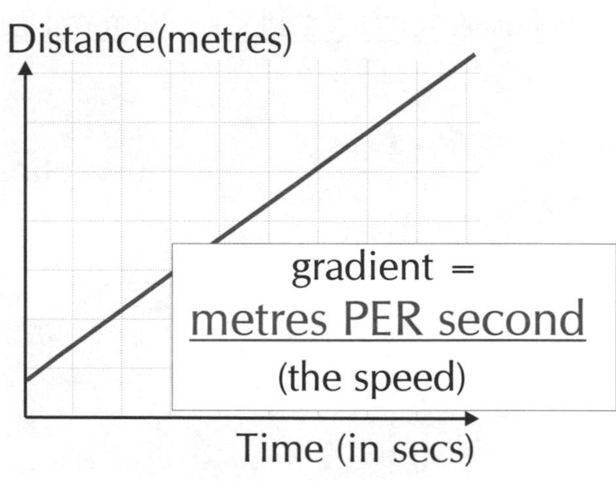

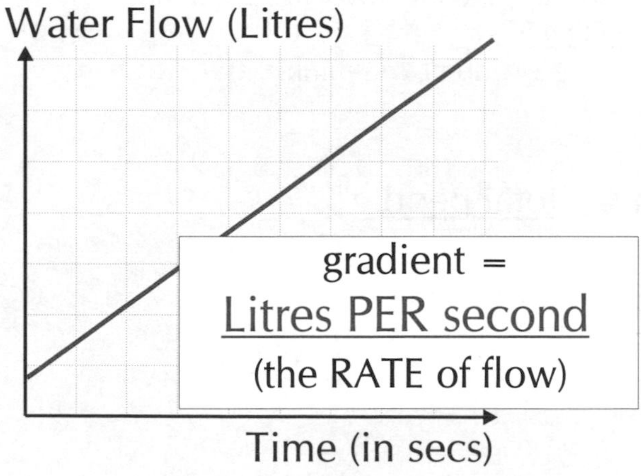

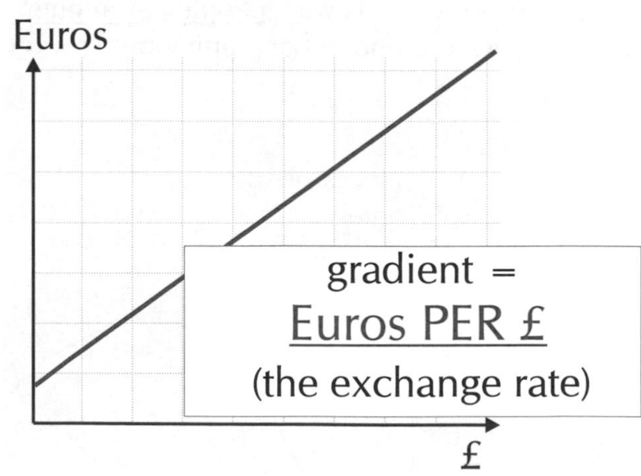

Gradients just mean something per something

You can start to see why gradients are so useful. Good examples are distance-time and velocity-time graphs where the gradients represent distance per time (speed) and speed per time (acceleration). (See pages 64-65)

The Meaning of Area

*The **area** under a graph **represents** the **total something***

The secret here is the UNIT of the Vertical Axis which will be a RATE of some sort, i.e. "SOMETHING PER ANOTHER-THING".
To find the *meaning* of the *area under the graph*, all you do is remove the "PER ANOTHER-THING" from those units and the "SOMETHING" that's left is what the area under the graph represents.
The area is the "TOTAL SOMETHING" in fact.

For this to work the units on the two axes need to MATCH. For example, speed in metres per second plotted against time in seconds. The 'seconds' match, so the area represents total metres.

*Two **examples:***

1) If the vertical axis is velocity, (measured in "METRES PER SECOND"), then remove the "per second" and the area must represent "metres", or rather TOTAL METRES, i.e. the TOTAL DISTANCE TRAVELLED.

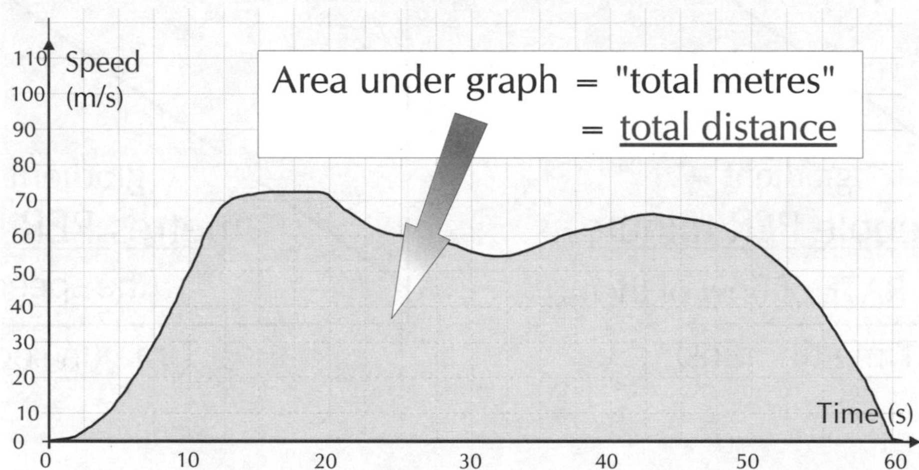

2) If the vertical axis was "people per minute" (entering a zoo, say), then remove the "per minute" and the area under that graph would simply be TOTAL PEOPLE.

(Easy, don't you think?)

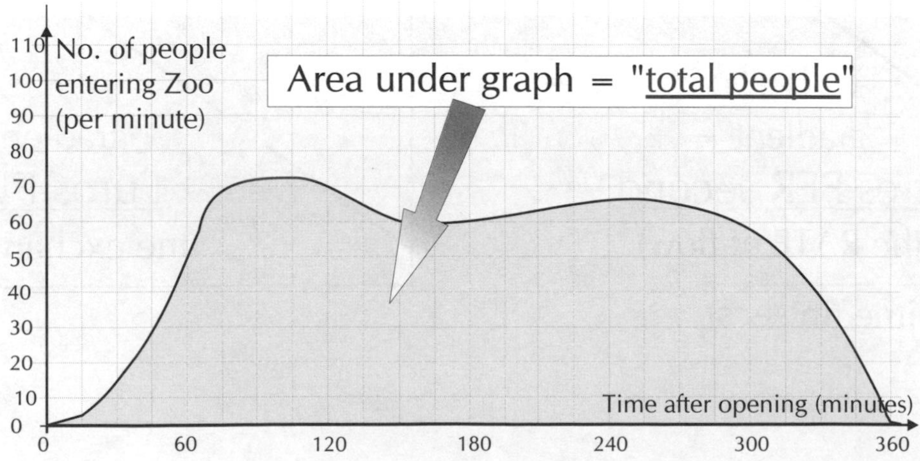

Who'd have thought the area under the graph would be so useful

Knock off the "per another thing" then the area under the graph gives the total of the something. Sounds pretty confusing, but if you've learnt these examples properly you'll see exactly what I mean.

Finding Equations from Graphs

The basic idea here is to *get the equation for a given curve* and there are *four main types* of equation/curve which you're likely to get in the Exam:

SQUARED FUNCTION: "$y = ax^2 + b$" **CUBIC FUNCTION: "$y = ax^3 + b$"**
EXPONENTIAL FUNCTION: "$y = pq^x$" **TRIG FUNCTION: "$y = d(\sin x) + e$"**

It can all seem quite tricky to the uninitiated, but once you've cottoned onto the method it's really pretty simple. It's the same easy method for all of them and this is it:

Method

1) You have to find TWO unknowns in the equation (e.g. a and b, or p and q, etc.), which means you'll need TWO pairs of x and y values to stick in the equation.
2) You find these simply by taking the *coordinates* of *two points on the graph*.
3) You should always try to *take points that lie on either the x-axis or y-axis*. (this makes one of the coordinates ZERO which makes the equations much easier to solve)

Example

The graph below has been obtained from experimental data and the curve appears to be of the form "$H = at^2 + b$". Use the graph to find values for the constants "a" and "b".

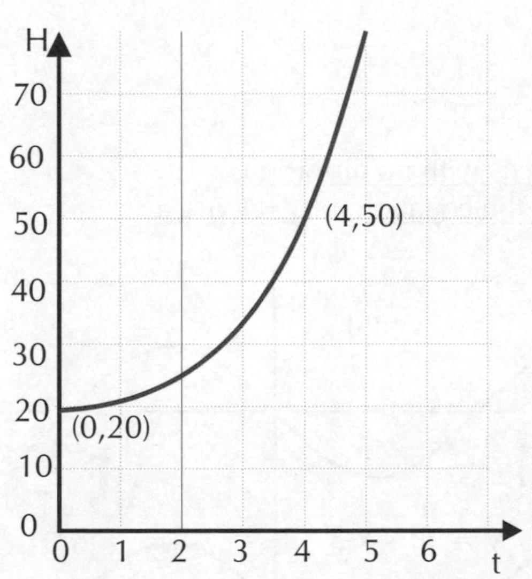

ANSWER:
We can choose any two points on the graph but the most obvious and sensible choices are the two indicated: (0, 20) and (4, 50). The best of these of course is (0, 20), and sticking these values for H and t in the equation gives:
$20 = 0 + b$
so straight away we know $b = 20$

Now using (4, 50), together with $b = 20$ gives: $50 = a \times 16 + 20$

which gives:
$a = (50 - 20)/16 = 1.875$ so $a = 1.9$ (to 2sf)

Hence the equation is $H = 1.9t^2 + 20$

If they give you one of the other equations, then the algebra will be a bit different. However, the basic method is always exactly the same so make sure you know it.

You have to plug two sets of points in — one to get each unknown

Remember to select the points you use carefully. If you can use points on the x or y axis then one of your values will be zero — and that'll make things much easier.

Graphs: Shifts and Stretches

Don't be put off by function notation involving f(x). It doesn't mean anything complicated — it's just a fancy way of saying "an equation in x".

In other words "y = f(x)" just means "y = some totally mundane equation in x, which we won't tell you, we'll just call it f(x) instead to see how many of you get in a flap about it".

In a question on transforming graphs they will either use function notation or they'll use a known function instead. There are only four different types of graph transformations so just LEARN them and be done with it. Here they are in order of difficulty:

1) y-stretch: $y = k \times f(x)$

This is where the original graph is stretched along the y-axis by multiplying the whole function by a number, i.e. y = f(x) becomes y = kf(x) (where k = 2 or 5 etc.). If k is less than 1, then the graph is squashed down in the y-direction instead:

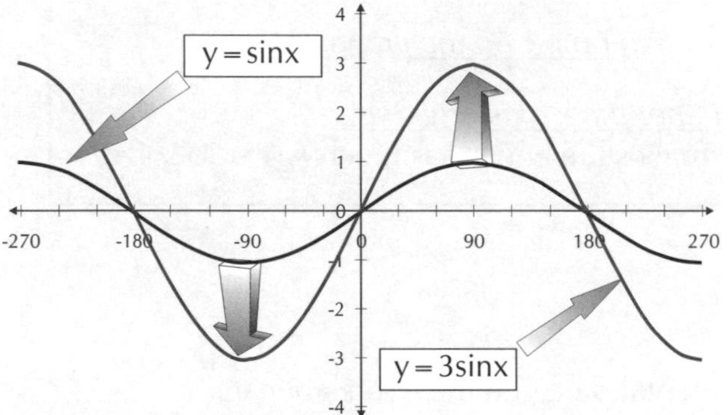

This graph shows y = f(x) and y = 3f(x)
(y = sin x and y = 3 sin x)

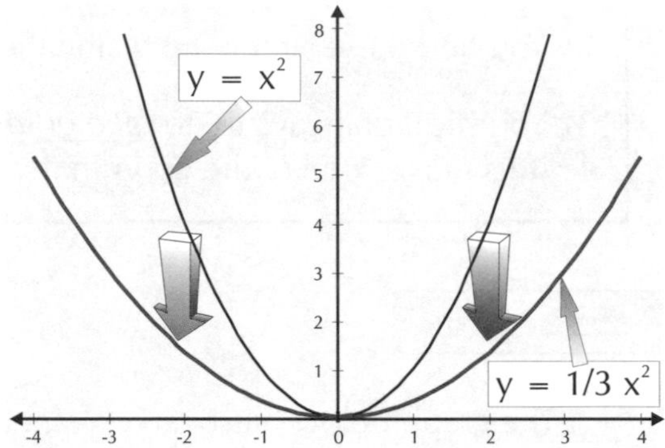

This graph shows y = f(x) and y = 1/3 f(x)
($y=x^2$ and $y=1/3\ x^2$)

2) y-shift: $y = f(x) + a$

This is where the whole graph is slid UP OR DOWN the y-axis with no distortion, and is achieved by simply adding a number onto the end of the equation: y = f(x) + a.

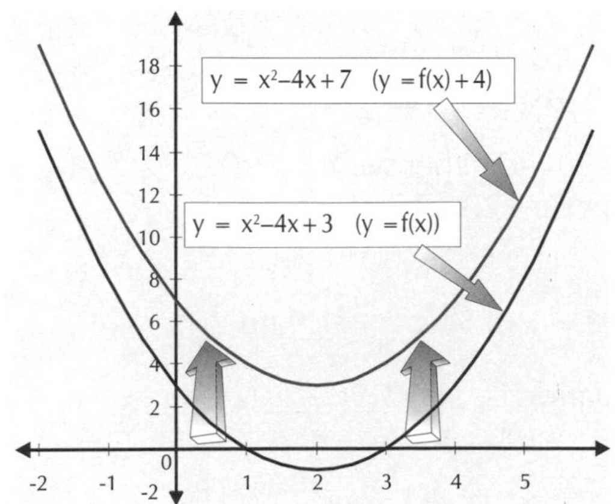

This shows y = f(x) and y = f(x) + 4
i.e. $y = x^2 - 4x + 3$, and
$y = (x^2 - 4x + 3) + 4$
or $y = x^2 - 4x + 7$

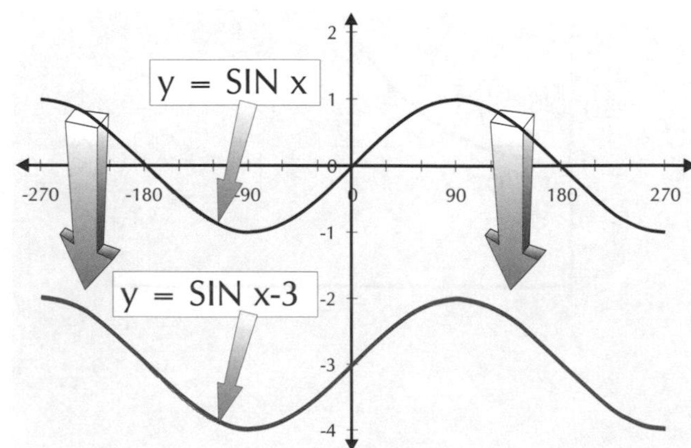

This shows y = f(x) and y = f(x) – 3
i.e y = sin x and y = sinx – 3

Remember f(x) is just some equation with x's in it

Graphs can be stretched or squashed along the y-axis by multiplying the whole function by a number. Or they can slide up or down by adding a number to the function. That's all I'm trying to say.

Graphs: Shifts and Stretches

3) x-shift: $y = f(x - a)$

This is where the whole graph slides to the left or right — it only happens when you replace "x" everywhere in the equation with "x – a". These are a bit tricky because they go "the wrong way". In other words, if you want to go from $y = f(x)$ to $y = f(x - a)$ you must move the whole graph a distance "a" in the POSITIVE x-direction → (and vice versa).

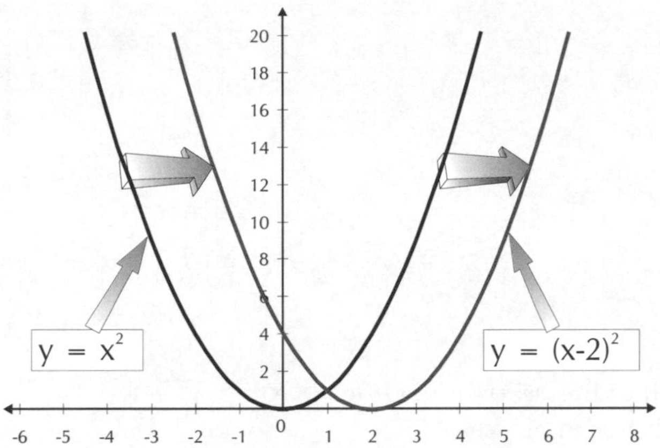

This graph shows $y = f(x)$ and $y = f(x–2)$
(i.e. $y = x^2$ and $y = (x - 2)^2$)

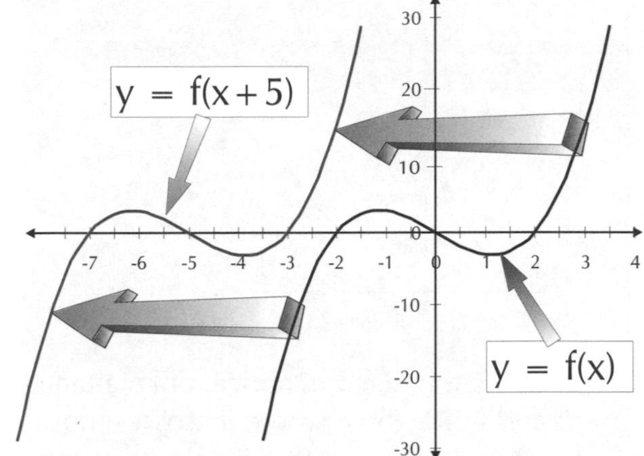

This graph shows $y = f(x)$ and $y = f(x+5)$
i.e. $y = x^3 - 4x$, and $y = (x+5)^3 - 4(x+5)$

4) x-stretch: $y = f(kx)$

These go "the wrong way" too — when k is a "multiplier" it *scrunches the graph up*, whereas when it's a "divider", it *stretches* the graph out. (The opposite of the y-stretch)

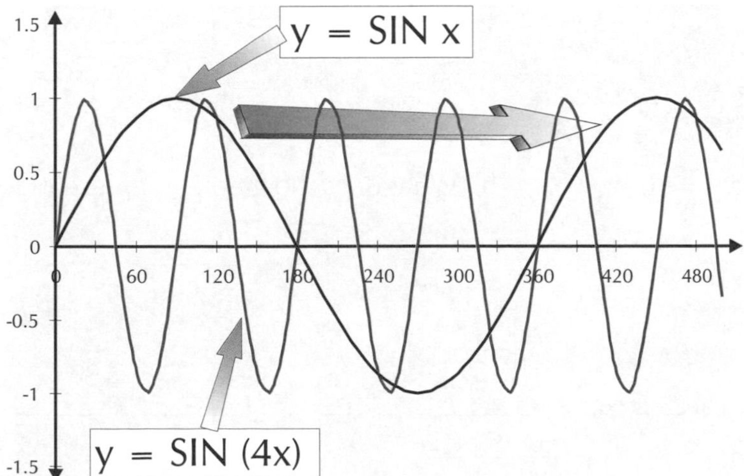

This graph shows
$y = \sin x$ and $y = \sin(4x)$
The one that is all squashed up is $y = \sin(4x)$
The way to sketch it is simply that with a multiplier of 4, it will be 4 times as squashed up.
(Each full cycle of up-and-down takes ¼ the amount of x-axis as the original graph, so you fit 4 of them into 1 of the other graph)

Remember, if k is a divider, then the graph spreads out. So if the squashed up graph above was the original, $y = f(x)$, then the more spread out one would be $y = f(x/4)$.

Two more slightly trickier shifts and stretches

Graphs can also slide left or right when x is replaced with x – a. Or be stretched or squashed along the x-axis when x is replaced with kx. These are slightly trickier than the last page but the principle is the same.

Warm-Up Questions

Take a deep breath and go through these warm-up questions one by one.
If you don't know these basic facts there's no way you'll cope with the exam questions.

Warm-Up Questions

1)

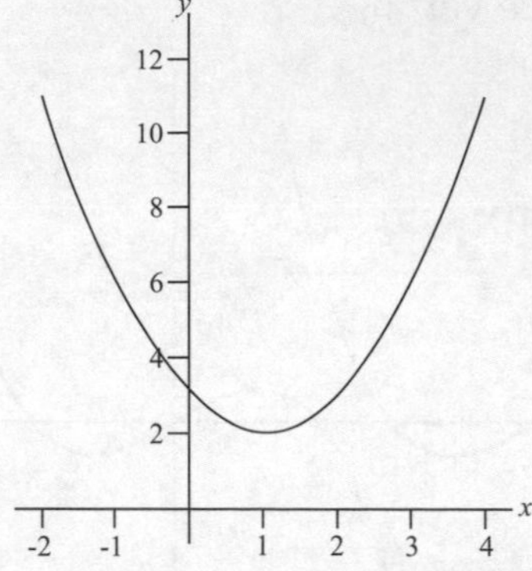

Using the diagram above, draw a tangent at each of the following values of x and write down where it crosses the x-axis (the horizontal axis).
(a) $x = 2$. (b) $x = -1$. (c) $x = 0$.

2)

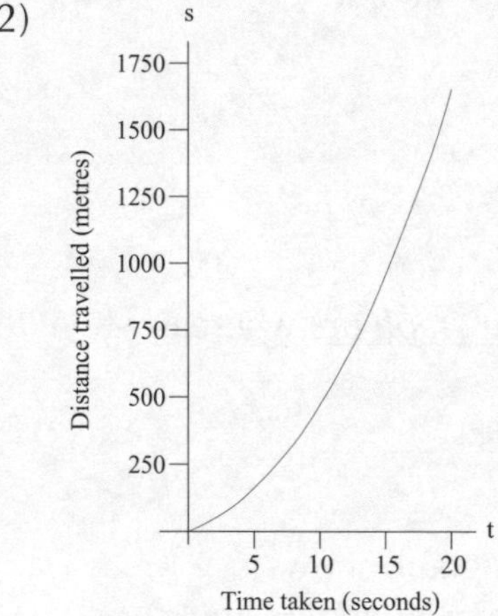

(a) Find the gradient of the curve at $t = 10$. (b) What does the gradient represent?

3)

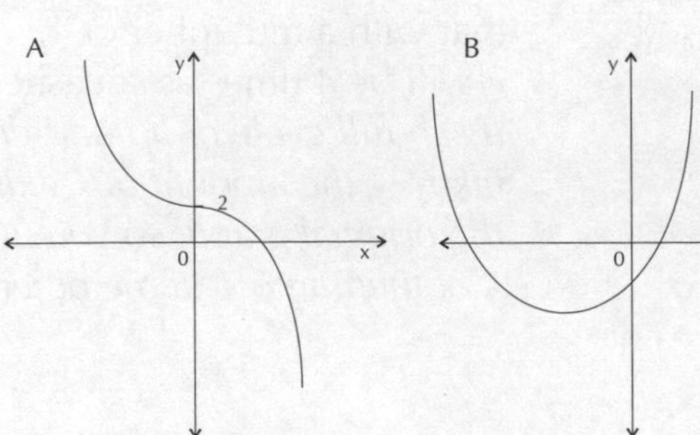

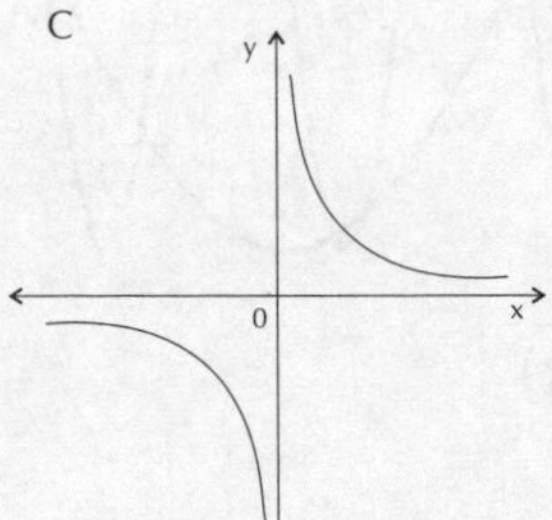

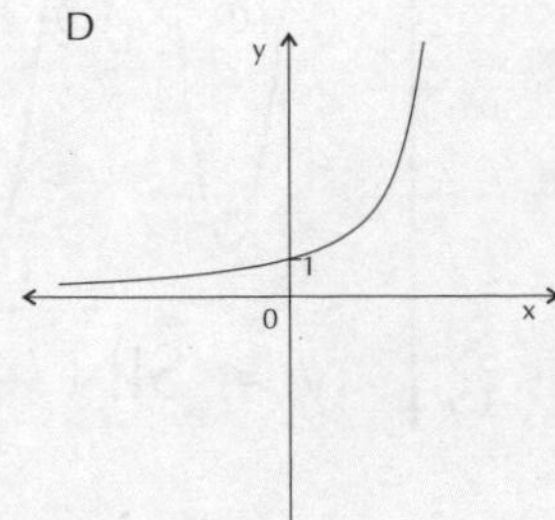

Match the graphs with their equations.

(a) $y = 2^x$ (b) $y = 2x^2 + 5x - 3$ (c) $y + x^3 = 2$ (d) $xy = 1/2$

Worked Exam Questions

Worked Exam Questions

Exam questions don't vary that wildly, the basic format is the same.
So you'd be mad not to spend a bit of time learning some model answers wouldn't you...

1 Below is the velocity-time graph for a minute of a cyclist's journey.

(a) Calculate an estimate for the acceleration of the cyclist after 30 seconds.

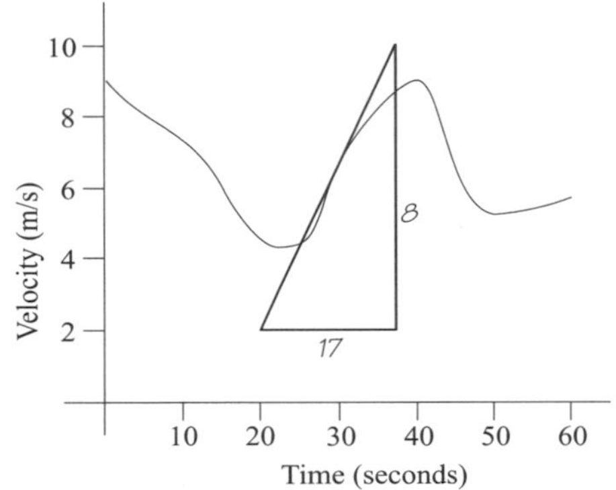

Hint: Write the change in y and the change in x on the graph.

8/17 = 0.47058... = 0.5 (1 d.p.)

(3 marks)

(b) What would the area under the graph represent?

Distance travelled in that minute of the journey.

(1 mark)

2 Below is a sketch of the curve with equation $y = f(x)$.

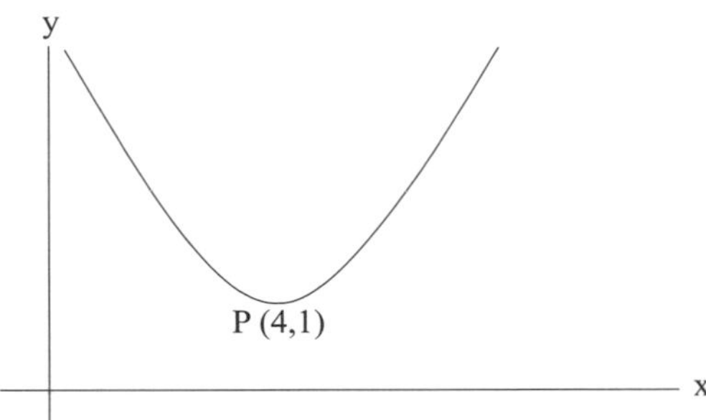

There is just one minimum point and that is P (4,1).
Write down the coordinates of the minimum point for curves with the following equations.

(a) $y = f(x - 2)$

X-shift to the right (in the positive X-direction). Min pt = (6,1).

(1 mark)

(b) $y = f(4x)$

X-stretch. The graph is 'scrunched up' along the x-axis. Min pt = (1,1).

It is an "X-Stretch", but it actually scrunches the graph up. This is because 'k' is a multiplier. If 'k' was a divider it would stretch the graph — strange but true (see p. 145).

(1 mark)

(c) $y = f(x) + 3$

Y-shift upwards. Min pt = (4,4).

(1 mark)

Exam Questions

3 The graph shown has the form $y = ax^3 - bx^2$.

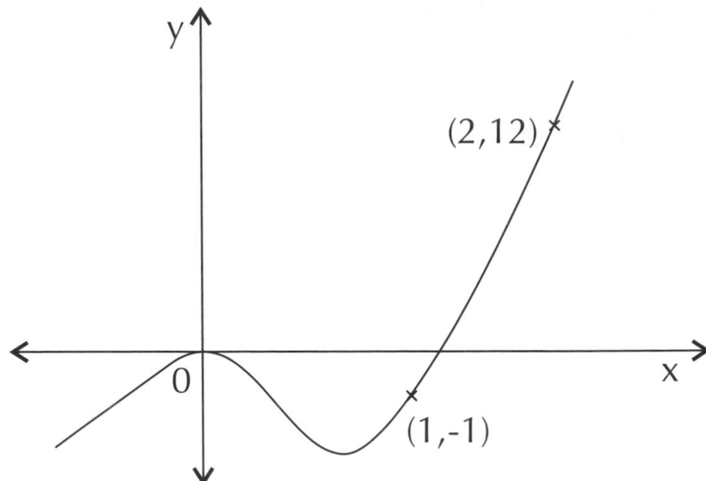

The curve passes through (1, -1) and (2, 12). Find the value of a and the value of b.

....

(3 marks)

4

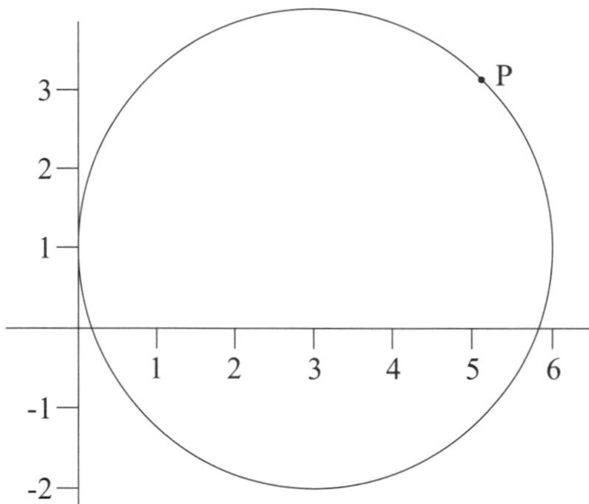

(a) Draw the tangent at P to the curve.

(1 mark)

(b) Calculate the gradient of the tangent you have drawn.
Give your answer correct to 1 decimal place.

....

(3 marks)

Revision Summary for Section Five

Aren't graphs great? I think everyone likes graphs.
Anyway, here are the questions to find out what you know. By the way, I hope you haven't started trying to kid yourself that these aren't proper maths questions so you don't have to bother with them. Maths is *packed* with *facts* — and you need to know them *to be able to do it*.
All these questions do is see how many of the simple facts you've learnt so far.
Try it now and scare yourself. Then learn some stuff and try again.

Keep learning the basic facts until you know them

1) What are the four types of straight lines you should know?
2) What does a straight-line equation look like?
3) What is the "x=0, y=0" method?
4) What is the "table of three values" method?
5) Describe how to find the length of a line, given the coordinates of the endpoints.
   Describe how to find the midpoint of the same line.
6) In which order do you write 3-D coordinates: a) (z, y, x) b) (y, x, z) c) (x, y, z)?
7) What does "y = mx + c" have to do with?
8) What do "m" and "c" represent?
9) List the five steps necessary to draw the graph of "5x = 2 + y" using "y = mx +c".
10) List the three steps for obtaining the equation from a straight line graph.
11) What are the three main stages of a linear programming question?
12) How do you draw a line from an inequality?
13) How do you decide which side of the lines should be shaded?
14) What bit of information in the question gives the equation for your ruler?
15) What is the tricky first step to getting a line you can put your ruler on?
16) What do you then do with your ruler? And where will the answer be?
17) List three important steps in filling in a table of values from an equation.
18) List four important points for plotting a graph.
19) Can graphs be used to obtain solutions to equations?
20) Detail the four steps for solving an equation using graphs.
21) Explain briefly how simultaneous equations can be solved using two graphs.
22) What is meant by a "merged equation", and how do you solve it with graphs?
23) What are the similarities and what is the main difference between "solving two simultaneous equations" and "solving a merged equation" using graphs?
24) State three key points for drawing a tangent.
25) What is the five-step method for finding the gradient of a line?
26) What is the rule for deciding what the area under a graph actually represents?
27) What is the rule for deciding what the gradient of a graph represents?
28) Describe in words and with a sketch the different forms of these graphs:
    $y = mx + c$; $y = ax^2 + bx + c$; $y = ax^3 + bx^2 + cx + d$; $xy = a$
29) What are the two steps for identifying "a and b" in an equation from its graph?
30) List the five types of graph/equation that you really need to know how to do.
31) What does the notation y = f(x) mean? Is it really complicated?
32) How many types of shift and stretch are there for graphs?
33) Illustrate each of the different types.
34) Explain how the equation is modified for each of these.
35) Give an example of each type, both the modified equation and a sketch.

Some Simple Bits and Bobs

When it comes to NEGATIVE NUMBERS, everyone knows Rule 1,
but sometimes Rule 2 applies instead, so make sure you know BOTH rules and when to use them.

Rule 1:

Only to be used when:

1) Multiplying or dividing:
   e.g. $-2 \times 3 = \underline{-6}$, $-8 \div -2 = \underline{+4}$ $-4p \times -2 = \underline{+8p}$

2) Two signs are together:
   e.g. $5 - -4 = 5 + 4 = \underline{9}$ $4 + -6 - -7 = 4 - 6 + 7 = \underline{5}$

+	+	makes	+
+	–	makes	–
–	+	makes	–
–	–	makes	+

Rule 2:

Use this when ADDING OR SUBTRACTING.

THE NUMBER LINE

Example:

"Simplify:

4X – 8X – 3X + 6X"

So

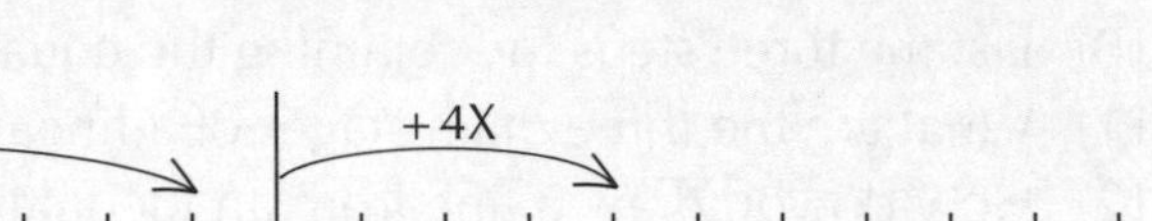

$4X - 8X - 3X + 6X = \underline{-1X}$

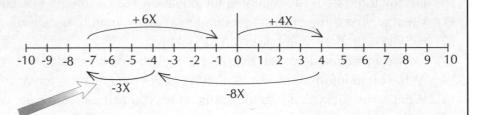

Letters multiplied together

Watch out for these combinations of letters in algebra that regularly catch people out:

1) abc means a×b×c. The ×'s are often left out to make it clearer.

2) gn^2 means g×n×n. Note that only the n is squared, not the g as well. e.g. πr^2

3) $(gn)^2$ means g×g×n×n. The brackets mean that BOTH letters are squared.

4) $p(q - r)^3$ means $p \times (q - r) \times (q - r) \times (q - r)$. Only the brackets get cubed.

5) -3^2 is a bit ambiguous. It should either be written $(-3)^2 = 9$, or $-(3^2) = -9$

These simple bits and bobs are the key to all algebra

Algebra gets people really phased at first. If you don't get these basics in your head you will be really baffled in a few pages' time. So scribble over and over again until this is crystal clear.

Difference of Two Squares

Questions on the difference of two squares are very popular in the Exam and you need to learn to recognise them at the drop of a hat.

D.O.T.S. - The Difference Of Two Squares:

$$a^2 - b^2 = (a + b)(a - b)$$

The "difference of two squares" (D.O.T.S. for short) is where you have:

"one thing squared" take away "another thing squared"

In the Exam you'll more than likely be asked to factorise a D.O.T.S. expression (i.e. put it into two brackets as above).

Too many people have more trouble than they should with this, probably because they don't make enough effort to learn it as a separate item in its own right. So you'd better learn it now before it's too late.

Make sure you LEARN these three important examples:

1) Factorise $9P^2 - 16Q^2$.

Answer: $9P^2 - 16Q^2 = (3P)^2 - (4Q)^2 = \underline{(3P + 4Q)(3P - 4Q)}$

2) Factorise $1 - T^4$.

Answer: $1 - T^4 = \underline{(1 + T^2)(1 - T^2)}$

3) Factorise $3K^2 - 75H^2$.

Answer: $3K^2 - 75H^2 = 3(K^2 - 25H^2) = \underline{3(K + 5H)(K - 5H)}$

This is straightforward as long as you recognise the pattern

Once you've seen one D.O.T.S. question you've seen them all because they all follow the same basic pattern. The third example is the trickiest one because it doesn't look like a D.O.T.S. However if you're on your guard you'll see that taking out the factor of three makes everything look d.o.t. ier straight away.

Basic Algebra

1) Terms

Before you can do anything else, you MUST understand what a TERM is:

1) **A TERM IS A COLLECTION OF NUMBERS, LETTERS AND BRACKETS, ALL MULTIPLIED/DIVIDED TOGETHER.**

2) TERMS are SEPARATED BY + AND – SIGNS

E.g. $4x^2 - 3py - 5 + 3p$

3) TERMS always have a + or – ATTACHED TO THE FRONT OF THEM

4) e.g.

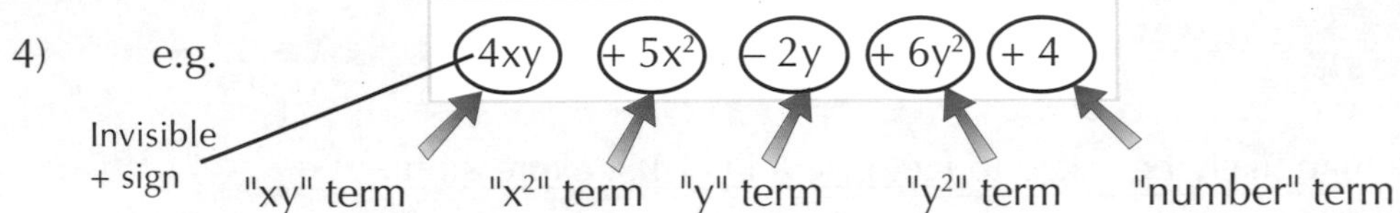

2) Simplifying

— or "Collecting Like Terms"

EXAMPLE: Simplify $2x - 4 + 5x + 6$

(2x) (–4) (+5x) (+ 6) = (+2x) (+5x) (–4) (+6)

Invisible + sign; x-terms; number terms

= 7x +2 = $7x + 2$

1) Put bubbles round each term — be sure you capture the +/– sign IN FRONT of each.

2) Then you can move the bubbles into the best order so that LIKE TERMS are together.

3) "LIKE TERMS" have exactly the same combination of letters, e.g. x-terms or xy-terms.

4) Combine LIKE TERMS using the NUMBER LINE (not the other rule for negative numbers).

You need to know what terms are — and how to collect like ones

Terms are a collection of numbers and letters separated by + and – signs. When you collect like terms together, you combine x terms, or y terms, or xy terms, or x^2 terms or y^2 terms or...

Basic Algebra — Brackets

3) **Multiplying** out brackets

1) The thing outside the brackets multiplies each separate term inside the brackets.

2) When letters are multiplied together, they are just written next to each other, pq.

3) Remember, $R \times R = R^2$, and TY^2 means $T\times Y\times Y$, whilst $(TY)^2$ means $T\times T\times Y\times Y$.

4) Remember a minus outside the bracket REVERSES ALL THE SIGNS when you multiply.

1) $3(2x + 5) = \underline{6x + 15}$ 2) $4p(3r - 2t) = \underline{12pr - 8pt}$

3) $-4(3p^2 - 7q^3) = -12p^2 + 28q^3$ (note both signs have been reversed — Rule 4)

5) DOUBLE BRACKETS — you get four terms, and usually two of them combine to leave three terms.

$(2P - 4)(3P + 1) = (2P\times 3P) + (2P\times 1) + (-4\times 3P) + (-4\times 1)$

$= 6P^2 + 2P - 12P - 4$

$= \underline{6P^2 - 10P - 4}$ (these two combine together)

6) SQUARED BRACKETS — ALWAYS write these out as TWO BRACKETS:

e.g. $(3d + 5)^2$ should be written out as $(3d + 5)(3d + 5)$ and then work them out as above.

YOU SHOULD ALWAYS GET <u>FOUR</u> TERMS from a pair of brackets.

The usual <u>WRONG ANSWER</u> is $(3d + 5)^2 = 9d^2 + 25$

It should be: $(3d + 5)^2 = (3d + 5)(3d + 5) = 9d^2 + 15d + 15d + 25 = \underline{9d^2 + 30d + 25}$

People often make mistakes multiplying out brackets

Remember the usual wrong answer for $(3d + 5)^2$. You should get four terms. As long as you write it out in full as $(3d + 5)(3d + 5)$ and do it like any other double brackets, then you won't go wrong.

Basic Algebra — Factorising

4) Factorising

— putting brackets in

This is the exact reverse of multiplying-out brackets.
Here's the method to follow:

1) Take out the biggest number that goes into all the terms.
2) Take each letter in turn and take out the highest power (e.g. x, x^2 etc) that will go into EVERY term.
3) Open the brackets and fill in all the bits needed to reproduce each term.

EXAMPLE:

"Factorise $15x^4y + 20x^2y^3z - 35x^3yz^2$"

Answer: $5x^2y(3x^2 + 4y^2z - 7xz^2)$

Biggest number that'll divide into 15, 20 and 35.

Highest powers of x and y that will go into all three terms.

z was not in ALL terms so it can't come out as a common factor.

REMEMBER:

1) The bits *taken out* and put at the front are the *common factors*.
2) The bits *inside the brackets* are *what's needed to get back to the original terms* if you multiplied the brackets out again.

Factorising is the opposite of multiplying out brackets

There's no excuse for making simple mistakes here because you can always check your answer by multiplying the brackets out again. If you've done it right then you will get back to the original expression.

Basic Algebra — Fractions

5) Algebraic fractions

The basic rules are exactly the same as for ordinary fractions (see P.2), and you should definitely be aware of the close similarity.

1) Multiplying (easy)

Multiply top and bottom separately and cancel if possible:

e.g. $$\frac{st}{10w^3} \times \frac{35s^2tw}{6}$$

$$= \frac{35s^3t^2w}{60w^3} = \frac{7s^3t^2}{12w^2}$$

2) Dividing (easy)

Turn the second one upside down, then multiply and cancel if possible:

e.g. $$\frac{12}{p+4} \div \frac{4(p-3)}{3(p+4)}$$

$$= \frac{\cancel{12}\,3}{\cancel{p+4}} \times \frac{3\cancel{(p+4)}}{\cancel{4}(p-3)} = \frac{9}{p-3}$$

3) Adding/subtracting (not so easy)

Always get a common denominator i.e. same bottom line (by cross-multiplying) and then ADD TOP LINES ONLY:

$$\frac{t-2p}{3t-p} - \frac{1}{3} = \frac{3(t-2p)}{3(3t-p)} - \frac{1(3t-p)}{3(3t-p)}$$

$$= \frac{3t-6p-3t+p}{3(3t-p)} = \frac{-5p}{3(3t-p)}$$

It's exactly the same as normal fractions

All this stuff should be second nature by now because all the rules are the same as those for normal fractions. OK, it might look a bit harder with all those letters instead of numbers, but that's algebra for you.

Solving Equations

Solving Equations means finding the value of x from something like: $3x + 5 = 4 - 5x$.

Now, not a lot of people know this, but exactly the same method applies to both solving equations and rearranging formulas, as illustrated on the next two double pages.

1) EXACTLY THE SAME METHOD APPLIES TO BOTH FORMULAS AND EQUATIONS.
2) THE SAME SEQUENCE OF STEPS APPLIES EVERY TIME.

To illustrate the sequence of steps we'll use this equation:

$$\sqrt{2 - \frac{x+4}{2x+5}} = 3$$

The *six steps* applied to equations

1) Get rid of any square root signs by

squaring both sides:

$$2 - \frac{x+4}{2x+5} = 9$$

2) Get everything off the bottom by

cross-multiplying up to EVERY OTHER TERM:

$$2 - \frac{x+4}{2x+5} = 9 \quad \Rightarrow \quad 2(2x+5) - (x+4) = 9(2x+5)$$

3) Multiply out any brackets:

$$4x + 10 - x - 4 = 18x + 45$$

That's the first three steps

This is great — all solving equation questions broken down into six simple steps. But hold your horses, make sure you've got these straight before you rush on to number four.

Solving Equations

4) Collect all <u>subject terms</u> on one side of the "=" and all <u>non-subject terms</u> on the other.

Remember to reverse the +/– sign of any term that crosses the "="

+18x moves across the "=" and becomes -18x
+10 moves across the "=" and becomes -10
-4 moves across the "=" and becomes +4

+/– +/– +/–

$$4x - x - 18x = 45 - 10 + 4$$

5) Combine like terms on each side of the equation,

and reduce it to the form "Ax = B", where A and B are just numbers (or bunches of letters, in the case of formulas):

$-15x = 39$ ("Ax = B": A = -15, B = 39, x is the subject)

6) Finally slide the A underneath the B

to give "$x = {}^{B}/_{A}$", divide, and that's your answer.

$x = {}^{39}/_{-15} = -2.6$

So $x = -2.6$

The Seventh Step (if you need it)

If the term you're trying to find is squared, don't panic.

Follow steps 1) to 6) like normal, but solve it for, x^2 instead of x:

7) Take the square root of both sides and stick a ± sign in front of the expression on the right:

$x^2 = 9$
$x = \pm 3$

Don't forget the ± sign...

That's it, all the steps you need to solve any of these equations

There's nothing like making life easy for you. By breaking down these questions into six (or seven) simple steps we're more or less giving you marks. All you have to do is learn them.

Rearranging Formulas

Rearranging Formulas means making one letter the subject,
e.g. getting "y= " from something like $2x + z = 3(y + 2p)$

Generally speaking "solving equations" is easier, but don't forget:

1) EXACTLY THE SAME METHOD APPLIES TO BOTH FORMULAS AND EQUATIONS.
2) THE SAME SEQUENCE OF STEPS APPLIES EVERY TIME.

We'll illustrate this by making "y" the subject of this formula:

$$M = \sqrt{2K - \frac{K^2}{2y+1}}$$

The *six steps* applied to formulas

1) Get rid of any square root signs by

squaring both sides:

$$M^2 = 2K - \frac{K^2}{2y+1}$$

2) Get everything off the bottom by

cross-multiplying up to EVERY OTHER TERM:

$$M^2 = 2K - \frac{K^2}{2y+1} \Rightarrow M^2(2y+1) = 2K(2y+1) - K^2$$

3) Multiply out any brackets:

$$2yM^2 + M^2 = 4Ky + 2K - K^2$$

Is it just me or does this seem a bit familiar?

Remember what I said — get the first three steps lodged firmly in your brain box before you rush off over eagerly on to step four. You've got to walk before you can run.

Rearranging Formulas

4) Collect all subject terms on one side of the "=" and all non-subject terms on the other.

Remember to reverse the +/– sign of any term that crosses the "="

+4Ky moves across the "=" and becomes –4Ky
$+M^2$ moves across the "=" and becomes $-M^2$

+/– +/–

$$2yM^2 - 4Ky = -M^2 + 2K - K^2$$

5) Combine like terms on each side of the equation,

and reduce it to the form "Ax = B", where A and B are just bunches of letters which DON'T include the subject (y). Note that the left hand side has to be FACTORISED:

$(2M^2 - 4K)y = 2K - K^2 - M^2$
("Ax = B" i.e. $A = (2M^2 - 4K)$, $B = 2K - K^2 - M^2$, y is the subject)

6) Finally slide the A underneath the B

to give "X = B/A", (cancel if possible) and that's your answer.

So $y = \dfrac{2K - K^2 - M^2}{(2M^2 - 4K)}$

The Seventh Step (if You Need It)

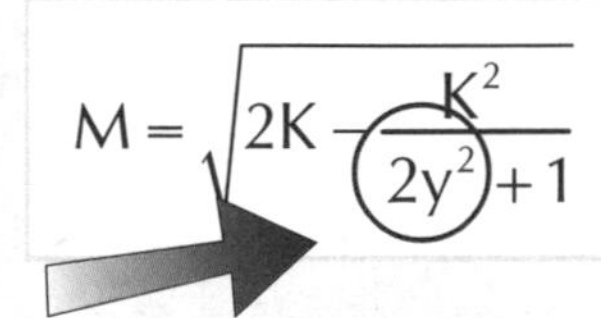

If the term you're trying to make the subject of the equation is squared, this is what you do:

Follow steps 1) to 6), and then...

$$y^2 = \frac{2K - K^2 - M^2}{(2M^2 - 4K)}$$

(I've skipped steps 1) - 6) because they're exactly the same as the first example — but with y^2 instead of y.)

7) Take the square root of both sides and stick a ± sign in front of the expression on the right:

$$y = \pm\sqrt{\frac{2K - K^2 - M^2}{(2M^2 - 4K)}}$$

Remember — square roots can be +ve or –ve.

It's the same method as solving equations — or did I say that already

I can't overstate how useful and important the last four pages are. Six (or seven) simple steps to solve all equations and rearrange all formulas. That's a lot of marks right there — take them or leave them.

Warm-Up and Worked Exam Questions

It's easy to think you've learnt everything in the section until you try the warm-up questions.
Don't panic if there are bits you've forgotten. Just go back over them until they're firmly fixed in your brain.

Warm-Up Questions

1) Make sure you know and can apply the rules of signs. Here's a quick test for you:
(a) $-1 + 3$ (b) $-1 - -3$ (c) $4 - -2$ (d) $4 + -2$
(e) -1×-3 (f) $-1 \div -3$ (g) 4×-2 (h) $4 \div -2$.
2) Multiply out:
(a) $4(2p + 7)$ b) $(4x - 2)(2x + 1)$ c) $a(5a - 3)$.
3) Factorise $x^2 - 4y^2$. *HINT: Remember D.O.T.S*
4) Simplify: (a) $4a + c - 2a - 6c$ (b) $3r^2 - 2r + 4r^2 - 1 - 3r$.
5) Factorise:
(a) $6p - 12q + 4$ (b) $4cd^2 - 2cd + 10c^2d^3$.
6) Express as single fractions:
(a) $\frac{x}{2} + \frac{3x}{5}$ (b) $\frac{abc}{d} \div \frac{b^2}{dc}$ *Algebraic fractions work like number fractions*
7) Solve these equations to find the value of x:
(a) $8x - 5 = 19$ (b) $3(2x + 7) = 3$ (c) $4x - 9 = x + 6$.
8) What is the subject of these formulae?
(a) $p = \sqrt{\frac{ml^2}{h}}$ (b) $t = px - y^3$.
9) (a) Write down the rule for the area of a rectangle, explaining any letters you use.
(b) How would you find the length if you know the area and width? Write this as a formula.

Worked Exam Questions

I've gone through these worked examples and written in answers, just like you'll do in the exam.
It should really help with the questions which follow, so don't say I never do anything for you.

1 (a) Simplify $4(3x + 4) - 3(x - 2)$.

Be careful — this is $-3 \times -2 = +6$

$4(3x + 4) - 3(x - 2) = 12x + 16 - 3x + 6 = 9x + 22$

(2 marks)

(b) Factorise $36p^2 - 25q^2$.

$36p^2 - 25q^2 = (6p + 5q)(6p - 5q)$

It's a squared thing minus another squared thing which means it's difference of 2 squares.

(2 marks)

(c) Expand and simplify $(3c + 4)(2c - 1)$.

$(3c + 4)(2c - 1) = 6c^2 - 3c + 8c - 4 = 6c^2 + 5c - 4$

(2 marks)

Worked Exam Questions

2 (a) Simplify $8p^2q - 3pq + 2pq^2 - 4p^2q - 7pq$.

pq^2 is a different term from p^2q so keep them separate

$8p^2q - 3pq + 2pq^2 - 4p^2q - 7pq = 4p^2q - 10pq + 2pq^2$

(2 marks)

(b) Factorise fully $16a^2b - 4ab^2 + 8abc$.

$16a^2b - 4ab^2 + 8abc = 4ab(4a - b + 2c)$

(2 marks)

(c) Expand and simplify $(5s - 2)^2$.

$(5s - 2)^2 = (5s - 2)(5s - 2) = 25s^2 - 10s - 10s + 4 = 25s^2 - 20s + 4$

(2 marks)

3 Solve for p:

(a) $\frac{500}{p} = 16$

This is just like normal fractions, e.g. 12/3 = 4 and 12/4 = 3

$\frac{500}{p} = 16$ so $\frac{500}{16} = p$ so $p = 31.25$

(2 marks)

(b) $10 - \frac{p+3}{2} = \frac{2p+1}{3}$

$10 - \frac{(p+3)}{2} = \frac{(2p+1)}{3} \Rightarrow 60 - 3(p+3) = 2(2p+1)$

$\Rightarrow 60 - 3p - 9 = 4p + 2$

$\Rightarrow 49 = 7p$

$\Rightarrow p = 7$

(3 marks)

4 (a) Expand $(3x + p)^2$.

$(3x + p)^2 = (3x + p)(3x + p) = 9x^2 + 6px + p^2$

(2 marks)

(b) Find the positive values of p and q that would make $(3x + p)^2 = 9x^2 + qx + 16$.

$9x^2 + 6px + p^2 = 9x^2 + qx + 16 \Rightarrow p^2 = 16$, so $p = 4$ (positive value)

and $6p = q$, so $q = 24$

(2 marks)

Exam Questions

5 Simplify these expressions:

(a) $3x^2y - 2xy^2 + x^2y - 4y^2x$.

....

(2 marks)

(b) $4(k + 2r) - 3k - 2(r + k)$.

....

(2 marks)

6 Multiply out the brackets and simplify if possible:

(a) $4(2x - 3) - 3(4 + 3x)$.

....

(2 marks)

(b) $(3c - 1)(2c + 6)$.

....

(2 marks)

7 Express as a single fraction:

(a) $\frac{8}{3x} + 2$.

....

(1 mark)

(b) $\frac{x^2y}{z} + \frac{xy^3}{3z}$.

....

(2 marks)

8 (a) Factorise $12c^2d^3 + 18cd^2 - 30c^3d^4$.

....

(2 marks)

(b) (i) Simplify $-2bc \times -4b^2d$.

....

(2 marks)

(ii) Simplify $t - t(t - 1)$.

....

(2 marks)

Exam Questions

9 Factorise:

(a) $2cx + xy + 2ac + ay$.

....

(3 marks)

(b) $16x^2 - 4p^2$.

....

(2 marks)

10 Solve these equations to find the value of x:

(a) $7x - 3(x + 1) = 7$.

....

(2 marks)

(b) $\frac{3x-1}{5} = \frac{x}{4} + \frac{1}{2}$.

....

(3 marks)

11 (a) Expand $(x - 3)^2$.

....

(2 marks)

(b) Simplify $(x - 3)^2 - x(x - 4)$.

....

(2 marks)

(c) Solve the equation $(x - 3)^2 - x(x - 4) = 7x + 18$.

....

(2 marks)

12 The cost of a blank CD is 35p and the admin charge for copying a CD is £7 per hundred. Postage of p pence per CD is added.

(a) Write a formula for the cost (£c) of copying and posting n CDs.

....

(2 marks)

(b) What will be the total cost of sending out 173 CDs, each using one first-class stamp of 32p?

....

(2 marks)

Inequalities

The main thing to remember about inequalities is that they're not half as difficult as they look.

The inequality symbols are very off-putting,
but most of the algebra for them is identical to ordinary equations
— you just need to learn a few tricks to go with them.

*The **inequality** symbols:*

$>$ means "Greater than" $\geqslant$ means "Greater than or equal to"

$<$ means "Less than" $\leqslant$ means "Less than or equal to"

REMEMBER, the one at the BIG end is BIGGEST

so $x > 4$ and $4 < x$ both say: "x is greater than 4"

*Algebra with **inequalities***

$5x < x + 2$

$5x = x + 2$

The thing to remember here is that
inequalities are just like regular equations in the sense that:

all the normal rules of algebra apply

There is ONE BIG EXCEPTION:

Whenever you MULTIPLY OR DIVIDE
BY A NEGATIVE NUMBER,
you must FLIP THE INEQUALITY SIGN.

Inequalities are just like normal equations — except the exception

Two things to remember here — "the one at the big end is the biggest" and "flip the inequality sign when you multiply or divide by a negative number". Otherwise it's the old algebra you know and love.

Inequalities

Three *important* examples

1) Solve $5x < 6x + 2$

The equivalent equation is $5x = 6x + 2$, which is easy — and so is the inequality:

First subtract 6x : $5x - 6x < 2$ which gives $-x < 2$

Then multiply both sides by -1: $x > -2$ (i.e. x is greater than -2)
(NOTE: The < has flipped around into a >, because we multiplied by a –ve number)

2) Find all integer values of x where $-4 \leq x < 1$

This type of expression is very common —
YOU MUST LEARN TO READ THEM IN THIS WAY:

" x is between -4 and +1, possibly equal to -4 but never equal to +1 ".
(Obviously the answers are -4, -3, -2, -1, 0 (but not 1))

3) Find the range of values of x where $x^2 \leqslant 25$

The trick here is: DON'T FORGET THE NEGATIVE VALUES.
Square-rooting both sides gives $x \leqslant 5$. However, this is ONLY HALF THE STORY, because $-5 \leqslant x$ is also true. There is little alternative but to simply LEARN this:

1) $x^2 \leqslant 25$ gives the solution $-5 \leqslant x \leqslant 5$,

(x is between -5 and 5, possibly equal to either)

2) $x^2 \geqslant 36$ gives the solution: $x \leqslant -6$ or $6 \leqslant x$

(x is "less than or equal to -6" or "greater than or equal to +6")

This stuff is straightforward as long as you learnt the last page

These three examples give you a really clear idea of what you need to do in the exam. The biggest stumbling block is forgetting the negative values when you have x^2, but now I've warned you, you won't.

Simultaneous Equations

Simultaneous equations tend to follow a pretty standard format and the rules are really quite simple, but you must follow ALL the steps, in the right order, and treat them as a strict method. Every step is vital. Miss one out and it's like forgetting to put the water in with the sand and cement — no matter how well you pummel the mixture, it won't stick your bricks together.

There are two types of simultaneous equations you could get — EASY ONES (where both equations are linear) and TRICKY ONES (where one's quadratic).

 $2x = 6 - 4y$ and $-3 - 3y = 4x$  $7x + y = 1$ and $2x^2 - y = 3$

1 Six steps for **easy simultaneous equations**

We'll use these two equations for our example: $2x = 6 - 4y$ and $-3 - 3y = 4x$

1) Rearrange both equations into the form $ax + by = c$ where a,b,c are numbers, (which can be negative). Also label the two equations —(1) and —(2)

$$2x + 4y = 6 \quad \text{—(1)}$$
$$-4x - 3y = 3 \quad \text{—(2)}$$

2) You need to match up the numbers in front (the "coefficients") of either the x's or y's in both equations. To do this you may need to multiply one or both equations by a suitable number. You should then relabel them: —(3) and —(4)

$$(1)\times 2: \quad 4x + 8y = 12 \quad \text{—(3)}$$
$$-4x - 3y = 3 \quad \text{—(4)}$$

3) Add or subtract the two equations to eliminate the terms with the same coefficient. If the coefficients are the same (both +ve or both –ve) then SUBTRACT. If the coefficients are opposite (one +ve and one –ve) then ADD.

$$(3) + (4) \quad 0x + 5y = 15$$

4) Solve the resulting equation to find whichever letter is left in it.

$$5y = 15 \quad \Rightarrow \quad \underline{y = 3}$$

5) Substitute this value back into equation (1) and solve it to find the other quantity.

$$\text{Sub in (1)}: \quad 2x + 4 \times 3 = 6 \;\Rightarrow\; 2x + 12 = 6 \;\Rightarrow\; 2x = -6 \;\Rightarrow\; \underline{x = -3}$$

6) Then substitute both these values into equation (2) to make sure it works out properly. If it doesn't then you've done something wrong and you'll have to do it all again.

Sub x and y in (2): $-4 \times -3 \;-\; 3 \times 3 = 12 - 9 = \underline{3}$, which is right, so it's worked.

So the solutions are: $\underline{x = -3}$, $\underline{y = 3}$

*And these are the **easy** simultaneous equations*

It might just be me, but I think simultaneous equation are quite fun... well maybe not fun... but quite satisfying... anyway it doesn't matter whether you like them or not — you've got to learn how to do them.

Simultaneous Equations

2 Seven steps for **tricky simultaneous equations**

Example: Solve these two equations simultaneously: $7x + y = 1$ and $2x^2 - y = 3$

1) Rearrange the quadratic equation so that you have one term on its own.
   And label the equations (1) and (2).

$7x + y = 1$ — (1)
$y = 2x^2 - 3$ — (2)

2) Substitute the quadratic expression into the other equation.
   You'll get another equation — label it (3).

$7x + y = 1$ — (1)
$y = 2x^2 - 3$ — (2)
$7x + (2x^2 - 3) = 1$ — (3)

In this example you just shove the expression for y into equation (1), in place of y.

3) Rearrange to get a quadratic equation.
   And guess what... You've got to solve it.

Remember — if it won't factorise, you can either use the formula or complete the square. Have a look at P.176 for more details.

$2x^2 + 7x - 4 = 0$
That factorises into:
$(2x - 1)(x + 4) = 0$
So, $2x - 1 = 0$ OR $x + 4 = 0$
In other words, $x = 0.5$ OR $x = -4$

Check this step by multiplying out again:
$(2x - 1)(x + 4) = 2x^2 - x + 8x - 4 = 2x^2 + 7x - 4$

4) Stick the first value back in one of the original equations (pick the easy one).

(1) $7x + y = 1$ Substitute in $x = 0.5$: $3.5 + y = 1$, so $y = 1 - 3.5 = -2.5$

5) Stick the second value back in the same original equation (the easy one again).

(1) $7x + y = 1$ Substitute in $x = -4$: $-28 + y = 1$, so $y = 1 + 28 = 29$

6) Substitute both pairs of answers back into the other original equation to check they work.

(2) $y = 2x^2 - 3$
Substitute in $x = 0.5$ and $y = -2.5$: $-2.5 = (2 \times 0.25) - 3 = -2.5$ — jolly good.
Substitute in $x = -4$ and $y = 29$: $29 = (2 \times 16) - 3 = 29$ — *smashing.*

7) Write the pairs of answers out again, *CLEARLY*, at the bottom of your working.
   The two pairs of answers are:

$x = 0.5$ and $y = -2.5$ OR $x = -4$ and $y = 29$

(Do this even if you think it's pointless and stupid. If there's even the remotest chance of the examiner getting the pairs mixed up, it's worth a tiny bit of extra effort, don't you think.)

Remember to write the two pairs out clearly

You are basically combining the two equations to make one quadratic equation. Solve that equation and then stick the solutions back in to get the other two corresponding answers. What could be easier?*

*Inventive answers on a postcard to "Entertain the editor", CGP, Cumbria. Examples of inventive answers do not include "falling off a log" or "pie".

Warm-Up and Worked Exam Questions

Simultaneous equations and inequalities — two lovely algebra topics, if you ask me... Anyway, love them or hate them, you have to do them. With both, it's just a case of learning the method and practising lots of questions... So let's start with some inequalities...

Warm-up Questions

1) List all integer values for x where $12 < x < 17$.
2) Find all integer values of n if $-3 \leq n \leq 3$.
3) Find all integer values of x such that $8 < 4x < 20$.
4) Solve the inequality $2q + 2 \leq 12$.
5) Solve the inequality $4p + 12 > 30$.

Worked Exam Questions

Inequality exam questions are all the same, more or less... than or equal to...

1 Find all integer values of n such that $6 < 3n < 20$.

Dividing by 3 gives $2 < n < 6.666...$; n must be an integer,

so the only values it can take are: 3, 4, 5, 6.

(2 marks)

2 Draw on a number line all values of n such that $1 < n \leq 5$.

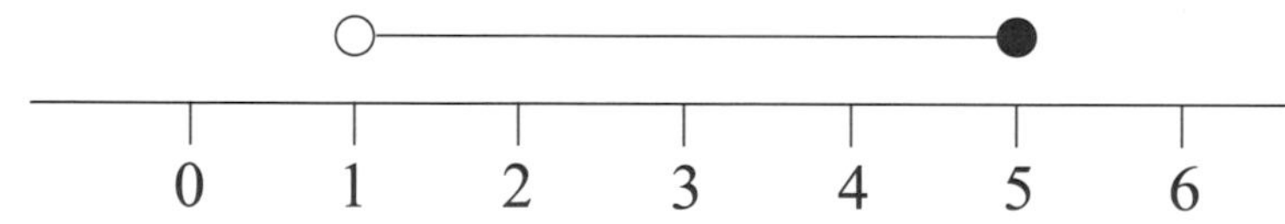

Remember, the circle above the number must be shaded in if that number IS allowed. If it is NOT allowed, it should be left hollow.

(2 marks)

3 Sketch on a graph the region specified by the inequality $2 \leq x \leq 4$.

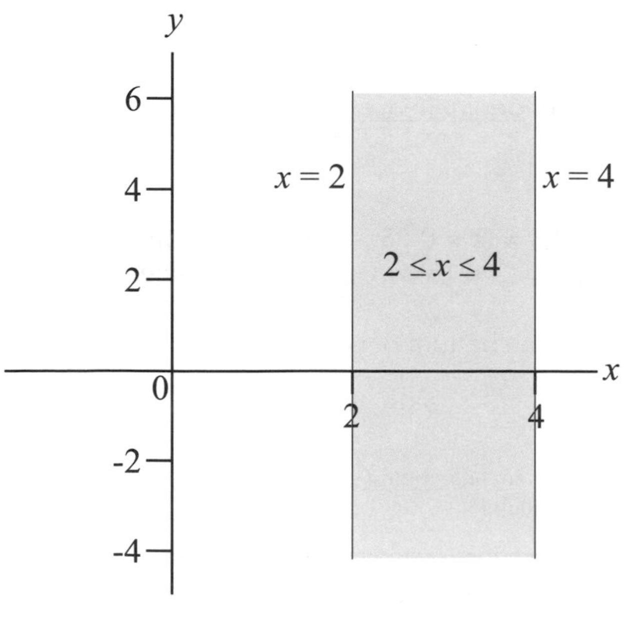

Use solid lines to draw x = 2 and x = 4, then shade between them.

(2 marks)

Warm-Up and Worked Exam Questions

Now it's time to practise some simultaneous equations. They're really not hard at all, so if you're struggling, all you need is more practice.

Warm-up Questions

1) Solve, by elimination, the simultaneous equations $2x + 3y = 19$ and $2x + y = 9$.
2) Solve simultaneously by elimination: $3x + 2y = 20$ and $x - 2y = -4$.

Worked Exam Questions

Have a good sift through these worked examples.
Make sure you understand the bottom one especially, it's of the tricky variety...

3 Solve by elimination the simultaneous equations $3x + 3y = 21$ and $5x - 2y = 14$.

$3x + 3y = 21$ (1) $5x - 2y = 14$ (2)

You need to multiply both equations to make the coefficient of either x or y the same. It's probably easier to go for y.

Equation (1) × 2: $6x + 6y = 42$ — (3)

Equation (2) × 3: $15x - 6y = 42$ — (4)

(3) + (4): $21x = 84$, so $x = 4$.

Once you've found x, just put it into one of the other equations to find y.

Now substitute $x = 4$ into equation (1):

$3x + 3y = 21 \Rightarrow 12 + 3y = 21 \Rightarrow 3y = 9 \Rightarrow y = 3$.

So $x = 4$, $y = 3$

(4 marks)

4 Solve simultaneously $8x + y = -3$ and $y = 2x^2 + 3$.

This is a tricky one because it contains a quadratic. You need to substitute the value of y, then rearrange and solve the resulting quadratic equation (by factorisation).

Substitute "$y = 2x^2 + 3$" into the first equation:

$8x + 2x^2 + 3 = -3 \Rightarrow 2x^2 + 8x + 3 = -3$

$\Rightarrow 2x^2 + 8x + 6 = 0$

You've got a normal quadratic eqn now, so try to factorise it.

Factorising: $(2x + 2)(x + 3) = 0$

So $x = -1$ or $x = -3$

Now to find y, just put your values for x into one of the equations.

Substitute values for x into second original equation to find values for y:

If $x = -1$: $y = 2x^2 + 3 = 5$ If $x = -3$: $y = 2x^2 + 3 = 21$

So answers are: $x = -1$ and $y = 5$ OR $x = -3$ and $y = 21$.

(6 marks)

Exam Questions

5 List all integer values of x such that $-4 < x \leq 2$.

....

(2 marks)

6 Draw a number line to represent those values of n where $10 < n \leq 15$.

(2 marks)

7 Solve the inequality $5a - 10 > 50$.

....

....

(2 marks)

8 Solve the inequality $13 < 4t + 3 < 27$.

....

....

....

(3 marks)

9 Solve the inequality $-3x > 12$.

....

....

(2 marks)

10 Sketch on a graph the region satisfied by all of the following inequalities:
$0 \leq x \leq 2$, $y \geq -1$ and $y \leq x - 1$.

(5 marks)

Exam Questions

11 Solve simultaneously by elimination $5x + 4y = 75$ and $2x + 4y = 54$.

....

....

(3 marks)

12 Solve by elimination the simultaneous equations $3x - 2y = 7$ and $4x - 4y = 8$.

....

....

(3 marks)

13 Solve simultaneously by elimination the equations $-2x - 5y = -6$ and $3x + 4y = 2$.

....

....

(3 marks)

14 Solve graphically the simultaneous equations $y = 3x + 5$ and $y = x^2 - 3$.

y
25
20
15
10
5
0
-10 -5 5 10 x
-5
-10

....

(3 marks)

15 Solve the simultaneous equations $x = 4y + 3$ and $3x^2 = y + 1$.

....

....

....

(5 marks)

Factorising Quadratics: a = 1

There are several ways of solving a quadratic equation which are covered on the following pages. You need to know all the methods.

Factorising a quadratic

"Factorising a quadratic" means "putting it into 2 brackets" — you'll need to remember that. (There are several different methods for doing this, so stick with the one you're happiest with. If you have no preference then learn the one below.)

The standard format for quadratic equations is: $ax^2 + bx + c = 0$
Most Exam questions have a = 1, making them much easier.
E.g. $x^2 + 3x + 2 = 0$ (See next page for when a is not 1)

Factorising method when a = 1

1) ALWAYS rearrange into the STANDARD FORMAT: $ax^2 + bx + c = 0$
2) Write down the TWO BRACKETS with the x's in: (x)(x)=0
3) Then find two numbers that MULTIPLY to give "c" (the end number) but also ADD/SUBTRACT to give "b" (the coefficient of x)
4) Put them in and check that the +/– signs work out properly.

An example

"Solve $x^2 - x = 12$ by factorising."

ANSWER:

1) First rearrange it (into the standard format): $x^2 - x - 12 = 0$
2) a=1, so the initial brackets are (as ever): (x)(x)=0
3) We now want to look at all pairs of numbers that multiply to give "c" (=12), but which also add or subtract to give the value of b:

1 × 12	*Add/subtract to give:*	13 or 11	
2 × 6	*Add/subtract to give:*	8 or 4	this is what we're
3 × 4	*Add/subtract to give:*	7 or (1) ←	after (=±b)

4) So 3 and 4 will give b = ±1, so put them in: (x 3)(x 4)=0
5) Now fill in the +/– signs so that the 3 and 4 add/subtract to give -1 (=b), Clearly it must be +3 and –4 so we'll have: $(x + 3)(x - 4)=0$
6) As an ESSENTIAL check, EXPAND the brackets out again to make sure they give the original equation: $(x + 3)(x - 4) = x^2 + 3x - 4x - 12 = x^2 - x - 12$
We're not finished yet mind, because $(x + 3)(x - 4) = 0$ is only the factorised form of the equation — we have yet to give the actual SOLUTIONS. This is very easy:
7) THE SOLUTIONS are simply the two numbers in the brackets, but with OPPOSITE +/– SIGNS: i.e. $x = -3$ or $+4$
Make sure you remember that last step. It's the difference between SOLVING THE EQUATION and merely factorising it.

Factorising quadratics is not easy — but it is important

The difficult bit is working out which numbers combine to give the right multiples and addition/ subtraction. Mind you, if you go through the possibilities logically you'll get there in the end.

Factorising Quadratics: $a \neq 1$

Factorising method when "a" is not 1

E.g. $3x^2 + 5x + 2 = 0$

The basic method is still the same but it's a lot messier. Chances are, the Exam question will be with a=1, so make sure you can do that type easily. Only then should you try to get to grips with these harder ones.

An example

"Solve $3x^2 + 7x = 6$ by factorising."

1) First rearrange it (into the standard format): $3x^2 + 7x - 6 = 0$

2) Now because a = 3, the two x-terms in the brackets will have to multiply to give $3x^2$ so the initial brackets will have to be: $(3x\quad)(x\quad)=0$
(i.e. you put in the x-terms first, with coefficients that will multiply to give "a")

3) We now want to look at all pairs of numbers that multiply with each other to give "c" =6, (ignoring the minus sign for now): i.e. 1×6 and 2×3

4) *Now the difficult bit*: to find the combination which does this:

   multiply with the 3x and x terms in the brackets and then add or subtract to give the value of b (=7):

   The best way to do this is by trying out all the possibilities in the brackets until you find the combination that works. Don't forget that EACH PAIR of numbers can be tried in TWO different positions:

   (3x 1)(x 6) multiplies to give 18x and 1x which add/subtract to give 17x or 19x
   (3x 6)(x 1) multiplies to give 3x and 6x which add/subtract to give 9x or 3x
   (3x 3)(x 2) multiplies to give 6x and 3x which add/subtract to give 9x or 3x
   (3x 2)(x 3) multiplies to give 9x and 2x which add/subtract to give 11x or (7x)

5) So (3x 2)(x 3) is the combination that gives b = 7, (give or take a +/–)

6) Now fill in the +/– signs so that the combination will add/subtract to give +7 (=b). Clearly it must be +3 and –2 which gives rise to +9x and -2x
So the final brackets are: $(3x - 2)(x + 3)$

7) As an ESSENTIAL check, EXPAND the brackets out again to make sure they give the original equation: $(3x - 2)(x + 3) = 3x^2 + 9x - 2x - 6 = 3x^2 + 7x - 6$

8) The last step is to get THE SOLUTIONS TO THE EQUATION: $(3x - 2)(x + 3)=0$ which you do by separately putting each bracket = 0 :
   i.e. $(3x - 2)=0 \Rightarrow x = 2/3$ $\qquad (x + 3)=0 \Rightarrow x = -3$
   Don't forget that last step. Again, it's the difference between SOLVING THE EQUATION and merely factorising it.

Factorising quadratics when a is not 1 is quite a bit harder

The problem is it's a lot harder to work out the right combination of numbers to go in the brackets. Don't get stressed out, just take your time and work through the possibilities as you did on the last page.

The Quadratic Formula

The solutions to any quadratic equation $ax^2 + bx + c = 0$ are given by this formula:

$$x = \frac{-b \pm \sqrt{b^2 - 4ac}}{2a}$$

LEARN THIS FORMULA —
If you can't learn it, there's no way you'll be able to use it in the Exam, even if they give it to you.

Using it should, in principle, be quite straightforward. As it turns out though, there are quite a few pitfalls, so TAKE HEED of these crucial details:

*Using the **quadratic formula***

1) Always write it down in stages as you go.

Take it nice and slowly — any fool can rush it and get it wrong, but there's no marks for being a clot.

2) MINUS SIGNS.

Throughout the whole of algebra, minus signs cause untold misery because people keep forgetting them. In this formula, there are two minus signs that people keep forgetting:

the -b and the -4ac.

The -4ac causes particular problems when either "a" or "c" is negative, because it makes the -4ac effectively +4ac — so learn to spot it as a HAZARD before it happens.
WHENEVER YOU GET A MINUS SIGN, THE ALARM BELLS SHOULD ALWAYS RING!

3) Remember you divide ALL of the top line by 2a, not just half of it.

4) Don't forget it's 2a on the bottom line, not just a.

This is another common mistake.

Looks nightmarish — but you'll soon be chanting it in your sleep

This formula looks difficult to use and learn but after you've said "minus b plus or minus the square root of b squared minus four a c all over 2 a" a few times you'll wonder what all the fuss is about.

The Quadratic Formula

An example

"Find the solutions of $3x^2 + 7x = 1$ to 2 decimal places."

(The mention of decimal places in exam questions is a VERY BIG CLUE to use the formula rather than trying to factorise it...)

Method

1) First get it into the form $ax^2 + bx + c = 0$:

$$3x^2 + 7x - 1 = 0$$

2) Then carefully identify a, b and c:

$$a = 3, \quad b = 7, \quad c = -1$$

3) Put these values into the quadratic formula and write down each stage:

$$x = \frac{-b \pm \sqrt{b^2 - 4ac}}{2a} = \frac{-7 \pm \sqrt{7^2 - 4 \times 3 \times -1}}{2 \times 3}$$

$$= \frac{-7 \pm \sqrt{49 + 12}}{6}$$

$$= \frac{-7 \pm \sqrt{61}}{6} = \frac{-7 \pm 7.81}{6}$$

$$= 0.1350 \text{ or } -2.468$$

So to 2 d.p., the solutions are: $x = 0.14$ or -2.47

4) Finally AS A CHECK put these values back into the original equation:

E.g. for $x = 0.1350$:

$3 \times 0.135^2 + 7 \times 0.135 = 0.999675$, which is 1, as near as ...

Not so nightmarish after all — just stick the numbers in the formula

Minus b plus or minus the square root of b squared minus four a c all over 2 a, minus b plus or minus the square root of b squared minus four a c all over 2 a, scream if you want to go faster...

Completing The Square

$$x^2 + 12x - 5 = (x + 6)^2 - 41$$

The SQUARE... ...COMPLETED

Solving quadratics by "completing the square"

This is quite a clever way of solving quadratics, but is perhaps a bit confusing at first. The name "Completing the Square" doesn't help — it's called that because of the method where you basically:

1) write down a SQUARED bracket, and then

2) stick a number on the end to "COMPLETE" it.

It's quite easy really, so long as you make an effort to learn all the steps — some of them aren't all that obvious.

Method

1) As always,

   REARRANGE THE QUADRATIC INTO THE STANDARD FORMAT:

   $ax^2 + bx + c = 0$

2) If "a" is not 1 then

   divide the whole equation by "a" to make sure it is.

3) Now

   WRITE OUT THE INITIAL BRACKET:

   $(x + b/2)^2$

   NB: THE NUMBER IN THE BRACKET is always HALF THE (NEW) VALUE OF "b"

4) MULTIPLY OUT THE BRACKETS and COMPARE TO THE ORIGINAL

   to find what extra is needed, and add or subtract the adjusting amount.

Make a SQUARE (bracket) and COMPLETE it (add or take away)

Completing the square basically means working out a squared bracket which is almost the same as your equation and then working out what has to be added or subtracted to make it right.

Completing The Square

An example

"Express $x^2 - 6x - 7 = 0$ as a completed square, and hence solve it."

The equation is already in the standard form and "a" = 1, so:

1) The coefficient of x is -6, so the squared brackets must be:

$(x - 3)^2$

2) Square out the brackets: $x^2 - 6x + 9$, and compare to the original: $x^2 - 6x - 7$.

To make it like the original equation it needs -16 on the end, hence we get:

$(x - 3)^2 - 16 = 0$ as the alternative version of $x^2 - 6x - 7 = 0$

Don't forget though, we wish to SOLVE this equation, which entails these three special steps:

1) Take the 16 over to get:

$(x - 3)^2 = 16$.

2) Then SQUARE ROOT BOTH SIDES:

$(x - 3) = \pm 4$ AND DON'T FORGET THE ±

3) Take the 3 over to get:

$x = \pm 4 + 3$ so $x = 7$ or -1 *(don't forget the ±)*

That's completing the square complete

This example should have been a piece of cake to follow, as should every other completing the square question from now on. If not I'd suggest you go back a page and make sure you've learnt the method.

Trial and Improvement

In principle, this is an easy way to find approximate answers to quite complicated equations. BUT... you have to make an effort to LEARN THE FINER DETAILS of this method, otherwise you'll never get the hang of it.

Method

1) SUBSTITUTE TWO INITIAL VALUES into the equation that give OPPOSITE CASES. *These are usually suggested in the question. If not, you'll have to think of your own. "Opposite cases" means one answer too big, one too small, or one +ve, one –ve, for example. If your values don't give opposite cases try again.*
2) Now CHOOSE YOUR NEXT VALUE IN BETWEEN THE PREVIOUS TWO, and SUBSTITUTE it into the equation. *Continue this process, always choosing a new value between the two closest opposite cases, (and preferably nearer to the one which is closest to the answer you want).*
3) AFTER ONLY THREE OR FOUR STEPS you should have two numbers which are to the right degree of accuracy but DIFFER BY 1 IN THE LAST DIGIT. *For example if you had to get your answer to 2 d.p. then you'd eventually end up with say 5.43 and 5.44, with these giving OPPOSITE results of course.*
4) At this point you ALWAYS take the Exact Middle Value to decide which is the answer you want. *E.g. for 5.43 and 5.44, you'd try 5.435 to see if the real answer was between 5.43 and 5.435 or between 5.435 and 5.44 (See below).*

An example

The equation $x^2 + x = 14$ has a solution between 3 and 3.5. Find this solution to 1 DP.

Try x = 3	$3^2 + 3 = 12$	(Too small)	← (2 opposite cases)
Try x = 3.5	$3.5^2 + 3.5 = 15.75$	(Too big)	

14 is what we want and it's slightly closer to 15.75 than it is to 12 so we'll choose our next value for x a bit closer to 3.5 than 3

Try x = 3.3	$3.3^2 + 3.3 = 14.19$	(Too big)

Good, this is very close, but we need to see if 3.2 is still too big or too small:

Try x = 3.2	$3.2^2 + 3.2 = 13.44$	(Too small)

Good, now we know that the answer must be between 3.2 and 3.3. To Find out which one it's nearest to, we have to try the EXACT MIDDLE VALUE: 3.25

Try x = 3.25	$3.25^2 + 3.25 = 13.81$	(Too small)

This tells us with certainty that the solution must be between 3.25 (too small) and 3.3 (too big), and so to 1 DP it must round up to 3.3. ANSWER = 3.3

It's like playing a game of higher and lower

You need to commit this method to memory, otherwise you've wasted your time even reading it. Luckily it's simple — like a guessing game where you guess a number too high, and then too low and get gradually closer until you get to the right answer. That's really all you're doing with this method.

Warm-Up and Worked Exam Questions

This algebra stuff isn't everyone's cup of tea. But once you get the knack of it, through lots of practice, you'll find the questions are all really similar. Which is nice.

Warm-up Questions

1) Which is the correct factorisation for $x^2 + 4x - 12$?
   a) $(x + 6)(x + 2)$ b) $(x + 6)(x - 2)$ c) $(x - 6)(x + 2)$.
2) Which is the correct factorisation of $3x^2 - 5x - 2$?
   a) $(3x - 2)(x + 1)$ b) $(3x + 1)(x - 2)$ c) $(3x - 1)(x + 2)$.
3) Factorise:
   a) $x^2 + 11x + 28$ b) $x^2 + 16x + 28$ c) $x^2 + 12x - 28$.
4) Solve by factorisation:
   a) $x^2 + 8x + 15 = 0$ b) $x^2 + 5x - 14 = 0$ c) $x^2 - 7x + 7 = -5$.
5) Complete the square for the expression $x^2 + 8x + 20$.
6) Express $x^2 - 10x + 9$ as a completed square, and hence solve $x^2 - 10x + 9 = 0$.

Worked Exam Questions

Now, the exam questions — the good news is, if you've got the hang of the warm-up questions, you'll find the exam questions pretty much the same.

1 Solve $x^2 - x = 30$ by factorising.

The first thing you need to do is get all the terms on the same side — otherwise you'll be stuck from the outset.

Rearrange to give $x^2 - x - 30 = 0$:

Factorise to give $(x + 5)(x - 6) = 0$:

Solve to give $x = -5$ or $x = 6$.

Once you've factorised, put each bracket equal to 0 to get the values for x.

(2 marks)

2 Solve $2x^2 + 6x = 20$ by factorisation.

Rearrange to give $2x^2 + 6x - 20 = 0$:

To get $2x^2$, you'll need to start with $(2x \quad)(x \quad)$. Then find numbers which multiply to 20. Just keep trying different pairs until you find the one that works...

Factorise to give $(2x - 4)(x + 5) = 0$:

Hence $(2x - 4) = 0$ or $(x + 5) = 0$:

Solve to give $x = 2$ or $x = -5$.

(3 marks)

Worked Exam Questions

Worked Exam Questions

You should definitely make an effort to learn the quadratic formula — the best way to make sure you remember it and can use it correctly is to practise it with lots of questions...

3 Solve $3x^2 + 13x + 3 = 0$ to 2 decimal places, using the quadratic formula.

The best way to start is to write down the quadratic formula and say what a, b and c are.

$$x = \frac{-b \pm \sqrt{b^2 - 4ac}}{2a} \qquad a = 3,\ b = 13,\ c = 3$$

Then just plug in all the numbers and be very careful...

$$x = \frac{13 \pm \sqrt{13^2 - 4 \times 3 \times 3}}{2 \times 3} = \frac{13 \pm \sqrt{169 - 36}}{6} = \frac{13 \pm 11.53...}{6}$$

$$x = \frac{-13 + 11.53...}{6} \text{ or } x = \frac{-13 - 11.53...}{6}$$

So $x = -0.24$ or $x = -4.09$ (both to 2 d.p.)

Don't forget to give your answer to 2 decimal places — it's very easy to throw away marks by forgetting this...

(3 marks)

4 Find a solution for $x^2 + 5x = 30$ $(3 < x < 4)$ to 2 decimal places by trial and improvement.

You know it's between 3 and 4, so start with 3.5.

x	$x^2 + 5x$
3.5	29.75
3.7	32.19
3.6	30.96
3.55	30.3525
3.54	30.2316
3.53	30.1109
3.52	29.9904
3.525	30.05063

Remember — you're just making guesses for x to get as close to the right hand side (30) as possible.

If it's too low, guess higher.
If it's too high, guess lower.

Keep going until you've guessed values either side of 30 using x values that round to the same number (to 2 d.ps). It sounds confusing, but it'll make sense when you get the hang of it.

We can see that x lies between 3.52 and 3.525.
So to 2 decimal places, x = 3.52 (because x is definitely less than 3.525, it must round down to 3.52).

(4 marks)

Exam Questions

Non-Calculator Exam Questions

5 (a) Factorise $x^2 - x - 20$.

....

(1 mark)

(b) Factorise $6x^2 + x - 12$.

....

(2 marks)

6 Factorise $2x^2 - 6x - 8$ and hence solve $2x^2 - 6x - 8 = 0$.

....

....

....

(3 marks)

7 Solve by factorisation $x^2 - 7x = -12$.

....

....

....

(3 marks)

8 Solve $x^2 + 9x + 9 = -9$.

....

....

....

(3 marks)

9 Complete the square for the expression $x^2 + 10x + 10$.

....

(2 marks)

10 Express $x^2 - 6x - 40 = 0$ as a completed square, and hence solve.

....

....

....

(3 marks)

Exam Questions

Calculator Exam Questions

11 Solve $x^2 + 8x - 4 = 0$ to 1 decimal place by completing the square.

....

....

....

(3 marks)

12 Find both solutions of $2x^2 + 3x - 4 = 0$ to 2 decimal places.

....

....

....

(3 marks)

13 Use the quadratic formula to find the solutions of $3x^2 - 5x = 12$ to 2 decimal places.

....

....

....

(3 marks)

14 $x^2 - 3x = 15$ has a solution between 5 and 6.
Use trial and improvement to find it to 2 decimal places.

....

....

....

....

....

....

....

(4 marks)

Compound Growth and Decay

This can also be called "Exponential" Growth or Decay.

The formula

This topic is simple if you LEARN THIS FORMULA. If you don't, it's pretty well impossible:

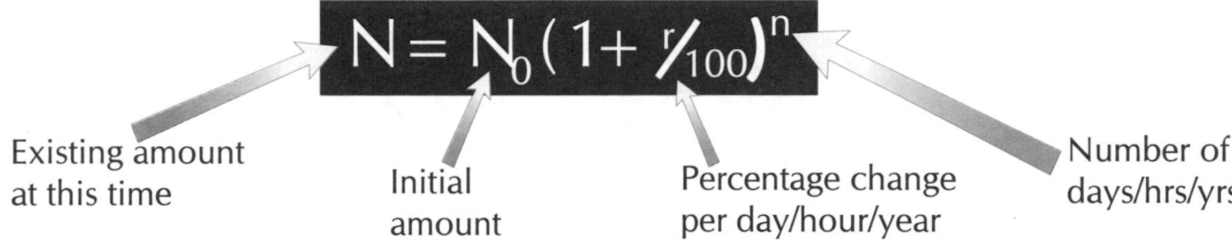

Percentage *increase* and *decrease*

The (1+ r/100) bit might look a bit confusing in the formula but in practice it's really easy:

e.g. 5% increase will be 1.05 5% decrease will be 0.95 (= 1 – 0.05)

26% increase will be 1.26 26% decrease will be 0.74 (= 1 – 0.26)

Three examples to show you how *easy* it is:

1) *"A man invests £1000 in a savings account which pays 8% per annum. How much will there be after 6 years?"*

ANSWER: Usual formula (as above): Amount = $1000(1.08)^6$ = £1586.87
(1000: Initial amount; 1.08: 8% increase; 6: 6 years)

2) *"The activity of a radio-isotope falls by 12% every hour. If the initial activity is 800 counts per minute, what will it be after 7 hours?"*

ANSWER: Same old formula: Activity = Initial value$(1 - 12/100)^n$
Activity = $800(1 - 0.12)^7 = 800 \times (0.88)^7$ = 327 cpm

3) *"In a sample of bacteria, there are initially 500 cells and they increase in number by 15% each day. Find the formula relating the number of cells, n and the number of days, d."*

ANSWER: Well stone me, it's the same old compound increase formula again:
$n = n_0(1+0.15)^d$ or finished off: $n = 500 \times (1.15)^d$

Compound growth and decay — percentages applied again and again

What this method does in effect is to get the original value, increase it by the percentage, then increase that amount by the percentage, then take that amount and increase it by the percentage, then... get it?

Direct and Inverse Proportion

Direct proportion: $y = kx$

BOTH INCREASE TOGETHER

1) The graph of y against x is *a straight line through the origin:*

$y = kx$

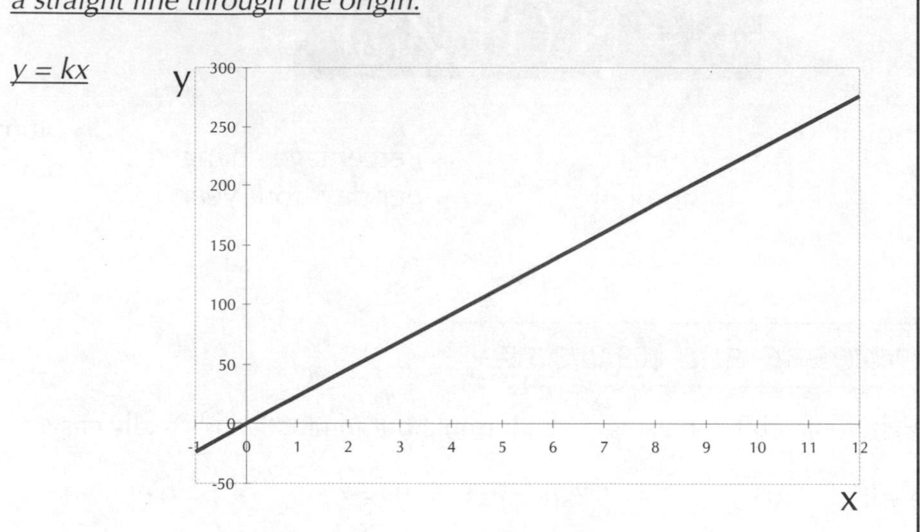

2) In a table of values *the MULTIPLIER is the same for X and Y*.
i.e. if you *double* one of them, you *double* the other;
if you *times one of them by 3*, you *times the other by 3*, etc.

X	2	6	8	12	14	56
Y	3	9	12	18	21	84

× 3 (2 → 6, 3 → 9) × 2 (6 → 12, 9 → 18) × 4 (14 → 56, 21 → 84)

3) The RATIO $^x/_y$ is the same for all pairs of values,
i.e from the table above:

$$\frac{2}{3} = \frac{6}{9} = \frac{8}{12} = \frac{12}{18} = \frac{14}{21} = \frac{56}{84} = 0.6667$$

Direct proportion means x and y increase together

There are three straightforward properties of direct proportion on this page.
I suggest you learn all three, no alarms and no surprises.

Direct and Inverse Proportion

Inverse proportion: $y = k/x$

One INCREASES , one DECREASES

1) The graph of y against x is the well known y=k/x graph:

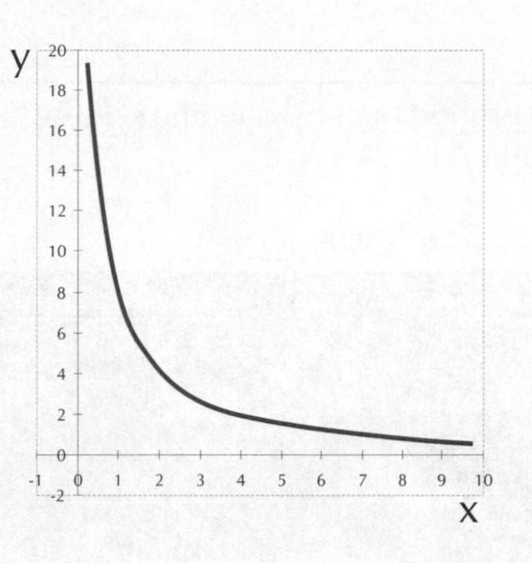

2) In a table of values the MULTIPLIER for one of them becomes a DIVIDER for the other, i.e. if you double one, you half the other, if you treble one, you divide the other by three, etc.

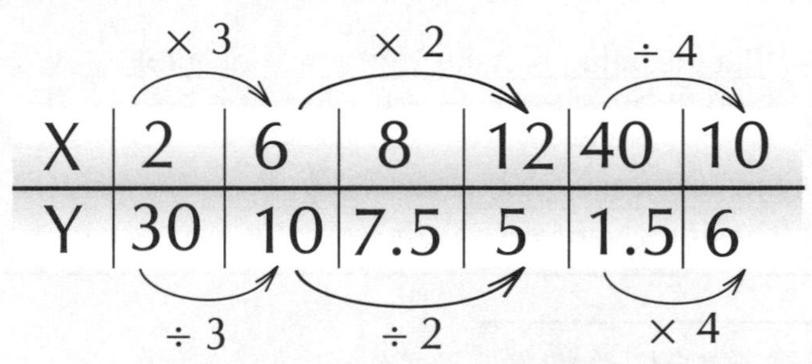

X	2	6	8	12	40	10
Y	30	10	7.5	5	1.5	6

3) The PRODUCT XY (X times Y) is the same for all pairs of values, i.e. in the table above

$2 \times 30 = 6 \times 10 = 8 \times 7.5 = 12 \times 5 = 40 \times 1.5 = 10 \times 6 = \underline{60}$

Inverse ***square*** *variation*

You can have all sorts of relationships between x and y, like $y = kx^2$ or $y = k/x^3$ etc. as detailed on P.186.

The most important type is $\underline{y = k/x^2}$ and is called "INVERSE SQUARE" variation. DON'T MIX UP THIS NAME with inverse proportion, which is just $y = k/x$.

With inverse proportion one increases, the other decreases

Here's the same three properties for inverse proportion; the shape of the graph, the table of values and the product xy (equivalent to the ratio for direct proportion). And don't forget inverse square variation either.

Variation

This concerns Exam questions which involve statements like these:

"y is proportional to the square of x"
"D varies with the cube of t"
"t is proportional to the square root of h"
"V is inversely proportional to r cubed"

To deal successfully with things like this you must remember this method:

Method

1) Convert the sentence into a proportionality using the symbol " $\propto$ ", which means "is proportional to"

2) Replace " $\propto$ " with "=k" to make an EQUATION:

The above examples would become:	Proportionality	Equation
"y is proportional to the square of x"	$y \propto x^2$	$y = kx^2$
"t is proportional to the square root of h"	$t \propto \sqrt{h}$	$t = k\sqrt{h}$
"D varies with the cube of t"	$D \propto t^3$	$D = kt^3$
"V is inversely proportional to r cubed"	$V \propto 1/r^3$	$V = k/r^3$

(Once you've got it in the form of an equation with k, the rest is easy)

3) Find a PAIR OF VALUES of x and y somewhere in the question, and SUBSTITUTE them into the equation with the sole purpose of finding k.

4) Put the value of k back into the equation and it's now ready to use. e.g. $y = 3x^2$

5) INEVITABLY, they'll ask you to find y, having given you a value for x (or vice versa).

An example

The time taken for a duck to fall down a chimney is inversely proportional to the square of the diameter of the flue. If she took 25 seconds to descend a chimney of diameter 0.3m, how long would it take her to get down one of 0.2m diameter?

(Notice there's no mention of "writing an equation" or "finding k" — it's up to YOU to remember the method for yourself)

ANSWER:

1) Write it as a proportionality, then an equation: $t \propto 1/d^2$ i.e. $t = k/d^2$

2) Sub in the given values for the two variables: $25 = k/0.3^2$

3) Rearrange the equation to find k: $k = 25 \times 0.3^2 = 2.25$

4) Put k back in the formula: $t = 2.25/d^2$

5) Sub in new value for d: $t = 2.25/0.2^2 = 56.25$secs

That's the last page to learn in the book

I'm afraid it's true — goodbye scribbling and scribbling, goodbye methods and formulas to learn.
But as the sun sets on the day of learning, a beautiful dawn is breaking — there's a practice exam waiting.

Warm-Up and Worked Exam Questions

Well, it's been a long journey, but you've made it to the last set of mini-questions in the book. So don't stop now, on with the final warm-up questions...

Warm-up Questions

1) 6% increase is the same as multiplying by 1.06. Write the following in the same way.
   a) 15% increase b) 9% decrease c) 10% increase
   d) 12.5% increase e) 24% decrease.
2) £3000 is invested at 3% compound interest (per year).
   Find the total investment at the end of 4 years.
3) Write each of the following as an equation:
   a) A is proportional to the square of r b) $D \propto \frac{1}{R}$
   c) H is inversely proportional to the cube of D d) $V \propto S^3$

Worked Exam Questions

Get through these exam questions, then it'll be time to put your feet up... for a well deserved break... a nice glass of ginger beer... a chocolate biscuit... mmm. (But don't relax too much, there's still the practice exam.)

1 Lotte invests £4000 in a savings account which pays 3.5% interest per year. The interest is added to the investment at the end of each year. She does not withdraw any money. Find out how much her investment is worth at the end of 5 years.

Using the formula on page 183... $4000 \times (1.035)^5 = 4750.74522... = £4750.75$ (nearest penny).

(N_0 = 4000, $(1+3.5/100)$ = 1.035, n = 5)

(2 marks)

2 £600 is invested for 3 years at 4% compound interest. Work out the total interest earned over the 3 years.

$600 \times (1.04)^3 = 674.9184 = £674.92$ (nearest penny)

Interest $= 674.92 - 600 = £74.92$

(3 marks)

3 y is inversely proportional to x^2. When $x = 4$, $y = 3$.

(a) Express y in terms of x.

$y \propto \frac{1}{x^2} \rightarrow y = \frac{k}{x^2}$ — *Start by writing an equation to show how x and y are inversely proportionally related (that's a mouthful).*

Now, putting in the given values of x and y will give you k. $x = 4$ when $y = 3$ gives: $3 = \frac{k}{4^2} \rightarrow k = 3 \times 16 = 48$, so $y = \frac{48}{x^2}$

(3 marks)

(b) (i) Calculate the value of y when $x = 8$.

$y = \frac{48}{8^2} = \frac{48}{64} = \frac{3}{4}$

Now, you've got the equation $y = 48 / x^2$. Just stick in values for y or x to answer these questions.

(ii) Calculate the value of x when $y = 75$.

$75 = \frac{48}{x^2} \rightarrow x^2 = \frac{48}{75} = 0.64 \rightarrow x = 0.8$

(3 marks)

Exam Questions

4 A car depreciates over the first five years at a regular rate of 8% each year.
The car was bought for £12,500. How much is it worth after 5 years?

....

(3 marks)

5 The company Etto Oil sells oil in various sized containers. The capacity, C litres, of an Etto oil container is always directly proportional to the cube of its diameter, d metres. One container size has a capacity of 270 litres and a diameter of 1.5 metres.

(a) Find the equation connecting C and d.

....

(3 marks)

(b) Another oil container is 1.8 metres in diameter.
Find out how many litres this container can hold.

....

(2 marks)

(c) Find the diameter of an oil container which holds 140 litres.

....

(2 marks)

6 Carolyn opens a savings account with £6000. It pays 3.8% interest per year.
How many years will it take for her investment to be more than £7000?

....

(3 marks)

7 F varies inversely as the square of t. F = 40 when t = 5.

(a) Express F in terms of t.

....

(3 marks)

(b) (i) Calculate the value of F when t = 200.

....

(1 mark)

(ii) Calculate the value of t when F = 50.

....

(2 marks)

Revision Summary for Section Six

Section Six is the really nasty one — algebra. But grisly or not, you still have to do it. The best way is by practising and practising until you can do each type of question in your sleep. Remember, the exam questions will be virtually exactly the same as the ones you've been practising, so it really is worth all the effort. This last set of questions is the final pitstop before the practice exam. So let's see you make a really good push for the finish...

Keep learning the basic facts until you know them

1) What are the two rules for negative numbers? When should each be used?
2) Write down four combinations of letters that regularly catch people out in algebra.
3) What does "DOTS" stand for? Give two examples of it.
4) What are "terms"? What two rules apply to them?
5) Describe the steps for simplifying an expression involving several terms.
6) What is the method for multiplying out brackets such as $3(2x + 4)$?
7) What is the method for multiplying pairs of brackets? What about squared brackets?
8) What are the three steps for factorising expressions such as $12x^2y^3z + 15x^3yz^2$?
9) Give details of the three techniques for doing algebraic fractions, with examples.
10) Which is the easiest and which is the most difficult? What makes it difficult?
11) What are the six steps for solving equations or rearranging formulas? What's the 7th step?
12) What do the four (or is it really two?) inequality symbols mean?
13) What are the two rules for doing algebra with inequalities?
14) Detail three important examples of it.
15) What does "factorising a quadratic" mean you have to do?
16) Write down five important details on the method for factorising quadratics.
17) What check should you do to make sure you've done it right?
18) What difference does it make when factorising a quadratic if "a" is not 1?
19) How exactly do you get solutions to a quadratic equation, once you've factorised it?
20) Write down the formula for solving quadratics.
21) What clue do you get that you should use it?
22) What are the three main pitfalls that catch people out with the quadratic formula?
23) What are the four main steps for turning a quadratic into a completed "square"?
24) What are the next three steps for solving an equation in this form?
25) Write down the six steps for doing easy (linear) simultaneous equations.
26) What are the seven steps for doing simultaneous equations where one's quadratic?
27) Write down the four steps of the trial and improvement method.
28) List the three key features of both direct proportion and inverse proportion.
29) What is the difference between inverse proportion and inverse square proportion?
30) What is the formula for compound growth and decay?
31) Give three important examples to show how the method is always the same.
32) What sort of statements are involved in the subject of "variation"?
33) What are the five essential steps involved in dealing with questions on variation?

Practice Exam

Once you've been through all the questions in this book, you should feel pretty confident about the exam. As final preparation, here is a practice exam to really get you set for the real thing. We've made a combined paper — one section of calculator and on of non-calculator questions. The paper is designed to give you the best possible preparation whichever syllabus you're following. If you're doing Foundation then you won't have learnt every bit — but it's still good practice.

General Certificate of Secondary Education

CGP Practice Exam Paper GCSE Maths

GCSE Maths

Section A: Calculator Allowed
Time allowed: 1 hour

Sections B: Calculator NOT Allowed
Time allowed: 1 hour

Instructions to candidates

- Answer the questions in the spaces provided.
- Do all rough work on the paper.

Information for candidates

- The marks available are given in brackets at the end of each question or part-question.
- Marks will not be deducted for incorrect answers.
- In calculations show clearly how you work out your answers.
- There are **10** questions in **Section A** of this paper.
  There are **9** questions in **Section B** of this paper.
  There are **no** blank pages.

Advice to candidates

- Work steadily through the paper.
- Don't spend too long on one question.
- If you have time at the end, go back and check your answers.

GCSE Mathematics Formulae Sheet

Volume of prism = area of cross-section × length

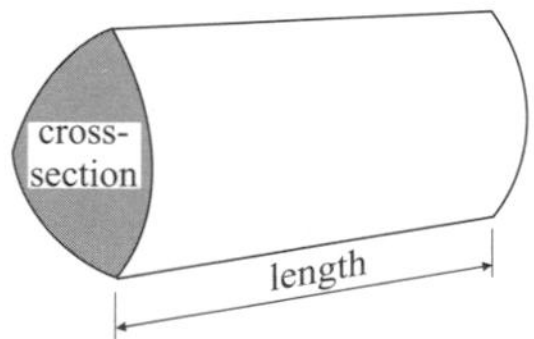

Volume of sphere $= \frac{4}{3}\pi r^3$

Surface area of sphere $= 4\pi r^2$

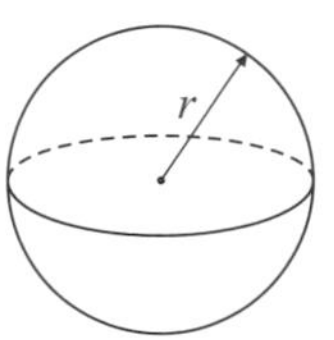

Volume of cone $= \frac{1}{3}\pi r^2 h$

Curved surface area of cone $= \pi r l$

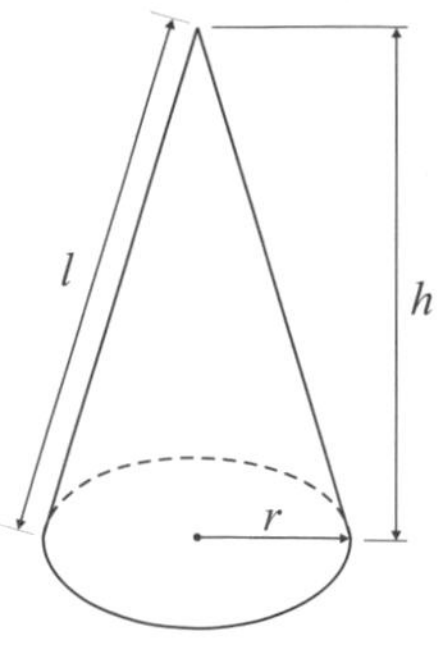

For any triangle *ABC*:

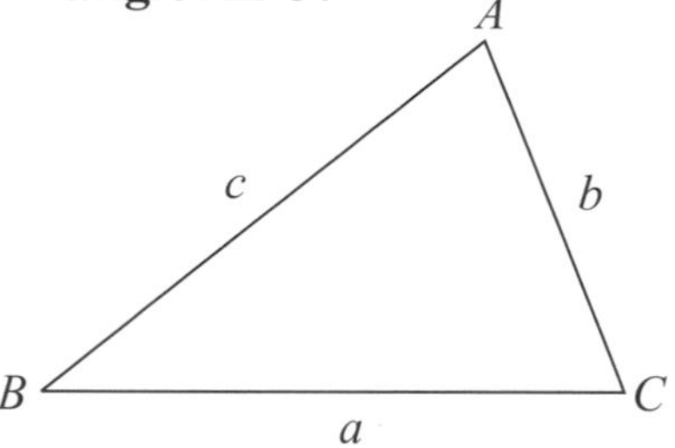

Sine rule: $\frac{a}{\sin A} = \frac{b}{\sin B} = \frac{c}{\sin C}$

Cosine rule: $a^2 = b^2 + c^2 - 2bc\cos A$

$$\cos A = \frac{b^2 + c^2 - a^2}{2bc}$$

Area of triangle $= \frac{1}{2}ab\sin C$

The quadratic equation:

The solutions of $ax^2 + bx + c = 0$, where $a \neq 0$, are given by:

$$x = \frac{-b \pm \sqrt{b^2 - 4ac}}{2a}$$

SECTION A - Calculator Allowed

Leave blank

1 (a) Calculate $\frac{131.4 - 0.73}{2 - 4.5^2}$.

....

....

Answer (a) ....

(2 marks)

(b) Using indices, write 1089 as a product of its prime factors.

....

....

....

Answer (b) ....

(2 marks)

OCR, Specimen 2003

2 Tracey and Wayne share £7200 in the ratio 5:4

Work out how much each of them receives.

Tracey £ ....

Wayne £ ....

(3 marks)

EDEXCEL, 2000

3 (a) The diagram shows two regular polygons

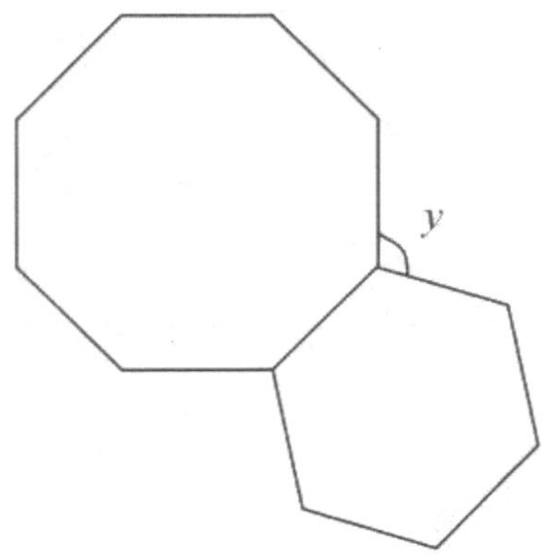

Not drawn accurately

Work out the size of angle y.

....

....

....

Answer ....degrees

(3 marks)

(b) This diagram shows a kite *ABCD*.

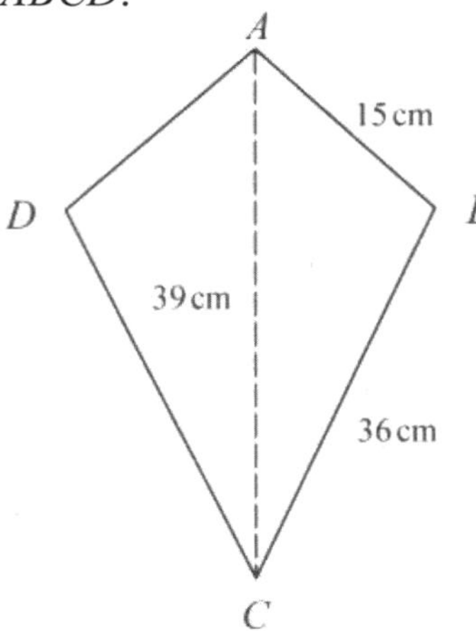

Not drawn accurately

$AB = 15$ cm, $BC = 36$ cm and $AC = 39$ cm.

Explain why angle $B = 90°$

....

....

....

....

(3 marks)

AQA, Specimen 2003

Leave blank

4 (a) Solve the equation

$$7p+3=3(p-1)$$

$p =$ ....

(2 marks)

q is an integer such that $0<3q\leq 16$

(b) List all the possible values of q.

....

(2 marks)

(c) Solve the inequality

$$\frac{r+1}{3}\leq r-2$$

....

(3 marks)

EDEXCEL, 2003

5 (a) Complete the table below for $y=x^3+5x$.

....

....

x	–2	–1	0	1	2	3
y	–18		0	6	18	

(1 mark)

(b) Draw the graph of $y = x^3 + 5x$ on the grid below

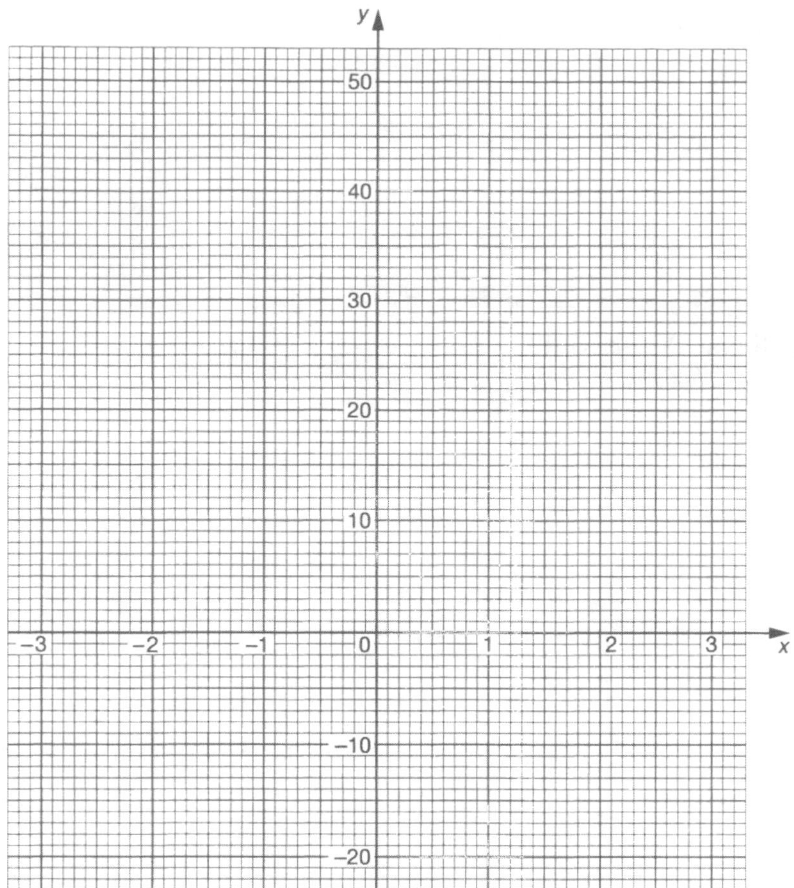

(3 marks)

(c) Use your graph to solve $x^3 + 5x = 10$

Answer (c) $x =$ ....

(1 mark)

OCR, 2001

6 The Andromeda Galaxy is 21 900 000 000 000 000 000 km from the Earth.

(a) Write 21 900 000 000 000 000 000 in standard form.

....

(1 mark)

Light travels 9.46×10^{12} km in one year.

(b) Calculate the number of years that light takes to travel from the Andromeda Galaxy to Earth.
Give your answer in standard form correct to 2 significant figures.

....

(2 marks)

EDEXCEL, Specimen 2003

Leave blank

7 Solve the simultaneous equations

$$4x + y = 4$$
$$2x + 3y = -3$$

$x =$ ....

$y =$ ....

(4 marks)

EDEXCEL, 2001

8 Aisha travels to work by bus on two days.
The probability that the bus is late on any day is 0.6.

(a) Complete the tree diagram to show the possible outcomes for the two days.

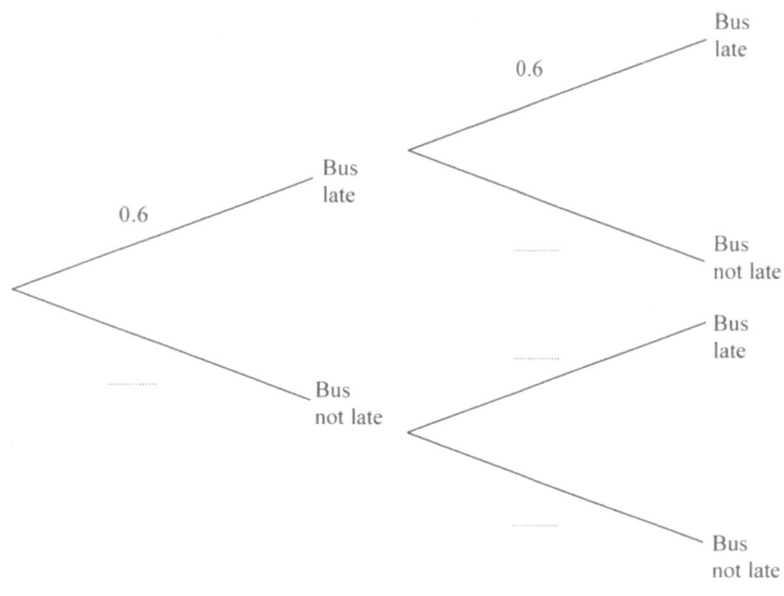

(1 mark)

Leave blank

(b) What is the probability that the bus is late on at least one of the two days?

....

....

....

....

....

....

Answer ....

(3 marks)

AQA, Specimen 2003

9 Some people took part in a Fun Run and their times to complete the course were recorded. Some of the data is shown in the table and some is shown in the histogram.

Time (t minutes)	$60 < t \leqslant 90$	$90 < t \leqslant 105$	$105 < t \leqslant 135$	$135 < t \leqslant 180$	$180 < t \leqslant 240$
Numbers of runners	40	50			30

(a) Using all the information, complete the table and the histogram.

(5 marks)

(b) What is the probability that two runners, selected at random, both took longer than 180 minutes?
Leave your answer as a fraction.

....

....

....

Answer (b) ....

(3 marks)

OCR, 2001

Leave blank

10

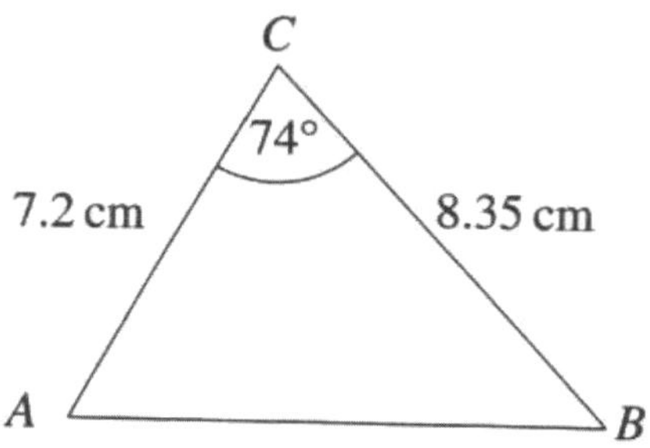

Diagram **NOT** accurately drawn

The diagram shows triangle ABC
$AC = 7.2$ cm.
$BC = 8.35$ cm.
Angle $ACB = 74°$.

(a) Calculate the area of triangle ABC.
Give your answer correct to 3 significant figures.
Give the units with your answer.

....
(3 marks)

(b) Calculate the length of AB.
Give your answer correct to 3 significant figures.

....cm
(3 marks)

EDEXCEL, 2002

SECTION B - Calculator NOT Allowed

1 The diagram shows triangles *P* and *Q*.

Leave blank

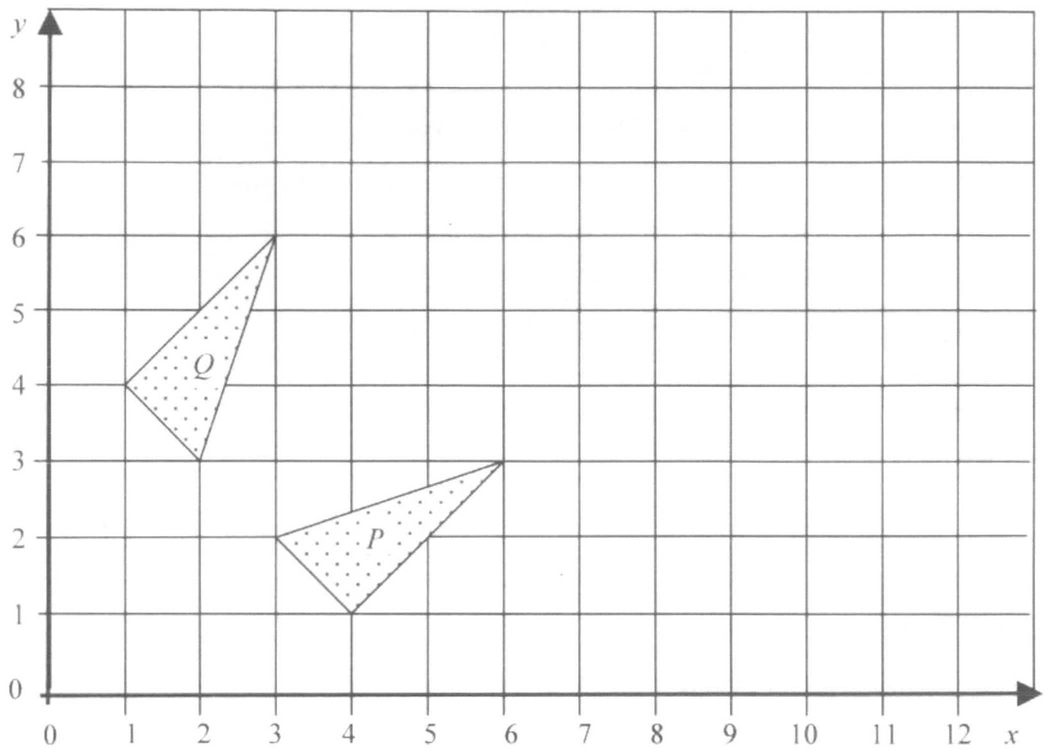

(a) Describe fully the **single** transformation which takes *P* onto *Q*.

....

....

....

....

....

(2 marks)

(b) On the diagram, draw an enlargement of shape *P* with scale factor 2, centre (3,2).

(2 marks)

AQA, Specimen 2003

Leave blank

2 In the game of "Soap", two fair dice, with the faces numbered 1 to 6, are thrown.
The total of the scores on the dice is the score for that turn.
The player then moves the same number of places as their score.
For example, if (3, 5) is thrown, the player moves 8 places.

(a) Khalid wants to land on the space marked "Albert Square". He is now on "Coronation Street" which is 6 spaces away.

By considering the possibility space (all possible outcomes), work out the probability that Khalid lands on "Albert Square" on his next turn.

....

....

....

....

....

....

....

....

Answer (a) ....

(3 marks)

Caroline does not want to land on "Ramsey Street" which is 7 spaces away.

(b) What is the probability that Caroline does not land on "Ramsey Street" on her next turn?

....

....

Answer (b) ....

(2 marks)

You can only escape from "Cell Block H" if you score the same number on each dice.
John is on "Cell Block H".

(c) What is the probability that John escapes on his next turn?

....

....

Answer (c) ....

(1 mark)

OCR, 2000

3 Write down the three inequalities which define the shaded region.

Leave blank

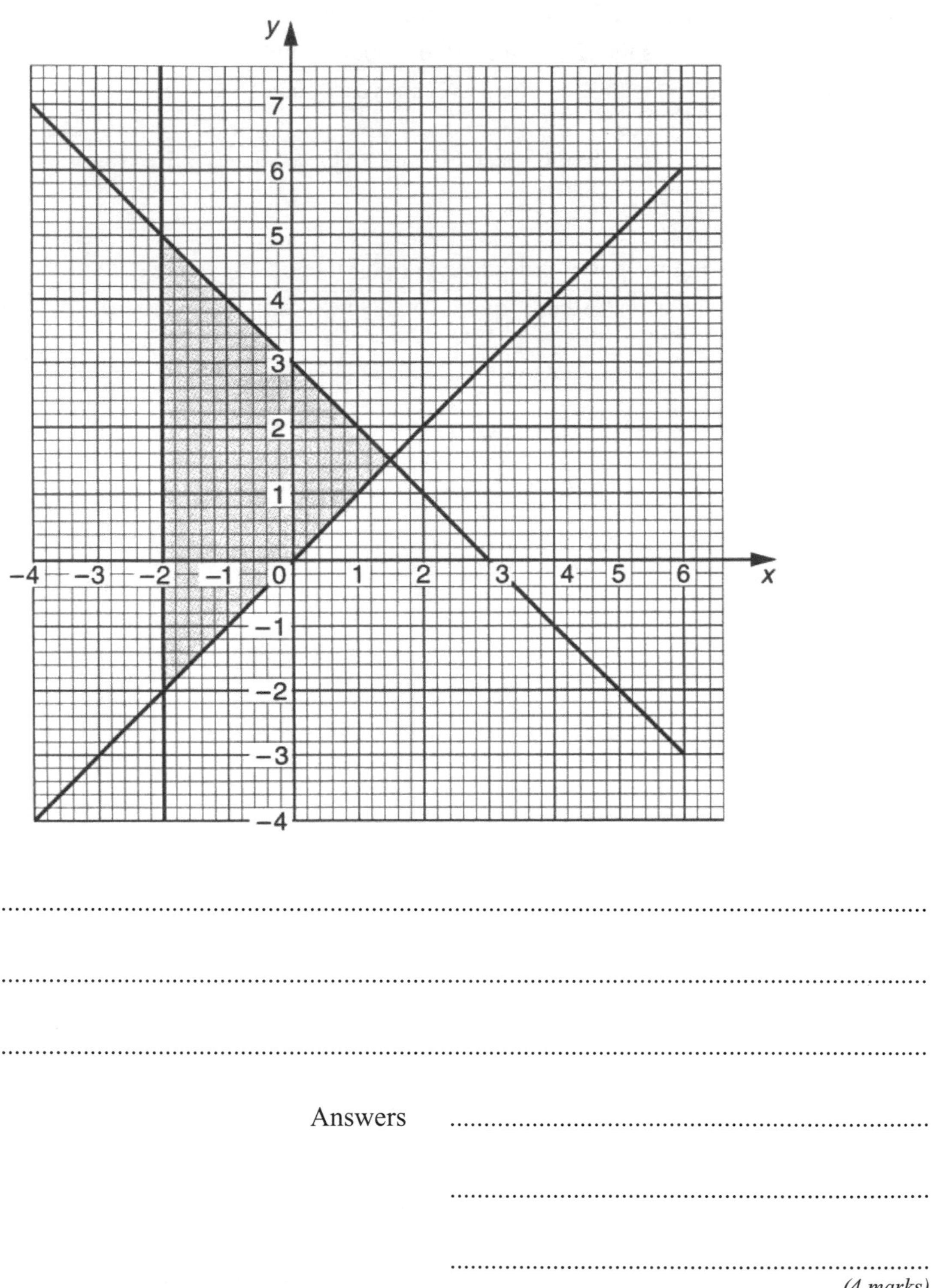

....

....

....

Answers ....

....

....

(4 marks)

OCR, 2001

Leave blank

4 The diagram is a plan of a field drawn to a scale of 1 cm to 20 m.

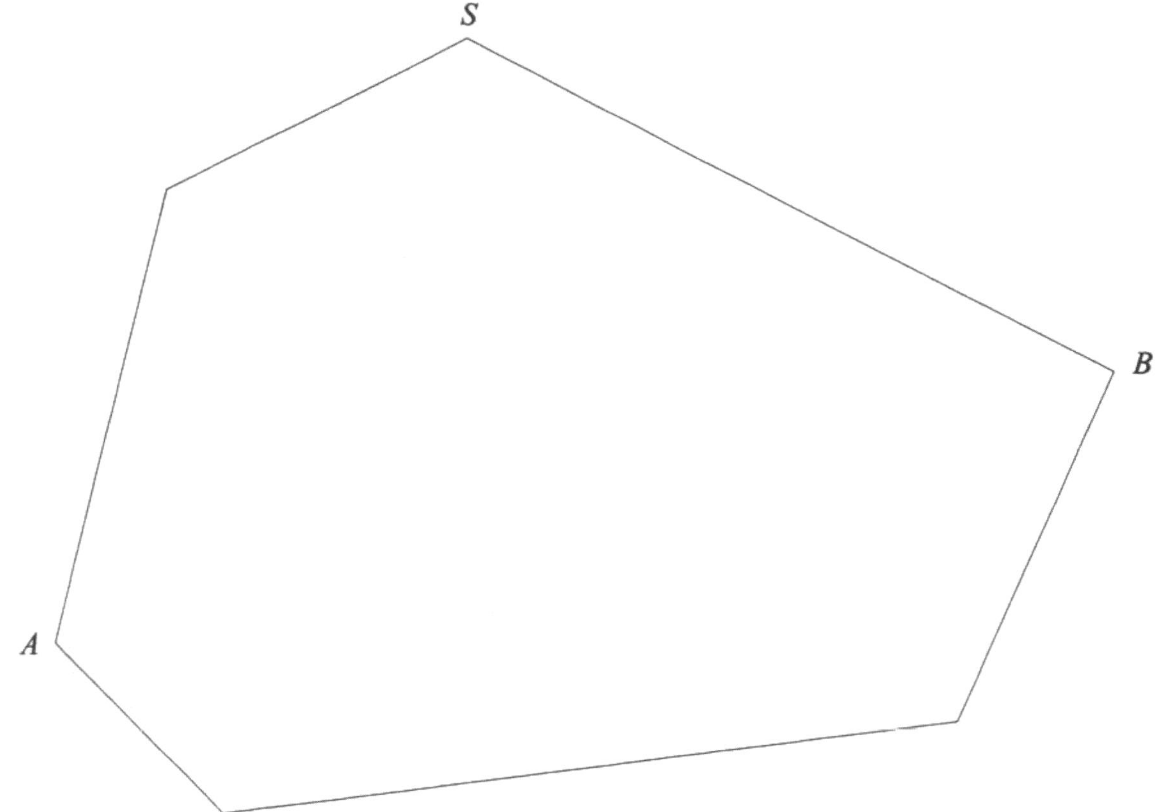

Scale: 1 cm to 20 m

There is a water sprinkler at *S*.
The sprinkler can water that region of the field which is 60 metres or less from the sprinkler.

(a) Shade, on the diagram, the region of the field which is 60 metres or less from the sprinkler.

(2 marks)

A farmer is going to lay a pipe to help water the field.
A and *B* are posts which mark the widest part of the field.
The pipe will cross the field so that it is always the same distance from *A* as it is from *B*.

(b) On the diagram draw a line accurately to show where the pipe should be laid.

(2 marks)

EDEXCEL, 2001

Leave blank

5 (a) Simplify

(i) $p^4 \times p^3$,

....

Answer (a) (i) ....

(1 mark)

(ii) $\frac{12t^5}{3t^2}$.

....

....

Answer (ii) ....

(1 mark)

(b) Solve $3x + 19 \geq 4$

....

....

....

Answer (b) ....

(2 marks)

(c) Rearrange the following formula to make w the subject.

$$s = \frac{w + y}{2}$$

....

....

....

Answer (c) ....

(2 marks)

(d) The nth term, t_n, of a sequence is given by the formula

$$t_n = \frac{n(n+1)}{2}$$

(i) Write down the values of t_1, t_2, t_3.

....

....

Answer (d) (i) ....

(2 marks)

(ii) This sequence of numbers has a special name. Write down that name.

Answer (ii) ....

(1 mark)

OCR, Specimen 2003

Leave blank

6 There are 12 boys and 15 girls in a class.
In a test the mean mark for the boys was n.
In the same test the mean mark for the girls was m.
Work out an expression for the mean mark of the whole class of 27 students.

....

(3 marks)

EDEXCEL, Specimen 2003

7 Pupils in Year 7 are all given the same test.
The test is marked out of 100.
The results for the boys are:

Lowest score	7 marks
Highest score	98 marks
Lower quartile	36 marks
Median	53 marks
Upper quartile	66 marks

(a) The diagram shows the box plot for the girls' results.
Draw a box plot to show the information for the boys on the same diagram.

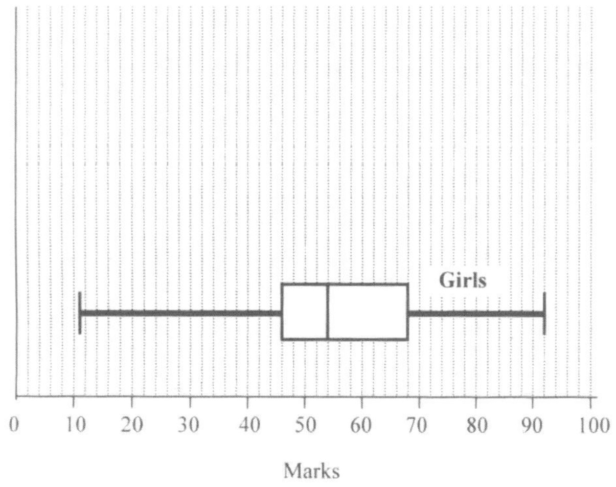

Girls

0 10 20 30 40 50 60 70 80 90 100

Marks

(2 marks)

(b) Comment on the differences between the boys' and girls' results.

....

....

....

....

....

....

(2 marks)

AQA, Specimen 2003

Leave blank

8

Diagram **NOT** accurately drawn

(x – 3) cm

(x + 4) cm

The length of a rectangle is $(x + 4)$ cm.
The width is $(x - 3)$ cm.
The area of the rectangle is 78 cm^2.

(a) Use this information to write down an equation in terms of x.

....
(2 marks)

(b) (i) Show that your equation in part (a) can be written as

$$x^2 + x - 90 = 0$$

(ii) Find the values of x which are solutions of the equation

$$x^2 + x - 90 = 0$$

$x =$ .... or $x =$ ....

(iii) Write down the length and the width of the rectangle.

length = ... cm

width = ... cm
(6 marks)

EDEXCEL, 2000

Leave blank

9 A is the point (2,3) and B is the point (–2,0).

(a) (i) Write $\overrightarrow{AB}$ as a column vector.

....

(ii) Find the length of vector $\overrightarrow{AB}$.

....
(4 marks)

D is the point such that

$\overrightarrow{BD}$ is parallel to $\binom{0}{1}$ and

the length of $\overrightarrow{AD}$ = the length of $\overrightarrow{AB}$.
O is the point (0,0).

(b) Find $\overrightarrow{OD}$ as a column vector.

....
(2 marks)

C is the point such that $ABCD$ is a rhombus.
AC is a diagonal of the rhombus

(c) Find the coordinates of C.

....
(2 marks)

EDEXCEL, 2001

Page 7 (Warm-Up Questions)

1) (a) 1, 4, 9 (b) 1, 8 (c) 1, 3, 6, 10
(d) 2, 4, 8 *(officially, 1 is also a power of 2, since $2^0 = 1$)*
(e) 2, 3, 5, 7
2) (a) 36 (b) There aren't any (c) 36 (d) 32 (e) 31, 37
3) 231 ÷ 3 = 77. 231 ÷ 7 = 33. 231 ÷ 11 = 21.
So 231 has more than 2 factors.
4) 1, 2, 4, 5, 8, 10, 20, 40
5) $2 \times 2 \times 2 \times 5$ (or $2^3 \times 5$)
6) (a) $\frac{4}{15}$ (b) $\frac{2}{5} \times \frac{3}{2} = \frac{6}{10} = \frac{3}{5}$ (c) $\frac{10}{15} + \frac{6}{15} = \frac{16}{15} = 1\frac{1}{15}$ (d) $\frac{10}{15} - \frac{6}{15} = \frac{4}{15}$
7) 40% *(one-fifth of 100% is 20%, so two-fifths is 40%)*
8) 66.66666…% or $66\frac{2}{3}$%
9) £13.50 *(10% of £90 = £9, so 5% of £90 = £4.50, then add these together. Can also do this by 0.15 × 90 = 13.50)*
10) 74% *(double both numbers to make it out of 100, which is a percentage)*

Page 9 (Exam Questions)

5) 400 *(These are the square numbers, so the 20th number is 20 × 20 = 400)* *[1 mark]*

6) (a)

924 → ② and 462
462 → ② and 231
231 → ⑦ and 33
33 → ③ and ⑪

So **924 = 2^2 × 3 × 7 × 11** *[1 mark]*

(b)

210 → 10 and 21
10 → ② and ⑤
21 → ③ and ⑦

So 210 = 2 × 3 × 5 × 7.

The common factors are 2, 3 and 7. So HCF of 924 and 210 = 2 × 3 × 7 = **42** *[2 marks]*

7) (a) $\frac{37}{7} - \frac{13}{5} = \frac{185}{35} - \frac{91}{35} = \frac{94}{35} = 2\frac{24}{35}$ *[2 marks]*
(b) $\frac{8}{3} \times \frac{15}{4} = \frac{120}{12} = \frac{10}{1} = 10$ *[2 marks]*

8) The amount of money she lost was £95 – £57 = £38
To find this as a percentage of what she paid: 38 ÷ 95 × 100 = 40% *[2 marks]*

9) *Remember to leave the interest in the account, and keep finding interest on the new balance. The easiest way, however, is to increase the money by 4% each year: an increase of 4% gives a total of 104%, which has a decimal equivalent of 1.04. Do this for 4 years:*
£5000 × 1.04 × 1.04 × 1.04 × 1.04 = £5849.29
But you were asked how much interest was earned:
Interest = £5849.29 – £5000 = £849.29 *[3 marks]*

Page 13 (Warm-Up Questions)

1) √10 and π are the only irrational ones.
2) √50 is a little bit more than 7 (since $7^2 = 49$), and √70 is just over 8 (since $8^2 = 64$), so any simple decimal number between, say, 7.5 and 8 would do.
3) The easiest irrational numbers to find are the square roots of non-square numbers. So the square root of any whole number between 50 and 70 would do (except 64, because 64 is a square number and therefore √64 = 8 which is rational).
4) Again you can use the square root of a non-square number. 8 is √64 and 9 is √81, so choose the square root of any whole number between 64 and 81.
5) (a) $\frac{4}{10}$ or $\frac{2}{5}$ (b) $\frac{4}{9}$ (c) $\frac{45}{99}$
6) (a) 0.7
(b) 0.7777777…
7) √30.
8) √36 = 6.

Page 15 (Exam Questions)

5) Irrational numbers are: $\frac{\pi}{2}$ and **√50**. *[2 marks]*
6) √25 = 5 and √36 = 6, so choose any square root between 25 and 36, **e.g. √30**. *[2 marks]*
7) √80 is just under 9, and √90 is more than 9 (since √81 = 9), so choose **9** as your answer. *(There are other possibilities.)* *[2 marks]*
8) You need to realise that a more accurate approximation for π = 3.142, so choose **3.141** as your answer. *(There are other possibilities.)* *[2 marks]*
9) (a) $\frac{3}{4} = \frac{6}{8}$ so we need a fraction between $\frac{6}{8}$ and $\frac{7}{8}$. By converting both fractions to sixteenths (by doubling both the numerator and the denominator), we can see that $\frac{13}{16}$ fits the bill. (Alternatively, turn both fractions to decimals — see (b) below — and choose a decimal number in between, e.g. 0.76). *[2 marks]*
(b) Use your calculator to turn both fractions into decimals:
$\frac{3}{4} = 0.75$ and $\frac{7}{8} = 0.875$.
We want a square root of something which is in between these two decimals, as then we know it will be irrational.
$0.75^2 = 0.5625$ and $0.875^2 = 0.765625$ so choose the square root of a number between 0.5625 and 0.765625, **e.g. √0.6**. *[2 marks]*
10) (a) √16 = 4 (rational) (b) √8 (irrational)
(c) √90 (irrational) (d) √2.5 (irrational)
[4 marks]
11) You need to realise that a more accurate approximation for π = 3.14159, so we need the square root of a number that gives us an answer between 3.14 and 3.141. Try various ones on your calculator until you come up with an answer, **e.g. √9.86**. *[3 marks]*

Page 18 (Warm-Up Questions)

1) (a) 8, 13, 18, 23, 28, 33
(b) 8, 11, 14, 17, 20, 23
2) 2, 6, 12, 20, 30, 42
3) (a) 5n (b) 3n + 4 (c) n^2
4) There is always one cross in the centre, and the number of other crosses is 4 times the pattern number (because there are 4 "arms" coming from the centre). So in the nth pattern there will be a total of 4n + 1 crosses.
(This method is a kind of 'common sense method'. You can get the same result by finding 'a' and 'd' and then using dn + (a – d).)

Page 19 (Exam Questions)

3) (a)

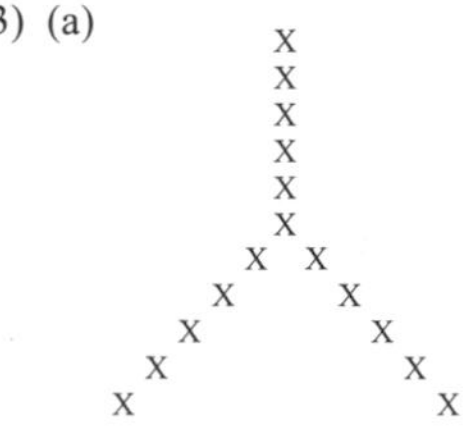

[1 mark]

(b) The missing numbers from the table are: **10, 13, 16**. *[1 mark]*
(c) 3 × 20 + 1 = **61**. *[1 mark]*
(d) 3 × n + 1 = **3n + 1**. *[2 marks]*
4) The gaps are 6 each time, so it's based on the 6 times table. You need to subtract 3 from the 6 times table to get the sequence we want, so the nth term is **6n – 3**. *(Again you can get the same result using dn + (a – d).)* *[2 marks]*

5) Compare the sequence to $n^2 = 1, 4, 9, 16, 25, ...$ The sequence in the question is just this sequence plus an extra 1 each time.
So the nth term is $\mathbf{n^2 + 1}$.
[2 marks]

6) (a)
X X X X X
X X X X X
X X X X X
X X X X X
X X X X X
● ● ● ● ●

[1 mark]

(b) **n** dots. *[1 mark]*

(c) $\mathbf{n^2}$ crosses. *[1 mark]*

(d) A total of $\mathbf{n^2 + n}$ crosses and dots. *[1 mark]*

Page 25 (Warm-Up Questions)

1) $12.7 \times 1000 = 12\ 700$ g.

2) $1430 \div 100 = 14.3$ m.

3) This little rhyme will help:
"Two and a quarter pounds of jam. Weighs about one kilogram".
So you need about 9 lbs to make 4 kg, so 10 lbs is approximately 4½ kg.

4) $$\frac{94 \times 1.9}{0.328 + 0.201} \rightarrow \frac{90 \times 2}{0.3 + 0.2} = \frac{180}{0.5} = 360$$

5) $\sqrt{49} = 7$ so $\sqrt{50}$ will be about 7.1 (actually 7.071...).

6) (a) 40.22.
(b) 39.9.
(c) 28.

Page 26 (Exam Questions)

4) 8 km is about 5 miles, so 24 km is about $3 \times 5 =$ **15 miles**. *[1 mark]*

5) 1kg is about 2¼ lbs, so 5 lbs is just over **2 kg**. *[1 mark]*

6) $312 \div 60 = 5.2$ hours. Two tenths of an hour is 2×6 minutes $= 12$ minutes. So 5.2 hours is **5 hours 12 minutes**. *[2 marks]*

7) $$\frac{29 \times 2.9}{9.1 - 6.9} \rightarrow \frac{30 \times 3}{9 - 7} = \frac{90}{2} = \mathbf{45}$$ *[2 marks]*

8) $495 \div 4 = 123.75 =$ **120 km/h** (2 sig. fig.). *[2 marks]*

9) 3½ metres = 350 cm. So the model car is $350 \div 40 =$ **8.75 cm** long.
[2 marks]

10) The upper bounds of a and b are 8.5 and 5.5, and the lower bounds are 7.5 and 4.5. We want the smallest possible answer in each case, so:
(a) $a + b = 7.5 + 4.5 =$ **12**.
(b) $a \div b = 7.5 \div 5.5 =$ **1.363636...**
[4 marks]

*Note that in (b) the smallest value is NOT given by the lower bounds.
It depends on the operation you are carrying out.
So the lowest value of a ÷ b is given by a small value for a and a big one for b.*

11) Upper bound $= 60.5 \times 60.5 \times 60.5 =$ **221445.125 mm³**.
Lower bound $= 59.5 \times 59.5 \times 59.5 =$ **210644.875 mm³**.
[3 marks]

12) Maximum width is 59.5 cm, so the maximum error is 0.5 cm.
Find this as a percentage of the extreme value:
$$\frac{0.5}{59.5} \times 100 = \mathbf{0.84\%}$$ (2 d.p.) *[3 marks]*

Page 39 (Warm-Up Questions)

1) 672 cm³ *(area of triangle × length = 1/2 × 12 × 8 × 14)*

2)
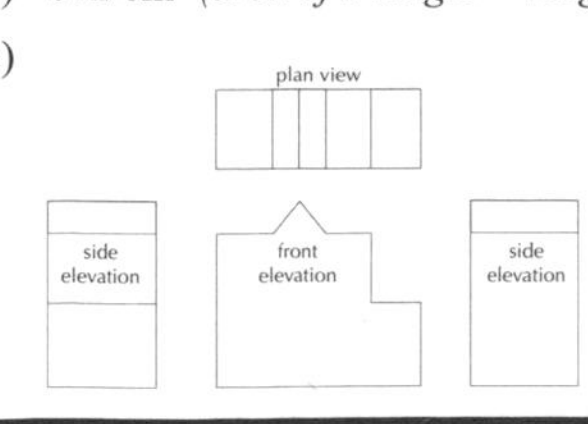

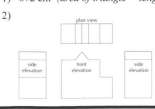

3) (a) 1963.5mm² *($\pi r^2 = 25^2 \times \pi$)*
(b) 37 146 mm² *(area of rectangle minus area of four circles)*
(c) 148 584 mm³ *(volume = area × thickness)*

Page 40 (Exam Questions)

2) Exterior angle = 360° ÷ number sides.
So for octagon = 360° ÷ 8 = 45°.
Interior angle = 180° – exterior = 180 – 45 = **135°**. *[2 marks]*

3)

pqr	2p(p+q)	p+q+r	2p+2r	pq(r-p)	p^2r
V	A	L	L	V	V

[3 marks]

4) (a) Area of metal = area whole circle – area of segment.
Area whole circle $= \pi r^2 = 15^2 \times \pi = 706.9$ mm²
Area segment $= (\theta \div 360) \times$ area circle $= (70 \div 360) \times 706.9 = 137.5$ mm²
Area metal $= 706.9 - 137.5 =$ **569.4 mm²**. *[3 marks]*

(b) Perim of metal = perim circle – perim arc segment + edges of segment.
Perim circle = $\pi \times$ diameter $= 30\pi = 94.2$ mm
Perim arc segment $= (\theta \div 360) \times$ perim circle $=$
$(70 \div 360) \times 94.2 = 18.3$ mm.
Perim metal $= 94.2 - 18.3 + (2 \times 15) =$ **105.9 mm** *[3 marks]*

Page 49 (Warm-Up Questions)

1)
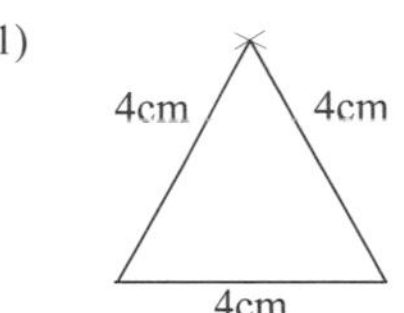

(Not to scale.)

2) a = 115°, *angles on a line add to 180°, so a = 180 – 65.*
b = 115°, *a and b are corresponding angles, so a = b.*
c = 65°, *c and 65° are also corresponding angles.*
d = 115°, *angles on a line add to 180°, so d = 180 – c.*
*There are often different ways of going about these angle questions.
Just keep scribbling down angles as you find them, it can make it easier to get the angle you want.*

3) EDC = 135°.
*(Sum of interior angles = (n – 2) × 180 = 540°.
So take all the angles away from 540°.)*

4)
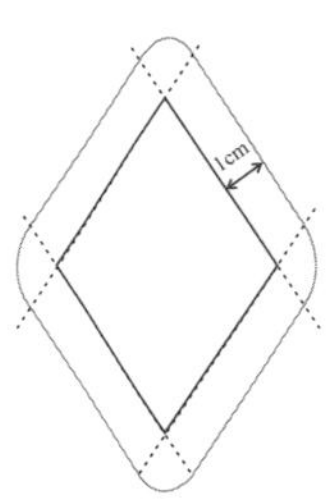

5) M = N = 64°,
(Angles M and N are equal — this is an extension to the "equality of tangents from a point" theorem on page 45, called the "Alternate Segment Theorem" — basically, triangle RQS is isosceles.)
L = 52°, *(Angles in a triangle add to 180, so 180 – 64 – 64)*

Page 51-52 (Exam Questions)

3)
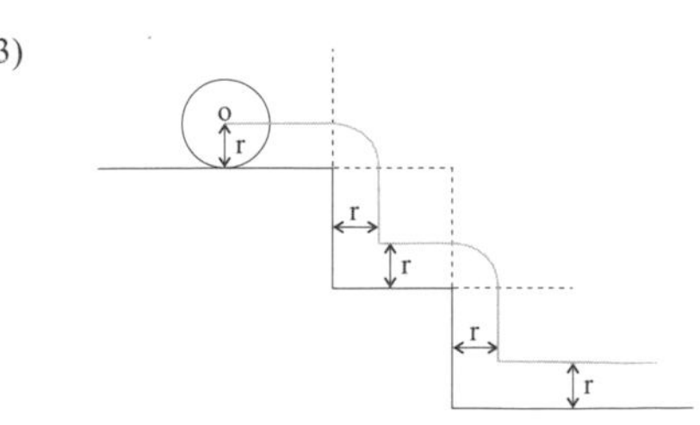

[3 marks]

4) (a) Angle OAT is 90°. OAB = 90 – 60 = 30°.
Triangle OBA is isosceles so $X = 180 - 30 - 30 =$ **120°**. *[3 marks]*
(b) Angle subtended at the centre is twice the angle subtended at the circumference. i.e. $X = 2Y$. $Y = X \div 2 = 120 \div 2 =$ **60°**. *[2 marks]*
(c) Triangle BAT is isosceles by "equality of tangents" rule.
Angle TAB = angle ABT = 60°. Therefore, Z = 180 – 60 – 60 = **60°**.
(so in fact triangle BAT is equilateral.) *[2 marks]*

5) Angles in a triangle add to 180°.
$180° = 110° + (180° - \alpha) + (180° - \beta)$
$180° = 470° - \alpha - \beta$
$\alpha + \beta = 290°$ as required. *[3 marks]*

Page 58 (Warm-Up Questions)

1) (a) a and e (b) b and f

2) (a) $\frac{1}{4.5}$ or 0.222 or $\frac{2}{9}$
Note that the enlargement scale factor is less than one — so the 'enlargement' actually makes the shape smaller.
(b) 2.6 cm

3) $\begin{pmatrix} -3 \\ 3 \end{pmatrix}$

Page 59 (Exam Questions)

3) 4.2 ÷ 2.5 = 1.68. 9.24 ÷ 1.68 = **5.5 cm** *[2 marks]*

4) 12 × 2.5 = 30 cm
8.5 × 2.5 = 21.25 cm
So dimensions are **30 cm × 21.25 cm** *[2 marks]*

5) (a)

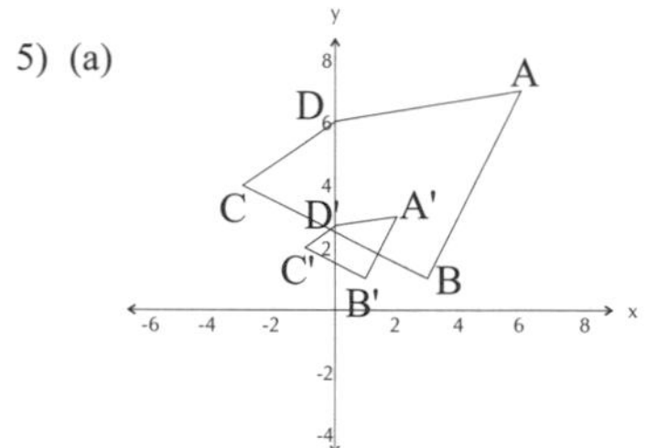

[2 marks]
(b) B' is the point (1, 1) *[1 mark]*

6) (a) Reflection in the line $y = 0$ (the x-axis) *[2 marks]*
(b)

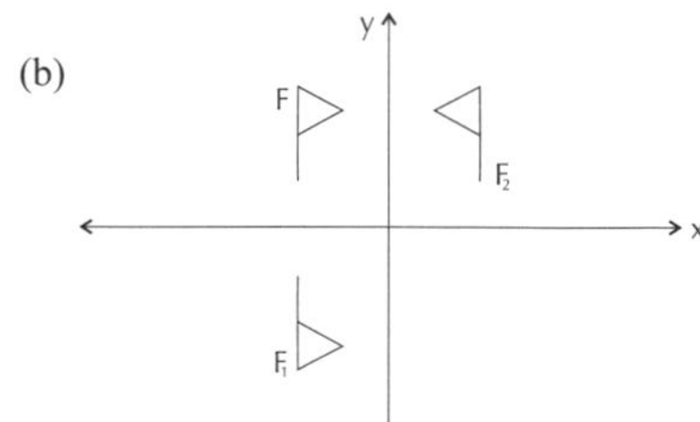

[1 mark]
(c) Rotation 180° centre (0, 0) *[2 marks]*

Page 66 (Warm-Up Questions)

1) 90 km/hr
(100 metres in 4 secs is 25 metres per second, then just multiply by 60 to get metres per minute, then again to get metres per hour and then finally divide by 1000.)

2) 9 km *(from formula triangle: speed × time = distance)*

3) 11.3 g/cm³ *(density = mass ÷ volume)*

4) 96 g *(volume = 5 × 4 × 6 = 120 cm³. Then use mass = density × volume.)*

Page 67 (Exam Questions)

3) Takes 2 hours 40 mins = $2\frac{2}{3}$ hours.
Distance is 30 km.
Average speed = Dist ÷ Time = $30 \div 2\frac{2}{3} =$ **11.25 km/h** *[2 marks]*

4) Volume is 4 × 4 × 4 = 64 cm³
Mass = Density × Volume = 13.55 × 64 = **867.2 g** *[3 marks]*

5) (a) **4 km** *[1 mark]*
(b) The points where the graph is horizontal are where Dominic has stopped. So the answers are **D** and **F**. *[2 marks]*
(c) The fastest leg of his journey was stage E (the slope is greatest here). The speed on a distance - time graph is the gradient, so work out the gradient at this point.
Gradient = change in y / change in x
Read the values off the graph:
the change in y is 17 – 9 = 8 km
the change in x is 30 minutes = 0.5 hours.
So the gradient is 8 / 0.5 = 16 km / h.
So his speed is **16 km / h**. *[3 marks]*
(d) To work out his average speed for the total journey, draw a straight line on the graph from his start point to finish point and work out the slope of this line, like above:
the change in y is 24 km.
the change in x is 9:40 am to 1:30 pm = 230 mins = 3.83 hours.
So the gradient is 24 / 3.83 = **6.26 km / h** (2 d.p.). *[3 marks]*

Page 72 (Warm-Up Questions)

1) 2.5×10^5 miles
2) 2.7×10^{-6} seconds
3) 0.0000000000000000000000027 g
4) 1.2×10^8
5) (a) 4^3 (b) 6^3 (c) 3^8
6) (a) 2 (b) $1\frac{32}{49}$ (c) 9

Page 74 (Exam Questions)

4) (a) 1 cubic mm of blood = 5×10^6 red blood cells
1 cubic cm of blood = $5 \times 10^6 \times 1000 = 5 \times 10^9$ red blood cells
1 litre of blood = $5 \times 10^9 \times 1000 = 5 \times 10^{12}$ red blood cells
6 litres of blood = $5 \times 10^{12} \times 6 =$ **3×10^{13} red blood cells**
[2 marks]
(b) $3 \times 10^{13} \div 120$
$= 3 \times 10^{13} \div 1.2 \times 10^2$
$= (3 \div 1.2) \times 10^{11}$
$= 2.5 \times 10^{11}$
[2 marks]

5) (a) p^7 (b) $2t^3$ (c) $36a^6d^4$ *[3 marks]*

6) (a) $4.0 \times 10^{10} + 3.72 \times 10^{11}$ m²
$= 4.0 \times 10^{10} + 37.2 \times 10^{10}$ m²
$= (4.0 + 37.2) \times 10^{10}$ m²
$= 41.2 \times 10^{10}$ m²
$= 4.12 \times 10^{11}$ m²
[2 marks]
(b) $(3.72 \times 10^{11}) \div (4.0 \times 10^{10})$
$= (37.2 \times 10^{10}) \div (4.0 \times 10^{10})$
$= 37.2 \div 4.0 = 9.3 = 9$ (to 1 s.f.)
1 : 9 *[2 marks]*

Page 83 (Warm-Up Questions)

1) (a) 13.1 cm *(by Pythagoras)*
(b) 40° *(tan x = 8.4 ÷ 10)*

2) AC = 9.6 cm *(by sin rule : $\frac{AC}{\sin 52} = \frac{12}{\sin 80}$)*

3) 104.5° *(by cos rule :* $\cos A = \frac{6^2+4^2-8^2}{2\times6\times4}$*)*

4 (a) Choose from:

similarities: they both have the same shape / same range (-1 and 1)

differences: they cross the x-axis at different places / translating the sine graph by 90° horizontally gives the cosine graph

(b) Choose from:

similarities:
tan 0°, 180°, 360°... = sin 0°, 180°, 360°... = 0

differences:
tan x is not a continuous graph / vertical axes:

y values for sin x go between -1 and 1, whereas y values for tan x go to infinity.

5)

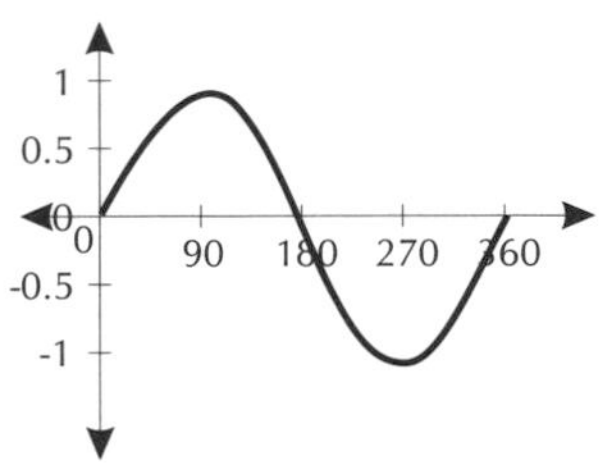

Page 85 (Exam Questions)

4) (a) $BD^2 = 6.4^2 - 5.5^2$ by Pythagoras.
Therefore $BD = \sqrt{(6.4^2 - 5.5^2)}$ = **3.27 m** *[3 marks]*

(b) AB = AD + DB = 8.7 + 3.27 = 11.97 = **12.0 m to 3 s.f.** *[1 mark]*

(c) $AC^2 = AB^2 + BC^2 = 12^2 + 5.5^2$. $AC = \sqrt{174.25}$ = **13.2 m** *[3 marks]*

5) (a) tan 52.1 = DC ÷ 24.
So DC = 24 tan 52.1 = **30.8 m high** *[3 marks]*

(b) Call the angle of elevation x.

tan x = 30.8 ÷ 31.

x = **44.8°** *[3 marks]*

Page 89 (Warm-Up Questions)

1) (a) $\vec{AB} = \begin{pmatrix}7\\2\end{pmatrix}$ (b) $\vec{BC} = \begin{pmatrix}6\\-3\end{pmatrix}$ (c) $\vec{ED} = \begin{pmatrix}8\\0\end{pmatrix}$

(d) $\vec{CD} = \begin{pmatrix}-2\\-4\end{pmatrix}$ (e) $\vec{AM} = \begin{pmatrix}12\\-3\end{pmatrix}$

2) (a) $\begin{pmatrix}4\\9\end{pmatrix}$ (b) $\begin{pmatrix}-1\\2\end{pmatrix}$ (c) $\begin{pmatrix}5\\7\end{pmatrix}$ (d) $\begin{pmatrix}-1\\-6\end{pmatrix}$ (e) $\begin{pmatrix}1\\10\end{pmatrix}$

These are straightforward, just deal with the top and bottom numbers separately, then it's a simple matter of addition and subtraction.

3) (a) $\begin{pmatrix}6\cos 40°\\6\sin 40°\end{pmatrix} = \begin{pmatrix}4.596\\3.857\end{pmatrix}$

(b) $\begin{pmatrix}28\cos 65°\\-28\sin 65°\end{pmatrix} = \begin{pmatrix}11.833\\-25.377\end{pmatrix}$

(c) $\begin{pmatrix}-2.4\cos 12°\\2.4\sin 12°\end{pmatrix} = \begin{pmatrix}-2.348\\0.499\end{pmatrix}$

4) Speed = 9.43 m/s (3 sig.fig.). Direction = 58.0° (3 sig.fig.).
(finding the speed by Pythagoras and using tan to get the direction)

Page 91 (Exam Questions)

2) (a) (i) a + 2b. (ii) ½ a + 2b

(b) (i) and (ii) both = a + b. *(this is easiest done by drawing a quick sketch)*

(c) The lines are parallel and of equal length *(they have the same vector).* *[5 marks]*

3) (a) This is basically a triangle question. Use Pythagoras to get the resultant speed $\sqrt{(6^2 + 5^2)}$ = **7.81 km/h (3 sig.fig.)**.
Then use tan x = 5 ÷ 6 = 39.8°. **So 50.2° to the bank (3 sig.fig.)**. *[2 marks]*

(b) Start by drawing a sketch:

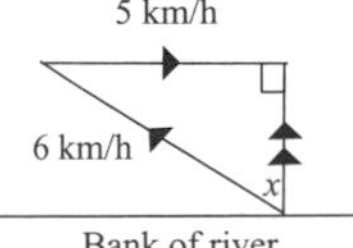

Bank of river

This time, the hypot. of the triangle is 6 km/h. So use sin x = 5 ÷ 6.
This gives x = 56.44° which means an angle of 90 – 56.44 = **33.6° to the bank (3 sig.fig.)**. *[2 marks]*

(c) Start with a sketch again:

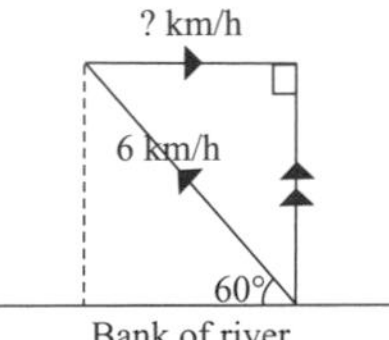

Bank of river

From the sketch, you can see that the river speed you want is the same (though in the opposite direction) as the horizontal component of the boat's speed vector. So the river's speed is 6 cos 60° = **3 km/h**. *[2 marks]*

For these vector questions, a quick labelled sketch will nearly always make your life a lot easier.

Page 95 (Warm-Up Questions)

1) 1/216 or 0.0046. *(1/6 × 1/6 × 1/6)*

2) 16/49 or 0.33. *(4/7 × 4/7)*

3) 1/8 or 0.125. *(1/2 × 1/2 × 1/2)*

4) 6/7 or 0.86.
(prob at least one of each colour = 1 – prob all blue – prob all red = 1 – (3/7 × 2/6 × 1/5) – (4/7 × 3/6 × 2/5) = 6/7.)

In a question like this, there are lots of ways of getting at least one of each colour, but there are only two ways that it can't happen, i.e. if all the balls are red, or all blue. So work out those probabilities and subtract them from 1.

Page 96 (Exam Questions)

2) P (grey, grey) P (black, black) P (red, red)

$$\left(\frac{12}{24}\times\frac{11}{23}\right)+\left(\frac{8}{24}\times\frac{7}{23}\right)+\left(\frac{4}{24}\times\frac{3}{23}\right)$$
$$=\frac{132}{552}+\frac{56}{552}+\frac{12}{552}$$
$$=\frac{200}{552}=\mathbf{\frac{25}{69}}$$

OR 0.3623. *[5 marks]*

3) (a)

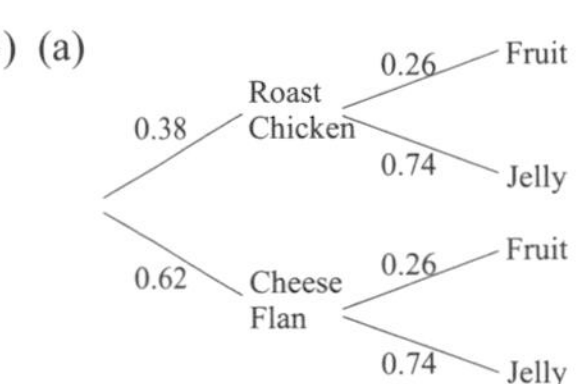

[1 mark]

(b) 0.38 × 0.74 = **0.2812**. *[2 marks]*

4)

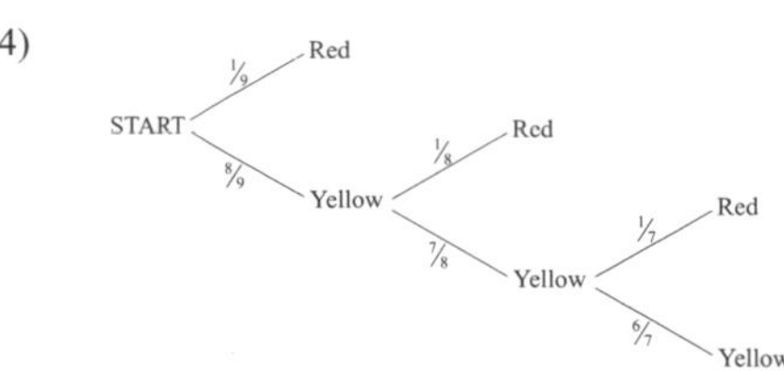

$\left(\frac{1}{9}\right)+\left(\frac{8}{9}\times\frac{1}{8}\right)+\left(\frac{8}{9}\times\frac{7}{8}\times\frac{1}{7}\right)=\frac{1}{3}$ *[3 marks]*

You should begin to see that all these questions boil down to drawing a tree diagram and then multiplying down the branches.

Page 105 (Warm-Up Questions)

1) Mode = most common.
Median = middle value.
Mean = total of items ÷ number of items
Range = how far from the biggest to the smallest.

2)

Number of cars	Frequency	No. of cars × F
0	1	0
1	24	24
2	36	72
3	31	93
4	22	88
5	9	45
6	1	6
	= 124	= 328

(a) Mean = 328 ÷ 124 = 2.645
(b) Median = 124 ÷ 2 = 62nd value = 3
(c) Mode = 2
(d) Range = 6 – 0 = 6.

3)

Height (cm)	Frequency	Midpoint	Midpoint × F
145 -	18	150	2700
155 -	22	160	3520
165 -	24	170	4080
175 - 185	15	180	2700
	= 79		= 13000

(a) Mean = 13000 ÷ 79 = 164.56
(b) Median = 79 ÷ 2 = 39.5th value = 155 - 165.
(c) Modal Group = 165-175

Page 106 (Exam Questions)

2) (a)

Time (t mins)	Frequency	Mid-point	Midpoint × F
0 < t ≤ 1	77	0.5	38.5
1 < t ≤ 2	142	1.5	213
2 < t ≤ 3	143	2.5	357.5
3 < t ≤ 4	60	3.5	210
4 < t ≤ 5	49	4.5	220.5
5 < t ≤ 6	29	5.5	159.5
	= 500		= 1199

Mean = 1199 ÷ 500 = 2.398 minutes.
[4 marks]

(b)

Time (≤ mins)	Cumulative Frequency
1	77
2	219
3	362
4	422
5	471
6	500

[3 marks]

(c)

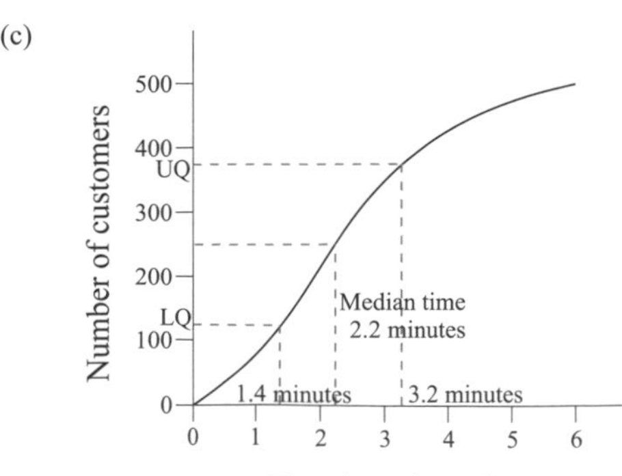

[4 marks]

(d) (i) 2.2 minutes (see graph). *[1 mark]*
(ii) IQ range = UQ – LQ = 3.2 mins – 1.4 mins = **1.8 mins** *[2 marks]*

Page 113 (Warm-Up Questions)

1)

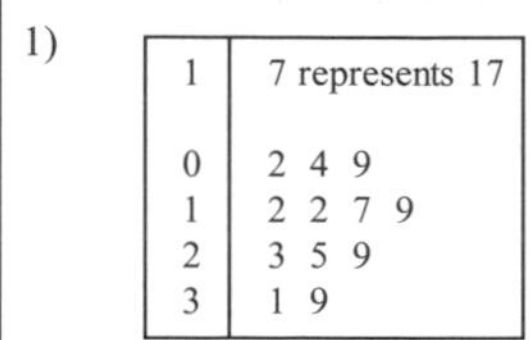

1	7 represents 17
0	2 4 9
1	2 2 7 9
2	3 5 9
3	1 9

2) Graph 1 — Moderate positive correlation.
Graph 2 — Weak negative correlation.

3) Systematic sampling.

4) The sample is made up of 600 residential addresses in Birmingham. We are not told how the sample is chosen. The results obtained are likely to be biased as the interview timing will exclude households where the occupants are at work during the normal working hours.

Pages 115-116 (Exam Questions)

3) (a) 80 ÷ 720 = **1/9**

(b) Divide each of the numbers of people by 9:
0-5 = 38 ÷ 9 = **4**; 6-12 = 82 ÷ 9 = **9**; 13-21 = 108 ÷ 9 = **12**; 22-35 = 204 ÷ 9 = **23**; 36-50 = 180 ÷ 9 = **20**; 51+ = 108 ÷ 9 = **12**.
Total = 80. **[Total 3 marks]**
In a stratified sample, you choose at random, but equally from each category. So here, you need to sample a ninth of the people from each category.

4) (a)

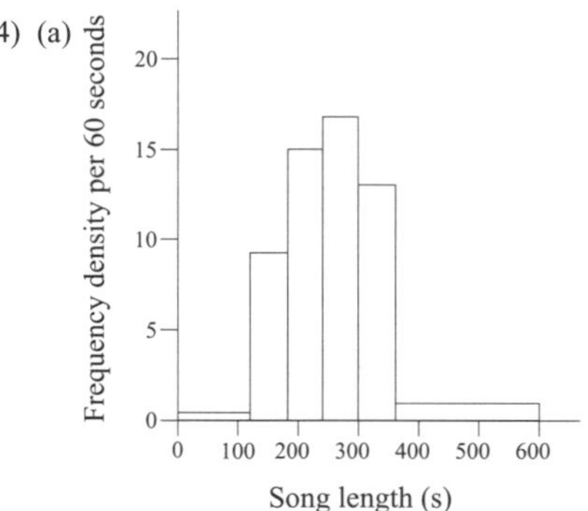

[2 marks]

(b) Work out the products of the mid point of each category and its frequency. Then add them all up to get an estimate of the total length of all the songs:
(60 × 1) + (150 × 9) + (210 × 15) + (270 × 17) + (330 × 13) + (480 × 5) = 15840.
Now divide this by the total number of songs, which is 60:
15840 ÷ 60 = **264 seconds**. *[2 marks]*
This is very much like producing the third and fourth columns in a grouped frequency table (see page 102).

5) (a)

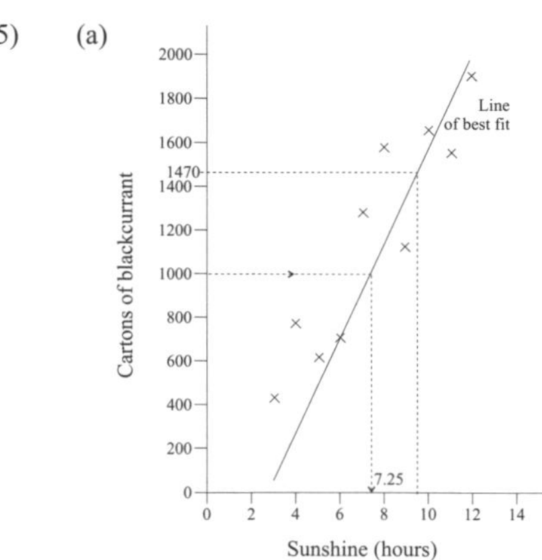

[1 mark]

(b) As the number of hours of sunshine increases, so does the number of cartons sold. This shows a positive correlation between the two quantities. *[1 mark]*

(c) See graph above. Any suitable line of best fit similar to the one shown would receive one mark. *[1 mark]*

(d) (i) About $7^1/_4$ hours. *[1 mark]*

(ii) Dependent on the line of best fit, answer in range of **1450** to **1550**. *[1 mark]*

Page 124 (Warm-Up Questions)

1) 1 in 4 *(this is equivalent to 25%).*

2) (a) $y = x$. (b) Horizontal line, $y = 4$.

(c) Vertical line, $x = -1$. (d) $y = -x$.

3) Positive: C, E. Negative: A, D. No gradient: B.

4) (a)

x	0	2	3
y	-4	2	5

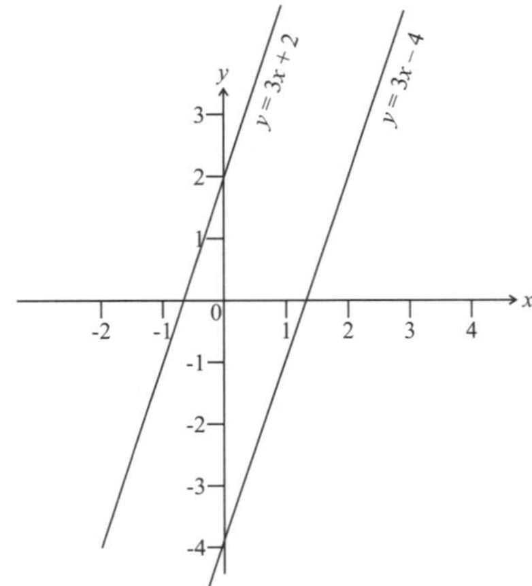

(b) See diagram. $y = 3x + 2$ will be parallel to $y = 3x - 4$ and will pass through the point (0, 2) on the y axis.

Page 125 (Exam Questions)

2) (a) **A and D**. *Have to find two lines with the same gradient, or in other words two with the same coefficient of x. This is not immediately obvious but by dividing D by two on both sides we see A & D both have the form y = 3x + c, and thus both have a gradient of three. Therefore A and D are parallel.* *[1 mark]*

(b) **B and E.**
Because they both have negative coef. of x in the format y = mx + c.
NB. for E you need to move the x to the other side to get it in this form.
[1 mark]

(c) **C**. *(Because when x = 0, y = 0)* *[1 mark]*

(d) **A and E.** *Put in the x = 4 and see which give a y value of 10 :*
A: y = 3x – 2, when x = 4, y = (3 × 4) – 2 = 10, so A has point (4, 10).
E: y = 14 – x, when x = 4, y = 14 – 4 = 10, so E has point (4, 10).
[1 mark]

3) Need to find the intersections of the lines: $y = 2x - 1$; $2y = x + 1$; $y = 3$.
$y = 2x - 1$ meets $2y = x + 1$ when $4x - 2 = x + 1$. $x = 1$. $y = (2 \times 1) - 1 = 1$
So **(1, 1)** is one of the points.

$y = 2x - 1$ meets $y = 3$ when $2x - 1 = 3$. $x = 2$. $y = 3$ (because on $y = 3$).
So **(2, 3)** is one of the points.

$2y = x + 1$ meets $y = 3$ when $6 = x + 1$. $x = 5$. $y = 3$ as above.
So **(5, 3)** is one of the points.
[3 marks]

Page 129 (Warm-Up Questions)

1)

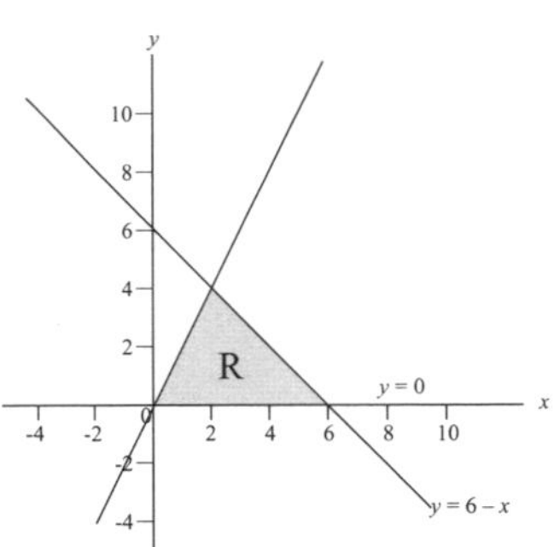

2)

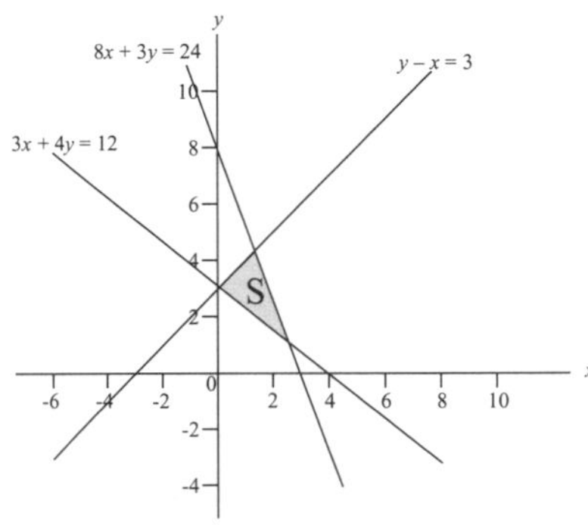

3) $m \geq 10$, $c \geq 6$, $m + c \leq 24$.

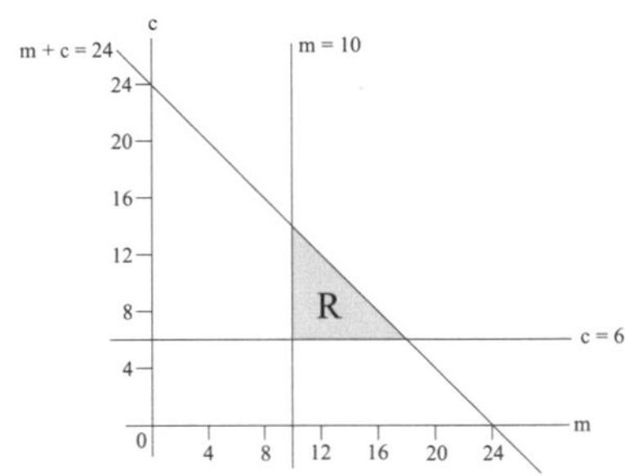

Page 130 (Exam Questions)

2) (a) $120x + 150y \leq 4200$ (or $12x + 15y \leq 420$ or $0.12x + 0.15y \leq 4.2$),
$x \leq 2y$, $x \leq 20$.
[2 marks]

(b)

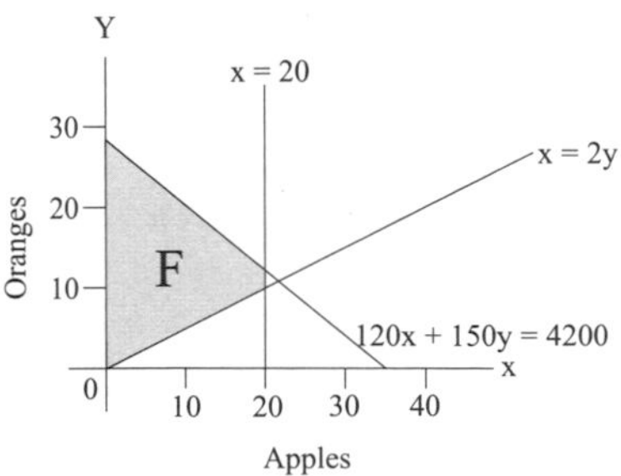

[3 marks]

(c) Use the equation $10x + 30y = 1000$
So $y = 1000/3 - x/3$ ie a line with gradient -1/3.
If you use a ruler to move that line through the region you get an optimum point of 20 apples and 12 oranges.
So (20 × 10) + (12 × 30) = £5.60.
So he would get 10.00 – 5.60 = **£4.40** change.
[4 marks]

3)

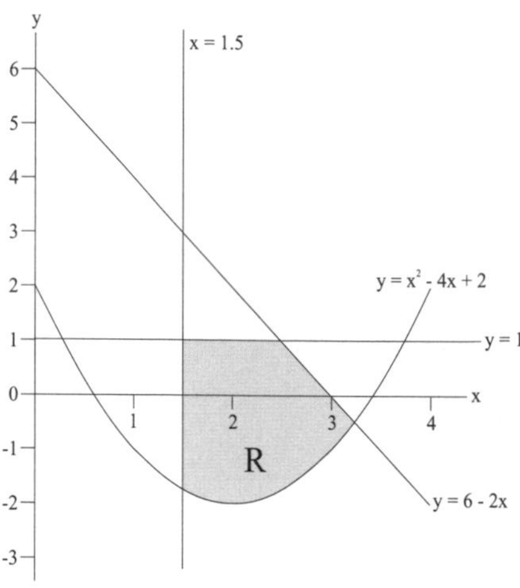

[4 marks]

Page 135 (Warm-Up Questions)

1) (a)

x	-2	-1	0	1	2	3	4	5
x^2	4	1	0	1	4	9	16	25
-2x	4	2	0	-2	-4	-6	-8	-10
-1	-1	-1	-1	-1	-1	-1	-1	-1
$y = x^2 - 2x - 1$	7	2	-1	-2	-1	2	7	14

(b)

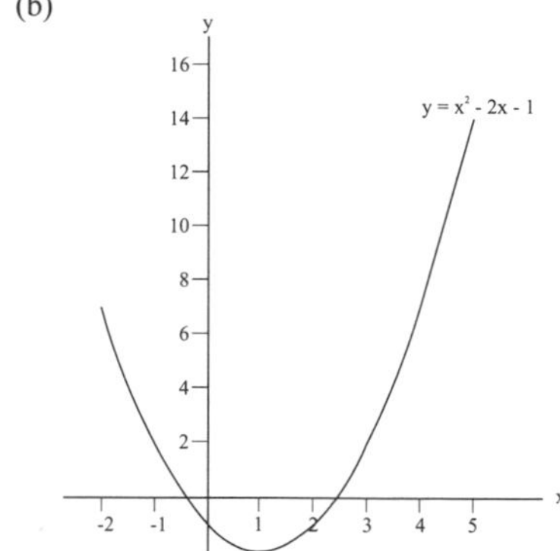

(c) 4.25 (a value between 4.2 and 4.3 is acceptable).

(d) $x = -1.65$ and 3.65 (values between -1.6 and -1.7 and between 3.6 and 3.7 are acceptable).

2) (a) $x = 6, y = 6$. (b) $x = 2, y = 4$. (c) $x = 3.1, y = 1.7$.
Just read off the points where the lines cross... erm, that's it.

3)

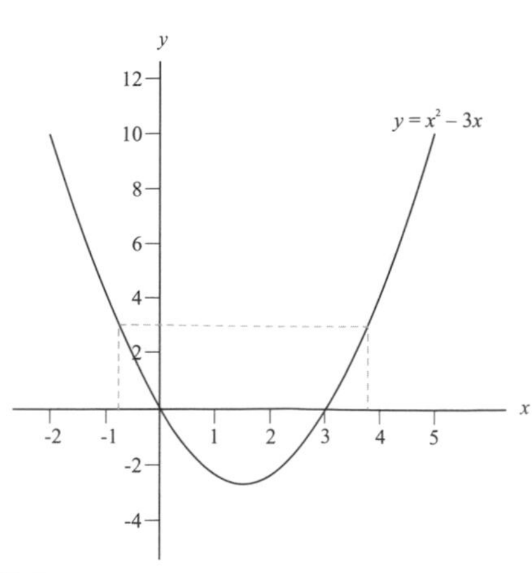

(a) $x = 0$ and 3.

(b) $x = -0.8$ and 3.8.

4)

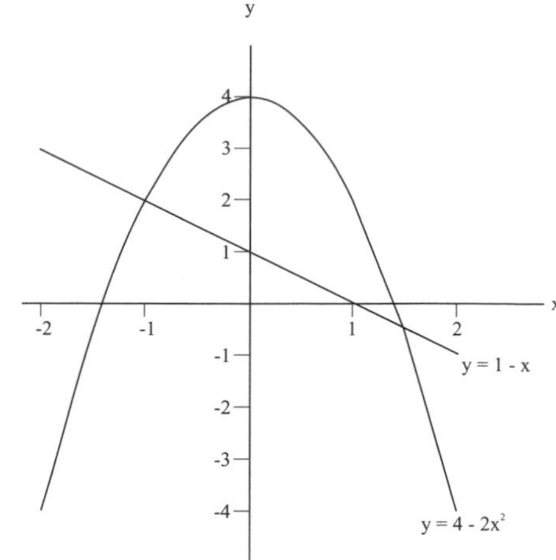

$x = -1$ and 1.5. *(The solution is just where the two graphs cross.)*

5) $y = 5 - x$.
(This is like the reverse process of question 4. You need to think which equation you can combine with the one given to get to the one you want. $y = 5 - x$ meets $y = x^2 - 3x + 2$ when $5 - x = x^2 - 3x + 2$, i.e. $x^2 - 2x - 3 = 0$ as required.)

Page 137 (Exam Questions)

3) (a)

t	0	1	2	3	4	5	6
$h = 4.2t - 0.7t^2$	0	3.5	5.6	6.3	5.6	3.5	0

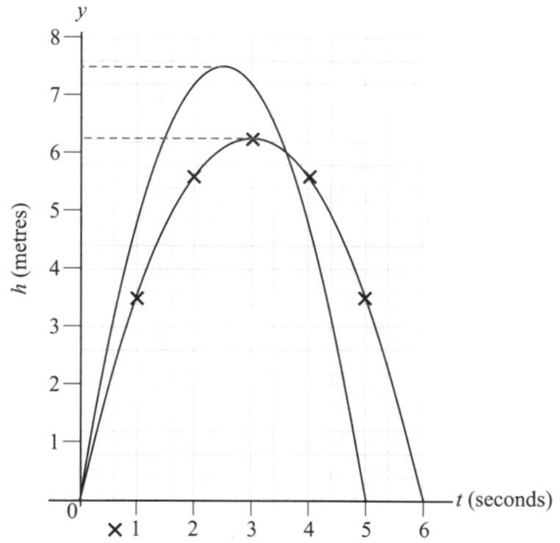

[4 marks]

(b) **Nick** (Nick's graph has a higher max pt). *[1 mark]*

(c) Read off the max values from the graph:
$7.5 - 6.3 =$ **1.2 m**.
[2 marks]

(d) Just read down from the point where the graphs intersect:
Answer: **3.6 s** (values between 3.5 - 3.7 s are acceptable).
[1 mark]

Once you've drawn the graph (and made sure you've done it accurately), all you need to do is read off the points, like the maximum height, and the point where they cross, showing they are at the same height.

4) (a) 5, 3, 2, 1.4.
[2 marks]

(b)

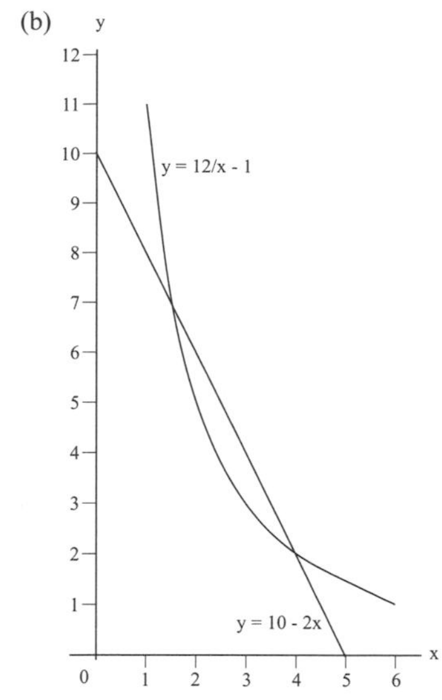

[2 marks]

c) $x = 4$ and $x = 1.5$
(values between $x = 3.9$ to 4.1 and $x = 1.4$ to 1.6 are acceptable).
[2 marks]

Page 146 (Warm-Up Questions)

1) (a) About $x = 0.5$ (b) About $x = 1$ (c) About $x = 1.5$
All of these are done by just drawing the tangent and seeing where it hits the x-axis.

2) (a) 80 (1 sig.fig.).
(Draw a tangent and work out difference in y ÷ difference in x for 2 points on the axis.)
(b) Velocity at time 10 seconds.
(It's the rate of change of distance — i.e. speed)

3) (a) D. (b) B. (c) A. (d) C.

Page 148 (Exam Questions)

3) (a) $y = ax^3 - bx^2$
$x = 1, y = -1$. So $-1 = a - b$. $a = b - 1$.
$x = 2, y = 12$. So $12 = 8a - 4b$. $3 = 2a - b$.
Combining the two $3 = 2b - 2 - b$. **b = 5**
a = b – 1 = 4.
[3 marks]

4) (a)&(b)

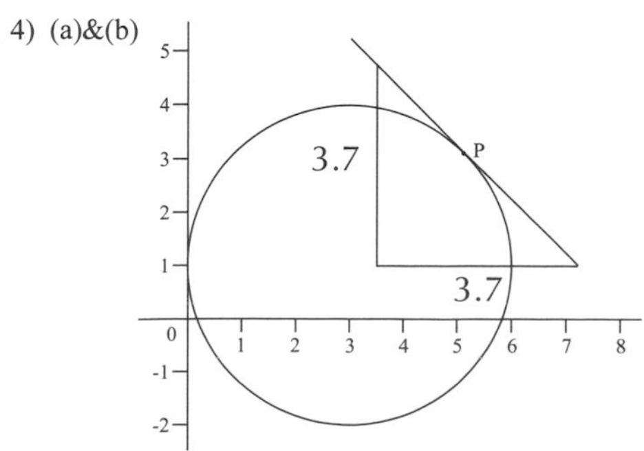

$-3.7 \div 3.7 =$ **–1.0 (to 1 d.p.)** *[4 marks]*
In the real exam these diagrams would be bigger and therefore clearer, we're just trying to squeeze more questions in again. So don't worry too much if your answer is a bit different from -1. The main thing is that you've done the method in the right way — drawn the tangent, made a triangle, worked out the change in y and x and then divided change in y by change in x.

Page 160 (Warm-Up Questions)

1) (a) 2 (b) 2 (c) 6 (d) 2
(e) 3 (f) $\frac{1}{3}$ (g) -8 (h) -2

2) (a) $8p + 28$ (b) $8x^2 - 2$ (c) $5a^2 - 3a$

3) $(x + 2y)(x - 2y)$

4) (a) $2a - 5c$ (b) $7r^2 - 5r - 1$

5) (a) $2(3p - 6q + 2)$ (b) $2cd(2d - 1 + 5cd^2)$

6) (a) $\frac{11x}{10}$ (b) $\frac{ac^2}{b}$ *(turn 2nd fraction upside down and multiply)*

7) (a) $x = 3$ (b) $x = -3$ (c) $x = 5$

8) (a) p (b) t

9) (a) $A = lw$ where A stands for area, l stands for length and w stands for width.
(b) To find the length you divide the area by the width: $l = \frac{A}{w}$

Pages 162-163 (Exam Questions)

5) (a) Collect like terms together:
$(3x^2y + x^2y) + (-2xy^2 - 4y^2x)$;
$\mathbf{4x^2y - 6xy^2}$
[2 marks]
(b) Collect together the r terms and k terms:
$(4k - 3k - 2k) + (8r - 2r)$;
6r – k
[2 marks]

6) (a) $8x - 12 - 12 - 9x$;
$\mathbf{-x - 24}$
[2 marks]
(b) $6c^2 - 2c + 18c - 6$;
$\mathbf{6c^2 + 16c - 6}$
[2 marks]

7) (a) $\mathbf{\frac{8 + 6x}{3x}}$
[1 mark]
(b) $\frac{x^2y}{z} + \frac{xy^3}{3z} = \frac{3x^2y + xy^3}{3z} = \mathbf{\frac{xy(3x + y^2)}{3z}}$
[2 marks]

8) (a) $\mathbf{6cd^2(2cd + 3 - 5c^2d^2)}$
[2 marks]
(b) (i) $\mathbf{8b^3cd}$
[2 marks]
(ii) $\mathbf{2t - t^2}$
[2 marks]

9) (a) This one is tricky — there are no factors common to all the terms.
But two terms have 2c in and the other two have y in them, so try taking these out: $2cx + xy + 2ac + ay = 2c(x + a) + y(x + a)$
Now both of these terms have $(x + a)$, so you can take that out as a common factor to get $\mathbf{(x + a)(2c + y)}$. *[3 marks]*
On this one, it's easy to get stuck and give up at the start, but if you just play with it a bit, the answer will suddenly pop out of nowhere...
(b) You've got a squared term minus another squared term, so use the "difference of 2 squares": $\mathbf{(4x - 2p)(4x + 2p)}$.
[2 marks]
Look back to page 151 if you've forgotten what the difference of 2 squares is all about.

10)(a) $7x - 3x = 7 + 3$;
$4x = 10$;
$\mathbf{x = 2.5}$.
[2 marks]
(b) First of all, multiply by 20 to get rid of the numbers on the bottom.
$4(3x - 1) = 5x + 10$;
$12x - 4 = 5x + 10$;
$7x = 14$;
$\mathbf{x = 2}$
[3 marks]

11)(a) $\mathbf{x^2 - 6x + 9}$.
[2 marks]
(b) $(x^2 - 6x + 9) - x^2 + 4x$;
$\mathbf{-2x + 9}$
[2 marks]
(c) Use your answer to part b) to get:
$-2x + 9 = 7x + 18$;
$-9x = 9$;
$\mathbf{x = -1}$
[2 marks]

12)(a) The cost of buying, copying and posting n CDs is:

c = cost of n blank CDs + admin charge for n CDs + postage for n CDs.

c = 0.35n + 0.07n + (p/100)n

$\mathbf{c = 0.42n + \frac{pn}{100} = n\left(0.42 + \frac{p}{100}\right)}$

[2 marks]

(b) Just put n = 173 and p = 32 into the formula:

c = 173(0.42 + (32 / 100)) = **£128.02**

[2 marks]

It's easy to get confused between pounds and pence on this one — in the formula you need to divide p by 100 because c is in pounds.
In part b), you put in p = 32, not p = 0.32 because p is in pence.
Just think carefully about what you're doing and you should be alright...

Page 168 (Warm-Up Questions)

1) x = 13, 14, 15, 16.

2) n = -3, -2, -1, 0, 1, 2, 3.

3) Dividing by 4 gives $2 < x < 5$, but x must be an integer so x = 3, 4.

4) $2q + 2 \leq 12 \Rightarrow 2q \leq 10 \Rightarrow q \leq 5$.

5) $4p + 12 > 30 \Rightarrow 4p > 18 \Rightarrow p > 4\frac{1}{2}$.

Page 169 (Warm-Up Questions)

1) $x = 2, y = 5$
(Subtract the equations to give 2y = 10, therefore y = 5. Substitute the y = 5 into the second equation to give 2x + 5 = 9, therefore x = 2.)

2) $x = 4, y = 4$
(Add the equations to give 4x = 16, therefore x = 4. Substitute x = 4 into the first equation to give 12 + 2y = 20, giving y = 4.)

Page 170 (Exam Questions)

5) **x = -3, -2, -1, 0, 1, 2.** *[2 marks]*

6) 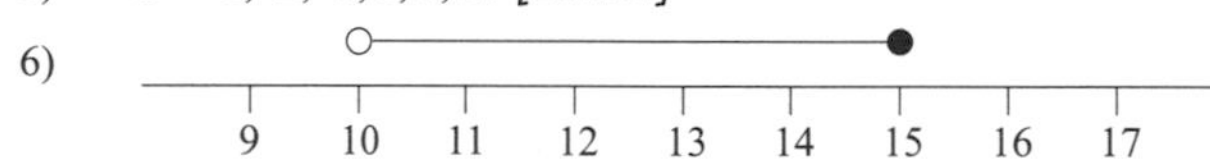

[2 marks]

Remember — a filled-in circle means "includes the value", an empty one means it doesn't...

7) 5a – 10 > 50; 5a > 60; **a > 12**. *[2 marks]*

8) Subtract 3 from both sides and the middle, then divide by 4:
13 < 4t + 3 < 27; 10 < 4t < 24; **2.5 < t < 6**. *[3 marks]*

9) You need to divide by -3, which means you need to flip the inequality sign around (dividing or multiplying by a negative number always flips the inequality sign):
$-3x > 12$; **$x < -4$**. *[2 marks]*

10) Use solid lines to draw $x = 0$, $x = 2$, $y = -1$ and $y = x - 1$.
Then shade the region bound by the inequalities:
You need to work out which side of the line $y = x - 1$ the inequality $y \leq x - 1$ falls on. To do this, try the point (0, 0) and see if this satisfies the inequality:
$x = 0$ and $y = 0$ in the inequality gives $0 \leq -1$, which is false, so (0, 0) is the wrong side of the line.

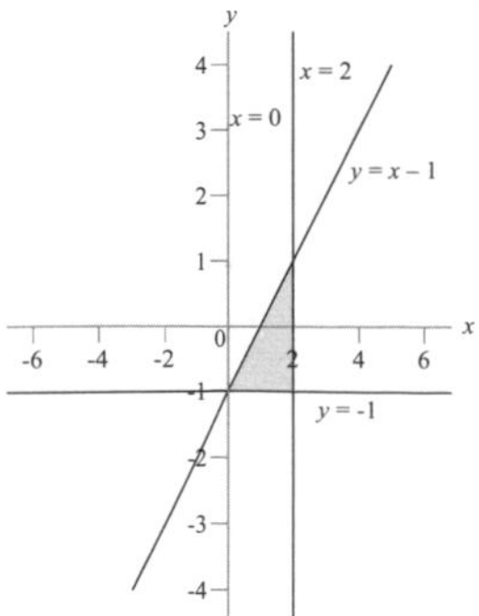

[5 marks]

Page 171 (Exam Questions)

11) $5x + 4y = 75$ $\quad 2x + 4y = 54$.
Subtract to give $3x = 21$, therefore $x = 7$.
Substitute $x = 7$ into first equation to give $35 + 4y = 75$, so $4y = 40$, therefore $y = 10$.
Answer: **$x = 7$ and $y = 10$.** *[3 marks]*

12) $3x - 2y = 7$ — (1) $\quad 4x - 4y = 8$ — (2).
Double the first equation to give: $6x - 4y = 14$ — (3).
Subtract equation (2) from equation (3) to give $2x = 6$, therefore $x = 3$.
Substitute $x = 3$ into the first equation to give $9 - 2y = 7$, therefore $y = 1$.
Answer: **$x = 3$ and $y = 1$.** *[3 marks]*

13) $-2x - 5y = -6$ (1) $\quad 3x + 4y = 2$ (2).
Multiply the first equation by 4 and the second by 5 to eliminate y:
$-8x - 20y = -24$ (3) $\quad 15x + 20y = 10$ (4).
Now add equations (3) and (4) to give $7x = -14$, therefore $x = -2$.
Substitute $x = -2$ into second equation (easier than the first because it has no minus signs) to give $-6 + 4y = 2$, so $4y = 8$, therefore $y = 2$.
Answer: **$x = -2$ and $y = 2$.** *[3 marks]*

14) Plot each graph. You will have 2 crossing points, so two sets of answers.

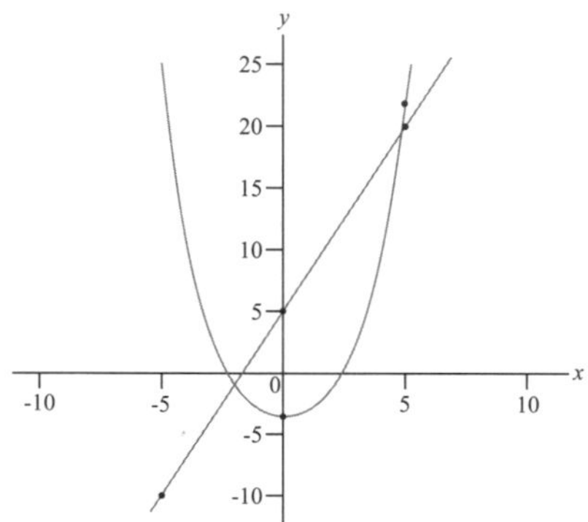

Approximate answers (cannot be exact because we are reading from a graph) are: **$x = 4.8$ and $y = 19.5$** AND ALSO **$x = -1.7$ and $y = -0.5$.**
[3 marks]

15) $x = 4y + 3$ — (1) $\quad 3x^2 = y + 1$ — (2)
The second equation is a quadratic — you need to rearrange this to get y on its own, then substitute that into the first equation:
(2) gives: $y = 3x^2 - 1$ — (3)
Now substitute equation (3) into equation (1):
$x = 4(3x^2 - 1) + 3$
$x = 12x^2 - 4 + 3$
$12x^2 - x - 1 = 0$
Factorise to solve for x:
$(4x + 1)(3x - 1) = 0$
So $x = -1/4$ or $x = 1/3$.
Now substitute these into equation (1) to find values for y:
$x = -1/4$ in (1): $-1/4 = 4y + 3$; $4y = -13/4$; $y = -13/16$.
$x = 1/3$ in (1): $1/3 = 4y + 3$; $4y = -8/3$; $y = -2/3$.
So the answers are: **$x = -1/4$ and $y = -13/16$** OR **$x = 1/3$ and $y = -2/3$.**
[5 marks]
These simultaneous equation questions involving quadratics might seem quite tricky, but it's just a set method, so once you've learnt it it's not hard at all. (Remember — if there's a quadratic in it, you're going to get <u>2 sets of values</u>.)

Page 179 (Warm-Up Questions)

1) Answer is (b); *$(x + 6)(x - 2) = x^2 + 4x - 12$.*

2) Answer is (b); *$(3x + 1)(x - 2) = 3x^2 - 5x - 2$.*

3) (a) $(x + 4)(x + 7)$.
(b) $(x + 14)(x + 2)$.
(c) $(x + 14)(x - 2)$.

4) (a) $x = -3$ or $x = -5$ *(it factorises to $(x + 3)(x + 5) = 0$)*
(b) $x = 2$ or $x = -7$ *(it factorises to $(x - 2)(x + 7) = 0$).*
(c) $x = 3$ or $x = 4$
(Rearrange to give $x^2 - 7x + 12 = 0$, then factorise to give $(x - 3)(x - 4) = 0$, so $x = 3$ or $x = 4$.)

5) $(x + 4)^2 + 4$
($(x + 4)^2$ gives $x^2 + 8x + 16$, so complete the square by adding 4.)

6) $x = 9$ or $x = 1$
($(x-5)^2$ gives $x^2 - 10x + 25$ so complete the square by subtracting 16;
$(x-5)^2 - 16 = 0$
$(x-5)^2 = 16$
$(x-5) = \sqrt{16}$
$(x-5) = 4$ or $(x-5) = -4$
$x = 9$ or $x = 1$.)

Pages 181-182 (Exam Questions)

5) (a) **$(x+4)(x-5)$**.
[1 mark]

(b) **$(3x-4)(2x+3)$**.
(This one's a tricky one — there's lots of different possible combinations of numbers — just keep trying and you'll get there sooner or later.
[2 marks]

6) Factorise to give $(2x+2)(x-4) = 0$, so **$x = -1$ or $x = 4$**.
[3 marks]

7) Rearrange to give $x^2 - 7x + 12 = 0$, then factorise to give $(x-3)(x-4) = 0$. **So $x = 3$ or $x = 4$.**
[3 marks]

8) Rearrange to give $x^2 + 9x + 18 = 0$, then factorise to give $(x+3)(x+6) = 0$. **So $x = -3$ or $x = -6$.**
[3 marks]

9) $(x+5)^2$ gives $x^2 + 10x + 25$, so complete the square by subtracting 15; so the answer is **$(x+5)^2 - 15$**.
[2 marks]

10) $(x-3)^2$ gives $x^2 - 6x + 9$, so complete the square by subtracting 49.
So $(x-3)^2 - 49 = 0$
$(x-3)^2 = 49$
$(x-3) = \sqrt{49}$
$x - 3 = 7$ or $x - 3 = -7$
$x = 10$ or $x = -4$
[3 marks]

11) $(x+4)^2$ gives $x^2 + 8x + 16$ so subtract 20 to complete the square.
So $(x+4)^2 - 20 = 0$
$(x+4)^2 = 20$
$(x+4) = \sqrt{20}$
$x + 4 = 4.5$ or $x + 4 = -4.5$ (to 1 d.p.)
$x = 0.5$ or $x = -8.5$ (to 1 d.p.)
[3 marks]

12) Since there are no hints about completing the square or trial and improvement, you should use the formula (the expression won't factorise, because the question asks for "2 decimal places").
Substitute a = 2, b = 3, c = -4:

$$x = \frac{-3 \pm \sqrt{3^2 - (4 \times 2 \times -4)}}{2 \times 2} = \frac{-3 \pm \sqrt{9+32}}{4} = \frac{-3 \pm \sqrt{41}}{4} = \frac{-3 \pm 6.40}{4}$$

so $x = \frac{-3+6.40}{4}$ or $x = \frac{-3-6.40}{4}$

so **$x = 0.85$ or $x = -2.35$** (both to 2 d.p.)
[3 marks]

13) Rearrange to give $3x^2 - 5x - 12 = 0$.
Substitute a = 3, b = -5, c = -12:

$$x = \frac{-(-5) \pm \sqrt{(-5)^2 - (4 \times 3 \times -12)}}{2 \times 3} = \frac{5 \pm \sqrt{25+144}}{6} = \frac{5 \pm \sqrt{169}}{6} = \frac{5 \pm 13}{6}$$

so $x = \frac{5+13}{6}$ or $x = \frac{5-13}{6}$

So **$x = 3.00$ or $x = -1.33$** (both to 2 d.p.)
[3 marks]
In these question, you need to give the first value of x to 2 decimal places ("3.00"), and not just "x = 3", because the question specifically asks for this level of accuracy. Always be careful to give your answer to the right number of decimal places, otherwise you'll lose marks needlessly.

14)

x	$x^2 - 3x$
5.5	13.75
5.7	15.39
5.6	14.56
5.65	14.9725
5.66	15.0556
5.655	15.014025

You can see that x lies between 5.65 and 5.655.
So to 2 decimal places, **$x = 5.65$** (because x is definitely less than 5.655, it must round down to 5.65 not up to 5.66).
[4 marks]

Page 187 (Warm-Up Questions)

1) (a) × 1.15.
(b) × 0.91.
(c) × 1.1.
(d) × 1.125.
(e) × 0.76.

2) £3376.53.

3) (a) $A = kr^2$.
(b) $D = k/R$.
(c) $H = k/D^3$.
(d) $V = kS^3$.

Page 188 (Exam Questions)

4) $2500 \times 0.92^5 =$ **£8238.52**.
[3 marks]
These question are very standard — if you're at all confused, look back to page 183.

5) (a) Start with the equation $C = kd^3$, where k is a constant to be found.
Now substitute in C = 270, d = 1.5 to find k:
$270 = k \times 1.5^3$; $k = 80$.
So the equation is **$C = 80d^3$**.
[3 marks]

(b) Just put d = 1.8 into the equation and find C:
$C = 80 \times 1.8^3 =$ **466.56 litres**.
[2 marks]

(c) Put C = 140 into the equation and solve for d:
$140 = 80d^3$; $d^3 = 1.75$; **d = 1.21 metres**.
[2 marks]
Don't forget the units in your answer, otherwise it's more easy marks down the drain...

6) Investment value is 6000×1.038^n, where n is number of years.
Just try different values of n until you find the lowest value for which investment is greater than £7000.
Answer: **n = 5**.
[3 marks]

7) (a) Start with the general equation:
$F = k/t^2$
Now put in F = 40, t = 5 to find k:
$40 = k / 5^2$; $k = 1000$.
So equation is **$F = 1000/t^2$**.
[3 marks]

(b) (i) $F = 1000 / 200^2 =$ **0.025**.
[1 mark]

(ii) $50 = 1000 / t^2$; $t^2 = 20$; **t = 4.47** (3 s.f.).
[2 marks]

EXAM PAPER ANSWERS

Please note: The answers to the past exam questions have not been provided or approved by the examining bodies (AQA, OCR and London Qualifications Ltd - Edexcel). As such AQA, OCR and London Qualifications Ltd do not accept any responsibility for the accuracy and method of the working in the answers given. CGP has provided suggested solutions — other possible solutions may be equally correct.

Section A — Calculator Allowed

1 (a) $131.4 - 0.73 = 130.67$. $2 - 4.5^2 = -18.25$
$130.67 \div -18.25 =$ **-7.16** ***(2 marks, 1 mark for 130.67 ÷ -18.25)***

(b)

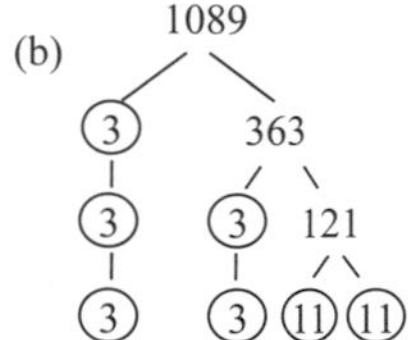

$3^2 \times 11^2$ ***(2 marks, 1 mark for 3 × 3 × 11 × 11)***

2 $7200 \div 9$ ***(1 mark)***
Tracey: $(7200 \div 9) \times 5 =$ **£4000**
Wayne: $(7200 \div 9) \times 4 =$ **£3200**
(1 mark each)

3 (a) Interior angle of octagon = 180 – exterior = 180 – 360 ÷ 8 = 135°.
Interior angle of hexagon = 180 – exterior = 180 – 360 ÷ 6 = 120°.
(1 mark for either correct)
angle $y = 360 - (135 + 120)$ ***(1 mark for this calculation, even if values for interior angles are not correct)***
So, angle $y =$ **105** ***(1 mark)***

(b) Looking at the two shorter sides: $15^2 + 36^2 = 225 + 1296 = 1521$ ***(1 mark)***
Looking at the longest side: $39^2 = 1521$ ***(1 mark)***
$\therefore 15^2 + 36^2 = 39^2$. This matches Pythagoras Theorem and $\angle ABC$ is opposite to longest side so $\angle$ is 90° ***(1 mark)***

4 (a) $7p + 3 = 3p - 3$ ***(1 mark)***
$7p - 3p = -3 - 3$. $p =$ **-1½** ***(1 mark)***

(b) Dividing through by 3 gives: $0 < q \le 5\frac{1}{3}$, *so q =* ***1,2,3,4,5***
(2 marks for correct answer, 1 mark if a single mistake is made, e.g. including q =0)

(c) Multiply by 3 on both sides: $r + 1 \le 3r - 6$ ***(1 mark for getting 3r – 6)***
Rearrange to get: $1 + 6 \le 3r - r$ ***(1 mark)***
$r \ge 3½$ ***(1 mark)***

5 (a)

x	-2	-1	0	1	2	3
y	-18	-6	0	6	18	42

(1 mark)

(b)

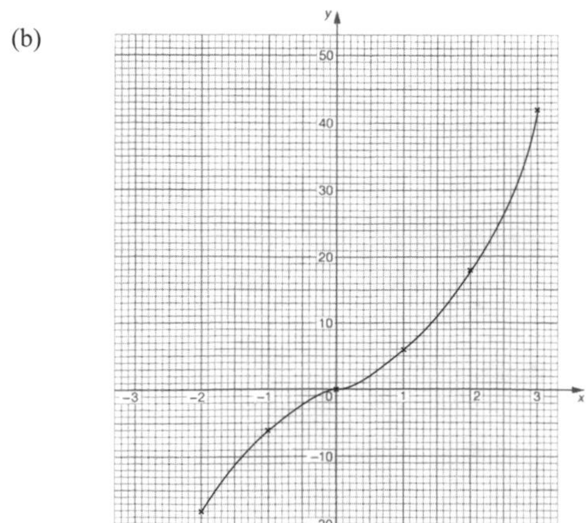

(2 marks for all points plotted correctly, 1 mark for 3 correctly plotted points. 1 mark for correct shape, drawn with a smooth curve.)

(c) Read off the value of the graph at $y = 10$. This gives $x =$ **1.4**.
(1 mark for an answer between 1.25 and 1.45)

6 (a) 2.19×10^{19} ***(1 mark)***
(b) $(2.19 \times 10^{19}) \div (9.46 \times 10^{12}) = 2.3 \times 10^6$
(1 mark for correct method, 1 mark for 2.3 × 10⁶)

7 e.g. eqn (1) × 3 : $12x + 3y = 12$.
Then subtract eqn (2): $10x = 15$ ***(1 mark for this method, allow 1 slip)***
[or eqn (2) × 2 and subtract leads to $5y = -10$]
$x = 1.5$ [or $y = -2$] ***(1 mark)***
Then substitute answer back in, eg. 4 × "1.5" + y = 4 ***(1 mark for this method)***
Answer x **= 1.5,** y **= –2** ***(1 mark)***

8 (a)

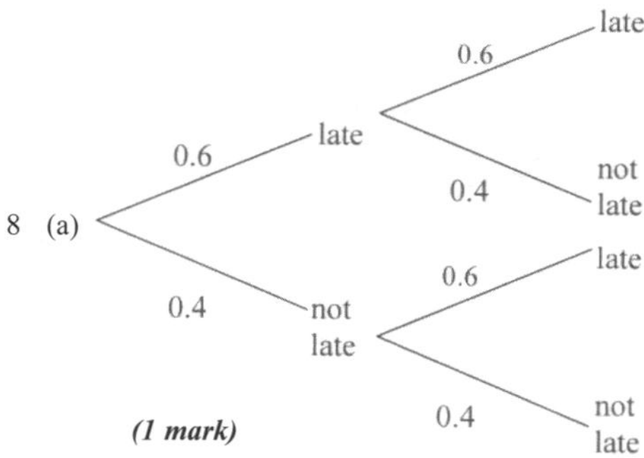

(1 mark)

(b) There are two possible ways to do this:
EITHER: Calculate prob that bus is on time both days
= 0.4 × 0.4 = 0.16 ***(1 mark),***
Then prob that late at least one day = 1 – prob on time both days
which = 1 – 0.16 ***(1 mark)*** = **0.84** ***(1 mark)***
OR Calculate prob that: (late, on time) + (on time, late) + (late, late)
= (0.6 × 0.4) + (0.4×0.6) + (0.6×0.6) ***(1 mark)***
= 0.24 + 0.24 + 0.36 ***(1 mark)*** = **0.84** ***(1 mark)***

9 (a) The first thing to do is work out how much one square represents.
All the other answers follow on from that:

Time (t minutes)	$60 < t \le 90$	$90 < t \le 105$	$105 < t \le 135$	$135 < t \le 180$	$180 < t \le 240$
Numbers of runners	40	50	**120**	**30**	30

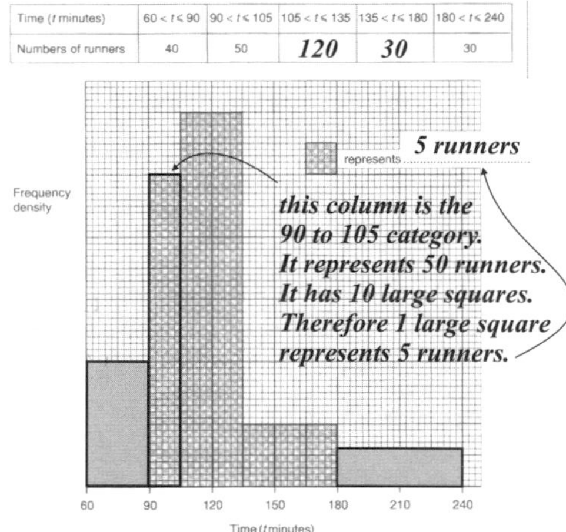

(5 marks in total. 1 for correct calculation of how much one square represents. If this is calculated incorrectly follow-on marks are available: 1 mark for correct method in drawing new bars. 1 mark for correct method for values in table. 1 mark for all values in table correct. 1 mark for both bars drawn correctly.)

(b) Total number of runners = 40 + 50 + 120 + 30 + 30 = 270. ***(1 mark)***
30 of them took longer than 180 minutes.
So prob of a runner taking longer than 180 min = 30/270 = 1/9. ***(1 mark)***
We want prob of 2 being over 180 min = 1/9 × 1/9 = **1/81** ***(1 mark)***

10 (a) Use area of triangle rule: Area $= \frac{1}{2} \times 7.2 \times 8.35 \times \sin 74°$ ***(1 mark)***
= **28.9 cm²**
(1 mark for 28.9, 1 mark for cm², lose 1 mark if answer not given to 3sf)

(b) Use cosine rule: $AB^2 = 7.2^2 + 8.35^2 - 2 \times 7.2 \times 8.35 \cos 74°$ ***(1 mark)***
$AB^2 = 51.84 + 69.7225 - 33.1426...$ (=88.419...) ***(1 mark for correct method here)***
AB = 9.40... (***1 mark for 9.40, lose 1 mark if answer not given to 3sf)***

Section A is marked out of a total of 50 marks

Section B — Calculator NOT Allowed

1 (a) Reflection *(1 mark)* in the line $y = x$ *(1 mark).*

(b) Vertices at (3, 2), (5, 0) and (9, 4). *(2 marks) (1 mark for freehand lines or 2 correct vertices)*

2 (a) There are 5 ways to get a total of 6:
(1 and 5), (2 and 4), (3 and 3), (4 and 2) and (5 and 1). *(1 mark)*
Are 6 × 6 = 36 possible outcomes (1,1)(1,2)...(1,6)(2,1), (2,2) etc *(1 mark)*

So Khalid can get 6 in 5 ways out of 36 outcomes so prob = **5/36** *(1 mark)*

Could also do this question by:

There are 5 ways to get a total of 6:
(1 and 5), (2 and 4), (3 and 3), (4 and 2) and (5 and 1). *(1 mark)*

The chances of any of these is 1/6 × 1/6 = 1/36. *(1 mark)*
The probability is therefore 5 × 1/36 = **5/36**. *(1 mark)*

(b) There are 6 ways to get a total of 7:
(1 and 6), (2 and 5), (3 and 4), (4 and 3), (5 and 2) and (6 and 1).
Therefore the prob of this is 6/36 = 1/6. *(1 mark)*
The probability of this NOT happening is 1– 1/6 = **5/6**. *(1 mark)*

(c) This time 6 possibilities (1 and 1), (2 and 2) etc.
Therefore prob = 6/36 = **1/6**. *(1 mark)*

3 First line $x \geq$ **-2**.
Second line: using $y = mx + c$: $y = 3 - x$. So $\boldsymbol{y \leq 3 - x}$.
Third line: using $y = mx + c$: $y = x$. So $\boldsymbol{y \geq x}$.
(1 mark each for the correct forms of the inequalities:
[x ? -2, y ? x and y ? 3 – x].
1 additional mark if all three inequality signs are the right way round.)

4 (a) and (b)

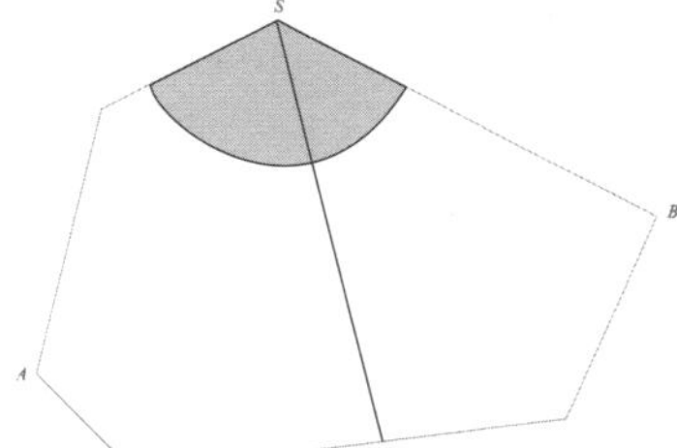

for (a) (2 marks - 1 for any recognisable complete arc which meets the field boundary, 1 for such an arc drawn accurately to the right scale)

for (b) (2 marks - 2 marks for accurately drawn line to the field boundaries or 1 mark for incomplete line—minimum length 6cm)

5 (a) (i) p^7 *(1 mark)*

(ii) $4t^3$ *(1 mark)*

(b) $3x \geq -15$ *(1 mark)* $\boldsymbol{x \geq -5}$ *(1 mark)*

(c) Multiply by 2: $2s = w + y$. *(1 mark)* $\boldsymbol{w = 2s - y}$ *(1 mark)*

(d) (i) $t_1 = 1(1 + 1) \div 2 = 1$
$t_2 = 2(2 + 1) \div 2 = 3$
$t_3 = 3(3 + 1) \div 2 = 6$
(2 marks for all 3 correct or 1 mark for 2 correct)

(ii) Triangular *(1 mark)* (accept triangle)

6 Total of boys marks = $12n$
Total of girls marks = $15m$ *(1 mark)*
Total marks for whole class = $12n + 15m$ *(1 mark)*

So mean = $\boldsymbol{\dfrac{12n + 15m}{27}}$ *(1 mark)*

7 (a) Correct plotting:

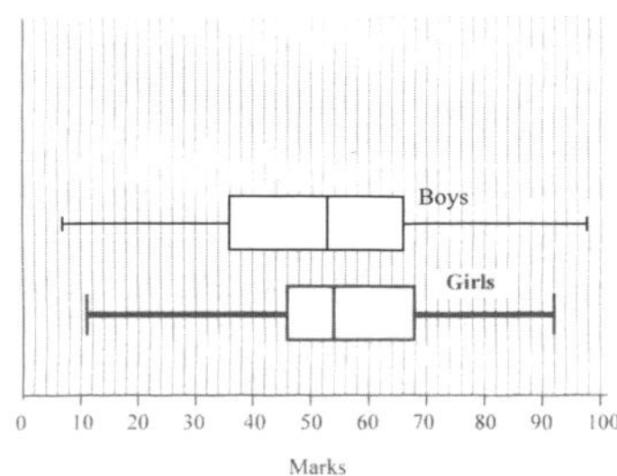

(2 marks for correct plot, lose 1 for each error)

(b) Any two valid comments ***(1 mark each)***, for example medians about the same, but girls have smaller IQR, or boys have wider range.

8 (a) $(x + 4)(x - 3) = 78$
(2 marks, 1 mark for just (x + 4)(x – 3))

(b) (i) multiplying out the brackets: $x^2 + 4x - 3x - 12 = 78$

$x^2 + x - 12 = 78$

$x^2 + x - 90 = 0$

(2 marks for: $x^2 + x - 90 = 0$, ***with evidence.***
1 mark for: $x^2 + 4x - 3x - 12$)

(ii) $(x - 9)(x + 10) = 0$ or $x = \dfrac{-1 \pm \sqrt{(1 - 4 \times -90)}}{2}$

$= 9$ or -10

(1 mark for correct method — factorisation or formula.
1 mark for answer)

(iii) length = 9 + 4 = **13**
width = 9 – 3 = **6**
(1 mark for each answer — accept even if (i) and (ii) are incomplete or incorrect)

9 (a) (i) $\begin{pmatrix} -2 \\ 0 \end{pmatrix} - \begin{pmatrix} 2 \\ 3 \end{pmatrix}$ *(1 mark)* $= \begin{pmatrix} -4 \\ -3 \end{pmatrix}$ *(1 mark).*

(ii) $\sqrt{(-4)^2 + (-3)^2} = 5$

(1 mark for use of pythagoras, 1 mark for correct answer)

(b) $\overrightarrow{BD} = \overrightarrow{BA} + \overrightarrow{AD} = \begin{pmatrix} 0 \\ k \end{pmatrix}$ *(1 mark)* because parallel to $\begin{pmatrix} 0 \\ 1 \end{pmatrix}$.

Therefore $\begin{pmatrix} 4 \\ 3 \end{pmatrix} + \overrightarrow{AD} = \begin{pmatrix} 0 \\ k \end{pmatrix}$. $\overrightarrow{AD} = \begin{pmatrix} -4 \\ k - 3 \end{pmatrix}$.

The length of $\overrightarrow{AD}$ = 5 because same as (a ii).

Therefore $(k - 3) = 3$ (because $4^2 + 3^2 = 5^2$). So $k = 6$.

Therefore $\overrightarrow{AD} = \begin{pmatrix} -4 \\ 3 \end{pmatrix}$.

Then we just work out $\overrightarrow{OD} = \overrightarrow{OA} + \overrightarrow{AD} = \begin{pmatrix} 2 \\ 3 \end{pmatrix} + \begin{pmatrix} -4 \\ 3 \end{pmatrix} = \begin{pmatrix} \mathbf{-2} \\ \mathbf{6} \end{pmatrix}$ *(1 mark)*

(c) $\overrightarrow{BC} = \overrightarrow{AD} = \begin{pmatrix} -4 \\ 3 \end{pmatrix}$ from (b). *(1 mark)*

$\overrightarrow{OC} = \overrightarrow{OB} + \overrightarrow{BC} = \begin{pmatrix} -2 \\ 0 \end{pmatrix} + \begin{pmatrix} -4 \\ 3 \end{pmatrix} = \begin{pmatrix} -6 \\ 3 \end{pmatrix}$.

Therefore C = **(-6, 3)**. *(1 mark)*

Section B is marked out of a total of 50 marks

Working out your Grade

- *Find your average percentage for the whole exam.*
- *Look it up in this table to see what grade you got. If you're borderline, don't push yourself up a grade — the real examiners won't.*

Average %	85+	74 – 84	61 – 73	47 – 60	37 – 46	29 – 36	22 – 28	15 – 21	under 15
Grade	A*	A	B	C	D	E	F	G	U

Important

- *This is a Higher paper — if you're doing Foundation you'll need more marks in the real exam. E.g. you'll generally need 26 marks or more to get a G grade.*
- *Obviously these grades are only a guide — and the more practice you do the better...*

Index

Index

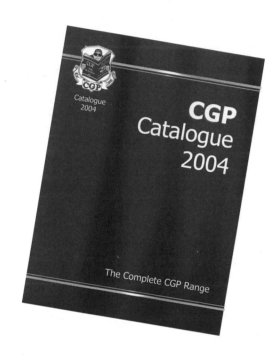